INCOME AND WEALTH
SERIES VIII

THE MEASUREMENT OF
NATIONAL WEALTH

INCOME AND WEALTH SERIES VIII

THE MEASUREMENT OF NATIONAL WEALTH

Papers by:

T. BARNA

P. J. BJERVE & MIKAEL SELSJORD

O. AUKRUST & JUUL BJERKE

NETHERLANDS CENTRAL BUREAU OF STATISTICS

F. GRÜNIG   I. VINSKI

ANTHONY SCOTT   A. GANZ

MANUEL BALBOA & ALBERTO FRACCHIA

D. FRANZSEN & J. J. WILLERS

J. M. GARLAND & R. W. GOLDSMITH

M. MUKHERJEE and N. S. R. SASTRY

with a statistical introduction
by the Editors and Th. van Der Weide

Edited by

RAYMOND GOLDSMITH

and

CHRISTOPHER SAUNDERS

QUADRANGLE BOOKS / CHICAGO

19748

International Association for Research
in Income and Wealth

INCOME AND WEALTH
SERIES VIII

ANALYTICAL TABLE OF CONTENTS

List of Papers submitted to the Fifth Conference of the International Association for Research in Income and Wealth

1

A Summary Survey of National Wealth Estimates

2

Alternative Methods of Measuring Capital

by T. BARNA

5

The Preparation of a National Balance Sheet: Experience in the Netherlands

By the Division of National Accounts of the Netherlands Central Bureau of Statistics

6

An Estimate of the National Capital Account of the Federal German Republic

by FERDINAND GRÜNIG

9

Problems and Uses of National Wealth Estimates in Latin America

by ALEXANDER GANZ

10

Fixed Reproducible Capital in Argentina, 1935–55

by *MANUEL BALBOA and ALBERTO FRACCHIA*

11

Capital Accumulation and Economic Growth in South Africa

by *D. G. FRANZSEN and J. J. D. WILLERS*

12

The National Wealth of Australia

by J. M. GARLAND and R. W. GOLDSMITH

13

An Estimate of the Tangible Wealth of India

by M. MUKHERJEE and N. S. R. SASTRY

of course, notoriously dubious because of the difficulties of allowing for changes in quality and, indeed, of defining what is meant by 'quality'.

The nature of the alternative methods of estimation vary considerably. The most common are: (a) *insurance valuations* (used, but for certain classes of assets only, for Belgium, Luxembourg, Norway, Sweden, India, and United Kingdom); (b) *censuses* of assets, usually in quantitative terms, to which prices are attached (used as the principal source of information by Yugoslavia and to some extent by almost all countries, especially for dwellings and land); (c) *balance sheets of enterprises*, which normally need adjustment to current replacement cost (again used to some extent by almost all countries). Some less commonly used methods, listed in Table V, are based on the capitalization of income and on tax statistics.

The differences that can arise from different methods of estimation are illustrated in the United Kingdom. The only comprehensive estimate for the United Kingdom, which is used throughout the tables in this chapter, is that made by Redfern, based wholly on the perpetual inventory method. But an alternative estimate, based on fire-insurance valuations, has been made by Barna for manufacturing industry only. The very wide difference between the results of the two methods is discussed by Barna in Paper 2 of the present volume.

Several of the statistical methods involve the estimation of depreciation rates. In addition to the major difficulties of estimating the useful lives of assets, referred to above, the choice arises between the various systems of depreciation. In most cases, straight-line depreciation is used. The declining-balance method, however, is used for South Africa and for certain assets in the United States. Both methods are applied in the calculations for Australia and the results compared (see p. 354).

The composition of national wealth

The estimates of national wealth in each country are summarized, in national currencies, in Table II, in accordance with the classification scheme set out above. A certain amount of additional detail is given where possible; thus the value of standing timber, which most countries omit, is given as a supplementary item (excluded from the total) for the countries recording it.

At the foot of Table I is given a number of alternative aggregates of 'national wealth'. Each aggregate is completed for each economy so far as the statistics are available.

In Table III the data of Table I are converted into percentages of three of the most commonly used aggregates, namely:

> Total reproducible tangible wealth of Enterprises and Government (A.I. + B.I. of classification scheme above)
> Total tangible wealth (A + B)
> Total tangible wealth plus net foreign assets (A + B + D)

One important distinction in the estimates is that between gross replacement cost (i.e. undepreciated values) of assets and their net values, and it is the net values that are given in the tables. For four countries, however, estimates have been made of both the gross and the net value, and the two sets of figures are shown in Table II.

For twelve countries information is available about the development over time of national wealth and its composition. These estimates are summarized in Table IV.

Capital–output ratios

Some authors have calculated capital–output ratios, exhibiting both average and marginal relationships. These are summarized in Table VII. In Table VI the development of average capital–output ratios over time is displayed for a number of countries. The relationship used in these tables, wherever possible, is that between *net* capital and *net* national product, but in certain cases the gross national product has necessarily been used as a measure of output. Consumers' durables have been excluded from both numerator and denominator.

The difficulties of interpreting these ratios within a single country are stressed by several authors; the drawing of conclusions from comparisons between different countries presents even greater obstacles.

II. STATISTICS OF NATIONAL WEALTH FOR EIGHTEEN COUNTRIES

BY TH. D. VAN DER WEIDE

TABLE I
National Wealth Estimates

Classification	Belgium	Luxembourg	Netherlands	Western Germany	France	United Kingdom
	1950	1950	1952	1955	1954	1953
	Current Prices	Current Prices	Current Prices	1950 Prices	Current Prices	1948 Prices
	Billions of B. francs	Billions of L. francs	Billions of guilders	Billions of D. mark	000 billions F. francs	Billions of pounds
A. *Enterprises* . . . total	1,031	73·18	77·6	405·5	44·55	..
I. Reproducible assets . total	851	59·89	61·2	305·5	(1) 35·05	(1) 28·28
1. Structures . . total	503	32·32	32·5	179·5	..	22·58
(a) Dwellings (1) .	400	17·70	18·3	100·0	(1) 8·90	10·20
(b) Agricultural .	} 103	2·31	3·1	10·9	..	
(c) Other . .		12·31	(1) 11·1	68·6	(2) 12·26	(2) 12·38
2. Equipment . total	273	26·06	18·9	84·0	..	..
(a) Agricultural .	23	(1) 0·92	(2) 1·5	7·9	8·10	0·20
(b) Other . .	(1) 250	(2) 25·14	17·4	76·1	..	..
3. Inventories . total	75	(1·51)	9·8	(1) 42·0	5·79	5·60
(a) Livestock. .	25	1·51	2·6	..	1·24	}
(b) Other agricultural	} 50	..	(3) 1·4	..	0·45	} 0·60
(c) Other . .		..	5·8	..	4·10	5·00
(d) (Standing timber) (2) .	(12)	(..)	(0·8)	(..)	(..)	(..)
II. Non-reproducible assets, land . . total	(2) 180	13·29	16·4	(2) 100·0	(3,4)9·50	..
(a) Agricultural .	..	6·27	13·1	..	(3) 8·55	..
(b) Forest . .	..	(3) 4·27	0·2	..	(5) 0·95	..
(c) Other . .	..	2·75	3·1	..	..	..
(Of which public enterprises) (6) total	..	9·89	6·1	..	10·82	..
(I. Reproducible assets) .	(5) 58	7·70	4·8	..	..	..
(II. Non-reproducible assets) .	..	2·19	1·3	..	..	..
B. *Government* (3) . . total	..	6·16	(4) 12·0	—	(6) 11·45	..
I. Reproducible assets . total	82	5·97	..	42·5	..	(3) 1·85
1. Structures (4) . .	..	5·71	..	(3) 35·0	..	} (3) 1·65
2. Equipment . .	..	} 0·26	..	7·5	..	
3. Inventories . .	..		..	..	..	0·20
II. Non-reproducible assets, land . . total	..	0·19	..	..	..	..
C. *Consumer durables* . total	165	..	20·2	(4) 60·0	6·90	..
1. Passenger cars and other vehicles (5) . . .	(3) 20	(·10)	0·2	..	0·50	..
2. Other . . .	(4) 145	..	(4) 20·0	..	6·40	..
D. *Foreign assets* . . total	110	−3·00	8·1	..	2·00	..
1. Monetary metals . .	30	0·00	2·2	..	2·00	..
2. Other net foreign assets .	80	−3·00	5·9	..	—	..
Total:						
1. Repr. tang. assets of Enterpr. + Govt. (AI + BI) . .	933	65·86	(5) 73·2	348·0	(7) 46·50	(4) 30·23
2. Repr. tang. assets (AI + BI + C)	1,098	..	(5) 93·4	408·0	(7) 53·40	..
3. Repr. tang. assets of Enterpr. + Govt. + net for. assets (AI + BI + D) . . .	1,043	62·86	(5) 81·3	..	(7) 48·50	..
4. Repr. tang. assets + net for. assets (AI + BI + C + D) .	1,208	..	(5) 101·5	..	(7) 55·40	..
5. Tang. assets of Enterpr. + Govt. (A + B) .	1,113	79·34	89·6	448·0	56·00	..
6. Tang. assets (A + B + C)	1,278	..	109·8	508·0	62·90	..
7. Tang. assets of Enterpr. + Govt. + net for. assets (A + B + D) .	1,223	76·34	97·7	..	58·00	..
8. Tang. assets + net for. assets (A + B + C + D) . .	1,388	..	117·9	..	64·90	..

TABLE I (*continued*)
National Wealth Estimates

Classification	Sweden 1952 Current Prices Billions of kroner	Norway 1953 Current Prices Billions of kroner	Yugo-slavia 1953 Current Prices Billions of dinars	Canada 1955 Current Prices Billions of Can. dollars	U.S.A. 1955 Current Prices Billions of dollars	Mexico 1950 Current Prices Billions of pesos
A. *Enterprises* . . . total	(1) 220·4	79·70	6,435	—	993·4	..
I. Reproducible assets . total	(1) 195·4	76·65	4,406	47·36	816·8	70·76
1. Structures . . total	..	45·97	2,726	26·71	550·2	(1) 57·23
(a) Dwellings (1) .	..	22·01	1,273	12·89	325·9	28·26
(b) Agricultural .	8·8	5·41	416	0·75	33·2	(2) 6·13
(c) Other . .	(1) 179·5	18·55	1,037	13·07	191·1	22·84
2. Equipment . . total	..	21·08	764	10·95	155·4	..
(a) Agricultural .	4·0	0·83	122	2·07	17·7	..
(b) Other . .	..	20·25	642	8·88	137·7	..
3. Inventories . total	..	9·60	916	9·70	111·2	13·53
(a) Livestock . .	3·1	1·30	223	1·49	10·7	4·33
(b) Other agricultural .	..	0·80	(1) 212	0·33	6·7	(3) 1·76
(c) Other . .	..	7·50	481	7·88	93·8	7·44
(d) (Standing timber) (2) .	(..)	(10·00)	(606)	(..)	(..)	(..)
II. Non-reproducible assets, land . . . total	25·0	3·05	2,029	..	176·6	..
(a) Agricultural . .	4·3	3·05	1,810	..	68·8	..
(b) Forest . .	(2) 12·0	..	147	..	(1) 10·2	..
(c) Other . . .	8·7	..	72	..	97·6	..
(Of which public enterprises) (6) total	..					..
(I. Reproducible assets) .	..	(3) 9·77		(2) 0·96	(3) 14·6	..
(II. Non-reproducible assets) .	..	..		..	..	..
B. *Government* (3) . . total	13·7	..	675	..	(2) 158·2	..
I. Reproducible assets . total	..	(1) 10·64	652	9·28	122·5	(4) 20·96
1. Structures (4) . .	..	10·64	} 652	(1) 8·50	118·0	..
2. Equipment . .	..	..		(1) 0·78	4·4	..
3. Inventories . .	..	..	—		0·1	..
II. Non-reproducible assets, land . . . total	..	..	23	..	35·7	..
C. *Consumer durables* . . total	(3) ..	..	714	10·93	143·7	..
1. Passenger cars and other vehicles (5) . .	..	0·55	12	2·80	51·6	..
2. Other . . .	..	..	702	8·13	92·1	..
D. *Foreign assets* . . . total	4·5	−1·37	−42	−7·86	41·5	..
1. Monetary metals .	1·2	0·19	(2) 112	1·14	26·1	1·79
2. Other net foreign assets .	3·3	−1·56	−154	−9·00	15·4	..
Total:						
1. Repr. tang. assets of Enterpr. + Govt. (AI + BI) . .	..	(1) 87·29	5,058	56·64	939·3	91·72
2. Repr. tang. assets (AI + BI + C) .	(4) 209·1	..	5,772	67·57	1,083·0	..
3. Repr. tang. assets of Enterpr. + Govt. + net for. assets (AI + BI + D) .	..	(1) 85·92	5,016	48·78	980·8	..
4. Repr. tang. assets + net for. assets (AI + BI + C + D) .	(4) 213·8	..	5,730	59·71	1,124·5	..
5. Tang. assets of Enterpr. + Govt. (A + B) .	..	(2) 90·34	7,110	..	1,151·6	..
6. Tang. assets (A + B + C) .	(4) 234·1	..	7,824	..	1,295·3	..
7. Tang. assets of Enterpr. + Govt. + net for. assets (A + B + D) .	..	(2) 88·97	7,068	..	1,193·1	..
8. Tang. assets + net for. assets (A + B + C + D) .	(4) 238·6	..	7,782	..	1,336·8	..

TABLE I (*continued*)
National Wealth Estimates

Classification	Australia	South Africa	Argentina	Colombia	Japan	India
	(1) 1956	1955	1955	1953	1955	1950
	Current Prices	Current Prices	1950 Prices	1950 Prices	Current Prices	Current Prices
	Billions of A. pounds	Millions of S.A. pounds	Billions of pesos	Billions of pesos	000 Billions yen	Billions of rupees
A. *Enterprises* . . . total	(2) 14·57	(1) 6,171	..	..	..	341·3
I. Reproducible assets . total	10·97	(1) 4,090	164·5	18·25	13·12	162·8
1. Structures . . total	5·58	(1) 2,209	..	11·44	7·04	85·3
(a) Dwellings (1) .	3·73	708		(1) 3·52	2·77	44·6
(b) Agricultural .	} 1·85	} 1,501	(1) 20·9	4·70	0·28	22·5
(c) Other . .			(2) 143·6	3·22	3·99	18·2
2. Equipment . . total	2·70	(1) 790	..	3·73	3·05	23·2
(a) Agricultural .	0·62	..	..	0·14	0·28	5·4
(b) Other . .	2·08	..	..	3·59	2·77	17·8
3. Inventories . total	2·69	(1) 1,091	..	..	3·03	54·3
(a) Livestock .	0·92	398	..	3·08	(1) 0·20	27·9
(b) Other agricultural	0·12	} 693	..	..	0·21	0·3
(c) Other . .	1·65		..	..	2·62	26·1
(d) (Standing timber) (2) .	(..)	(..)	(..)	(..)	(..)	(..)
II. Non-reproducible assets, land . . total	3·60	(1) 2,081	..	..	..	178·5
(a) Agricultural .	2·00	} 1,182	..	..	..	157·5
(b) Forest . .	..		..	..	..	..
(c) Other . .	(3) 1·60	899	..	..	..	21·0
(Of which public enterprises) (6) total	..	..	..	..	..	..
(I. Reproducible assets) .	..	..	..	..	1·33	21·6
(II. Non-reproducible assets) .	..	..	..	..	..	..
B. *Government* (3) . . total	..	(2) 2,449	..	..	..	..
I. Reproducible assets . total	(4) 5·43	(2) 2,120	52·3	4·01	3·20	8·0
1. Structures (4) . .		1,579	..	3·41	2·26	8·0
2. Equipment . .		479	..	0·60	0·46	..
3. Inventories . .		62	..	..	0·48	..
II. Non-reproducible assets, land . . total	..	(2) 329	..	..	..	..
C. *Consumer durables* . . total	1·73	..	..	..	4·01	..
1. Passenger cars and other vehicles (5) . . .	(5) 0·52	188	..	..	..	0·6
2. Other . .	1·21	..	..	..	..	..
D. *Foreign assets* . . . total	−1·02	..	..	..	0·20	..
1. Monetary metals . .	0·11	75	..	..	0·01	..
2. Other net foreign assets .	−1·13	..	..	..	0·19	..
Total:						
1. Repr. tang. assets of Enterpr. + Govt. (AI + BI) . .	16·40	6,210	(3) 216·8	(2) 22·26	16·32	170·8
2. Repr. tang. assets (AI + BI + C)	18·13	..	..	..	20·33	..
3. Repr. tang. assets of Enterpr. + Govt. + net for. assets (AI + BI + D)	15·38	..	..	..	16·52	..
4. Repr. tang. assets + net for. assets (AI + BI + C + D)	17·11	..	..	..	20·53	..
5. Tang. assets of Enterpr. + Govt. (A + B)	20·00	8,620	..	..	..	(1) 349·3
6. Tang. assets (A + B + C)	21·73	..	..	..	..	..
7. Tang. assets of Enterpr. + Govt. + net for. assets (A + B + D)	18·98	..	..	..	..	..
8. Tang. assets + net for. assets (A + B + C + D) . .	20·71	..	..	..	..	..

General notes

Sources: see appendix; United Kingdom, estimates of Redfern.

Classification:

(1) All dwellings.
(2) Not included in total.
(3) Only general government (military assets not included). For the distinction between general government, and government enterprises and public corporations (which are entered under A Enterprises, public) see *A System of National Accounts and Supporting Tables*, United Nations, pp. 11 and 12.
(4) Roads, bridges, canals, dikes, and public schools included.
(5) Only privately owned cars, wholly or partly in use for private consumption.
(6) Government enterprises and public corporations; for further explanation see (3).

Year: 31 December.

Conventions:

.. Not available
— Zero or less than half the final digit shown
billions = thousand millions

Country notes

Belgium
(1) Inventories of corporations (Sociétés Anonymes) included.
(2) Government land included.
(3) All passenger cars.
(4) Jewellery included.
(5) Structures and equipment only.

Luxembourg
(1) Agricultural inventories included.
(2) Inventories and some structures included.
(3) Standing timber included.

Netherlands
(1) Land and harbours included.
(2) Forestry included.
(3) Sown seeds, growing crop and perennial plants included.
(4) Rough estimate.
(5) Government land included.

W. Germany
(1) Rough estimate, government inventories included.
(2) Rough estimate, government land included.
(3) Roads, bridges, and canals excluded.
(4) Rough estimate.

France
(1) Agricultural dwellings excluded.
(2) Equipment and land included.
(3) Agricultural dwellings and structures included.
(4) Land of enterprises and building sites excluded.
(5) Rough estimate.
(6) Museums and art collections included.
(7) Instead of B I, B is taken (land of enterprises included, agricultural dwellings and structures excluded).

United Kingdom
(1) Inventories and structures of agriculture and coal-mining excluded.
(2) Equipment included, structures of coal-mining excluded.
(3) Only part of government services and public-owned schools and universities included, most central government structures excluded.
(4) See other notes.

Sweden
(1) Equipment, inventories, dwellings, consumers durables, and subsoil resources included (total of mining, reprod. assets included, 4·5 mld. kr.).
(2) Standing timber included.
(3) Included in enterprises.
(4) Subsoil resources included.

Norway
(1) Government equipment and inventories excluded.
(2) Government equipment, inventories, and land excluded.
(3) Inventories excluded.

Yugoslavia
(1) Perennial plants and growing crops included.
(2) Claims for reparations included.

Canada
(1) Military airports, barracks, wharves, etc., included (not equipment as weapons, aircraft, etc.).
(2) Rough estimate of dwellings and inventories only.

United States
(1) Standing timber included.
(2) Some public enterprises (of local authorities) included.
(3) See (2).

Mexico
(1) Equipment included.
(2) Soil improvements included.
(3) Standing crop and perennial plants included.
(4) Some military buildings and government enterprises included.

Australia
(1) 30 June.
(2) Government enterprises and public corporations excluded.
(3) Some government land included.
(4) Government enterprises and public corporations included.
(5) Rough estimate.

South Africa
(1) Government enterprises and public corporations excluded.
(2) Government enterprises and public corporations included.

Argentina
(1) Equipment included.
(2) Dwellings and equipment included.
(3) Inventories excluded.

Colombia
(1) Urban housing only.
(2) Inventories: livestock only.

Japan
(1) Growing crop included.

India
(1) Government land excluded.

Germany, France, South Africa, India } Standing timber is included in land.

TABLE II
Gross and Net National Wealth Estimates [1]

Classification	Western Germany 1955, 1950 Prices, Billions of D. mark			Netherlands 1952, Current Prices, Billions of guilders			Yugoslavia 1953, Current Prices, Billions of dinars			Australia (1) 1956, Current Prices, Billions of A. pounds		
	Gross (a)	Net (b)	(b) as % of (a)	Gross (a)	Net (b)	(b) as % of (a)	Gross (a)	Net (b)	(b) as % of (a)	Gross (a)	Net (b)	(b) as % of (a)
A. *Enterprises* . total	601·0	405·5	67	112·6	77·6	69	9,104	6,435	71	(2) 21·11	(2) 14·57	69
I. Reproducible assets . total	501·0	305·5	61	96·2	61·2	64	7,075	4,406	62	17·51	10·97	63
1. Structures . total	313·0	179·5	57	53·4	32·5	61	4,717	2,726	58	9·99	5·58	56
(a) Dwellings (i)	168·0	100·0	60	30·1	18·3	61	2,500	1,273	51	6·52	3·73	57
(b) Agricultural	21·7	10·9	50	5·1	3·1	61	636	416	65			
(c) Other.	123·3	68·6	56	(1) 18·2	11·1	61	1,581	1,037	66	3·47	1·85	53
2. Equipment . total	146·0	84·0	58	33·0	18·9	57	1,361	764	56	4·83	2·70	56
(a) Agricultural	11·5	7·9	69	(2) 2·8	1·5	54	248	122	49		0·62	..
(b) Other.	134·5	76·1	57	30·2	17·4	58	1,113	642	58		2·08	:
3. Inventories . total	(1) 42·0	42·0	100	9·8	9·8	100	997	916	92	2·69	2·69	100
(a) Livestock	..	..	..	2·6	2·6	100	223	223	100	0·92	0·92	100
(b) Other agricultural	..	..	..	(3) 1·4	1·4	100	(1) 293	212	72	0·12	0·12	100
(c) Other.	..	..	..	5·8	5·8	100	481	481	100	1·65	1·65	100
(d) (Standing timber (2) .	(..)	(..)	(..)	(0·8)	(0·8)	(100)	(606)	(606)	(100)	(..)	(..)	(..)
II. Non-reproducible assets, land . total	(2) 100·0	(2) 100·0	100	16·4	16·4	100	2,029	2,029	100	(3) 3·60	3·60	100
(a) Agricultural	..	..	:	13·1	13·1	100	1,810	1,810	100	3·60	3·60	100
(b) Forest.	..	..	:	0·2	0·2	100	147	147	100	2·00	2·00	100
(c) Other.	..	..	:	3·1	3·1	100	72	72	100	(3) 1·60	(3) 1,60	100

	(1)	(2)	(3)	(4)	(5)	(6)	(7)	(8)	(9)	(10)	(11)	(12)
B. *Government* (3) . . total	:	:	:	(4) 24·0	(4) 12·0	50			58 / 57	(4) 9·47	(4) 5·43	: / 57
I. Reproducible assets . total	85·0	42·5	50	:	:	:	1,172 / 1,149	675 / 652	57	:	:	:
1. Structures (4)	(3) 70·0	(3) 35·0	(3) 50	:	:	:	1,149	652	57	:	:	57
2. Equipment	15·0	7·5	50	:	:	:				:	:	:
3. Inventories	:	:	:	:	:	:				:	:	:
II. Non-reproducible assets, land . . total	:	:	:	:	:	:	23	23	100	:	:	:
C. *Consumer durables* . . total	(4) 90·0	(4) 60·0	67	33·3	20·2	61		714	:	3·52	1·73	49
1. Passenger cars and other vehicles (5)	:	:	:	(4) 0·3	0·2	45		12		(5) 0·89	(5) 0·52	58
2. Other	:	:	:	33·0	20·0	61		702	:	2·63	1·21	46
D. *Foreign assets* . . total	:	:	:	8·1	8·1	100	(2) −42	−42	100	−1·02	−1·02	100
1. Monetary metals	:	:	:	2·2	2·2	100	(2) 112	112	100	0·11	0·11	100
2. Other net foreign assets	:	:	:	5·9	5·9	100	−154	−154	100	−1·13	−1·13	100
Total:												
1. Repr. tang. assets of Enterpr. + Govt. (AI + BI)	586·0	348·0	59	(5) 120·2	73·2	61	8,224	5,058	62	26·98	16·40	61
2. Repr. tang. assets (AI + BI + C)	676·0	408·0	60	(5) 153·5	93·4	61		5,772	:	30·50	18·13	59
3. Repr. tang. assets of Enterpr. + Govt., + net for. assets (AI + BI + D)	:	:	:	(5) 128·3	81·3	63	8,182	5,016	61	25·96	15·38	59
4. Repr. tang. assets + net for. assets (AI + BI + C + D)	:	:	:	(5) 161·6	101·5	63		5,730	:	29·48	17·11	58
5. Tang. assets of Enterpr. + Govt. (A + B)	686·0	448·0	65	136·6	89·6	66	10,276	7,110	69	30·58	20·00	65
6. Tang. assets (A + B + C)	776·0	508·0	65	169·9	109·8	65		7,824	:	34·10	21·73	64
7. Tang. assets of Enterpr., + Govt. + net for. assets (A + B + D)	:	:	:	144·7	97·7	68	10,234	7,068	69	29·56	18·98	64
8. Tang. assets + net for. assets (A + B + C + D)	:	:	:	178·0	117·9	66		7,782	:	33·08	20·71	63

[1] See notes to Table I.

TABLE III
Structure of National Wealth [1]

Classification	Reproducible tangible wealth (AI + BI) = 100					
	Belgium	Luxem-bourg	Nether-lands	W. Ger-many	France	United Kingdom
	1950	1950	1952	1955	1954	1953
A. *Enterprises* . . . total	110	111	106	117	96	..
I. Reproducible assets . total	91	91	84	88	(1) 75	(1) 94
1. Structures . . total	54	49	44	52	..	75
(a) Dwellings (1)	43	27	25	29	(1) 19	34
(b) Agricultural	} 11	4	4	3	..	..
(c) Other . .	}	19	(1) 15	20	(2) 26	(2) 41
2. Equipment . . total	29	40	26	24	..	..
(a) Agricultural .	2	(1) 1	(2) 2	2	17	1
(b) Other. . .	(1) 27	(2) 38	24	22	..	..
3. Inventories . total	8	..	13	(1) 12	12	19
(a) Livestock .	3	2	4	..	3	} 2
(b) Other agricultural	} 5	..	(3) 2	..	1	} 2
(c) Other. . .	}	..	8	..	9	17
(d) (Standing timber) (2) .	(1)	..	(1)	(..)	(..)	(..)
II. Non-reproducible assets, land . . . total	(2) 19	20	22	(2) 29	(3, 4) 20	..
(a) Agricultural .	..	10	18	..	(3) 18	..
(b) Forest . .	..	(3) 7	—	..	(5) 2	..
(c) Other . .	..	4	4	..	..	..
(Of which public enterprises) (6) total	..	15	8	..	23	..
(I. Reproducible assets)	(5) 6	12	6	..	..	..
(II. Non-reproducible assets) .	..	3	2	..	..	..
B. *Government* (3) . total	..	9	(4) 16	..	(6) 25	..
I. Reproducible assets . total	9	9	..	12	..	(3) 6
1. Structures (4)	..	9	..	(3) 10	..	(3) 5
2. Equipment . .	..	} —	..	2	} ..	(3) 5
3. Inventories .	..	—	..	..	..	1
II. Non-reproducible assets, land . . total	..	—	..	..	..	..
C. *Consumer durables* . total	18	—	28	(4) 17	15	..
1. Passenger cars and other vehicles (5) . .	(3) 2	—	—	..	1	..
2. Other . . .	(4) 16	..	(4) 27	..	14	..
D. *Foreign assets* . . total	12	−5	11	..	4	..
1. Monetary metals .	3	—	3	..	4	..
2. Other net foreign assets .	9	−5	8	..	—	..
Total:						
1. Repr. tang. assets of Enterpr. + Govt. (AI + BI) . .	100	100	(5) 100	100	(7) 100	(4) 100
2. Repr. tang. assets (AI + BI + C) .	118	..	(5) 128	117	(7) 115	..
3. Repr. tang. assets of Enterpr. + Govt. + net for. assets (AI + BI + D) .	112	95	(5) 111	..	(7) 104	..
4. Repr. tang. assets + net for. assets (AI + BI + C + D) .	129	..	(5) 139	..	(7) 119	..
5. Tang. assets of Enterpr. + Govt. (A + B) .	119	121	122	129	120	..
6. Tang. assets (A + B + C) .	137	..	150	146	135	..
7. Tang. assets of Enterpr. + Govt. + net for. assets (A + B + D) .	131	116	134	..	125	..
8. Tang. assets + net for. assets (A + B + C + D) . .	149	..	161	..	140	..

[1] See notes to Table I.

TABLE III (*continued*)
Structure of National Wealth [1]

Classification	Reproducible tangible wealth (AI + BI) = 100					
	Norway	Yugoslavia	Canada	U.S.A.	Australia (1)	South Africa
	1953	1953	1955	1955	1956	1955
A. *Enterprises* . . . total	91	127	..	106	(2) 89	(1) 99
I. Reproducible assets . total	88	87	84	87	67	(1) 66
1. Structures . total	53	54	47	59	34	(1) 36
(a) Dwellings (1)	25	25	23	35	23	11
(b) Agricultural	6	8	1	4	} 11	} 24
(c) Other	21	21	23	20		
2. Equipment . total	24	15	19	17	17	(1) 13
(a) Agricultural	1	2	4	2	4	..
(b) Other	23	13	16	15	13	..
3. Inventories . total	11	18	17	12	16	(1) 18
(a) Livestock	1	4	3	1	6	6
(b) Other agricultural	1	(1) 4	1	1	—	} 11
(c) Other	9	10	14	10	10	
(d) (Standing timber) (2)	(12)	(12)	(..)	(..)	(..)	(..)
II. Non-reproducible assets, land . total	4	40	..	19	22	(1) 34
(a) Agricultural	4	36	..	7	12	} 19
(b) Forest	..	3	..	(1) 1	..	
(c) Other	..	1	..	10	(3) 10	14
(Of which public enterprises) (6) total						
(I. Reproducible assets)	(3) 11		(2) 2	(3) 2	..	..
(II. Non-reproducible assets)	..				..	..
B. *Government* (3) . total	..	13	..	(2) 17	..	(2) 39
I. Reproducible assets . total	(1) 12	13	16	13	(4) 33	(2) 34
1. Structure (4)	12	} 13	(1) 15	13	..	25
2. Equipment	..		(1) 1	1	..	8
3. Inventories	..	—	..	—	..	1
II. Non-reproducible assets, land . total	..	1	..	4	..	(2) 5
C. *Consumer durables* . total	..	14	19	15	11	..
1. Passenger cars and other vehicles (5)	1	—	5	6	(5) 3	3
2. Other	..	14	14	10	7	..
D. *Foreign assets* . . total	−2	−1	−14	4	−6	..
1. Monetary metals	—	(2) 2	2	3	1	1
2. Other net foreign assets	−2	−3	−16	1	−7	..
Total:						
1. Repr. tang. assets of Enterpr. + Govt. (AI + BI)	(1) 100	100	100	100	100	100
2. Repr. tang. assets (AI + BI + C)	..	114	119	115	111	..
3. Repr. tang. assets of Enterpr. + Govt. + net for. assets (AI + BI + D)	(1) 98	99	86	104	94	..
4. Repr. tang. assets + net for. assets (AI + BI + C + D)	..	113	105	120	104	..
5. Tang. assets of Enterpr. + Govt. (A + B)	(2) 104	146	..	123	122	139
6. Tang. assets (A + B + C)	..	155	..	138	133	..
7. Tang. assets of Enterpr. + Govt. + net for. assets (A + B + D)	(2) 102	140	..	127	116	..
8. Tang. assets + net for. assets (A + B + C + D)	..	154	..	142	126	..

[1] See notes to Table I.

TABLE III (*continued*)
Structure of National Wealth [1]

Classification	Reproducible tangible wealth (AI + BI) = 100				
	Argentina	Colombia	Japan	India	Mexico
	1955	1953	1955	1950	1950
A. *Enterprises* . . . total	..	..	..	200	..
I. Reproducible assets . total	76	82	80	95	77
1. Structures . total	..	51	43	50	(1) 62
(a) Dwellings (1)	..	16	17	26	31
(b) Agricultural	(1) 10	21	1	13	(2) 7
(c) Other	(2) 66	14	24	11	25
2. Equipment . total	..	17	19	14	..
(a) Agricultural	..	1	1	3	..
(b) Other	..	16	17	10	..
3. Inventories . total	..	..	19	32	15
(a) Livestock	..	14	(1) 1	16	5
(b) Other agricultural	..	..	1	—	(3) 2
(c) Other	..	..	16	15	8
(d) Standing timber) (2)	..	(..)	(..)	(..)	(..)
II. Non-reproducible assets, land . total	—	..	..	105	(..)
(a) Agricultural	..	..	..	} 92	..
(b) Forest	..	..	..		..
(c) Other	..	..	..	12	..
(Of which public enterprises) (6) total	..	..	..	..	..
(I. Reproducible assets)	..	..	8	13	..
(II. Non-reproducible assets)	..	..	..	..	..
B. *Government* (3) . total	..	..	..	..	..
I. Reproducible assets . total	24	18	20	5	23
1. Structure (4)	..	15	14	5	..
2. Equipment	..	3	3	..	..
3. Inventories	..	..	3	..	..
II. Non-reproducible assets, land . total	..	..	..	..	..
C. *Consumer durables* . total	..	..	25	..	..
1. Passenger cars and other vehicles (5)	..	..	..	—	..
2. Other	..	..	..	..	..
D. *Foreign assets* . total	..	..	1	..	..
1. Monetary metals	..	..	—	..	2
2. Other net foreign assets	..	..	1	..	..
Total:					
1. Repr. tang. assets of Enterpr. + Govt. (AI + BI)	(3) 100	100	100	100	100
2. Repr. tang. assets (AI + BI + C)	..	..	125	..	..
3. Repr. tang. assets of Enterpr. + Govt. + net for. assets (AI + BI + D)	..	..	101	..	..
4. Repr. tang. assets + net for. assets (AI + BI + C + D)	..	..	126	..	..
5. Tang. assets of Enterpr. + Govt. (A + B)	..	..	..	(1) 205	..
6. Tang. assets (A + B + C)	..	..	..	..	..
7. Tang. assets of Enterpr. + Govt. + net for. assets (A + B + D)	..	..	..	..	..
8. Tang. assets + net for. assets (A + B + C + D)	..	..	..	..	..

[1] See notes to Table I.

TABLE III (*continued*)
Structure of National Wealth [1]

Classification	Tangible wealth (A + B) = 100					
	Belgium	Luxembourg	Netherlands	W. Germany	France	Norway
	1950	1950	1952	1955	1954	1953
A. *Enterprises* . . total	93	92	87	91	80	88
I. Reproducible assets . total	76	75	68	68	(1) 63	85
1. Structures . total	45	41	36	40	..	51
(a) Dwellings (1)	36	22	20	22	(1) 16	24
(b) Agricultural	} 9	3	3	2	..	6
(c) Other .		16	(1) 12	15	(2) 22	21
2. Equipment . total	25	33	21	19	..	23
(a) Agricultural	2	(1) 1	(2) 2	2	14	1
(b) Other .	(1) 22	(2) 32	19	17	..	22
3. Inventories . total	7	2	11	(1) 9	10	11
(a) Livestock .	2	2	3	..	2	1
(b) Other agricultural	} 5	..	(3) 2	..	1	1
(c) Other .		..	6	..	7	8
(d) (Standing timber) (2)	(1)	(..)	(1)	(..)	(..)	(11)
II. Non-reproducible assets, land . total	(2) 16	17	18	(2) 22	(3,4) 17	3
(a) Agricultural .	..	8	15	..	(3) 15	3
(b) Forest .	..	(3) 5	0	..	(5) 2	..
(c) Other .	..	4	3	..	..	..
(Of which public enterprises) (6) total	..	12	7	..	19	..
(I. Reproducible assets) .	(5) 5	10	5	..	..	(3) 11
(II. Non-reproducible assets) .	..	3	1	..	..	..
B. *Government* (3) . total	..	8	(4) 13	..	(6) 20	..
I. Reproducible assets . total	7	8	..	9	..	(1) 12
1. Structures (4)	..	7	..	(3) 8	..	12
2. Equipment .	..	}	..	2	..	..
3. Inventories	..	—	..	..	..	..
II. Non-reproducible assets, land . total	..	—	..	..	..	..
C. *Consumer durables* . total	15	..	23	(4) 13	12	..
1. Passenger cars and other vehicles (5) .	(3) 2	—	—	..	1	1
2. Other .	(4) 13	..	(4) 22	..	11	..
D. *Foreign assets* . total	10	—4	9	..	4	—2
1. Monetary metals .	3	—	2	..	4	0
2. Other net foreign assets	7	—4	7	..	—	—2
Total:						
1. Repr. tang. assets of Enterpr. + Govt. (AI + BI) .	84	83	(5) 82	78	(7) 83	(1) 97
2. Repr. tang. assets (AI + BI + C)	99	..	(5) 104	91	(7) 95	..
3. Repr. tang. assets of Enterpr. + Govt. + net for. assets (AI + BI + D)	94	79	(5) 91	..	(7) 87	(1) 95
4. Repr. tang. assets + net for. assets (AI + BI + C + D) .	108	..	(5) 113	..	(7) 99	..
5. Tang. assets of Enterpr. + Govt. (A + B) .	100	100	100	100	100	(2) 100
6. Tang. assets (A + B + C) .	115	..	123	113	112	..
7. Tang. assets of Enterpr. + Govt. + net for. assets (A + B + D)	110	96	109	..	104	(2) 98
8. Tang. assets + net for. assets (A + B + C + D) . .	125	..	132	..	116	..

[1] See notes to Table I.

TABLE III (continued)
Structures of National Wealth [1]

Classification	Tangible wealth (A + B) = 100				
	Yugo-slavia	U.S.A.	Aus-tralia (1)	South Africa	India
	1953	1955	1956	1955	1950
A. *Enterprises* . . . total	91	86	(2) 73	(1) 72	98
I. Reproducible assets . total	62	71	55	(1) 47	47
1. Structures . . total	38	48	28	(1) 26	24
(a) Dwellings (1)	18	28	19	8	13
(b) Agricultural	6	3	} 9	} 17	6
(c) Other	15	17			5
2. Equipment . total	11	13	14	(1) 9	7
(a) Agricultural	2	2	3	..	2
(b) Other	9	12	10	..	5
3. Inventories . total	13	10	13	(1) 13	16
(a) Livestock .	3	1	5	5	8
(b) Other agricultural	(1) 3	1	1	} 8	—
(c) Other . .	7	8	8		7
(d) (Standing timber) (2) .	(9)	(..)	(..)	(..)	(..)
II. Non-reproducible assets, land . . . total	29	15	. 18	(1) 24	15
(a) Agricultural	25	6	10	} 14	} 45
(b) Forest . . .	2	(1) 1	..		
(c) Other . . .	1	8	(3) 8	10	6
(Of which public enterprises) (6) total	—	..	..	..	..
(I. Reproducible assets) . .		(3) 1	..	..	6
(II. Non-reproducible assets) .	—		..	..	..
B. *Government* (3) . . total	9	(2) 14	..	(2) 28	..
I. Reproducible assets . total	9	11	(4) 27	(2) 25	2
1. Structures (4) . .	} 9	10	..	18	2
2. Equipment . .		—	..	6	..
3. Inventories . .	—	—	..	1	..
II. Non-reproducible assets, land . . . total	—	3	..	(2) 4	..
C. *Consumer durables* . . total	10	12	9	..	..
1. Passenger cars and other vehicles (5) . .	0	4	(5) 3	2	—
2. Other . . .	10	8	6	..	..
D. *Foreign assets* . . . total	—1	4	—5	..	..
1. Monetary metals . .	(2) 2	2	1	1	..
2. Other net foreign assets	—2	1	—6	..	..
Total:					
1. Repr. tang. assets of Enterpr. + Govt. (AI + BI) . .	71	82	82	72	49
2. Repr. tang. assets (AI + BI + C)	81	94	91	..	..
3. Repr. tang. assets of Enterpr. + Govt. + net for. assets (AI + BI + D) . . .	71	85	77	..	..
4. Repr. tang. assets + net for. assets (AI + BI + C + D)	81	98	86	..	..
5. Tang. assets of Enterpr. + Govt. (A + B) . . .	100	100	100	100	(1) 100
6. Tang. assets (A + B + C) .	110	112	109	..	..
7. Tang. assets of Enterpr. + Govt. + net for. assets (A + B + D)	99	104	95	..	..
8. Tang. assets + net for. assets (A + B + C + D) . .	109	116	104	..	..

[1] See notes to Table I.

TABLE III (continued)
Structure of National Wealth [1]

Classification	Tangible wealth + net foreign assets (A + B + D) = 100							
	Belgium	Luxembourg	Netherlands	France	Norway	Yugoslavia	U.S.A.	Australia (1)
	1950	1950	1952	1954	1953	1953	1955	1956
A. *Enterprises* . . total	84	96	79	77	90	91	83	(2) 77
I. Reproducible assets . total	69	78	63	(1) 60	86	62	68	58
1. Structures . total	41	42	33	..	52	39	46	29
(a) Dwellings (1)	33	23	19	(1) 15	25	18	27	20
(b) Agricultural	} 8	3	3		6	6	} 3	} 10
(c) Other		16	(1) 11	(2) 21	21	15	16	
2. Equipment . total	22	34	19	..	24	11	13	14
(a) Agricultural	2	(1) 1	(2) 2	14	1	2	1	3
(b) Other	(1) 20	(2) 33	18	..	23	9	12	11
3. Inventories . total	6	2	10	10	11	13	9	14
(a) Livestock	2	2	3	2	2	3	1	5
(b) Other agricultural	} 4	..	(3) 1	1	1	(1) 3	1	1
(c) Other		..	6	7	8	7	8	9
(d) (Standing timber) (2)	(1)	..	(..)	(..)	(11)	(9)	(..)	(..)
II. Non-reproducible assets, land . . total	(2) 15	17	17	(3,4) 16	3	29	15	19
(a) Agricultural	..	8	13	(3) 15	3	26	..	11
(b) Forest	..	(3) 6	—	(5) 2	..	2	(1) 6	..
(c) Other	..	4	3	..	..	1	8	(3) 8
(Of which public enterprises) (6) total	..	13	6	19	..	..	..	..
(I. Reproducible assets)	(5) 5	10	5	..	(3) 11	..	(3) 1	..
(II. Non-reproducible assets)	..	3	1	..	..		..	..
B. *Government* (3) . total	..	8	(4) 12	(6) 20	..	10	(2) 13	..
I. Reproducible assets . total	7	8	..	..	(1) 12	9	10	(4) 29
1. Structures (4)	..	7	..	..	12	} 9	9	..
2. Equipment	..	} —	..	..	}		—	..
3. Inventories	..	}	..	..	}		—	..
II. Non-reproducible assets, land . . total	..	—	..	..	..	—	3	..
C. *Consumer durables* . total	13	..	21	12	..	10	12	9
1. Passenger cars and other vehicles (5)	(3) 2	—	—	1	1	—	4	(5) 3
2. Other	(4) 12	..	(4) 20	11	..	10	8	6
D. *Foreign assets* . total	9	—4	8	3	—2	—1	3	—5
1. Monetary metals	2		2	3	—	(2) 2	2	1
2. Other net foreign assets	7	—4	6	—	—2	—2	1	—6
Total:								
1. Repr. tang. assets of Enterpr. + Govt. (AI + BI)	76	86	(5) 75	(7) 80	(1) 98	72	79	86
2. Repr. tang. assets (AI + BI + C)	90	..	(5) 96	(7) 92	..	82	91	96
3. Repr. tang. assets of Enterpr. + Govt. + net for. assets (AI + BI + D)	85	82	(5) 83	(7) 84	(1) 97	71	82	81
4. Repr. tang. assets + net for. assets (AI + BI + C + D)	99	..	(5) 104	(7) 96	..	81	94	90
5. Tang. assets of Enterpr. + Govt. (A + B)	91	104	92	97	(2) 102	101	97	105
6. Tang. assets (A + B + C)	104	..	112	108	..	111	109	114
7. Tang. assets of Enterpr. + Govt. + net for. assets (A + B + D)	100	100	100	100	(2) 100	100	100	100
8. Tang. assets + net for. assets (A + B + C + D)	113	..	121	112	..	110	112	109

[1] See notes to Table I.

C

TABLE IV

Structure of National Wealth over Time (Percentages)

Belgium (current prices)

	Land	Agriculture	Industry		Dwellings	Government	Consumers' durables	Gold	Net foreign assets	Total
			Structures	Equipment						
1939	14	3	6	18	25	8	10	5	11	100
1950	14	3	7	21	28	7	12	2	6	100

Luxembourg (current prices)

	Land		Agriculture Equipment, Livestock	Steel Industry	Other Industry, Commerce, Equipment	Industry, Commerce, Structures, Dwellings	Government Structures, Roads, etc.	Net Foreign Assets	Total
	Agriculture, Forest	Building Sites							
1934	22	4	4	27	18	31	5	−19	100
1950	14	4	3	14	25	27	8	−4	100

W. Germany (1950 prices; land, inventories, net foreign assets excluded)

	Agriculture	Electricity, Gas, Water,	Manufacturing Industry	Other Enterprises	Transport	Dwellings	Government	Total
1913	10	2	9	6	18	42	13	100
1939	6	4	11	7	18	37	17	100
1955	6	5	18	9	16	32	14	100

TABLE IV (continued)

France (current prices)

	Agriculture		Manufacturing Industry, Commerce	Transport, Communications	Dwellings, other Industrial Buildings	Government	Consumer Durables	Monetary Gold	Net Foreign Assets	Total
	Land, Structures	Equipment, Livestock								
1913	23	5	9	9	22	8	7	3	14	100
1954	14	4	21	11	17	20	10	3	—	100

United Kingdom (1948 prices; land, inventories, agricultural structures, government (partly) excluded)

	Agriculture Equipment	Coal, Gas, Water, Electricity	Manufacturing Industry, Trade	Transport, Communications	Dwellings	Public and Social Services	Total
1938	—	9	25	18	42	6	100
1953	1	9	27	14	42	7	100

Sweden (current prices, subsoil resources and exploitable water power included)

	Agriculture			Mining	Other Industry	Transport, Communications	Dwellings, Buildings, Equipment, Consumers' Durables included	Government	Monetary Metals	Net Foreign Assets	Total
	Land Structures	Equipment, Livestock	Forestry Land included								
1908	4	24	11	4	15	8	36	4	1	−7	100
1952	2	7	5	2	21	4	51	6	1	1	100

Norway (1938 prices; land, inventories, net foreign assets excluded)

	Agriculture, Forestry	Mining, Manufacturing Industry	Electricity, Gas	Fishing, Merchant Fleet, Harbours	Transport, Communications	Other Enterprises, Trade	Dwellings	Government, Roads, Bridges	Total
1899	15	8	—	6	6	8	15	42	100
1939	11	13	6	9	8	7	13	33	100
1953	9	16	8	9	8	7	14	29	100

TABLE IV (continued)

Canada (1949 prices, land excluded)

	Agriculture	Industry		Transport, Communications	Dwellings	Government	Consumer Durables	Monetary Metals	Net Foreign Assets	Total
		Structures, Equipment	Inventories							
1947	9	24	17	11	26	18	14	1	−20	100
1955	8	28	15	9	21	15	17	2	−15	100

U.S.A. (current prices)

	Land		Agriculture			Other Enterprises			Government	Consumers' Durables	Monetary Metals	Net Foreign Assets	Total
	Agriculture	Other	Livestock	Structural Equipment	Inventories	Structures	Equipment	Inventories					
1900	21	23	4	4	2	20	7	8	3	9	2	−3	100
1922	15	19	2	3	1	19	10	9	6	11	2	3	100
1939	8	21	2	2	1	20	10	7	11	11	6	1	100
1949	8	15	2	4	1	17	13	9	10	14	4	3	100
1955	7	14	1	5	1	19	13	9	12	14	3	2	100

Australia (current prices; net foreign assets excluded)

	Land	Agriculture Equipment Livestock	Enterprises Equipment	Inventories	Dwellings, Agriculture, Industry, Buildings	Motor Vehicles	Consumers' Durables	Government	Monetary Metals	Totals
1915	22	6	5	7	30	4		24	2	100
1929	21	6	4	8	31	3	3	23	1	100
1947	22	6	8	8	29	1	4	21	1	100
1956	16	7	9	8	26	3	6	25	—	100

TABLE IV (continued)

South Africa (current prices, land, net foreign assets excluded)

	Agriculture		Mining	Manufacturing Industry		Dwellings	Other Private Assets			Railways, Harbours	Other Public Assets	Total
	Fixed Assets	Inventory		Fixed Assets	Inventory		Fixed Assets		Inventories			
1910	9	21	12	3	1	15			9	19	11	100
1922	13	13	12	4	2	11	5		7	19	14	100
1938	12	10	11	6	4	12	5		7	15	18	100
1947	11	8	9	7	6	13	5		7	14	20	100
1955	11	6	10	10	6	13	6		6	12	20	100

Argentina (1950 prices; land, inventories, net foreign assets excluded)

	Agriculture	Manufacturing Industry, Mining, Construction	Transport, Communications, Electricity, Housing, Personal Services	Public Works	Total
1938	13	11	58	18	100
1948	11	12	56	21	100
1955	10	13	53	24	100

Colombia (1950 prices; land, inventories, net foreign assets excluded)

	Agriculture		Mining	Manufacturing Industry		Transport, Communications, Energy		Housing	Services	Total
	Fixed Assets	Livestock		Structures	Equipment	Structures	Equipment			
1925	26	15	2	2	6	5	1	17	26	100
1938	25	16	2	2	7	8	3	15	22	100
1945	25	17	2	3	6	8	3	16	20	100
1953	22	14	2	5	9	8	6	16	18	100

TABLE V
Methods of Valuation

Components	(Part 1. Mainly Perpetual-inventory Method)		
	Canada	U.S.A.	Argentina
A. *Enterprises*			
I. Reproducible assets			
1. Structures:			
(a) Dwellings .	D	D	(See other structures) ..
(b) Agricultural	D	(See other structures) ..	Agricult. dwell. A1
(c) Other. .	D	D	D
			Electricity B2
			Shipping A1
2. Equipment:			
(a) Agricultural	D	D	(See structures) ..
(b) Other. .	D	D	(See structures) ..
3. Inventories:			
(a) Livestock .	A2	A2	..
(b) Agricultural	A2	A2	..
(c) Other. .	B2	B2	..
	(Sample)		
(d) (Standing timber) .	..	(See forest land) ..	..
II. Non-reproducible assets, land			
(a) Agricultural	..	(Land + buildings) J2	..
(b) Forest .	..	A4	..
(c) Other. .	..	J1	..
B. *Government*			
I. Reproducible assets			
1. Structures . .	D	D	D
2. Equipment .	D	D	D
3. Inventories .	..	D	..
II. Land . . .	..	(Land + buildings) J1	..
C. *Consumers' durables*			
1. Passenger cars .	D	D	..
2. Other . . .	D	D	..
D. *Foreign assets*			
1. Monetary metals .	K	K	..
2. Other . . .	K	K	..
		Panama Canal D	

NOTES TO TABLE V

Methods of valuation, symbols used.

A – Quantity × price.
    1. Replacement cost minus depreciation.
    2. Market price.
    3. Market price of used goods.
    4. Expert price (or estimated price).

B – Balance sheet figures.
    1. Book value.
    2. Book value of assets adjusted for current price level, or book value = current price level.
    3. Value of net worth.

C – 1. Direct expert valuation of value after depreciation.
    2. Census valuation of value after depreciation.

D – Perpetual-inventory method.
E – Capitalization of net income (or rent).
F – Valuation of net worth on the basis of stock-exchange value of stocks and bonds.

G – Insurance data (fire, marine, and aviation insurance).
    1. Insurance premiums capitalized.
    2. Insurance expert valuation (+ correction for possible undervaluation).

H – Tax data.
    1. Valuation by tax authorities.
    2. Capitalization of cadastral levy.

TABLE V (continued)
Methods of Valuation

Components	(Part 1. Mainly Perpetual-inventory Method)		
	Colombia	South Africa	Australia
A. *Enterprises*			
I. Reproducible assets			
1. Structures:			
(a) Dwellings .	Urban dwellings A1	D	D
(b) Agricultural	(See other structures) ..	(See other structures) ..	(See other structures) ..
(c) Other .	Electricity ⎱ B2 / Railways ⎰ / Shipping A1	D	D
2. Equipment:			
(a) Agricultural	D	(See other equipment) ..	D
(b) Other .	D	D	D
3. Inventories:			
(a) Livestock .	A2	A2	A2
(b) Agricultural	..	(See other inventories) ..	A2
(c) Other .	..	B2	B2
(d) (Standing timber) .	..	(Sample) ..	..
II. Non-reproducible assets, land			
(a) Agricultural	..	—	A4
(b) Forest .	..	—	
(c) Other .	..	—	A4
B. *Government*			
I. Reproducible assets			
1. Structures .	D	D	D
2. Equipment .	D	D	(See structures) ..
3. Inventories .	..	D	(See structures) ..
II. Land .	..	—	..
C. *Consumers' durables*			
1. Passenger cars .	..	D	D
2. Other .	..	..	D
D. *Foreign assets*			
1. Monetary metals	..	K	K
2. Other .	..	..	K

NOTES TO TABLE V (continued)

Methods of valuation, symbols used.

I – Other methods.
1. Labour force × floor space per man.
2. Capital invested per man (based on limited research).
3. Valuation of monetary gold by adding gold imports and issues.

J – 1. Value as a percentage of other assets.
2. Value as a ratio of other economic data.

K – Official data, not further specified (Government, Central Bank, etc.).

Additional symbols.

One of the above-mentioned methods $+ a$ = estimate of a past year continued by means of price and (or) quantity indexes.

A⎱ B⎰ both methods used as a check.

— no information on methods available.

.. no estimates available (see Table I).

Country notes.
(1) Estimates of Redfern.
(2) Estimates of Barna.
(3) After correction for structures, holdings and foreign participations.

TABLE V (*continued*)
Methods of Valuation

Components	(Part 1. Mainly Perpetual-inventory Method)	(Part 2. Mainly Other Methods)			
	(1) United Kingdom	Belgium		Luxembourg	
A. *Enterprises*					
I. Reproducible assets					
1. Structures:					
(a) Dwellings .	D		A3		G1
(b) Agricultural	..	See other structures)	..		G1
(c) Other .	D	(1939 + a)	H2		G1
				Electricity ⎫	F
				Railways ⎪	
				Water ⎬	B1
				G.P.O. ⎭	
2. Equipment:					
(a) Agricultural	D	(1939 + a)	C1		A1
(b) Other .	(See structures)	(3) Corporations	F		G1
	..	Railways	B1	Railways ⎫	
		Non-corporation	I2	G.P.O. ⎬	B2
		(Rough est.)		Water ⎭	
3. Inventories:					
(a) Livestock .	(See agricult. invent.)		C1	(See equipment)	A2
(b) Agricultural	D	(See other invent.)	..	(See equipment)	..
(c) Other .	D	(1939 + a)	C1	(See equipment)	..
(d) (Standing timber) .	..	—		(See forest land)	..
II. Non-reproducible assets, land					
(a) Agricultural	..		A4		A4
(b) Forest . .	..		A4		A4
(c) Other . .	..		A4		A4
B. *Government*					
I. Reproducible assets:					
1. Structures .	D	(1948 + a)	C1		G1
				Repres. build.	C1
				Roads	A4
2. Equipment .	D	(See structures)	..	(Structures)	J1
3. Inventories .	D	(See structures)	..	(See equipment)	..
II. Land . .	..		..		A4
C. *Consumers' durables*					
1. Passenger cars .	..		A1		A1
2. Other . . .	..	(Dwellings)	J1		..
D. *Foreign assets*					
1. Monetary metals .	..		K		..
2. Other . . .	..	Rough est.		(Govt. and large enterprise)	K

TABLE V (*continued*)
Methods of Valuation

Components	(Part 2. Mainly Other Methods)					
	Netherlands		West Germany		France	
A. *Enterprises*						
I. Reproducible assets						
1. Structures:						
(a) Dwellings .		A1		A1		A1
(b) Agricultural		A1		A1	(See land)	..
(c) Other. .	(1948 + a)	I2		D	Mining	
	Transport	A1	Transport }		Electricity }	B1
	Electricity		Electricity }	C2	Gas	
	Govt. enterpr. }	B2			Transport	A1
	Trade				Railways	{ A1 / D
					Other (rough est.)	BDF
					(Product. wages)	J2
2. Equipment:						
(a) Agricultural		A4		A1		A1
(b) Other. .		I2		D	(See structures)	..
	Transport	A1	Transport }			
	Electricity		Electricity			
	Govt. enterprise }	B2	Trade }	C2		
	Trade		Banking			
			Services			
3. Inventories:						
(a) Livestock .		A2		..		A2
(b) Agricultural		A2	(See other invent.)	..		—
(c) Other. .	(1947 = 0)	D	(Gr. nat. prod.)	J2		—
(d) (Standing timber) .		A4		..		..
II. Non-reproducible assets, land						
(a) Agricultural .		E		..		A4
(b) Forest . .		A4		..		A4
(c) Other . .	(Dwellings)	J1		..		..
B. *Government*						
I. Reproducible assets:						
1. Structures .	State	B2	Rough est. (partly)	D	(1913 + a)	C1
	Other (State)	J1			Schools }	A1
					Roads }	
2. Equipment .	(See structures)	..	(See structures)	..	(See structures)	..
3. Inventories .	(See structures)	..		..	(See structures)	..
II. Land . . .	(See structures)	..		..	(See structures)	..
C. *Consumers' durables*						
1. Passenger cars .		A1	(See other c.d.)	..		A1
2. Other . .	(1948 + a)	C2	(Gr. nat. prod.)	J2	Furniture (rent)	J2
					Clothing (consumption)	J
D. *Foreign assets*						
1. Monetary metals .		K		..		I3
2. Other . .		E		..		..

TABLE V (*continued*)
Methods of Valuation

Components		(Part 2. Mainly Other Methods)					
	(2) United Kingdom	Sweden		Norway		Yugoslavia	
A. *Enterprises*							
I. Reproducible assets							
1. Structures:							
(a) Dwellings .	G2	(See other struct.)	..		A1	A1	
(b) Agricultural	..	(Minus land)	H1		—	A1	
(c) Other. .	G2		G2		G2	A1	
		Electricity	D	Transport	A1		
		Railways	B1	G.P.O. }	B1		
		Govt. enterprise	B3	Railways }			
		Mining	E				
2. Equipment:							
(a) Agricultural	G2		H1		—	A1	
(b) Other. .	G2	(See structures)		(See structures)	..	A1	
3. Inventories:							
(a) Livestock .	..		A2		A2	A2	
(b) Agricultural	..	(See structures)	..		A2	A2	
(c) Other. .	..	(See structures)	..		A2	A2	
					C2		
(d) (Standing timber) .	..	See forest land)	..		—	A1	
II. Non-reproducible assets, land							
(a) Agricultural .	..	(Agr. structures)	J1		A4	A2	
(b) Forest . .	..		G2		..	(Standing timber) J1	
(c) Other . .	..		H1		..	A2	
B. *Government*							
I. Reproducible assets:							
1. Structures. .	..		C1		A1	I1	
					D		
2. Equipment .	..	(See structures)	..		..	A1	
3. Inventories	..	(See structures)	..		..	..	
II. Land . . .	..	(See structures)	..		..	A2	
C. *Consumers' durables*							
1. Passenger cars .	..		A3		A1	A1	
2. Other . . .	..		A3		..	A3	
D. *Foreign assets*							
1. Monetary metals .	..		K		K	K	
2. Other . . .	..	(1943 + a)	C2		K	K	
			K				

TABLE V (*continued*)
Methods of Valuation

Components	(Part 2. Mainly Other Methods)				
	Japan	India		Mexico	
A. *Enterprises*					
I. Reproducible assets					
1. Structures:					
(a) Dwellings .	A1	Urban dwell.	E		I2
		Agric. dwell.	{ A1 / C2		
(b) Agricultural	B2	(Of land)	J1		C2
(c) Other. .	(Sample) B2	(+ a)	B1		C2
				Oil industry }	D
				G.P.O. (partly) }	
				G.P.O. (partly) ..	A1
2. Equipment:					
(a) Agricultural	B2	(Per househ.)	{ A1 / C2	(See structures)	..
(b) Other. .	B2	(See structures)	..	(See structures)	..
3. Inventories:					
(a) Livestock .	B2	(Per househ.)	{ A2 / C2		C2
(b) Agricultural	(See other inventories)		—	(= product 1950)	J2
(c) Other. .	B2	Trade (net output)	J2		C2
(d) (Standing timber) .	..		..		..
II. Non-reproducible assets, land					
(a) Agricultural	..	(+ a)	C2		..
(b) Forest .	..	(See Agric. land)	..		..
(c) Other. .	..		C2		..
B. *Government*					
I. Reproducible assets:					
1. Structures .	B2	(1946 + a)	B1		D
		Roads	A1	Roads	A1
2. Equipment .	(See structures)		..	(See structures)	..
3. Inventories .	B2		..	(See structures)	..
II. Land . . .	..		..		..
C. *Consumers' durables*					
1. Passenger cars .	(Sample) C2		A1		..
2. Other . .	(Sample) C2		..		..
D. *Foreign assets*					
1. Monetary metals .	K		..		K
2. Other . . .	—		..		..

Year	Belgium Current Prices			West Germany 1950 Prices					Norway 1938 Prices		
				Wealth			Ratio				
	Wealth 1	Income 2	Ratio $\frac{1}{2}$	Net 1	Gross 2	Product 3	$\frac{1}{3}$	$\frac{2}{3}$	Wealth 1	Product 2	Ratio $\frac{1}{2}$
1846	10·75	1·159	9·3	—	—	—	—	—	—	—	—
96	29·83	3·280	9·1	—	—	—	—	—	—	—	—
97	—	—	—	—	—	—	—	—	—	—	—
98	—	—	—	—	—	—	—	—	—	—	—
99	—	—	—	—	—	—	—	—	—	—	—
1900	—	—	—	—	—	—	—	—	7,417	1,821	4·1
1	—	—	—	—	—	—	—	—	7,583	1,860	4·1
2	—	—	—	—	—	—	—	—	7,724	1,882	4·1
3	—	—	—	—	—	—	—	—	7,840	1,858	4·2
4	—	—	—	—	—	—	—	—	7,970	1,850	4·3
5	—	—	—	—	—	—	—	—	8,075	1,860	4·4
6	—	—	—	—	—	—	—	—	8,212	1,931	4·3
7	—	—	—	—	—	—	—	—	8,395	2,019	4·2
8	—	—	—	—	—	—	—	—	8,581	2,085	4·1
9	—	—	—	—	—	—	—	—	8,741	2,119	4·1
1910	—	—	—	—	—	—	—	—	8,961	2,213	4·0
11	—	—	—	—	—	—	—	—	9,239	2,302	4·0
12	—	—	—	—	—	—	—	—	9,567	2,406	4·0
13	50·95	6·488	7·9	215	341	63	3·4	5·4	9,905	2,528	3·9
14	—	—	—	—	—	—	—	—	10,224	2,589	3·9
15	—	—	—	—	—	—	—	—	10,550	2,726	3·9
16	—	—	—	—	—	—	—	—	10,904	2,870	3·8
17	—	—	—	—	—	—	—	—	11,098	2,605	4·3
18	—	—	—	—	—	—	—	—	11,340	2,455	4·6
19	—	—	—	—	—	—	—	—	11,745	3,084	3·8
1920	—	—	—	—	—	—	—	—	12,203	3,171	3·8
21	—	—	—	—	—	—	—	—	12,403	2,734	4·5
22	—	—	—	—	—	—	—	—	12,573	3,037	4·1
23	—	—	—	—	—	—	—	—	12,804	3,127	4·1
24	—	—	—	—	—	—	—	—	13,070	3,099	4·2
25	—	—	—	—	—	—	—	—	13,351	3,245	4·1
26	—	—	—	—	—	—	—	—	13,536	3,241	4·2
27	—	—	—	—	—	—	—	—	13,736	3,380	4·1
28	—	—	—	—	—	—	—	—	14,082	3,573	3·9
29	—	—	—	245	401	68	3·6	5·9	14,500	3,888	3·7
1930	445·00	66·50	6·7	—	—	—	—	—	14,990	4,196	3·6
31	—	—	—	—	—	—	—	—	15,317	3,791	4·0
32	—	—	—	—	—	—	—	—	15,482	3,999	3·9
33	—	—	—	—	—	—	—	—	15,662	4,093	3·8
34	—	—	—	—	—	—	—	—	15,926	4,253	3·7
35	—	—	—	—	—	—	—	—	16,319	4,480	3·6
36	—	—	—	—	—	—	—	—	16,851	4,808	3·5
37	—	—	—	—	—	—	—	—	17,564	5,012	3·5
38	443·00	65·20	6·8	—	—	—	—	—	18,192	5,102	3·6
39	—	—	—	299	476	104	2·9	4·5	18,874	5,353	3·5
1940	—	—	—	—	—	—	—	—	—	—	—
41	—	—	—	—	—	—	—	—	—	—	—
42	—	—	—	—	—	—	—	—	—	—	—
43	—	—	—	—	—	—	—	—	—	—	—
44	—	—	—	—	—	—	—	—	—	—	—
45	—	—	—	—	—	—	—	—	—	—	—
46	—	—	—	—	—	—	—	—	17,157	5,555	3·1
47	—	—	—	—	—	—	—	—	18,256	6,311	2·9
48	—	—	—	212	412	68	3·1	6·1	19,311	6,567	2·9
49	—	—	—	—	—	—	—	—	20,413	6,772	3·0
1950	1430·0	265·0	5·4	226	440	97	2·3	4·5	21,587	7,073	3·1
51	—	—	—	—	—	—	—	—	22,760	7,322	3·1
52	—	—	—	—	—	—	—	—	24,051	7,629	3·2
53	—	—	—	—	—	—	—	—	25,435	7,812	3·3
54	—	—	—	—	—	—	—	—	26,868	7,915	3·4
55	—	—	—	306	544	150	2·0	3·6	28,284	8,323	3·4
56	—	—	—	—	—	—	—	—	—	—	—

NOTES TO TABLE VI.
Country notes
Belgium – Wealth: total net wealth (see source 13).
Income: national income at factor cost (see source 13).
W. Germany – Wealth: gross and net fixed assets (see source 5).
Product: gross national product (see source 5).
Norway – Wealth: net fixed assets (see source 9).
Product: net domestic product (see source 9).

U.S.A. Current Prices			Australia Current Prices			South Africa Current Prices			Argentina 1940 Prices			Colombia 1950 Prices	Year
Wealth 1	Income 2	Ratio ½	Wealth 1	Product 2	Ratio ½	Wealth 1	Product 2	Ratio ½	Wealth 1	Product 2	Ratio ½	Wealth Product Ratio	
—	—	—	—	—	—	—	—	—	—	—	—	—	1846
—	—	—	—	—	—	—	—	—	—	—	—	—	96
71·6	12·1	5·9	—	—	—	—	—	—	—	—	—	—	97
76·2	12·4	6·1	—	—	—	—	—	—	—	—	—	—	98
82·5	14·5	5·7	—	—	—	—	—	—	—	—	—	—	99
87·7	15·5	5·7	—	—	—	—	—	—	—	—	—	—	1900
92·0	17·2	5·4	—	—	—	—	—	—	—	—	—	—	1
98·6	17·7	5·6	—	—	—	—	—	—	44·6	10·76	4·1	—	2
04·1	19·4	5·4	1309	204	6·4	—	—	—					3
09·0	18·5	5·9	—	—	—	—	—	—					4
17·1	20·2	5·8	—	—	—	—	—	—					5
26·7	24·1	5·3	—	—	—	—	—	—					6
33·8	26·6	5·0	—	—	—	—	—	—	68·3	15·89	4·3	—	7
37·5	22·6	6·1	—	—	—	—	—	—					8
44·8	26·9	5·4	—	—	—	—	—	—					9
52·0	28·5	5·3	—	—	—	—	—	—					1910
57·7	28·1	5·6	—	—	—	—	—	—					11
65·2	30·5	5·4	—	—	—	—	—	—	102·1	19·90	5·1	—	12
71·8	31·9	5·4	—	—	—	—	—	—					13
75·8	30·2	5·8	—	—	—	—	—	—					14
91·8	33·7	5·7	2137	380	5·6	—	—	—					15
26·8	42·1	5·4	—	—	—	—	—	—					16
74·4	56·0	4·9	—	—	—	—	—	—	110·2	19·13	5·8	—	17
44·4	66·7	4·7	—	—	—	1,226	176	7·0					18
73·0	73·5	5·1	—	—	—	1,142	214	5·3					19
74·4	77·2	4·8	—	—	—	1,275	219	5·8					1920
28·6	59·9	5·5	—	—	—	1,062	189	5·6					21
34·2	60·1	5·6	—	—	—	782	192	4·1	116·4	25·49	4·6		22
57·1	71·5	5·0	—	—	—	769	211	3·6					23
57·6	71·4	5·1	—	—	—	778	222	3·5					24
34·2	75·1	5·1	—	—	—	766	232	3·3					25
98·9	80·9	4·9	—	—	—	774	241	3·2					26
13·9	78·8	5·3	—	—	—	790	258	3·1	140·3	33·18	4·2	4·4	27
30·6	79·9	5·4	—	—	—	796	270	2·9					28
39·1	85·7	5·1	4,350	844	5·2	816	264	3·1					29
10·1	73·8	5·6	—	—	—	817	249	3·3					1930
50·1	58·2	6·2	—	—	—	770	230	3·3					31
23·1	41·8	7·7	—	—	—	704	232	3·0	160·3	33·86	4·7	4·2	32
30·2	39·6	8·3	—	—	—	761	258	2·9					33
41·8	48·2	7·1	—	—	—	828	290	2·9					34
44·9	56·4	6·1	—	—	—	882	315	2·8					35
66·6	64·2	5·7	—	—	—	954	348	2·7					36
33·4	72·7	5·3	—	—	—	1,141	373	3·1	166·0	39·75	4·2	3·7	37
34·4	66·4	5·8	—	—	—	1,226	389	3·2					38
95·6	71·6	5·5	—	—	—	1,291	420	3·1					39
24·2	80·3	5·3	—	—	—	1,607	460	3·5					1940
73·1	102·3	4·6	—	—	—	1,900	507	3·7					41
05·2	134·8	3·7	—	—	—	2,106	554	3·8	173·1	45·91	3·8	3·6	42
22·9	166·9	3·1	—	—	—	2,215	600	3·7					43
38·1	180·6	3·0	—	—	—	2,261	644	3·5					44
70·6	179·3	3·2	—	—	—	2,271	686	3·3					45
79·5	176·3	3·9	—	—	—	2,417	730	3·3					46
97·8	192·0	4·2	7018	1819	3·9	2,807	803	3·5	188·0	57·01	3·3	3·1	47
55·8	215·2	4·0	—	—	—	3,142	886	3·5					48
98·2	208·8	4·3	—	—	—	3,423	978	3·5					49
—	—	—	—	—	—	3,784	1,153	3·3					1950
—	—	—	—	—	—	4,721	1,283	3·7					51
—	—	—	—	—	—	5,668	1,387	4·1	217·6	63·15	3·4	2·9	52
—	—	—	—	—	—	5,513	1,533	3·6					53
—	—	—	—	—	—	5,687	1,668	3·4					54
—	—	—	—	—	—	6,209	1,778	3·5	231·7	68·77	3·4	—	55
—	—	—	21,763	5,460	4·0	—	—	—	—	—	—	—	56

U.S.A.   – Wealth: total net national wealth (see source 18).
Income: national income at factor cost (see source 18).

S. Africa   – Wealth: fixed reproducible assets (see source 10).
Product: gross national product at factor cost (see source 10).

Argentina   – Wealth: fixed reproducible assets (five-year averages, see source 4, Table XV).
Product: gross domestic product at market price (five-year averages, see source 4, Table XVI).

Colombia   – Wealth: fixed reproducible assets (see source 4, Table XXVIII).
Product: gross national product (see source 4, Table XXVIII).

TABLE VII
Capital–Output Ratios

Country	Year	Currency	Capital (1)			4 Output (2)	Ratios		
			1 AI + BI	2 A + B	3 A + B + D		1/4	2/4	3/4
Belgium	1950	bln. francs	933	1113	1223	276	3·4	4·0	4·4
Luxembourg	1950	bln. francs	65·86	79·34	76·34	9·667	6·8	8·2	7·9
Netherlands	1952	bln. guilders	73·2	89·6	97·7	17·83	4·1	5·0	5·5
W. Germany (3)	1955	bln. mark	348·0	448·0	..	(4) 150	2·3	3·0	..
France	1954	000 bln. francs	46·50	56·00	58·00	11·51	4·0	4·9	5·0
United Kingdom (5)	1953	bln. pounds	30·23	..	..	(6) 10·836	2·8	..	..
Norway	1953	bln. krones	87·29	90·34	88·97	16·871	5·2	5·4	5·2
Yugoslavia	1953	bln. dinars	5058	7110	7068	(7) 990	5·1	7·2	7·1
Canada	1955	bln. C. dollars	56·64	..	..	20·535	2·8	..	..
U.S.A.	1955	bln. dollars	939·3	1151·6	1193·1	322·7	2·9	3·6	3·7
Mexico	1950	bln. pesos	91·72	..	..	37·50	2·4	..	..
Australia (8)	1956	bln. A pounds	16·40	20·00	18·98	(9) 4·510	3·6	4·4	4·2
S. Africa	1955	mln. S.A. pounds	6210	8620	..	(10)1505	4·1	5·7	..
Argentina	1950	bln. pesos	193·8	..	..	51·9	3·7	..	..
Japan	1955	000 bln. yen	16·32	..	..	6·795	2·4	..	..
India	1950	bln. rupees	170·8	349·3	..	95·3	1·8	3·7	..

Notes to Table VII.

(1) See Totals of Table 1.
(2) National income at factor cost, source: *Statistics of National Income and Expenditure*, Statistical Papers, Series H, No. 10, United Nations, New York, 1957.
(3) 1950 prices.
(4) Gross national product, 1950 prices, source: see appendix, papers, no. 5.
(5) 1948 prices.
(6) Net domestic product at factor cost, 1948 prices, source: *National Income and Expenditure 1957*, Central Statistical Office, London, 1957.
(7) Source: see Appendix, Paper 12.
(8) June.
(9) Rough estimate based on 1955 (Series H, No. 10) and figures for 1955 and 1956 of *Monthly Bulletin of Statistics*, United Nations, March 1958.
(10) Rough estimate based on 1954 (Series H, No. 10) and figures for 1954 and 1955 of *Monthly Bulletin of Statistics*, United Nations, March 1958.

APPENDIX OF SOURCES

PAPERS PRESENTED AT THE FIFTH CONFERENCE OF THE
INTERNATIONAL ASSOCIATION FOR RESEARCH IN INCOME
AND WEALTH, HELD IN AUGUST 1957 IN THE
NETHERLANDS

1. *Argentina.* Manuel Balboa and Alberto Fracchia, 'Fixed Reproducible Capital in Argentina'.
2. *Australia.* J. M. Garland and R. W. Goldsmith, 'The National Wealth of Australia'.
3. *Canada.* Anthony Scott, 'Canada's Reproducible Wealth'.
4. *Colombia.* Alexander Ganz, 'Problems and Uses of National Wealth Estimates in Latin America'.
5. *W. Germany.* Ferdinand Grünig, 'Versuch einer Volksvermögensrechnung der Deutschen Bundesrepublik'.
6. *India.* M. Mukherjee and N. S. R. Sastry, 'An Estimate of the Tangible Wealth of India'.
7. *Japan.* Satoru Yoshiue, 'The National Wealth Estimates of Japan' (*The Outline of 1955 National Wealth Survey in Japan*, Statistics Section, Research Division, Economic Planning Board, Japanese Government, 1957).
8. *Netherlands.* Division of National Accounts, Netherlands Central Bureau of Statistics, 'The Preparation of a National Balance Sheet. Experience in the Netherlands'.
9. *Norway.* Odd Aukrust and Juul Bjerke, 'Real Capital in Norway'.
10. *South Africa.* D. G. Franzsen and J. J. D. Willers, 'Capital Accumulation and Economic Growth in South Africa'.
11. *United Kingdom.* Tibor Barna, 'Alternative Methods of Measuring Capital'.
12. *Yugoslavia.* Ivo Vinski, 'National Wealth of Yugoslavia'.

OTHER SOURCES

13. *Belgium.* Fernand Baudhuin, 'Placements, principes permanents d'économie privée', Louvain, 1949 and 1951.
14. *France.* Divisia–Dupin–Roy. 'A la recherche du franc perdu', 3. *Fortune de la France*, Paris, 1957.
15. *Luxembourg.* 'La Fortune Nationale du Grand–Duché de Luxembourg en 1950', *Cahiers économiques du Service d'Etudes et de Documentation Economiques*, Luxembourg, 1951.
16. *Sweden.* Karl Englund, 'Försök till en uppskattning av Sveriges nationalförmögenhet omkring år 1952', *Statistisk Tidskrift.* Statistiska Centralbyrån (Stockholm), October 1956, p. 493.
17. *United Kingdom.* (i) Philip Redfern, 'Net Investment in Fixed Assets in the United Kingdom, 1938–1953', *Journal of the*

Royal Statistical Society (London), Series A, Vol. 118, 1955, Part II, p. 141. (ii) *National Income and Expenditure*, 1957. H.M.S.O. 1957.

18. *U.S.A.* (i) R. W. Goldsmith, *A Study of Saving in the United States*, Princeton, 1956. (ii) R. W. Goldsmith, 'A Perpetual Inventory of National Wealth since 1896, *Studies in Income and Wealth*, Volume 14, National Bureau of Economic Research, New York, 1951.

19. *Mexico*. 'El desequilibrio externo en el desarollo economico Latino-Amiricano', *El caso de Mexico* (Volumen I), Naciones Unidas, La Paz, 1957.

2

ALTERNATIVE METHODS OF MEASURING CAPITAL

By T. Barna

I. THE TWO CONCEPTS OF CAPITAL

THE term 'capital' is generally given one of two alternative meanings. First, it can mean the individual's command over resources in the financial sense. This concept comprises the value of all assets belonging to an individual, including non-reproducible assets like land and natural resources and intangible assets like patent rights and trade-marks. The assets included are valuable simply because they can be sold to other individuals. The definition of *financial capital* thus depends on social institutions which determine the extent to which rights in property can be transferred between individuals. This concept of capital, which is primarily applicable to the individual, is extended to economic units such as business organizations and to the nation itself.

Secondly, the term 'capital' can mean a factor of production, one of the three major factors – Land, Labour, and Capital – distinguished in economic theory. In this sense, capital consists of physical objects which have been produced by the economic system and which are, in their turn, used for the production of other commodities. *Real capital* excludes land and natural resources; and it is difficult to work with a concept which includes intangible assets. Real capital is essentially a social concept, but it can be extended to economic units such as industries or firms.

The distinction made here between financial capital and real capital is important, and it should help to clarify the discussion of definitions and methods of measurement. There are a number of different purposes for measuring capital and a number of approaches to the problem of measurement; it will be found that each alternative is associated with one or the other of the two main concepts.[1]

This last point will be more fully developed in the next section, while subsequent sections discuss the principles of some statistical techniques; Section 3 deals with survey methods aiming at

---

[1] It is, of course, possible to reconcile the statistical difference between the two concepts.

a direct measurement of the value of capital, Section 4 with aspects of the index-number problem which especially affect the measurement of capital, and Section 5 with the so-called 'perpetual inventory' method of estimation.[1]

II. THE PURPOSE OF MEASURING CAPITAL

Today the chief interest in estimates of capital is not so much to obtain a measure of 'national strength' or of 'welfare' but rather to analyse the social and economic structure. In practice this means that the aim is to obtain not just a comprehensive and unique total of national capital but to estimate a set of analytically significant components; whether a uniquely defined and measured total is possible or not, is no longer regarded as an important issue. The set of estimates of capital can be analysed *either* by examining the interrelation of different components *or* by relating it to measures of income or output flows and measures of other factors of production (that is, labour and natural resources).

The purposes for which estimates of capital are made can be divided into three broad categories connected with the problems of the distribution of wealth; social accounting; and economic development and growth.

The problem of the distribution of wealth and of taxable capacity

The purpose of estimates falling into this category is to establish the relative shares of individuals or groups of individuals in total wealth. This also gives a measure of taxable capacity and the basis for proposals for the taxation of wealth. Estimates of the value of public property are incidental to the main purpose but are an important complement in so far as they indicate the relative importance of public and private property.

For the purpose of indicating the distribution of wealth, capital is understood in the financial sense, and therefore it follows that valuation must be based on market prices. The relevant statistical sources are normally a by-product of the ad-

---

[1] Much of this paper is an exposition of familiar views, and I have not disturbed the text by references to standard works. For a more systematic account of the problem of national capital cf. S. Kuznets 'On the Measurement of National Wealth', *Studies in Income and Wealth*, Vol. 2, N.B.E.R., New York, 1938, and R. W. Goldsmith, 'Measuring National Wealth in a System of Social Accounting', *Studies in Income and Wealth*, Vol. 12, N.B.E.R., New York, 1950.

ministration of taxation, and the main problems discussed by the estimators are technical rather than theoretical ones. These technical problems arise under two headings: the interpretation of tax statistics and the adjustments to be made to them; and estimates for the area not covered by tax statistics.

Estimates of the distribution of wealth are well developed and easily understood in countries which have capital taxation of one form or another. From the point of view of the statistics to be derived from them, capital taxation can be of two types: annual taxes or specific levies on capital, or taxes on capital passing at death from one owner to another. The latter type of tax (death duties) gives rise to interesting problems of estimation in so far as the amount of capital assessed for taxation in a particular period (a year or the average of several years) can be regarded as a sample of all capital in personal ownership. Such estimates have been particularly popular in England during the past fifty years.[1] It should be emphasized, however, that most of the discussion around this method was concerned with the sampling problem rather than with the central problems of measuring capital.

The most effective form to analyse the distribution of wealth is by fitting Lorenz curves or log-normal curves, when the distribution can be described by one or two parameters (such as the Gini-coefficient).[2] Put into this form, the different distributions should be comparable through time and between countries.

The problem of social accounting and of economic research based on social accounts

Striking attempts were made in recent years to extend the system of national income accounts to embrace capital accounts. The reason for these attempts is a dissatisfaction with the existing system of national income accounts as a sufficient basis for the analysis of the behaviour of the economy. For the fuller understanding of the movements of the economy capital accounts, as well as income accounts, are necessary. In other

[1] Cf., for instance, H. Campion, *Public and Private Property in Great Britain*, Oxford, 1939.

[2] Although originally started in connection with distributions of income and wealth, the study of these parameters received a stimulus from the recent interest in the measurement of business concentration. Cf. P. E. Hart and S. J. Prais, 'The Analysis of Business Concentration: A Statistical Approach', *Journal Royal Statistical Society*, Series A, 1956.

words, a stock-flow type of dynamic analysis requires the support of a more extensive system of social accounts.

The need for capital accounts was, of course, always recognized in connection with the banking sector. Here behaviour is usually explained in terms of the items of the capital account – the various 'liquidity ratios'. In other sectors of the economy, though the influence of stock items on behaviour may not be as dominant as of flow items, capital accounts are essential for the measurement of rates of growth.

The logical problems of extending social accounting to include an articulate system of capital accounts are not difficult to solve. Instead of incomings and outgoings, the accounts will show assets and liabilities. Capital accounts can be drawn up for each sector for which we have income–expenditure accounts. The items in the capital accounts can be classified in various ways, including the degree of liquidity of the asset or liability, legal criteria, or physical characteristics.

A number of problems, analogous to those encountered in national income accounting, remain to be solved, and we need generally agreed conventions on their treatment. It is not within the scope of this paper to discuss these problems, but two illustrations are given.

First, in an articulate system of accounts the classification of items ought to be consistent between accounts, but there are difficulties. An individual shareholder, for instance, regards shares in a first-class company as an easily marketable asset, but from the point of view of the company the corresponding liability is of a long-term nature. In an analogous way, in national-income accounting the individual may regard payments of death duties as on capital account, but the Government may regard the corresponding receipt as on revenue account.

Secondly, we have to decide how far assets and liabilities shown on a given account should be 'gross'. For instance, if an industrial undertaking is using rented buildings or plant, should it show their value among its assets and liabilities? In ordinary commercial accounting this is not done, but when comparing one industry with another it might be an advantage to show rented assets on both sides of the balance sheet. There is nothing illogical in this procedure, since the firm is normally responsible for the asset rented by it. The analogous problem in national-income accounting is the routing of transactions in input–output tables. Alternative solutions are possible, but, in some instances, a particular solution is generally accepted as the most convenient one.

For social-accounting purposes capital is conceived again in the financial rather than in the real sense. Since assets and liabilities derive from ownership, valuation can in principle be based on recorded transactions. There are, however, two alternative valuations possible, at cost or at market price. The values of some, but not all, items in the capital accounts will be different according to which method is chosen, and this difference can be quantitatively large with long-lived assets, especially in periods of changing prices and interest rates.

In practice, neither market prices nor costs are fully available. Market prices are typically available only for a relatively small proportion of capital items, and the value of the bulk is estimated from this proportion or is imputed. Costs, on the other hand, have often been lost in the records or superseded by the last recorded price when there was a change in ownership. Thus balance sheets are generally at cost, but when assets are acquired second-hand it is the cost of acquisition and not original cost which is recorded. Further, balance sheets are subject to revaluations.

It should be noted that capital accounts with items valued in terms of cost are generally consistent with income–expenditure accounts,[1] but capital accounts based on market prices are not. Revaluations disrupt the simple arithmetic connection between the accounts. However, this is not a reason for preferring one basis to the other. The chief criteria for choice should be impact on behaviour rather than simplicity of calculation.

It is probably true that on the whole market prices rather than original cost affect the behaviour of individuals, business, or the Government. For instance, the ease with which a company can raise new money from shareholders is a function of the market value rather than of the cost of its assets. If this is so, then the system of capital accounts ought to be in terms of market prices.

At the same time, it is recognized by those who study economic behaviour that the original cost of assets also influences behaviour. Tax laws, for instance, are generally based on cost,

---

[1] This is so if realized capital gains or losses are brought into the income statement.

and for this reason valuation at cost is relevant. Hence, occasionally, a concession must be made and items valued at cost, but this ought to be a supplement to the main principle of valuing at market price rather than a substitute for it.

Market price in this context need not be understood in the literal sense as the price at the end of the year. In so far as prices are volatile or subject to special temporary influences, it is not so much the price of the moment as the 'normal' price which is relevant. This, of course, introduces further difficulties of measurement. 'Normal' price is generally understood as an average over a period, but it can also mean the price that would obtain under certain conditions regarded as normal. Such an estimate of normal price is made, for instance, by the expert who values a business 'as a going concern'.

The problem of economic development and growth

Beside the construction of an articulate system of social accounts, current interest in the measurement of capital stems from its importance as a symptom and a cause of economic development. For this purpose capital is understood in the real sense. We are interested in a group of physical assets, called capital, as a factor of production and in the contribution it makes to output.

Most current work in this field is not concerned with the whole economy but with the industrial sector only. The chief reason for this concentration of interest is the relative ease with which statistics for the industrial sector can be obtained, but it is also true that some of the theoretical problems are less difficult in the industrial than in the other sectors of the economy.

There are two main approaches to the valuation of capital – identifying claims to assets and identifying physical objects. The former is eminently suitable when capital is conceived in the financial sense, but only the latter approach is possible when capital is conceived as a factor of production. This is an important qualification which implies a restriction on the statistical sources and methods available.

For the purpose of measuring real capital, we must form groups of physical objects rather than groups of claims to assets. One grouping is not readily translatable into terms of the other, for two reasons. First, the grouping of physical objects is accord-

ing to location but the grouping of claims according to ownership. Thus physical capital employed in an industry is not
identical to the sum of claims of the owners of that industry;
some assets may be rented from other sectors. Secondly, for
business firms the market may provide a valuation of the total
net claims of the firm, but this cannot be broken down according
to physical objects: we cannot, for instance, infer from a stock-
exchange quotation of a company's securities the value of its
fixed assets.

The customary classification of capital is into fixed capital
and inventories, but for many purposes it is more useful to
revert to Adam Smith's fourfold classification distinguishing
fixed capital, circulating capital, durable consumer goods, and
perishable goods in the hands of the consumer. The last category
is hardly measurable, nor is it analytically important to deal with
it. Durable consumer goods include, on Adam Smith's definition, dwellings, and should also include all kinds of social
capital, such as schools and hospitals. Circulating capital is then
identical to inventories as commonly understood and fixed
capital to structures and equipment other than dwellings and
social capital. It is an advantage to keep these three categories –
inventories, durable consumer goods and social capital, and
other fixed assets – separate, since in many respects a different
economic analysis is appropriate to each, and the problems of
valuation and of measurement are also likely to be to some extent different.

The rest of the paper will apply specifically to the last category
only, the tangible fixed assets of industry (in the broad sense).
The problems of valuation and measurement arise in the most
acute form in connection with this category of capital, partly because of the relatively long life of fixed assets and partly because
of their enormous heterogeneity.

Almost all business firms compute balance-sheet values for
fixed assets, although these figures are not necessarily published.
The rules for these computations are determined partly by law,
partly by accounting convention. In some instances firms compute more than one balance-sheet value; for example, depthis
tion for taxation may differ from the figure adopted by the firm
for its own use. The principles by which the values are computed
for taxation are generally known, although the resulting figures
are generally not published for individual firms. On the other

hand, the methods used in arriving at published balance-sheet values are not always known.

In balance sheets – published or filed with the authorities – we have a mass of data which often tempts the statistician. For certain practical purposes balance sheet data are of real economic significance; for instance, taxation or governmental price fixing may be based on them. But it is doubtful whether these data are acceptable in studies of real capital.

There are two main reasons against the use of balance-sheet values. First, they are in terms of original cost (or, rather, cost of acquisition). Secondly, depreciation always tends to err on the conservative side, and in consequence a significant proportion of assets may not be represented in the balance sheet or represented at a value which is unduly low in relation to its cost of acquisition. The fact that occasional revaluations take place makes the task of the statistician more difficult rather than easier, because comparison between firms and industries becomes subject to further qualification.[1]

Balance-sheet values are relevant only in so far as they influence market values. As already mentioned, original cost does to some extent affect behaviour and thereby the market value of assets. If, for instance, price control based on original cost operates, this will depress the profitability and hence the market value of assets. In so far as business-men in reaching investment decisions take into account the original cost of old investment and accumulated depreciation provisions, this also would affect market values. But while these factors may help to explain price formation, they do not make balance-sheet values a suitable basis for measuring capital.

The obvious answer to the search for 'realistic' valuation is market price. The difficulty is that market price is not always available or, when available, is not necessarily accepted as typical.

In Western industrial countries a large proportion of industrial capital is valued on the stock exchange. Apart from a number of technical problems, there are three major difficulties in using stock-exchange quotations in the present context. First, prices are too sensitive to short-term influences, and averages

---

[1] A survey of the larger British industrial firms would suggest that the ratio between some 'realistic' value of fixed assets and published balance-sheet values varies enormously from firm to firm, industry to industry, and through time.

would have to be taken over rather long periods. Secondly, as already mentioned, stock-exchange prices reflect capital owned rather than capital employed in production, and an analysis of the total by type of asset is logically impossible. Thirdly, these prices reflect not only the value of physical assets but also the good luck or misfortune of the industry in which they are used and the efficiency of management.

Hence only the market for buildings and equipment can give guidance. As only a fraction of fixed assets are new, it is in fact the second-hand market which is relevant. This market can seldom give a readily acceptable quotation. In any reasonable period only a small proportion of assets passes through the market, or with many kinds of assets none at all, and there is always a suspicion that these are not typical of the classes which they represent. For most industrial assets there are very heavy costs attached to the transfer of ownership, and to a large extent the second-hand market represents exceptional cases, such as assets sold by bankrupt firms or by leading firms whose policy is always to have new assets. Moreover, second-hand prices are volatile, and a change from a sellers' to a buyers' market can bring about a disproportionate change in price.

Even though observed market prices are not always acceptable, in principle the equivalent of 'normal' price can be imputed. In everyday life such estimates are frequently made by experts for the purpose of, for instance, fire insurance, adjustments to the balance sheet, offers of purchase, or public price fixing. Balance-sheet values and recorded market prices are deceptively accurate. The expert, frankly, estimates or guesses, but this process may give results which are economically more significant.

The expert tries to estimate the market price that would obtain under certain hypothetical conditions. He assumes, for instance, that the transaction takes place as between willing seller and willing buyer. The study of the processes by which experts arrive at valuation opens up the possibility of obtaining a new source of economically valid data. One interesting instance is the study of legal cases involving disputes about valuation when the evidence of experts is available to the public.[1]

This type of valuation, which seems to be the only satisfactory

[1] For an excellent example of such studies, cf. J. C. Bonbright, *The Valuation of Property*, New York, 1937.

one for the measurement of real capital, is discussed more fully in the next section.

III. SURVEY METHODS

Estimates of capital are generally based on published statistics of capital formation, on published balance sheets, or on calculations of physical capacity and costs of construction. The direct method of collecting data for the specific purpose of measuring capital is seldom used. Such data are, however, available, since they are needed in everyday affairs.

Economic theory provides the general formula for rational valuation: the value of an asset is equal to the sum of the discounted future income stream expected from it. This formula focuses attention on expectations, which are subjective, and on the fact that the future is always discounted compared to the present. But the application of the formula is not generally practicable. Men of affairs do not use formulae; this is just the economist's way of rationalizing their implicit methods.

The general method followed by the expert is to estimate replacement cost, and this can be done in two steps. First, he estimates the cost of replacement with a brand-new asset and, second, he makes an allowance for age, wear and tear, and obsolescence. The difficulty is that replacement, if it were to take place, would not be by identical units. As a result of inventions, capital undergoes an almost continuous and steady improvement, and hardly any two assets produced at different times are identical. The expert has to find a modern substitute for the existing asset and has to take account of differences in the profitability of the two types of asset. Lastly, when he takes age into account, he has to look forward and estimate the likely future life of the asset, rather than look into the past to determine expired life. Expert valuation is an art which consists of finding the amount of new and modern assets which is the equivalent of the old and obsolete asset in the economic rather than in the engineering sense. Different experts will, of course, arrive at different results, but this is no more than to say that the estimates are subject to error.

Replacement cost should include, in addition to the cost of acquisition of assets, also the cost of installation and other incidental costs. There is an important difference between the value of assets as installed in certain relation to each other and the break-up value when each asset might be sold separately. For our purpose assets should be valued at their worth to the existing management on the assumption that they want to continue in business.

The estimate also depends on the units into which assets are divided for valuation, and it is a recognized principle of property valuation that the value of the sum total of assets may differ from the sum total of the value of each asset. A machine consists of different parts which wear out at different times; the life of the machine may well be determined by a relatively short-lived component. If the lay-out of a factory is obsolete, its value may even be less than the break-up value. On the whole, however, the value of a complex unit is higher than that of its component parts because of the labour necessary to create the complex. The choice of a suitable unit for valuation is important in, for instance, valuation for fire insurance. This is especially so in modern factories, where the insured is more concerned with the possibility of partial loss than with total destruction. The usual practice is to value neither a whole factory or workshop as a unit, nor the smallest possible items, but something intermediate, such as a machine with all its attachments or a complex plant which operates as a single entity.

It was stated that the expert, in general, makes his estimate in two steps: he estimates the cost of a new asset, which is then adjusted (written down) to take account of the actual state of the asset to be replaced.[1] Hence two different concepts of replacement cost are distinguished: the cost of replacement with new and the cost of replacement with second-hand assets. It is the second concept which corresponds to the value of capital in economic theory, but the first has great practical importance. Very often experts estimate *replacement cost new* only. Sometimes, when the asset is near the end of its useful life, they estimate *written-down replacement cost* (which is a better term than 'net replacement cost') directly, without taking two separate steps.

Replacement cost new sets an upper limit to replacement cost, as it is normally possible to replace by new assets, though, exceptionally, an allowance must be made for scarcities (when the asset is not readily obtainable at the ruling price). The

---

[1] The rate at which the expert writes down new assets is not necessarily identical to the conventional rate of depreciation.

manufacturer would clearly be better off, apart from the disturbing effects of the change, if he were to replace old assets by new.

The value of assets declines with age partly because the expectation of further life declines and partly because of falling efficiency (in an economic or in a technical sense). It logically follows that value declines faster than efficiency, and indeed for important classes of assets efficiency does not decline at all. For this reason replacement cost new is a useful concept when examining the relationship of assets to current output, and certainly more relevant than written-down replacement cost in forecasting requirements of incremental capital.

One particular purpose for which replacement cost is estimated is fire insurance. The estimate of the insurable value can be the result of an elaborate procedure by experts or simply a guess by the business-man. This valuation ought to be realistic, and in the great majority of cases it is, as on its appropriateness the survival of the firm may well depend.

Since fire insurance is general, it is a possible source for statistical data. This was realized for a long time, as evident, for instance, from the interest shown in fire-insurance statistics by the St. Petersburg Congress of the International Statistical Institute in 1872. But to be able to interpret fire-insurance statistics, a direct survey of insurance policies is needed.

In a project into the measurement of capital in British industry at the National Institute of Economic and Social Research in London the empirical problem was tackled in two stages, corresponding to the two steps of the expert valuation process. In the first stage the replacement cost new of fixed assets was investigated, and in the second the length of life of assets and their declining efficiency with age. In the first stage a sample inquiry into replacement cost was undertaken and its chief results are shown in Table I.[1]

The inquiry concluded that the valuation of fixed assets for fire insurance does give a good basis for estimating, in an economically significant sense, the value of assets. But the figures which can be obtained from manufacturers are meaningless without an adequate explanation of the basis of valuation

[1] For a full account of the inquiry cf. T. Barna, 'The Replacement Cost of Fixed Assets in British Manufacturing Industry in 1955', *Journal of the Royal Statistical Society*, Series A, 1957.

and of the coverage. In certain instances supplementary information is required on uninsured assets and on the degree of under-insurance. Uninsured assets are confined to a small number of industries, and the problem was by-passed through obtaining insurable (as against insured) values and other estimates of replacement cost. Some firms disclosed the degree of under-insurance and, in general, under-insurance is unlikely to have greatly affected the results. This is so because small firms, which are more likely to under-insure, were not sufficiently represented in the sample and also because firms who were aware of defects in their insurance valuation tended to refuse to participate in the inquiry.[1]

The second stage of the inquiry, into the life of assets, aims mainly at the description in qualitative terms of the relevant characteristics of assets, but a certain amount of statistical data was also collected from a sample of firms (which is not necessarily representative for British industry). The statistics collected can be translated into terms of demographic statistics – life tables, mortality rates, average expected life, age distribution, etc.[2]

The questions asked seek to obtain information on the life of assets: (a) as implied in the firm's depreciation policy, and (b) as shown by past experience. Although the past is not necessarily a guide to the future, the returns received invariably indicated that assets acquired in the past lasted significantly longer than implied in depreciation policies.[3]

IV. VOLUME INDEXES

The problem of splitting changes in the value of capital into changes in price and changes in volume is the general index-number problem in a very acute form. This is so because of the great heterogeneity of capital assets. A given commodity can be produced by more than one technique, each employing a different set of equipment, and, moreover, assets of the same type differ in age, and this makes them different from an economic point of view even if measurable physical wear and tear is negligible. But the real difficulty is that because of technical

---

[1] On the nature of fire insurance, see also Appendix A below.
[2] A full report on this stage of the inquiry is not yet available.
[3] It should be noted that, as regards assumptions for the length of life of assets, on the whole, company depreciation policies do not differ substantially from normal tax depreciation.

TABLE I

Replacement Cost New of Fixed Assets in Manufacturing, United Kingdom, Mid-1955

Standard Industrial Classification Minimum List Heading	Industry	Employment 000's	Employment on Sample Returns %	Total Fixed Assets			Fixed Assets per Person Employed			Error in All Fixed Assets p.h. £
				Buildings, etc. £ million	Plant, etc. £ million	All £ million	Buildings, etc. £	Plant, etc. £	All £	
21	China and earthenware	73	78	23	22	45	310	310	620	100
22, 23	Glass	77	3	42	50	92	550	650	1,200	200
24	Cement	13	31	20	20	40	1,570	1,530	3,100	300
	Other	159	8	118	146	264	740	920	1,660	200
Order III	Treatment of non-metalliferous mining products	322	24	203	238	441	630	740	1,370	110
30	Coke ovens	20	5	20	158	178	1,000	7,900	8,900	1,000
31, 33	Chemicals, etc.	203	43	199	869	1,068	980	4,280	5,260	600
32	Drugs and toilet preparations	64	17	52	50	102	810	790	1,600	300
34	Paint and varnish	40	16	32	27	59	790	680	1,470	100
35(i)	Soap, etc.	23	44	24	38	62	1,040	1,660	2,700	300
36	Mineral oil refining	18	96	67	170	237	3,760	9,590	13,350	500
	Other chemicals	47	24	49	41	90	1,040	880	1,920	300
Order IV	Chemicals and allied trades	415	34	443	1,353	1,796	1,070	3,260	4,330	300
40, 41, 43	Iron and steel	276	33	216	791	1,007	780	2,880	3,660	300
42, 44	Foundries, tubes, etc.	171	1	86	188	274	500	1,100	1,600	300
49	Non-ferrous metals	113	30	119	164	283	1,050	1,450	2,500	400
Order V	Metal manufacture	560	23	421	1,143	1,564	750	2,040	2,790	190
50	Shipbuilding	223	—	89	112	201	400	500	900	400
51, –69	Mechanical engineering, etc.	990	5	455	1,030	1,485	460	1,040	1,500	300
70–79	Electrical engineering, etc.	800	29	376	512	888	470	640	1,110	100
Order VI	Engineering, etc.	2,013	14	920	1,654	2,574	460	820	1,280	160
80, 82, 83	Motor and aircraft	647	23	394	788	1,182	610	1,220	1,830	200
	Other vehicles	248	—	124	124	248	500	500	1,000	300
Order VII	Vehicles	895	16	518	912	1,430	580	1,020	1,600	170

		608	5	255	414	669	420	680	1,100	200
Orders VIII and IX	Metal goods, n.e.s., precision instruments									
113	Rayon, etc. production	38	80	62	112	174	1,630	2,940	4,570	200
	Other textiles	902	6	1,100	1,342	2,442	1,220	1,490	2,710	400
Order X	Textiles	940	9	1,162	1,454	2,616	1,240	1,550	2,790	380
Orders XI and XII	Leather, fur, clothing, etc.	641	3	257	192	449	400	300	700	200
150	Grain milling	37	4	66	117	183	1,770	3,170	4,940	500
151	Bread, etc.	215	6	133	132	265	620	610	1,230	200
152	Biscuit	60	11	24	25	49	400	420	820	200
155	Sugar and glucose	19	76	28	75	103	1,470	3,950	5,420	200
156	Cocoa, chocolate, etc.	105	12	73	82	155	700	780	1,480	300
	Other food industries	219	10	182	243	425	830	1,110	1,940	300
163–168	Drink industries	138	1	310	242	552	2,250	1,750	4,000	600
169	Tobacco	37	87	30	30	60	810	820	1,630	100
Order XIII	Food, drink, and tobacco	830	13	846	946	1,792	1,020	1,140	2,160	160
Order XIV	Manufactures of wood and cork	276	1	138	110	248	500	400	900	200
180, 181	Paper and pulp	88	22	123	291	414	1,400	3,300	4,700	300
182, 183	Cardboard and paper products	109	17	81	107	188	740	980	1,720	200
186	Newspaper printing	112	10	69	146	215	620	1,300	1,920	300
189	Printing	210	4	141	189	330	670	900	1,570	300
Order XV	Manufactures of paper	519	11	414	733	1,147	800	1,410	2,210	150
190	Rubber	110	33	55	138	193	500	1,250	1,750	100
	Other manufacturing	131	1	83	98	181	630	750	1,380	200
Order XVI	Other manufacturing	241	16	138	236	374	570	980	1,550	120
Orders III–XVI	Total manufacturing	8,260	13·4	5,715	9,385	15,100	690	1,140	1,830	70

development the nature and quality of capital equipment is constantly changing, and this process is irreversible.

In measuring the volume index of a bunch of commodities we generally rely on the fact that there are situations in which the prices of the commodities constituting the bunch are comparable, and it is on this basis that Professor Stone devised a basis for allowing for quality change.[1] With capital, however, the chief difficulty is that such situations do not exist, and cannot exist unless the technique of production of each industry were fixed, because quality change is not a reversible process, though for some consumer goods it is. Professor Stone also assumes that more than one quality of a given commodity is marketed at the same time, which is likely to be so in the case of consumer goods, where the market provides for the differing tastes of the public, but less likely in the case of capital goods, which are purchased not for subjective reasons but to make profit; here the latest model completely supersedes the earlier one, except during a transitional period when price comparisons might be misleading.

If we compare two economies, the sets of equipment used are likely to be different in them precisely because economic circumstances are different. If technological knowledge is the same in the two economies, the chief determining factors in the choice of equipment are real wages and the rate of profit ruling in the economy. Comparison is possible only if we revalue capital in one country on the assumption that the real wages and the rate of profit of the other are ruling – and this, of course, may lead to absurd results.

If, on the other hand, we take the same country at different times, technological knowledge has changed, bringing in its train changes in real wages and/or rates of profit. The difficulties are there again. Comparison is only possible through imputed prices and not by measurement of market prices. Even if the out-of-date and the newly invented equipment are produced simultaneously, this will be during a transitional period when relative prices represent neither relative costs nor relative value to the user but something between the two.

It is clear that if we make comparisons either between economies or through time, the outcome will be different according to whether we measure capital in terms of resource inputs or in

[1] R. Stone, *Quantity and Price Indexes in National Accounts*, O.E.E.C., 1956.

terms of final output – in terms of effort or in terms of efficiency. The more primitive economy has to make a greater effort to produce a given result.

Capital in terms of investment effort – that is, accumulation in the classical sense – ought to be measured by a value index deflated by a cost index. The chief constituents of the cost index are wage-rates and the rate of interest or profit.[1] The rate of interest affects the cost of brand-new equipment, since this required other, already existing, equipment for its production. Further, the rate of interest also enters the formula which relates equipment of a given age to the cost of brand-new equipment of the same type.[2]

Capital in terms of productive efficiency, on the other hand, should be measured as a refined volume index which takes account of improvements in 'quality'. But while such an index for consumer goods can be attempted with reference to market prices, for capital it must, in general, be imputed. We require a set of technical data, wages, and interest rates to compare one technique with another.

There are, then, two main alternative measures of the volume of capital – capital conceived in terms of effort or in terms of efficiency. It is not possible to compromise between the two, since technical progress, by its very nature, continually widens the gap between them. For different purposes we need a different concept, and it should prove useful to compute both indexes.[3]

A survey of econometric literature indicates that the chief attempts which have been made to measure capital were neither in terms of input nor in terms of output, but, somehow, in terms of its own 'price'. To compute a price index for capital goods is not easy – partly because it is not clear what such an index should measure – and often very primitive calculations (such as price per ton of machinery) are incorporated. The authors, as far

---

[1] The cost of materials can also be resolved into wages and interest or profit.

[2] For the solution of the index-number problem, which arises from the need to take account of both wage-rates and interest, Professor Champernowne suggested a chain method.

Mrs. Joan Robinson, on the other hand, is more inclined to deflate by wages only. The latter is admittedly a cruder method, but it is much simpler, and it is probable that not much is lost in accuracy. It can be argued that in the most interesting comparisons the differences in wage-rates are large but in rates of profits perhaps not. See articles by D. G. Champernowne, R. F. Kahn, and J. Robinson in *Review of Economic Studies, 1953–54*.

[3] I did not mention other indexes – such as the index of capacity – which are one-dimensional and do not take account of the economic essence of capital.

E

as can be seen, do not correct for 'quality change'. In other words, the index of the 'price of capital goods' implicitly takes account of inventions which reduce costs in the first instance in the investment-goods sector but not of inventions which reduce costs indirectly in the consumption-goods sector. For obvious reasons the movements of such an index must be between those of the two other indexes.

V. AN INDIRECT METHOD

The direct method of comparison is to take the value of capital in two situations and to correct for price differences. The so-called perpetual-inventory method, which was pioneered by Dr. Goldsmith in the United States, achieves the same end indirectly.[1] Here one takes capital formation year by year, corrected for price changes, and then the figures are cumulated and suitable deductions are made for capital consumption. The conceptual problems connected with the basis of valuation and with the price deflator, which were discussed in previous sections of this paper, are present but perhaps less easily recognized. All in all, the perpetual inventory method differs from the direct method only as regards statistical technique. The method was developed and used to exploit readily available statistical data. It suffers from the disadvantage of all indirect methods of measurement that its results may be subject to large error.

The method estimates both replacement cost new and the written-down replacement cost of capital, and changes in their volume over time. The results obtained depend on: (a) annual statistics of capital formation; (b) price index-numbers for capital, and (c) estimates of the length of life of assets. The conceptual problems are subsumed in the type of price index used, which was already discussed at the end of the preceding section.

The quantitatively crucial factor in the method is the estimate of the length of life of assets. In the United States the estimates of Dr. Goldsmith, and more recently of the Department of Commerce, and in the United Kingdom those of Mr. Redfern,[2] are based on lives implied in typical (but not universally adopted) depreciation rates for income-tax purposes.

For the United Kingdom I could adjust Mr. Redfern's esti-

[1] R. W. Goldsmith, 'A Perpetual Inventory of National Wealth', *Studies in Income and Wealth*, Vol. 14, N.B.E.R., New York, 1951.
[2] P. Redfern, 'Net Investment in Fixed Assets in the United Kingdom, 1938–1953', *Journal of the Royal Statistical Society*, Series A, 1955.

mates to make them comparable with my own estimates, which are based on the direct method. The disturbing gap between the two estimates is shown in Table II. The dividing line between buildings, on the one hand, and plant, on the other, is not un-ambiguous, and too much attention should not be paid to the separate figures. The error in my estimate due to sampling and the errors in my adjustments to Mr. Redfern's estimates are, probably, of a smaller order of magnitude than the gap between the two sets of figures. As regards conceptual differences, these tend to cause a gap in the opposite direction to the one actually found.

TABLE II

Comparison of Two Estimates of Fixed Assets in Manufacturing, United Kingdom, Mid-1955

(in £ thousand million, 1955 prices)

	Buildings	Plant and Machinery	Total (exc. vehicles)
Redfern [1]	3·5	6·6	10·1
Barna [2]	5·8	9·5	15·3
Difference as percentage of Redfern	66	44	51

[1] Original coverage increased to include: (a) factories built by the Government during the War and now leased to private firms, and (b) assets for government research and development.

[2] As in Table I, plus Atomic Energy Authority.

The discrepancy is thus due to statistical factors which in-clude, in order of importance, the following:

(a) The length of life of assets is longer than implied in the income-tax depreciation rates, and this is consistently con-firmed by the results of more recent research.

(b) Capital formation is under-reported in annual statistics. In general, a proportion of assets is charged to revenue, and such assets are not represented in statistics of capital formation but are included in estimates based on a direct inventory. A unique instance is the subsidy element in private capital formation, which is the result of govern-ment-financed asset creation during the War; this, itself, might explain one-fifth of the gap shown in the table.

(c) Statistics of capital formation are subject to the usual statistical errors, which might have been important in the earlier years utilized by the perpetual-inventory method.

It is probably true to say that the perpetual-inventory method is subject in all countries to the same kinds of error as in the United Kingdom, though it is difficult to generalize about the magnitude of these errors.

VI. CONCLUSIONS

In recent decades the popularity of national-income estimates far exceeded that of estimates of national wealth. This was not so in the eighteenth and the earlier parts of the nineteenth centuries, when estimates of the national wealth were frequently made and the 'strength of nations' was often compared in terms of capital rather than in terms of output.

The inherent difficulties in measuring national capital are obvious. The logical difficulties are equally present in the measurement of national income (taken as the equivalent of consumption *plus* additions to the stock of assets) but are, quantitatively, far less important. It is probably true to say that individual income is more difficult to define and measure than social income, but social capital is a more difficult concept than individual capital, which represents an individual's share in total wealth.

But there are also deeper reasons for the fluctuating fortunes of estimates of capital, and these derive from changing emphasis in economic policies and in economic theory. In the eighteenth and early nineteenth centuries the use of national wealth, as against national income, estimates was not unconnected with economic theories, which assumed that wages were determined by the subsistence level. In these theories the cost of labour is fixed, and labour itself is produced by the system in the same way as commodities are produced. The aim of the economy is to maximize the surplus produced over the cost of materials and labour. National capital is not an unsatisfactory measure of the results of this activity, and in many respects it is a better measure than the sum of capitalist incomes (rent, interest, and profits), since it includes durable goods which yield no money income (such as furniture, jewellery, and precious metals).

With the growth of interest in the standard of living of the people, attention became concentrated on estimates of national income. The main purpose of statisticians, for many years, was social rather than economic. The deliberate construction of national-income estimates for purposes of economic analysis became customary only in the inter-war period, and received its final impetus during and after the last war. The system of national-income accounts, as we have come to know it, is intimately connected with the economic problems of the developed Western countries in the last twenty-five years and with Keynesian economic theory. In fact, the system of accounts is, ultimately, a statistical analogue of the Keynesian fiscal policy model. The chief purpose of this model is to prescribe fiscal policies for curing either unemployment caused by lack of demand or inflation caused by excess demand for resources.

There are limitations of this approach in two main directions. First, the national income accounts are in themselves insufficient when one is dealing with problems requiring monetary as against fiscal policy measures. Secondly, they are obviously insufficient in dealing with problems of economic development which have become one of the pre-occupations of contemporary economics. In both instances we require capital as well as income estimates. In the first instance we require estimates of claims and liabilities, that is estimates of capital understood in terms of finance. In the second instance we require estimates of 'real' capital. These estimates are required not in substitution of estimates of income but as a complement to them.

The chief difficulties with studies of real capital are partly conceptual and partly statistical, although the two kinds of difficulties interact. The purpose for which estimates of real capital are needed must be explicitly stated, since different purposes require a different approach. On the statistical side there is need for direct and more detailed studies of capital and its effect on productivity.

A particularly undesirable possibility is the use of estimates for developed Western countries, which are either inaccurate or prepared for a different purpose, for the planning of economic development in other countries. Clearly a structural analysis, if necessary based on detailed engineering data, should be superior to the much-abused method of indirect statistical inference.

APPENDIX A

A fire policy is a contract whereby the insurer undertakes to compensate the insured for direct losses incurred in the event of fire. There are a number of different types of policy but, in the United Kingdom, they commonly embody the following principles:

(i) The policy gives cover for the destruction or physical deterioration of assets and not for consequential losses due to fire damage: production may be interrupted as a result of fire and profits may consequently suffer, but this loss is not covered by a fire policy. Another policy may be taken out to cover for loss of profits, including such items as the salaries of a nucleus staff and prestige advertising while production is interrupted, but such policies need not concern us here.

(ii) It is universal practice to place a definite value on the assets insured, the determination of this value depending on the type of policy.

(iii) In the event of fire the insured cannot receive more than full compensation, in terms of a given policy, even if he has placed an excessive value on the asset; but he can be under-compensated if he has placed an insufficient value on the assets.

Generally, fixed assets are specified separately from stock, and the technique of valuation is also different for the two types of assets. Seldom is a detailed list of items attached to the policy, but more commonly a factory is insured as a whole, specifying separately buildings and plant. In larger factories there is a tendency to insure by zone. There is also a tendency on the part of the insurer to insert the 'average' clause in certain types of policy under which all parts of a whole are deemed to be valued on the same basis. This means that if in the event of a loss the value insured is less than the true value, the insured is required to bear a proportionate part of the loss himself. In other words, if the rate insured is £10,000, the true value £20,000 and the loss £4,000, then the insured can only recover £2,000.

Two main types of policy exist: insurance for reinstatement and insurance for indemnity. The values to be insured under the former type correspond to replacement cost new. Under the latter type current market values are insured: in fact, the most frequent procedure is to determine current values as equivalent to written-down replacement cost. The choice between the different types of policy is left to the insured. He may, of course, always replace items lost with new assets, but under an indemnity policy he would not recover the full cost.

The insured generally excludes assets which he regards as indestructible. Apart from land, foundations to buildings fall into this category: they may account for 7–15 per cent of the value of buildings. Most other uninsured assets are in heavy industry, and include roadways, railway sidings, blast furnaces, coke ovens, and similar assets which are not inflammable. The extent to which these assets are in fact indestructible is debatable. Cases are known when foundations have cracked as the result of fire and had to be replaced at great cost. Properly, the values insured ought to allow even for the demolition of damaged buildings and for the clearing of debris. The practice of excluding so-called indestructible assets varies from firm to firm, but the impression was gained that the majority exclude foundations to buildings.

In industries where a significant proportion of assets, if not the bulk, is uninsured, fire-insurance values would give a misleading indication of the value of fixed assets. Fortunately, in most of such cases firms are able to supply information on the replacement cost of all fixed assets, whether insured or not. Indeed, it appears that an increasing number of firms is interested in possessing information on the replacement cost of assets quite apart from the need for such information for fire insurance. These figures are used for estimating depreciation in excess of normal balance-sheet depreciation and for assessing the profitability of the business in relation to real capital employed. Only a few of the firms possessing this information did re-value assets in the balance sheet.

Whether for fire insurance, or for other purposes, the technique of valuation can be divided into three categories:

(i) A detailed valuation may take place based on an expert assessment of physical assets either by a firm of valuers or by the manufacturer's own engineers. This procedure is slow and expensive, and takes place only infrequently.

(ii) The replacement cost of assets may be estimated by finding in the records the cost of acquisition and the date of purchase of each item, and by applying price indexes to bring these values up to date. The price indexes may be general or specifically prepared for the firm, and may or may not differentiate between different types of assets.

(iii) Short-cut methods may be used for bringing previously established values up to date by applying some index of prices.

In principle, policies are annual, but values insured are altered in the course of the year as additional assets are acquired or sold. It is not customary to make changes during the year to allow for the effect of changing prices, but such changes should be made annually.

It is known, however, that the latter kind of change is not made as regularly as it should be, and the valuation, especially of the smaller enterprises, is often brought up to date only once in several years.

The question of under-insurance is the most difficult to discuss. Over-insurance may perhaps be ignored, as the insured is not allowed to benefit by it: over-insurance, if it exists, is due to errors in valuation rather than to choice. But many firms are known to under-insure in order to save on the premium. Although rates are differentiated according to trade, and whether or not the factory has a sprinkler system, many insured feel that in their particular case the risk is less than is implied by the rate. An important element in the manufacturer's own judgment is the consideration of total loss, and therefore close attention is paid to factors such as the location of the factory (in relation to water supply or fire brigades) and the closeness of workshops to each other. For a large firm the wisest course is to prepare a good valuation of assets and then try to obtain a reduction in the rate, but this way may not be open to a small firm. Some firms under-insure by a given percentage with the express approval of the insurer. Here the difficulty can be overcome by asking for insurable values rather than for the actual sums insured. The problem is really confined to firms who under-insure in relation to the provisions of the policy. It should be made clear that the insurer is not trying to discover whether or not manufacturers under-insure so long as no fire takes place, and in the event of fire he would reduce the claim in proportion to the degree of under-insurance.

The existence and often the extent of under-insurance can be discovered by questioning the insured on the technique used to arrive at valuation. Under-insurance must be understood, of course, strictly in relation to what is meant to be insured, and account must be taken of:

(a) the basis of valuation, whether for reinstatement or for indemnity;
(b) how far certain types of assets are not covered; and
(c) the method of appraisal.

For instance, an insured having a reinstatement policy and assets only a few years old may insure original cost even though the cost of replacement has risen since he bought the assets. He may exclude foundations and make an excessive deduction for them. But more generally, in a period of rising prices values are not regularly revised upwards, or revised by only an insufficient percentage. Some firms, even though they have a reinstatement policy, assume that the annual rise in prices just about offsets the depreciation of assets through age. Others add 50 per cent to pre-war values instead of 300 per cent. The largest firms employ at least one clerk whose business is to report to the insurer the acquisition of new assets, and policies are frequently revised, pretending to accuracy; yet the policy may be substantially different from the correct value. The impression gained is that in a number of instances manufacturers take out a reinstatement policy and in the course of time allow it to approach the value of an indemnity policy, without, however, explicitly admitting this.

3

FINANCIAL ACCOUNTING WITHIN A
SYSTEM OF NATIONAL ACCOUNTS

By Petter Jakob Bjerve and Mikael Selsjord

The Central Bureau of Statistics of Norway

I. INTRODUCTION

THE interest in statistics on money and credit has increased
sharply in recent years. There are several reasons why this is so.
Monetary and credit policy has assumed new importance in
many countries, and governments feel a great need for current
statistical information relating to monetary matters. The same is
true of financial institutions, such as banks and insurance companies. In modern economic theory there is a strong tendency to
treat financial and real economic relationships within one and
the same model. This has created a need for statistics on money
and credit which are comparable and consistent with data on
the real economic sphere.

The traditional system of national accounts now gives a fairly
systematic description of the real economy. However, no room
has yet been found for financial variables within this system; nor
have statistics on money and credit as a rule been designed within the framework of a consistent logical accounting system. In
most countries these statistics take the form of incidental series
spread over a number of different publications. Since they are
based on different definitions, it is difficult to compare these
series. Nor do the statistics cover all the fields which it is desirable to include. This is probably due to the fact that the basic
data are collected for purposes of legal control, rather than with
a view to throwing light on aspects of monetary conditions of
interest to the national economy.

If statistics on money and credit are to meet present requirements, they must be based on a comprehensive system of
accounting. This is essential in order to provide complete and
comparable data giving an overall view and in order to be able
to check whether the figures are correct. The traditional real
economic accounts should be adapted as far as possible to this
comprehensive system so that the real economic as well as the
financial trend and position of the individual sectors are brought
out. Secondly, the basic statistics must be extended and co-

60

ordinated within this system, uniform definitions and standards of classification must be adopted, and the data must be extended to areas not covered at present.

The purpose of this paper is to consider the first of these two problems, namely, the construction of an accounting system for statistics on money and credit. The emphasis will be mainly on capital-balance accounts, i.e. accounts showing claims and debts and net changes in these items over the accounting period. In order to place these accounts in a broader accounting framework some problems relating to matters of principle will be discussed in connection with the gross accounts which show gross changes in claims and debts, i.e. the individual transactions. Problems of co-ordinating financial accounts with the traditional national accounts are also considered in this connection.

These problems are treated from a general point of view in Part II. First, the ideas underlying the accounting framework and relationships are considered, then the concrete drawing up of accounts, sector classification, classification of claims and debts, and the choice of evaluation principles are briefly discussed. Finally, some problems of reconciliation of accounts are considered. Part III endeavours to give a concrete illustration of the system outlined in Part II. Here a system of Norwegian financial accounts is considered in detail.

II. THE FINANCIAL ACCOUNTS

(1) *General analysis*

A systematic classification of statistics on money and credit may take the following form: (a) data on holdings of financial objects, i.e. financial assets and liabilities, presented in the form of balance sheets for groups of institutions; (b) data showing the flows into and out of such holdings which result from specific types of transactions; (c) data relating to quotations and interest rates. The financial accounts should endeavour to provide an accounting framework for the first two mentioned types of statistics.

If such an accounting system is to be meaningful it must be based on sector accounts showing the structure of claims and debts for the most important economic groups and the main inter-sector transactions. The structure of claims and debts is best described by drawing up financial balances for the sector system chosen. Such financial balances would distinguish the different types of financial objects, and should, furthermore, give details on the distribution by debtor and creditor of each sector's claims and debts respectively. This is necessary in order to make possible the consolidation of accounts.

Net changes in claims and debts will be brought out by a comparison of the balance-sheet items at the end and the beginning of the accounting period. This is sufficient for a number of analytical purposes, but in some cases it may be desirable to know the gross changes, i.e. the individual transactions underlying the decline and increase in the claims and debts of the different groups. Such a system of gross accounts would have to record all transactions involving financial means of payment or credit.

A system of gross financial accounts shows financial transactions between sectors, while the traditional national accounts consider the real aspects of these transactions. For practical as well as for theoretical purposes it is important that a way should be found of integrating these two systems. A solution which readily presents itself is to draw up an overall accounting system which is sufficiently detailed to permit, with suitable regrouping and supplementing of data, the construction of special series meeting different requirements. If such an overall system is to take the form of the traditional national accounts, tabulations such as, for instance, input–output relationships and the gross financial accounts could be incorporated by way of special accounts.

The drawing up of a system of gross financial accounts on the basis of the traditional national accounts would require regrouping of some of the data, the inclusion of supplementary statistics, and the introduction of certain correctives and estimates of statistical error needed in consolidating statements. The traditional national accounts are based on a functional sector classification, whereas the financial accounts are based on sectors classified according to their institutional characteristics. The data would therefore have to be regrouped to obtain consistency with the sector classification used in the financial accounts. Some items, which properly belong in the financial accounts, are not included in the traditional national accounts. This is true, for instance, of the purely financial transaction, i.e. transactions involving the exchange of financial objects. It would, therefore, be necessary to include data of this type. On the other hand, the traditional national accounts include imputed transactions which are of little relevance to a system of financial accounts. This complication is, however, of minor importance for many analytical purposes. These transactions are recorded both on the debit and the credit side of the income account and will not affect the balance of the statement. For the purpose of reconciling the capital account with the balance sheet, it is necessary to introduce estimates of statistical error and certain correctives, the most important of which would correct for actual or imputed profits and losses resulting from revaluation.

(2) *The accounting structure and accounting relationships*

A simplified accounting structure for a complete system of gross financial accounts drawn up along the lines considered above may consist of: (a) an income account; (b) a real capital account; and (c) a financial capital account.

(a) The income account records transactions relating to production and consumption as well as unilateral transfers, such as taxes, subsidies, gifts, and donations. All these transactions (other than depreciation) are assumed to have a counterpart in the financial capital account. It would then have to be imagined that transactions which involve an exchange of real objects, unilateral transfers of real objects, and imputed transactions involve financial counterpayments. The balance on the income account would correspond to the sector's savings, which is derived as the difference between income and expenditure during the period excluding expenditure on capital (the income method).

The income relationship of an arbitrary sector i may be expressed as follows:

$$(1) \qquad \Sigma^a \, \Sigma^j \, T_a^{ij} - \Sigma^a \, \Sigma^j \, T_a^{ji} - D^i = S^i$$

where T denotes the transactions on income account, the first top lettering the sector rendering real objects or receiving financial objects, and the second top lettering the sector receiving real objects or rendering financial objects. The foot lettering indicates the type of transaction. D^i and S^i designate depreciation and savings in sector i.

(b) The real capital accounts record all transactions bringing about changes in the sector's stock of real capital. Also these transactions, with the exception of depreciation, are assumed to have a counterpart in the financial accounts. The balance on the real capital account corresponds to the net real investment of the sector. The real capital relationships of sector i may be expressed as follows:

$$(2) \qquad \Sigma^j J^{ji} - \Sigma^j J^{ij} - D^i = I^i$$

where J denotes gross real investment and I net real investment. $\Sigma^j J^{ji}$ indicates real investment at cost prices, and the sale of capital equipment at balance-sheet value (evaluated in accordance with the principles used in traditional national accounting) are shown by $\Sigma^j J^{ij}$. Net real investment is shown here net of any profit arising in the sale of capital equipment at prices exceeding the balance-sheet value.

(c) The financial capital accounts record the financial counterparts of all transactions carried over the income account and the real capital account (depreciation excepted) as well as the purely financial transactions. The balance on this account corresponds to the net financial investment of the sector. The financial capital relationships of sector i may be expressed as follows:

$$(3) \quad (\Sigma^a \Sigma^j T_a^{ij} - \Sigma^a \Sigma^j T_a^{ji}) - [\Sigma^j J^{ji} - (\Sigma^j J^{ij} + \Sigma^j A^{ij})] \\ + (\Sigma^b \Sigma^j P_b^{ij} - \Sigma^b \Sigma^j P_b^{ji}) = G^i$$

where $\Sigma^j A^{ij}$ denotes profit arising from sale of capital equipment at prices exceeding the balance-sheet value. This magnitude must be included in the financial capital account in addition to the balance-sheet value $\Sigma^j J^{ij}$. The purely financial transactions are denoted by P. The foot lettering indicates the type of object. The expression $\Sigma^b \Sigma^j P_b^{ij}$ denotes ingoing financial objects at cost price and $\Sigma^b \Sigma^j P_b^{ji}$ outgoing financial objects at the balance-sheet value. The difference between these two items equals the profits arising from sale of financial objects at prices exceeding the balance-sheet value $(\Sigma^j \overset{*}{A}{}^{ij})$. G^i is net financial investment which, *inter alia*, includes all realized profits arising from revaluation.

If we insert $\Sigma^j A^{ij} = A^i$ and $\Sigma^j \overset{*}{A}{}^{ij} = \overset{*}{A}{}^i$ into (3) we derive the following equation from (1), (2), and (3):

$$(4) \qquad S^i = I^i + G^i - (A^i + \overset{*}{A}{}^i) = I^i + \overset{*}{I}{}^i$$

where $\overset{*}{I}{}^i = G^i - (A^i + \overset{*}{A}{}^i)$.

A schematic illustration of the sector accounts is given in diagram 1.

DIAGRAM 1. Sector Accounts

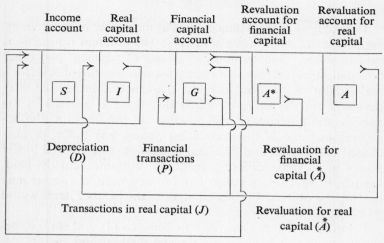

The financial capital account here gives a gross account for those changes in the claims and debts of the sectors which result from transactions. If, on the other hand, one wants a net statement of accounts showing changes in the holdings of financial objects, one may proceed by way of the balance sheet.

DIAGRAM 2. Sector Balances

Assets	Liabilities
Claims ($\Sigma^c \Sigma^j F_c^{ij}$) Real capital ($R^i$)	Debts ($\Sigma^c \Sigma^j F_c^{ji}$) Balance = Equity capital (E^i)

The balance sheet for sector i defines:

$$(5) \qquad F^i + R^i = E^i$$

where $F^i = \Sigma^c \Sigma^j F_c^{ij} - \Sigma^c \Sigma^j F_c^{ji}$

and where F denotes financial objects, the first top lettering the creditor sector and the second top lettering the debtor sector. The foot lettering indicates the type of object. R^i and E^i denote real capital and equity capital (net worth) of sector i.

As regards changes in the balance items we get the following relationship:

$$(6) \qquad \Delta E^i = \Delta R^i + \Delta F^i$$

The changes in the balance items in the course of an accounting period are due to several factors: The different transactions lead to inflows and outflows of means of payment and other financial objects. If these transactions involve sale of a sector's real capital or financial objects, the amount transacted may deviate from the value at which the object is entered in the balance sheet. Secondly, the valuation of the object at the beginning and end of the accounting period may differ, or purchased real capital and financial objects may be entered in the books at a value differing from the amount actually paid. Finally, extraordinary events like fire or a natural disaster may destroy the objects. The net changes in the balance items would comprise all these components.

In order to establish a relation between (4) and (6), i.e. between savings derived by the income method and savings derived by the balance-sheet method some corrections have to be taken into account. If differences resulting both from revaluation (non-realized profit) and profit due to extraordinary events are denoted by O and $\overset{*}{O}$ for real capital and financial capital respectively, we get:

$$(7) \qquad \Delta R^i - O^i = I^i$$

$$(8) \qquad \Delta F^i - \overset{*}{O}{}^i = G^i$$

$$(9) \qquad S^i = \Delta E^i - (A^i + \overset{*}{A}{}^i) - (O^i + \overset{*}{O}{}^i)$$

Here we get three different definitions of net financial investments corresponding to three different definitions of sector savings as the sum total of net real investment and net financial investment. If net financial investment is defined exclusive of realized and non-realized revaluation profit $(\overset{*}{I})$, the saving will correspond to the balance on the income account, i.e.:

$$(10) \qquad S_1{}^i = I^i + \overset{*}{I}{}^i = I^i + [G^i - (A^i + \overset{*}{A}{}^i)] =$$
$$\Delta E^i - (A^i + \overset{*}{A}{}^i) - (O^i + \overset{*}{O}{}^i)$$

If we include realized profit in net financial investment (G), savings, too, will comprise these profit components, i.e.:

$$(11) \qquad S_2{}^i = I^i + G^i = \Delta E^i - (O^i + \overset{*}{O}{}^i)$$

If, in addition, we include non-realized profits due to revaluation and extraordinary events in net financial investment (ΔF) and in net real investment (ΔR), savings will correspond to the net increase in equity capital as derived by the balance method, i.e.:

$$(12) \qquad S_3{}^i = I^i + [G^i + (O^i + \overset{*}{O}{}^i)] = \Delta E^i$$

(3) *The drawing up of accounts*

A large part of the statistics on money and credit now available throw light on the financial holdings of groups of institutions. It is therefore natural that the financial accounts show mainly the financial balances and the net changes in them. In the case of some financial objects both gross and net recording may be of interest. This applies in particular to long-term loans with different dates of maturity and age distribution. The gross changes in such balance items should therefore be shown to the extent that available statistics permit. At the outset it will hardly be practical to aim at drawing up a complete gross accounting system for all financial transactions. The gross accounts for the other transactions are here assumed to be incorporated in the traditional national accounts as indicated under II above.

The accounts relating to the financial balance items must be organized within a clearly delimited system of economic sectors. Furthermore, the balances must be arranged in a standardized form so as to make comparisons and aggregation of the figures possible. The balances must give details by debtor and creditor sectors and by types of claims and debts. It will then be possible to consolidate sector balances where this is desired for purposes of analysis. Moreover, it will be possible to study the financial structure of the sectors.

Organized in this manner, the financial accounts will show the sector's financial capital, i.e.:

$$(13) \qquad F^i = \Sigma^c \Sigma^j F_c{}^{ij} - \Sigma^c \Sigma^j F_c{}^{ji}$$

F

as well as the sector's financial investment (including realized and non-realized profits due to revaluation and extraordinary events), i.e.:

$$(14) \qquad \Delta F^i = \Sigma^c \, \Sigma^{j\Delta} F_c^{ij} - \Sigma^c \, \Sigma^{j\Delta} F_c^{ji}$$

(4) *Sector classification*

Since the financial accounts, *inter alia*, are to illustrate the structure of claims and debts, the sectors must be based on reporting units with independent accounts. Such units will normally be independent legal–economic units, such as enterprises, different kinds of institutions and individuals, such as wage and salary earners, pensioners, etc. Accounting units of this type (for instance, productive enterprises) may be composed of several functional units (for example, establishments defined in accordance with the International Standard Industrial Classification in the production sector) so that they may lend themselves to several economic functions. Thus, the combination production–consumption characterizes all unincorporated and non-co-operative enterprises. Since the sector classification must largely depend on existing institutional conditions, we shall consider only some general principles here which concern the problem. The discussion will otherwise be closely related to institutional conditions in Norway.

Since the financial accounts are intended, *inter alia*, to facilitate monetary and financial policy, it is natural that public administrative agencies are singled out in a special main sector. This is necessary if the monetary effects of public transactions on the rest of the economy are to be brought out. The sector Public Administration includes the central and local governments, and closely related agencies and administrative institutions. Public enterprises may, for some analytical purposes, usefully be included in the producing sectors. Another sector which is important from the point of view of monetary policy is financial institutions. These should be grouped in one main separate sector. The sector described as Financial Institutions should be restricted to institutions whose main function consists of granting credit or otherwise making liquid funds available to other sectors of the economy. A third main group includes units whose main function is the production of goods and services. This sector, which we call productive enterprises, should include enterprises owned by the State and the municipalities as well as private enterprises. Private individuals who are not self-employed form a fourth main sector, namely wage and salary earners, pensioners, etc. Finally, non-profit making organizations and institutions constitute a fifth main group. In order to bring out the economic relations of the home sectors with abroad, a sixth main sector – the rest of the world – should be introduced.

In splitting up the sectors it is particularly within the enterprise sector that problems involving matters of principle arise. Here it may be of interest to have several types of subdivision and possibly also cross-divisions. The enterprises may be distinguished according to ownership, i.e. state-owned, municipality-owned, and privately owned enterprises. Secondly, the private enterprises should be split up according to their form of organization into enterprises with limited liability (corporations and co-operatives) and other private enterprises. The entire enterprise sector ought, furthermore, to be split up according to industry. Since the statistical unit is the enterprise and not the establishment, the classification will be made according to the main activity of the enterprise. To facilitate international comparisons, the sector classification should follow as far as possible the ISIC.[1]

The following sector classification is an example of a possible solution along the lines discussed above:

I. Public administration
II. Financial institutions
III. Productive enterprises

   1. State-owned enterprises

      (i) agriculture and forestry
     (ii) fisheries, etc.
        etc.

   2. Municipal enterprises

      (i) agriculture and forestry
     (ii) fisheries, etc.
        etc.

[1] International Standard Industrial Classification of all Economic Activities.

3. Private enterprises
    (a) Corporations and co-operatives
        (i) agriculture and forestry
        (ii) fisheries
            etc.
    (b) Non-corporate enterprises (excluding co-operatives)
        (i) agriculture and forestry
        (ii) fisheries
            etc.

IV. Wage and salary earners, pensioners, etc.
V. Non-profit-making organizations and institutions
VI. The rest of the world.

(5) *Classification of financial objects*

The term 'financial object' is here meant to include all financial items which constitute assets in one sector and liabilities in another. There are many different types of financial objects. In spite of their differences, however, they have certain common features which enable us to bring them into a relatively small number of object groups which are uniform with regard to certain properties. It is particularly in the case of cross classifications according to debtor and creditor sectors that it is necessary, for practical reasons, to have a small number of object groups. On the other hand, the marginal classifications (i.e. classification of claims by creditor sectors or debts by debtor sectors) permit a more varied selection of financial objects.

In economic analyses it is important to know the degree of liquidity of financial objects, and each group of objects should be so established that they are as uniform as possible with regard to their degree of liquidity. Liquidity is usually related to the marketability of the financial object, which in turn normally has some connection with the legal form of the object. There is no perfect conformity between the degree of liquidity of the financial object and its legal form, but the latter may serve as a practical criterion in the classification of the objects. Since the nature of the financial objects depends very much on the institutional conditions in the various countries, our discussion of the classification will be based on the special conditions prevailing in Norway. The most liquid financial objects are the generally recognized means of payment, such as bank-notes and cheques. Since in Norway ordinary time deposits may easily be transferred to cheque accounts, there is reason to treat all bank deposits as one group. Another group of liquid financial objects comprises those which may be exchanged for cash at a given rate of discount. Here the degree of liquidity is somewhat reduced in as much as the rate of discount may rise during the life of the bill. Treasury bills belong to this group. For many objects there exists in most countries a well-organized market. This is true particularly of bearer bonds and shares. In such a market there is always a certain risk of fluctuations in quotations, and this may considerably reduce the liquidity of the objects concerned. Moreover, within these groups of financial objects the degree of liquidity may vary a great deal between the different kinds of securities. As regards claims which are not intended for negotiation, there exist a number of types. The degree of liquidity of these objects is determined largely by their life. Here it may be useful to segregate credits and loans in a separate group. It may also be of interest to show separately insurance claims on insurance companies and pension funds. Claims which are not interesting enough to deserve separate classification may be brought together in a residual group. Since the choice of object classification will depend on institutional conditions in individual countries, we shall not go into these problems of definition in further detail.

In cross-classifying the balance-sheet items along the basis discussed above, the following types of objects could be distinguished:

   I. Means of payment
  II. Discountable objects
 III. Marketable objects
  IV. Non-negotiable objects
   V. Other financial objects

The groups IV and V should be so defined that the former includes the objects which are most relevant for analytical purposes.

In tables giving marginal distributions it may be useful for many analytical purposes to give details by type of financial object. This will provide a more detailed picture of different features of the financial structure, such as the period of maturity of claims, their degree of security (mortgages, state guaranteed, etc.) or the manner in which the claims have arisen (trading credit, advance payment, etc.).

The financial objects must be distinguished from real capital and from equity capital. In the distinction from real capital it must be decided whether real means of payment, gold and coins, should be considered as financial or real objects. The distinction from equity capital, on the other hand, raises the question of whether an item which is regarded as a financial object by the debtor but not by the creditor (or vice versa) is to be regarded as a financial object or not.

In distinguishing financial objects from real capital, the following points of view may be relevant: Coins and gold are by their nature real objects. If, however, gold as a raw material in production is disregarded, both these objects are means of payment which perform the same function as bank-notes and other means of payment. For analytical purposes it is therefore natural to treat coins and gold as financial objects. If gold is regarded as a real object, an inflow of gold will increase the stock of real capital and consequently become a component of real capital investment. In the case of countries which do not produce gold, this is not a very suitable solution. If gold and coins are regarded as financial objects, the rest of the world must be considered debtor with respect to the gold and the central bank debtor with respect to the coins.

The way in which the problem of distinguishing financial objects from equity capital is solved will affect the determination of net financial investments and thereby also savings of the different sectors. It is impossible to give any objective criterion for this distinction. Each separate case must be decided on its merits, and the decision made must be adhered to consistently from one period to another. In the last instance analytical considerations, such as the allocation of savings to the different sectors, will be the decisive factor. Savings in the form of life insurance may be taken as an example. If it is desired, for analytical reasons, to include such savings in the sector of insurance-policy holders, then allocations to insurance reserves in life-insurance companies must be regarded as a financial object, i.e. as a debt to the policy-holders. If, on the other hand, allocations to reserves in the companies are regarded as capital reserves or equity capital, savings in the form of life-insurance policies must be allocated to the insurance sector.

(6) *Choice of evaluation principles*

As a rule, financial objects have a specific face value indicating the amount which the debtor declares to owe the creditor. This *nominal price* is usually the amount at which the object is redeemed at maturity. Financial objects are frequently traded on the market and then get a *market price*, which is not necessarily identical with their nominal price. By *self cost* is meant the sum of money which has actually been paid for the financial object when it was purchased. This is the amount which as a rule, after possible adjustment for revaluation, is entered in the accounts of the creditor as the balance-sheet value.

For a number of financial objects, and in particular for means of payment, all these principles of evaluation will produce the same result. For others, for instance, bonds and shares, on the other hand, different principles of evaluation may give rather different results. Estimates of net financial investment according to the balance-sheet method will therefore depend on the choice of evaluation principles.

The principles which can be used for the evaluation of financial objects, the most important of which have been mentioned above, fall into two main groups, i.e. principles giving identical evaluation for debtor and creditor, and principles giving different evaluations for these two parties. If the first group of evaluation principles is used, total net financial investment in a closed system of sectors will be nil. The same will also be true of the sum total of profit components. When the second group of evaluation principles is used, total net financial investment, as well as the sum total of profit components, will in general be different from nil.

The principles of evaluation may differ, depending on the purpose of analysis. For most analyses the main interest is probably in determining as exactly as possible the liquidation value of the financial objects. The meaning of the term 'liquidation value' depends on whether a short- or long-term point of view is adopted. From a short-term point of view the liquidation value equals the market value, i.e. the amount of money which can be obtained for the financial object if it is immediately sold on the market. Generally speaking, the principle of market evaluation can in practice be used only by the creditor. From a short-term point of view it therefore seems desirable that creditors should evaluate their financial objects at the market price. For debtors, on the other hand, it would be reasonable to use the nominal price. If a long-term view of the problem is taken, the liquidation value will equal the settlement value, which is usually the same as the nominal value. If the liquidation value is to be decisive, therefore, the nominal price must, according to a long-term view, be chosen as evaluation principle for the creditor as well as for the debtor.

Statistically, the nominal price is a simple and practical evaluation principle. Moreover, this principle gives identical results for debtor and creditor, and provides good opportunities for arriving at statistical consistency. If the nominal price is known, it is possible by appropriate methods of estimation to derive approximate figures for the market price. In a balance sheet based on nominal values, differences between market values and nominal values can be included as supplementary information for the objects in respect of which such differences may occur. In tabular form, the financial balance will take the following form:

DIAGRAM 3. Financial Sector Balance

Assets	Liabilities
1. Claims (nominal value) ($\Sigma^c \Sigma^j F_c{}^{ij}$)	4. Debts (nominal value) ($\Sigma^c \Sigma^j F_c{}^{ji}$)
2. Deviation from market quotation ($\Sigma^c \Sigma^j K_c{}^{ij}$)	5. $= 1 - 4$ Net financial capital (nominal value) ($F_1{}^i$)
3. $= 1 + 2$ Claims (market value)	6. $= 3 - 4$ Net financial capital (market value) (F^{2i})

Similarly, the balance of changes in the balance-sheet items will give net financial investment, excluding or including, as the case may be, non-realized profit due to revaluation. On the other hand, realized profit will always be included in net financial investment according to the balance-sheet method. These profits can only be specified on the basis of 'agio account' (profits and loss account) in the gross accounts (see Diagram 1 above).

If F_c indicates financial objects evaluated at nominal price, and K_c the difference between market value and nominal value, the financial balance may be expressed as follows:

$$(15) \qquad \Sigma^c \Sigma^j F_c{}^{ij} - \Sigma^c \Sigma^j F_c{}^{ji} = F_1{}^i$$

and

$$(16) \qquad \Sigma^c \Sigma^j (F_c{}^{ij} + K_c{}^{ij}) - \Sigma^c \Sigma^j F_c{}^{ji} = F_2{}^i$$

Similarly, the net financial investments may be expressed as follows:

$$(17) \qquad \Sigma^c \, \Sigma^j \, \Delta F_c^{ij} - \Sigma^c \, \Sigma^j \, \Delta F_c^{ji} = \Delta F_1^{\ i} = G^i$$

and

$$(18) \qquad \Sigma^c \, \Sigma^j \, (\Delta F_c^{ij} + \Delta K_c^{ij}) - \Sigma^c \, \Sigma^j \, \Delta F_c^{ji} = \Delta F_2^{\ i}$$

where $\qquad \Sigma^c \, \Sigma^j \, \Delta K_c^{ij} = \overset{*}{O}{}^i$

(7) *Problems of reconciling the accounts*

Even if a uniform system of classification is used and evaluation principles giving identical results for debtor and creditor are chosen, there will be discrepancies between the accounts of the various sectors. This is due partly to the lack of conformity in respect of the timing of entries (float) and partly to statistical errors. Only in exceptional cases therefore will debtors' returns agree with the corresponding statements of creditors. In order to obtain a clear statement of accounts these returns must be reconciled. A reconciliation is necessary if the balance is to be shown in matrix form. The reconciliation should be made on the basis of statements assumed to have small statistical errors. The difference between the reconciled figures and sectors' own figures may, if so desired, be specified in a corrective item which will consist partly of a statistical discrepancy and partly of a difference due to different dates of entry for creditor and debtor.

III. EXAMPLES ILLUSTRATING NORWEGIAN FINANCIAL ACCOUNTING

In Norway the Central Bureau of Statistics has been working for some time on the drawing up of a system of financial accounts.[1] It may also be mentioned in this connection that problems relating to the organization of statistics on money and credit into an accounting system have been dealt with by a special inter-Scandinavian committee. The Norwegian work started with the computation of financial sector balances. It is hoped that the work will be concluded by integrating this system of sector balances with the traditional national accounts within a general system of accounts based on the principles outlined in Sections (1) and (2) of Part II above. For the time being the

[1] The first results are published in *Kredittmarkedsstatistikk 1955* (Credit Market Statistics 1955), which appeared in January 1958 in the series 'NOS'.

theoretical diagram for the gross accounts is used only as an auxiliary instrument in solving the problems of principle which have arisen in connection with the work on the balance-sheet accounts. This section gives a short survey of the general principles underlying the approach.

(1) *Sector classification*

The classification of sectors is on the whole in accordance with the principles outlined in Part II, Section (3) above. The following classification has been adopted:

I. Public administration
   1. The Treasury
   2. Public funds
   3. Social insurance funds
   4. Municipalities

II. Financial institutions
   1. Bank of Norway
   2. Postal checking and savings accounts
   3. State banks
   4. Commercial and savings banks
   5. Credit associations, etc.
   6. Insurance

III. Other domestic sectors
   1. State enterprises
   2. Municipal enterprises
   3. Other Norwegian sectors

IV. Rest of the world

Since the basic statistics are still inadequate, it has not been possible to single out private companies, other private enterprises, wage and salary earners, pensioners, etc., and non-profit-making institutions. Sector III is broken down into industrial activities.

The classification of sectors has given rise to considerable practical problems. The definitions have to be so clear-cut that the reporting units will have no difficulty in classifying their financial objects. Moreover, the definitions must be adapted according to the possibilities of procuring returns. Finally, one must pay due consideration to the type of information needed for analytical purposes. The delimitation of sectors adopted in Norway is briefly outlined as follows: The Treasury is delimited in accordance with the capital balance account of the State in the state budget. Public funds comprise funds which are closely connected with the Government, but which submit independent accounts, such as different types of funds for lending money, other funds established to serve particular purposes, price-regulation funds, etc. Social insurance funds comprise the public insurance and pension schemes which operate as independent legal entities. Municipalities comprise local, rural, and urban governments and county governments. The different groups of financial institutions are delimited in accordance with the statutory laws underlying the activities of these institutions. The insurance sector comprises life-insurance companies, non-life-insurance companies, and private pension schemes and funds. State enterprises include state enterprises which are not separate legal subjects, but which submit special accounts; other enterprises entirely owned by the Government and joint-stock companies in which the Government or government enterprises own 50 per cent or more of the share capital, or for other reasons appoint the majority of board members. Municipal enterprises comprise enterprises which enter the accounts of the munici-palities but which also submit special accounts, municipal com-panies, and enterprises owned jointly by several municipalities. The group 'Other Norwegian sectors' is found as a residual.

(2) *Classification of financial objects*

The following main groups of financial objects have been adopted:

    I. Gold
   II. Bank-notes
  III. Bank deposits
  IV. Treasury bills
   V. Bearer bonds
  VI. Shares
 VII. Loans and advances
VIII. Capital participation
  IX. Insurance claims
   X. Other financial objects

Gold gives the Bank of Norway's holding of gold cover for bank-notes as well as temporary investment in gold. Bank deposits are delimited in accordance with the provisions given in banking legislation. Bearer bonds include debenture bonds issued to the holder. The group described as 'shares' also includes documents of participation in co-operative societies. Loans and advances include all kinds of loans, advances, and credits which do not concern bearer bonds. This group also includes commercial bills of exchange. By 'Capital participation' is meant long-term financial investment, e.g. state capital participation in dependent state enterprises, contributions to the International Bank for Reconstruction and Development and the International Monetary Fund. Insurance claims concern life-insurance companies and private pension schemes, and are classified with the insurance reserves of these institutions. The technical reserves of the non-life-insurance companies, on the other hand, are not considered to be financial objects.

(3) *Choice of evaluation principles*

The nominal price has been used in all the main figures. No attempt has been made at estimating the market value of shares and bearer bonds; wherever possible the balance-sheet value has been used as an approximation. This has been done by introducing in some tables corrective items giving the difference between balance-sheet value and nominal value.

(4) *The accounting structure and the available statistics* [1]

The financial balances of the sectors have been drawn up in such a manner that for each group of financial objects claims are specified according to debtor sectors and debts according to creditor sectors. By giving cross-classifications for the entire system of sectors and all financial objects, a very concentrated picture of the financial structure is obtained. By reading the table vertically a general picture of the claims of the various sectors is obtained, while when read horizontally, the table brings out the distribution of debts over the same sectors. The bottom part of the balance summarizes all the claims and all debts.

A similar table showing movements in the balance items is obtained by taking the differences between figures for the end

[1] The tables described in this section are published in *Credit Market Statistics 1955*, Nos. X1281. Oslo 1955.   Tables 89 and 90.

and the beginning of the period. This shows financial investment by sectors, according to financial objects. Financial investment in this table includes the realized profit on the sale of securities, but not non-realized profit. An indication of this latter magnitude is, however, obtained by considering the changes in the corrective items which show the difference between balance-sheet and nominal value.

In many cases it may be desirable to observe the balance figures or the movement figures for a certain sector over a longer period of time. The table must then be set up in the form of a time series, and it shows the financial balance of the sector 'Commercial and savings banks' at the end of each half-year period in 1952–55. Here it is necessary to have two tables, one for claims and one for debts.

The data relating to Sectors I, II, and III (Sub-sectors 1 and 2) have been obtained by direct returns from the individual units comprised by these sectors. These balances have been aggregated, and thus also show the position with regard to internal claims and debts. The balance for Sector III, Sub-sector 3, 'Other Norwegian sectors', has, on the other hand (except for bearer bonds), been consolidated and shows only claims and debts versus the specified sectors. The data, apart from claims and debts abroad, which are obtained from the annual financial census, have been taken from the other sector balances.

Sector III 'Other domestic sectors' is subdivided into industries. It has not been possible to establish complete balances for each individual industry, but a few important groups of financial objects, such as loans of financial institutions, bearer bonds, and share issues, have been included in these balances. The work on obtaining statistics of bank deposits by industry is under way.

4

REAL CAPITAL AND ECONOMIC GROWTH IN NORWAY 1900–56

By Odd Aukrust and Juul Bjerke

The Central Bureau of Statistics of Norway

INTRODUCTION

THE main purpose of this article is to present a review of the growth of real capital in Norway since the turn of the century. Attention has also been devoted to the relationship between the growth of real capital, employment, and net national product, however.[1]

In Section I some of the fundamental problems involved in computations of the value of the real capital are discussed. Attention is drawn to some of the defects and limitations which often are attached to estimates of the real capital stocks. Section II gives a description of the main features of the methods which have been applied for the Norwegian computations. Section III contains a summary of the principal results of the real capital computations. A more detailed statement of results is given in the Appendix. The last two sections comprise a closer analysis of the figures derived. Section IV is devoted to an analysis of the variations in the marginal capital–output ratio since 1900, with special emphasis on the remarkable post-war trend. Since 1948 the marginal capital–output ratio has been of the order of magnitude 5:1 as against 3:1 in earlier periods. In Section V it is pointed out that this may be explained by a production function of the Cobb–Douglas type with a trend component.

I. DEFINITION AND VALUATION PROBLEMS

In computations of the value of the stocks of real capital there are two vital questions which must be decided. The first is the question of defining the real objects one wants to include in the term real capital. The second, and far more difficult, problem consists in selecting a system of weights ('prices') which can be used in the aggregation of highly divergent real objects on the basis of a common unit of measurement.

[1] The work on this study has been carried out with the financial assistance of the Social Science Research Council.

The capital concept

In this study the concept of real capital is given a somewhat narrow scope. It embraces *all man-made durable real objects in private and public enterprises, including dwellings, and buildings and constructions of general government with the exception of military installations.* Durables are all real objects with a life expectancy of one year or more. Inventories, livestock, land, standing forests, and real objects in the hands of consumers have been excluded from the real capital concept, mainly because statistical sources do not permit annual estimates of these items to be made with any accuracy. The reader should bear this in mind when reading the analytical sections of the paper.

In order to permit some comparisons of the Norwegian figures with figures of other countries, rough estimates of the omitted items have been attempted for one single year, viz. for the end of 1953. These estimates, which are in current prices only, are included in Appendix, Table V. Apart from cars, the figures given do not include estimates of the value of durables in the hands of households, however.

The aggregation problem

To arrive at a convenient system of weights ('prices') for use in the aggregation of real objects of highly different nature it is necessary to operate on the basis of properties which the real objects have in common and which can be measured. Moreover, it is essential that the weight system be based on properties which are relevant from an economic-analytical point of view. However, we are immediately faced with the problem that there are almost no two real objects which are entirely identical in a technical sense. Even highly standardized categories of capital, such as automobiles, etc., will often have different technical qualities. In addition to these purely technical diversities, differences as regards total life and remaining life will make a comparison of various categories of real objects difficult. For these reasons one can hardly hope to arrive at a weight system on the direct basis of the technical properties of real objects.

There seems, however, to be two characteristics of capital objects as defined above which might serve as a basis for an economic measurement of the real capital. The first is that the production of capital objects entails a certain absorption of real resources (production costs). The second characteristic is that a certain production or earning capacity [1] is connected with the capital objects. These qualities seem to permit two different solutions to the aggregation problems. One method, which may be termed the *retrospective method*, implies looking back and using the costs of production as basis for the weight system. The second method, *the prospective method*, implies looking ahead and attempting to determine the weight system on the basis of the future earning capacity of the various real objects. Market prices, or substitutes for these in the absence of market prices, may be taken as an approximation to the latter weight system.

It is the first aggregation method, the retrospective, which has been applied in the Norwegian capital computations, and in the following section some features of this method will be analysed. The second method will also be discussed, however, as a comparison of the results derived from the two different methods is of interest.

The retrospective method

As has already been mentioned, this method implies that the costs of production for the various capital objects are taken as a starting-point. We are then faced with the choice between use of historical costs of capital and replacement costs in the valuation. For well-known reasons replacement costs are preferable. By the use of replacement costs a set of figures is derived for real capital in current value.

These figures will reflect the volume of real productive resources incorporated in the capital equipment as well as the current prices of these resources. To arrive at a volume concept for real capital (meaning by this the volume of accumulated productive resources absorbed) the current-value figures must be deflated with an appropriate cost index, that is an index reflecting the price trend for productive resources. To provide reliable expressions for such indices is not easy, but in principle it presents similar problems to those involved in other forms of price or cost indices.

Special problems arise in the estimation (in current value) of objects which are partly obsolete. To estimate all real objects,

---

[1] See Raymond W. Goldsmith, 'The Growth of Reproducible Wealth of the United States of America from 1805 to 1950', *Income and Wealth, Series II*, p. 249.

old as well as new, at full replacement cost would be tantamount to giving partly obsolete objects the same weight as completely new objects of the same category. The only way to avoid this is to base the valuation of partly obsolete objects on depreciated replacement costs. There is the difficulty, however, that several depreciation methods are possible (linear, progressive, and degressive). The choice between these will affect the computation result and lead to capital concepts of somewhat different content. Within the retrospective method, therefore, a number of variants are possible, depending on the depreciation system used. The choice among these variants can be made on a conventional basis only.[1] In the Norwegian computations constant depreciation allowances have in principle been used, i.e. equally large depreciation allowances each year through the life of the capital objects (the 'straight-line method').[2]

At a given time there will always be some real objects in use which have been rendered obsolete by technological and economic development, so that there can be no question of replacing them with identical units. For such objects it seems reasonable to base the estimates on the replacement costs of real objects by which the obsolete objects may be replaced, with proper adjustments for differences in the potential earning capacity of the two types of capital objects.

The prospective method

Under *the prospective method* the value of the capital items should reflect their future earning capacity. This must be determined on the basis of the future input and output flows which are associated with the different items. If we regard the prices of the various input and output categories and the discounting factors as given quantities at all times, and the future

---

[1] From the point of view of the individual company it may seem reasonable to provide for depreciation so that the value of the capital objects decreases in step with their remaining earning capacity. If this principle is to be strictly applied, it would be necessary to know the development over time of the output and input factors connected with the various capital objects. In practice, one will have to be content with more or less satisfactory approximations. *Stuvel* has pointed to linearly decreasing depreciation as a possible method. See G. Stuvel, 'The Estimation of Capital Consumption in National Accounting', *Review of Economic Studies*, 1955–56, Vol. XXIII (3), No. 62, pp. 183–185. Provided that the time function for the earning capacity of the capital objects decreases parabolically over the period, this method will be in agreement with the principle mentioned above. If, on the other hand, the earning capacity decreases linearly over the life period, the straight-line procedure will produce the desired result.

[2] Actually this principle may not always be fulfilled, cf. p. 90.

G

input and output flows are known, the earning capacity of the different capital items may in principle be estimated.

When the prospective method is used, one would in practice base the valuation on the market prices of the capital items, since as these can be taken as approximate expression of their earning capacity. Problems arise for the (quite numerous) categories of capital objects which are not usually sold in the market. In such cases one will have to guess what the market prices would have been if a market had existed. Another point in the prospective method is that no fundamental problems arise in the valuation of partly outworn capital objects, or objects which have been rendered obsolete by the technological and economic developments. The earning capacity or market prices give us the solution directly in both cases.

To arrive at figures for the value of the real capital measured in fixed prices under the prospective method one should in principle take the starting-point in a set of given (fixed) prices on all input and output factors and a set of discounting factors. In practice, the usual procedure is to deflate the figures in current prices by price indices designed to reflect the price trend for capital objects with a given potential earning capacity.

Comparison of the two methods

There is reason to believe that the results obtained under the two methods, in so far as the value of capital in terms of current prices is concerned, will not show very large deviations. The reason is that in most cases the market prices of capital goods are not likely to deviate much from their (depreciated) replacement costs as calculated by any standard method of depreciation under the retrospective method. It is obvious, for example, that the market price of new capital equipment cannot be far from its costs of production. But for partly obsolete objects, market prices may also be assumed to be fairly close, on an average, to depreciated replacement costs. This will be the case if and when the depreciation method actually used approximates, on an average, to the falling earning capacity of capital goods with increasing age.[1] With most of the standard depreciations methods discussed above this may not be too far from the truth.

For the value of capital in terms of *fixed* prices, on the other hand, the two methods will usually produce different results.

[1] See Raymond W. Goldsmith, *loc. cit.*, p. 251.

This is a consequence of the different meaning of the price-change concept in the two valuation methods. Under the *retrospective method* a series of figures for the value of the real capital in terms of fixed prices will reflect the quantity of productive resources which are incorporated in the capital equipment at various times. But the figures are not supposed to be influenced by the fact that as a result of increased technological knowledge it has gradually become possible to combine these productive resources in a more effective technique. Under the *prospective method*, on the other hand, one tries to compute figures in fixed prices which take into account both the increase in the volume of incorporated productive resources and improvements in technique. For here one uses price indices for capital objects which as far as possible are equal from a technological efficiency viewpoint. It is reasonable to assume that gradually increasing technological knowledge will make it possible to produce more effective capital objects with given investment of productive resources. It is to be expected, therefore, that the real capital volume will show a sharper increase over a period if the computations are performed under the *prospective valuation method* than if they are based on the *retrospective method*.

The choice between the two evaluation methods also depends on the objective of the computations. If the purpose is to study the role of capital as a factor of production, the *prospective method* may seem preferable. Volume figures for the capital computed on the basis of this method will, as pointed out above, also reflect improvements in the productive capacity of the capital as a result of more effective technique. That will not be the case to the same extent with volume figures computed under the *retrospective method*. This point is of significance if we want to use figures for the real capital in a production function to 'explain' the production trend over a lengthy period. If in this case we use capital data computed under the *retrospective method* we must include in the production function a special variable in order to allow for the effects of the gradual change in the technological level.[1]

[1] When real capital is to be used as explanatory variable in a production function there may be reason to question both of the valuation methods mentioned here. Under both methods partly obsolete capital objects will be given a substantially lower value than corresponding new objects, on the assumption that they have a lower *remaining* production capacity. But this probably does not give

If the primary purpose of the capital computations is regarded as part of the work on what Ingvar Ohlsson [1] terms 'statement of results' the *retrospective method* seems to be the most satisfactory. Two arguments may, as far as we can see, be raised in support of this:

(i) It is natural to require of our capital data that they (in terms of fixed prices) be consistent with the national account figures (also expressed in fixed prices), i.e. that the capital growth over a period according to the capital estimates shall equal the accumulated net investments over that period according to the national accounts. But in a national accounting system, prepared for the purpose of measuring 'economic results', net investments have to be estimated so as to give a measure of the volume of the productive resources which have been used to increase the capital of the society. It follows that in the capital computations also we must regard the capital as 'accumulated productive resources', which means that the *retrospective method* must be applied. Provided that the same principles are applied in the estimation of the depreciation in both cases, this will result in capital stock figures at constant prices which are consistent with the current national accounting figures at constant prices.

(ii) In analysing economic results it is often necessary to use stock data and current data together, for example, in analyses where the capital is regarded as the accumulated result of the production of earlier periods. It is therefore desirable that the two sets of data be based on identical valuation principles, i.e. that the capital data, like the current data, are computed on the basis of the production costs of the commodities.

In both cases a deeper reason for the choice of valuation principle lies in the fact that the production costs express a fundamental transformation relationship between the objects, as they

---

a satisfactory expression of the relation between the *current* production capacity of old and new equipment, for example, a ten-year-old railroad car in the short run may be of as good service as a completely new one. It is presumed that this factor may be disturbing for short-term analyses, where the age structure of the capital may vary appreciably, and where changes in the value of the capital therefore will not always provide a good measure for the changes in its production capacity.

[1] Ingvar Ohlsson, *On National Accounting*, Stockholm, 1953.

approximately measure the quantities of productive resources which are incorporated in them.

II. COMPUTATION METHODS

In this section a brief outline will be given of the computation methods of the Norwegian capital estimates. The employment data which are used in sections III–V will also be described in some detail.

Capital computations

Figures for the real capital volume have been computed on an annual basis for the period 1900–55 with the exception of the war years 1940–45. For all years the real capital has been classified into the following four groups: buildings and constructions in private and public enterprises; buildings and constructions of general government; ships and boats; machinery, tools, and transportation equipment excluding ships. More detailed data by industry as well as by type are available for three years, viz. the years 1900, 1939, and 1953. All results are expressed in 1938 prices.

The computations have been performed in three steps, or by three different types of computations. Step (1) was to determine figures for gross investment, measured in 1938 prices, for each year in the period under review and for each capital group. Step (2) consisted in direct and detailed computations of the value of the real capital stocks (in 1938 prices) at a few bench-mark points, namely at the end of the years 1899, 1920, 1939, and 1953. Steps (1) and (2) together gave the data required to compute (separately for each capital group) the total net investments and the total capital consumption within each of the periods 1900–20, 1921–39. In step (3) these preliminary results were used to compute annual figures for the capital consumption in each capital group, also in terms of 1938 prices. Together with the annual gross investment figures (step (1)) and directly computed capital data for bench-mark years (step (2)), this permitted a simple determination of the annual stock data. The computations at the various steps have been described in further detail in the following.

It is characteristic of the computation method applied that it is based on computations of gross investments for all years and independently derived estimates of capital stocks for bench-mark years, and that the results of these computations are controlled against each other by studying the implications they entail for the development of capital consumption. The capital-consumption data are useful *per se*, and will be used in the Norwegian national accounts.[1]

Step (1): Computation of annual gross investment figures

The gross investment data used in this study have been taken from earlier published national accounting data and are mainly estimated by the commodity-flow approach, i.e. on the basis of import statistics and Norwegian production of capital goods. Further details on the computations in fixed and current prices may be obtained from official publications.[2] The lack of gross investment data for the years 1940–45 is the main reason why this article contains no capital-stock figures for these years.

Step (2): Capital computations for bench-mark years

For no year are census results available which permit a computation of capital stocks based on complete and homogeneous material. The computations for bench-mark years made for this study are therefore based on data collected from highly variable sources, often supplemented with approximate corrections and estimates. As a general rule, total figures must be presumed subject to smaller relative margins of error than the more detailed specifications presented.

For the years 1899, 1939, and 1953 the capital-stock figures are based on detailed computations for each single group of capital objects, made separately for each individual industry. The computations for 1920 are more summary, and their main purpose has been to provide some basis for judging whether capital consumption over the fifty-year period have developed proportionally with the capital volume (see p. 90 below). The

---

[1] In our opinion it would be difficult to find a better method for computation of the level of capital consumption, as it guarantees that the national accounting data on capital consumption will be consistent with the gross investment data and with the best estimates that can be made of the size of the capital stocks at different points of time. The need for capital consumption data for the national account was, as a matter of fact, one of the main reasons for undertaking this study.

[2] Organization of European Economic Co-operation, *National Accounts Studies – Norway*, Paris, 1953, pp. 100–101. Central Bureau of Statistics of Norway, *National Accounts 1900–1929* (NOS. XI. 143), pp. 10–13, *National Accounts 1930–1939 and 1946–1951* (NOS. XI. 109), pp. 50–51, and *National Accounts 1938 and 1948–1953* (NOS. XI. 185), pp. 37–38.

nature of the statistical sources used in the direct capital computations vary from industry to industry and from capital object to capital object.

For some categories of capital it has been possible to base the computations on direct volume data and production costs data, sometimes supplemented by data on the age structure of capital. Dwellings, ships and boats, automobiles, roads and railroads are examples of groups of capital objects for which we have been able to make direct use of volume and cost data.

For other categories of capital objects the computations are based on value data, generally measured in current prices. These data are sometimes fire-insurance values, in other cases book values. The book values represent in some cases depreciated capital values, in others cumulated historical costs before depreciation. Manufacturing and mining are examples of industries where data on fire-insurance values have been available. For post, telegraph and telephone, and for railway and tramway rolling stock the computations are based on book values.

For the components of the capital equipment where computations are based on value data in current prices one of the difficult problems has been the conversion from current prices into 1938 prices. The price indices used for these computations have in most cases been those used for the fixed-price estimates for gross investment in the national accounts for the period 1900–55.

Step (3): Computation of annual capital consumption data

With the aid of data from step (1) and step (2) the sum total of the capital consumption over a period of years can be determined.[1] In our case the computations provide figures for the total capital consumption for the period 1900–39 and for the two sub-periods 1900–20 and 1921–39, separately for each of the four object groups of real capital discussed in paragraph 20. (A computation of capital consumption by industry is not possible, however, as gross investment data by industry are not available for the whole period 1900–39.)

---

[1] We have $D_{t/t+\theta} = J_{t/t+\theta} - (C_{t+\theta} - C_t)$, where $D_{t/t+\theta}$ and $J_{t/t+\theta}$ denote capital consumption and gross investment respectively in the period from t to $t + \theta$ and $C_{t+\theta}$ and C_t the size of the real capital at the end of the period and at the beginning of the period. $D_{t/t+\theta}$ can be set as balance when the right hand elements are known.

The next problem is to distribute the total of capital consumption thus estimated over the different years in the period. This can be done by assuming that each year's capital consumption varies in a given way with the depreciated value of the real capital at the beginning of the year (both expressed in 1938 prices).[1] The simplest assumption would be to assume that capital consumption throughout the period has been proportional to the capital value. However, the computations for the two sub-periods 1900–20 and 1921–39 indicate that the capital-consumption ratios (capital consumption in 1938 prices as a percentage of the real capital measured in 1938 prices) must have been higher after 1920 than before 1920 for all categories of capital objects. It seems natural to deduce from this that in the course of the period 1900–39 a gradual shortening of the 'normal' life of capital has taken place. We have therefore based our computations on the assumption that capital consumption as a percentage of the capital value has shown a linear rise over this period. In other words, we have assumed, for each kind of capital, that the capital consumption ratio p_t can be written

$$p_t = a + bt$$

where a and b are positive constants, and where t denotes the time. The magnitude t may assume values from 0 (in 1900) to 39 (in 1939).

We now have sufficient data to be able to determine the absolute magnitude of the capital consumption in each year and the capital at the beginning of each year. The procedure is as follows: It is possible to determine the constants a and b for each group of capital through the figures derived for the value of the real capital at the end of 1899, 1920, and 1939 and the capital consumption figures for the sub-periods 1900–20 and 1921–39. The capital-consumption ratios for each year then follow automatically from the above formula. But when the capital-consumption ratios are known and data are available for gross in-

---

[1] The straight-line method which was chosen for the present study requires the value of capital as new to be used as a basis for this distribution. Unfortunately, this could not be done for lack of data, and the method actually used must be viewed as an approximation to the former..It is justified in that the two methods will give identical results when applied to a stock of capital goods with a given age distribution. However, since the distribution by age of the various categories of capital cannot be expected to have remained constant over the period in question, the results obtained must be assumed to deviate somewhat from the values one should have got, had the straight-line method been strictly applicable.

vestments in each year it is a simple matter to compute annual capital-stock figures and annual capital-consumption data, starting from a direct estimate of the capital stock of one year, say the end of 1899.[1]

The computations for the post-war period are based on a form of extrapolation of bench-mark data for 1953. It is assumed that the capital-consumption percentages for the years 1946–56 can be determined through the same formula (with the same constants) as for 1900–39. Annual capital-consumption figures and stock figures for the real capital have then been computed as before, on the basis of these depreciation ratios, the already available annual investment figures, and the direct estimate of the capital stock in 1953.

Computation of employment data

For the period 1930–56, with the exception of the war years, annual employment figures in terms of man-years have been published in the official national accounts.[2] These figures are based on detailed computations for individual industries.

The employment data used in this article for the years prior to 1930 have a far weaker statistical foundation. They are not based on detailed computations for each individual industry. The data have been derived largely by backward extrapolation of the national accounting total for man-years in 1930. In the extrapolation the size of the working population, estimated on the basis of population censuses for 1900, 1910, 1920, and 1930, has been used as an indicator. A correction has been attempted for variations in unemployment, however. These corrections are based on data on unemployment among trade-union members.[3]

III. MAIN FINDINGS

The real capital data derived from the computations are presented in detail in the Appendix and in excerpts in Tables I–III below. Some comments on the figures are given in the following paragraphs.

---

[1] Capital consumption in 1900 is derived by applying the capital-consumption ratio for 1900 to the estimate of the real capital at the end of 1899. When gross investments for 1900 are known the size of the capital at the end of 1900 follows from this. With this as basis, the capital consumption for 1901 and the capital at the end of 1901 can be determined, and so on.

[2] See *National Accounts 1930–1939 and 1946–1951* (NOS. XI. 109) and *National Accounts 1938 and 1948–1953* (NOS. XI. 185), table 39.

[3] See *Statistiske oversikter 1948* (NOS. X. 178).

The growth of the total volume of real capital

The volume of capital has grown continuously since 1900, apart from the war period 1940–45. On the basis 1900 = 100, the volume of capital at the end of 1955 was 390 (Table I). This implies an average rate of growth of 2·4 per cent per annum.

TABLE I

Real Capital [1] by Type at the End of Selected Years

| Year | Value of Fixed Real Capital | As Percentage Value Fixed Real Capital at 1938 Prices | | | | Index of Total Fixed Real Capital 1900 = 100 |
	Million krona in 1938 prices	Buildings and Constructions of General Government	Buildings and Constructions of Enterprises	Machinery and Transportation Equipment Excl. Ships and Boats	Ships and Boats	
1899	7,250	14·5	73·5	6·8	5·2	100
1905	8,075	14·3	72·3	7·7	5·7	111
1910	8,961	13·4	71·5	9·1	6·0	124
1915	10,550	12·7	70·7	10·2	6·4	146
1920	12,203	11·9	72·0	10·5	5·6	168
1925	13,351	13·2	70·9	10·1	5·8	184
1930	14,990	13·2	68·2	10·5	8·1	207
1935	16,319	13·6	68·4	10·9	7·1	225
1939	18,874	13·2	66·4	12·5	7·9	260
1945	16,461	15·5	69·4	10·1	5·0	227
1950	21,578	14·1	64·9	12·7	8·3	298
1955	28,284	13·0	62·3	16·7	8·0	390

The rate of growth of capital shows large variations as between quinquennia (Table II). The most rapid growth in real capital before the last world war occurred between 1910 and 1920 and in the years 1935–39. In both these periods the rate of growth was well over 3 per cent per annum. The growth was notably slow in the five-year periods 1900–5 (1·7 per cent per annum), 1920–25 (1·8 per cent), and 1930–35 (1·7 per cent).

Between 1939 and 1945 there was a decline in total real capital of some 13 per cent.[2] The decline was due not so much to the

[1] Structures and equipment only.

[2] This is a somewhat lower figure than that computed by the Central Bureau of Statistics in 1946. The Bureau at that time arrived at an estimated capital reduction of 18·5 per cent, but this estimate included inventories, personal furniture, and movables, where the capital reduction was particularly large (Statistisk Sentralbyrå, *Nasjonalinntekten i Norge 1935–1943* (NOS. X. 102), p. 159).

decrease in the number of capital objects as to the fact that the average remaining life of capital dropped sharply. This fact must be borne in mind in considering changes in the real capital volume in relation to the net national product (the capital–output ratio) from 1939 up to the first post-war years.[1]

TABLE II

Growth of Real Capital [2] by Groups. Average Rates of Growth for Five-year Periods

Period	Increase in Real Capital, Absolute Figure — Million krona in 1938 prices	As Percentages of Increase in Real Capital			Average Rate of Growth, All Groups — Per cent per annum
		Buildings and Con-structions	Machinery and Trans-portation Equipment, Excl. Ships	Ships and Boats	
1900–05	658	71·0	17·8	11·2	1·7
1905–10	886	70·0	21·6	8·4	2·1
1910–15	1,589	74·5	16·6	8·9	3·3
1915–20	1,653	87·1	12·7	0·2	2·9
1920–25	1,148	87·5	4·7	7·9	1·8
1925–30	1,639	59·1	13·9	26·9	2·3
1930–35	1,329	88·0	15·3	−3·3	1·7
1935–39	2,555	64·2	23·0	12·8	3·7
1939–45	−2,413	43·6	28·5	27·9	−2·3
1945–50	5,117	60·0	20·9	19·1	5·6
1950–55	6,706	64·0	29·3	6·7	5·6

After the last world war the growth of real capital has been considerably stronger than for any other period in this century, viz. 5·6 per cent per annum on the average for the period 1945–55. It is remarkable that in spite of the capital reduction during the War we find the same rate of growth for the period 1939–55 as a whole as for the period 1900–39. The growth of capital in the years 1946–55 has, in other words, been sufficiently rapid to offset entirely the setback due to World War II.

Capital structure by type

The growth has not been equally strong for all groups of real capital. Estimated for the period 1900–55 as a whole, we find average rates of growth of 4·2 per cent per annum for machinery

[1] See p. 102.
[2] Structures and equipment only.

and transportation equipment (ships excluded), 3·3 per cent per annum for ships and boats, and 2·2 per cent per annum for buildings and constructions. To some extent the figures reflect the extensive mechanization which has taken place over the period in question

As a result of this there has been a marked change in the composition of capital. Buildings and constructions still represent the largest group, but have dropped from 88·0 per cent of total real capital (measured in 1938 prices) in 1900 to 75·3 per cent in 1955. In the same period the ratio for machines and transportation equipment (ships excluded) increased from 6·8 to 16·7 per cent and for ships and boats from 5·2 to 8·0 per cent.

The relative decline in the building and construction capital has been a stable feature in the development through the whole century. Only during the two world wars has there been a temporary increase in the relative importance of this capital group, and exclusively because the merchant fleet was substantially reduced through war losses.

The growing relative importance of machinery and transportation equipment (ships excluded) has also been a comparatively stable feature of the picture. Apart from a time of relative stagnation at the beginning of the twenties, it is only for the war years 1939–45 that the ratio for machinery and transportation equipment shows decline.

For ships and boats the trend has been more irregular. In this group we find periods of progress as well as periods of decline. The progress was most pronounced in the periods 1900–16, 1924–31, and 1945–55. There was an absolute decline towards the end of, and immediately after, World War I and in the period 1931–34.

Government building and construction measured as a proportion of total real capital has shown a slight downward trend through the period. The growth of real capital in this group has nevertheless been somewhat more rapid than for building and construction as a whole.

Real capital by industries

As pointed out earlier, it has not been possible to compute annual figures for real capital by industries, as pre-1930 gross investment data by industry are not available. Directly computed capital figures for the years 1900, 1939, and 1953, however, show the main lines of the development.

There has been increase in real capital within all industries, but the growth has been somewhat varied. The growth has been relatively weak within agriculture and forestry and housing, and particularly strong for mining, manufacturing, electricity development, and shipping.

TABLE III

Real Capital [1] by Main Industry Groups in 1900, 1939, and 1953

| Industry Group | Absolute Figures | | | Percentage Distribution | | |
| | Million kroner in 1938 prices | | | | | |
	1900	1939	1953	1900	1939	1953
Agriculture and forestry	1,112	2,090	2,382	15·3	11·1	9·4
Fishing and whaling	113	352	385	1·6	1·9	1·5
Mining and manufacturing	555	2,552	4,067	7·6	13·5	16·0
Electricity and gas	30	1,100	2,083	0·4	5·8	8·2
Dwellings	3,062	6,200	7,289	42·3	32·8	28·7
Sea transport	340	1,389	1,932	4·7	7·4	7·6
Other transport	446	1,418	2,038	6·1	7·5	8·0
Merchandise trade and services	540	1,281	1,815	7·5	6·7	7·1
General government	1,052	2,492	3,444	14·5	13·3	13·5
Of which: Highways and bridges	540	1,320	1,726	7·4	7·0	6·8
Total	7,250	18,874	25,435	100·0	100·0	100·0

The trend is reflected in the individual industries' ratio of the total real capital. For agriculture and forestry this ratio dropped from 15·3 per cent in 1900 to 9·4 per cent in 1953. (It should be observed that the figures do not include land and ground, livestock and standing forests. The relative decline would probably have been even bigger if these items had been included.) For housing there is a decrease from 42·3 per cent in 1900 to 28·7 per cent in 1953, or relatively a slightly weaker decrease than for agriculture and forestry. For all other sectors the ratio shows a rise or standstill.

The increase is particularly marked for electricity, mining, and manufacturing. For these sectors as a whole the ratio has trebled between 1900 and 1953, namely from 8 to 24 per cent. These

[1] Structures and equipment only.

industries accounted for almost one-third of the total net investment in the period. The growth has been most rapid in electricity, where the ratio advanced from 0·4 per cent in 1900 to 5·8
per cent in 1939 and to 8·2 per cent at the end of 1953.

Sea transport has also increased its ratio of the total real
capital quite appreciably. The ratio rose from not quite 5 per
cent in 1900 to about 7·5 per cent in 1939, a level reached again
in 1953, when the effects of the tonnage loss during the War had
been overcome.

The ratio has increased for other transport as well, viz. from
6·1 to 8·0 per cent. The rise is small, however (from 13·5 to
14·8 per cent), if capital of general government in highways and
highway bridges is included in this group. The entire growth relates to highway and air transport, and post, telephone, and telegraph. The railroad ratio of the total real capital has remained
unchanged.

For service trades other than transport the ratio has dropped.
For machinery and transport, however, there is also a strong
relative rise.

The data presented above on the composition of the real
capital by industry and object do not alter the picture suggested
by other evidence on economic developments in this century. It
confirms the view that the most marked feature of the picture is
the relative decline of agriculture, the rapid relative growth of
manufacturing, and the exploitation of water-power as a source
of energy. The relative expansion in sea transport and the increasing role of machinery and transport equipment compared
with building capital are also points worth noting.

Relation between real capital, employment, and production

In the course of the fifty-six years under review the real capital
in Norway has almost quadrupled. The average rate of growth
has been 2·4 per cent per annum. In *per capita* terms the corresponding rate of growth has been about 1·6 per cent per annum.
The tables give a strong impression of the extent to which the
wealth of a modern society is a result of the efforts of the latest
generation. About three-quarters of the real capital in existence
in Norway today has been created since the turn of the century,
only one-quarter is a heritage from earlier times.

The growth in employment has been considerably slower. The
number of man-years in 1956 was only about 60 per cent higher

than in 1900, corresponding to an average annual rate of growth of some 0·8 per cent. This, of course, means that production has become more 'capital-intensive'. In 1956 there was over 2·5 times as much capital behind each worker as at the turn of the century. The growth of real capital per man-year has been a relatively stable feature since 1900. It is only during the last world war and exceptionally in the 1920s that employment has risen more rapidly than the capital, so that the capital–labour ratio has dropped.

Production has risen more rapidly than both capital and employment. With 1900 = 100 the net national product in 1955 was 457. This corresponds to an average rate of growth of 2·8 per cent per annum, or 2·0 per cent if the growth is calculated per man-year and 2·0 per cent if estimated *per capita*. Thus, while production has undoubtedly become more 'capital-intensive' in the sense that the capital–labour ratio has risen, it has not also become more 'round-about', if by that we mean that the real capital represents more years of 'accumulated production' now than half a century ago. On the contrary, while the real capital expressed in fixed prices in 1900 represented about four years' national product, the average capital–output ratio in 1956 had dropped to approx. 3·3.

TABLE IV

Average Rates of Growth for Net National Product, Real Capital,[1] *and Employment in Selected Periods*

Period	Average Percentage Growth per Annum in Real Capital Volume	Average Percentage Growth Per Annum in Number of Man-years	Average Rates of Growth for Real Capital Volume per Man-year	Average Rates of Growth for Net National Product
1900–05	1·7	0·4	1·3	0·4
1905–10	2·1	0·8	1·3	3·5
1910–15	3·3	1·3	2·0	4·3
1915–20	2·9	1·6	1·3	3·1
1920–25	1·8	−0·6	2·5	0·4
1925–30	2·3	0·4	2·0	5·3
1930–35	1·7	0·9	0·8	1·3
1935–39	3·7	2·3	1·3	4·6
1930–46	−1·4	0·4	−2·0	0·5
1946–48	6·0	2·7	3·3	8·7
1948–51	5·5	0·9	4·7	3·7
1951–55	5·6	0·4	5·1	3·3

[1] Structures and equipment only.

The growth in the period 1900–56 has by no means been steady. Table IV indicates that there have been sharp fluctuations in the rates of growth of both real capital, employment, and national product. The table further shows that there is a comparatively high degree of co-variation between the three series. On the whole, we find that periods of rapid capital increase have also been periods of rapid growth in employment, and these are naturally also the periods when the rise in production has been greatest. Particularly striking is the co-variation between the rate of growth of real capital and the rate of growth of national product. It is worth noting, however, that the period following the last war is different both in this and other respects. One point often made is, for example, that the growth in the national product after 1948 does not seem to be in any reasonable proportion to the exceptionally rapid growth in the real capital in these years. In the remainder of this paper the co-variation between capital, employment, and production will be subjected to closer analysis.

IV. THE CAPITAL–OUTPUT RATIO

The idea of a constant marginal capital–output ratio

Studies from several countries, particularly the United States and Great Britain, have shown that a remarkable stability can be found in historical data in the relationship between the volume of capital and the volume of national product, totally or marginally. Sometimes this stability is interpreted as an economic law, from which the impression is gained that the size of production is determined by the volume of capital alone. Economic growth models of the Domar–Harrod type are examples of models which characteristically assume a constant marginal capital–output ratio.

It should be stressed, however, that *a priori* we have no reason to expect such a simple connection between increments in real capital and national product. On the contrary, production theory suggests that the marginal productivity of capital is not likely to be a constant, but a quantity which will vary with the size of the capital itself, as well as with employment and the technological level. Consequently, we cannot expect that a given increase of real capital will always lead to a proportionate increase of the national product, irrespective of what is happening to employment and to technology. Yet another argument may be added. Various kinds of capital will as a rule have different marginal productivity from a social point of view. The effects on the national product of a particular capital increase is therefore not independent of the 'mix' in which the capital increase takes place. 100 million kroner more invested in highways, for example, might lead to a different increase in the national product than the same amount invested in new housing.[1]

Against this background we shall in the following pages consider the actual trends in real capital and national product in Norway for the period after 1900. The main features are

TABLE V

Increments in Real Capital [2] and Net National Product for Bench-Mark Periods

(Figures in 1938 prices)

Period	Real Capital Increment	Net National Product Increment	Marginal Capital–Output Ratio
	Million kroner	Million kroner	$1 \div 2 = 3$
	1	2	3
1900–16 . .	3,300	1,049	3·15
1916–30 . .	3,950	1,326	2·99
1930–37 . .	2,351	816	2·88
1939–56 . .	10,136	3,199	3·17
1900–56 . .	21,078	6,731	3·13
1946–51 . .	5,126	1,767	2·90
1947–51 . .	4,430	1,011	4·38
1951–56 . .	6,741	1,230	5·48

illustrated in Graph 1 below, where correlated values of national product and real capital have been drawn for each year except the war years 1940–45 (the fine line). The graph should be studied together with Table V, where the increment in real capital and national product is shown for bench-mark periods.

The period 1900–39

For the period before the last world war real capital and national product have risen largely in step. This is particularly clear if we focus our attention on boom years in the period

[1] For an elaboration of this reasoning see Odd Aukrust, 'Effect of Investments on National Product', *Statsøkon. Tidsskrift*, 1957, No. 2.

[2] Structures and equipment only.

H

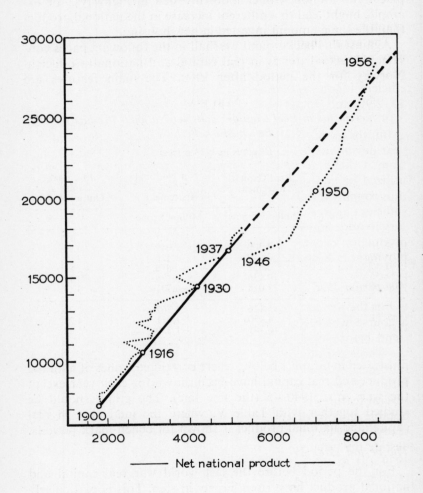

Growth of real capital and net national product 1900-39 and 1946-56

(which in Norway were 1900, 1916, 1930, and 1937) and disregard intermediate years when production capacity was not fully utilized. By and large, an increase in real capital of 300 million kroner (in fixed prices) has resulted in a rise in the annual national product of 100 million kroner, i.e. the marginal capital coefficient has been 3·0 for the period as a whole. This is shown by the fitted, fully drawn-in straight line in the graph.[1]

The graph further indicates that this ratio has kept remarkably constant in the different cyclical periods, measured from peak to peak. Table V shows that the marginal capital coefficient for the period 1900–16, was 3·15, for the period 1916–30, 2·99, and for 1930–37, 2·88. For the period 1930–39 it was 3·19.

But the graph also indicates that there are substantial year-to-year deviations from the straight line. It is justified to conclude from it that the physical production potentials were not fully utilized in inter-peak periods. The area above the fitted line thus roughly measures the 'loss in production' resulting from insufficient aggregate demand in the inter-war period. It is necessary to add, however, that not even in 1930 and 1937 was actual production capacity fully utilized, as there was extensive unemployment in both these years.

The period 1946–56

For the period following World War II the historical line has a course which on several points deviates radically from the trend before 1939. True, the marginal capital–output ratio for the whole period 1939–56 (3·17) does not differ much from the ratio derived for the pre-war period. But within this period the ratios shows substantial variations. Altogether, there are several features of the trend which seem peculiar: (i) There is a notable shift in the historical line between 1939 and 1945. Already in 1946 production was well above the pre-war level, despite the fact that real capital was considerably lower than in 1939. (ii) At the same time the national product showed a very rapid growth in the first two post-war years. For these years we find considerably lower values both for the average and the

---

[1] The line is a regression line for real capital (C_+) with respect to national product (Y_+), estimated on the basis of observations for 1900, 1916, 1929, and 1937. The formula of the line is $C_t = 3·00\ Y_t + 1,840$.

marginal capital–output ratio than those we know from the pre-war years. (iii) A change occurs in 1948. From then on the marginal capital–output ratio has been decidedly higher than in the inter-war period and at the same time increasing. It was 4·38 for the years 1947–51 and 5·48 for the years 1951–56, or 4·99 for the whole period 1947–56.

How are these facts to be explained? The most simple ex-planation is perhaps to regard the course of the historical line in the early post-war years as an 'accidental and transitory' de-viation to the right from the underlying long-run trend, followed by a normalization, e.g. as a consequence of variations in total demand. This is tantamount to acceptance of the hypothesis that the long-run marginal capital–output ratio is a constant and suggests that for coming years we must again expect to find the value of the marginal capital–output ratio at around 3·0.

As we have pointed out on p. 98, however, there is no reason to expect the marginal capital–output ratio to remain stable over time, rather the contrary. In particular, we have to assume that this ratio will itself be a function of employment, volume of capital, and production technique. A more subtle explanation for the post-war trend than that suggested in the previous para-graph is therefore required.

The following factors provide an explanation for the shift in the historical line from 1939 to 1946: (i) Employment was some-what higher in 1946 than in 1939. (ii) Parallel with the rise in employment there was an extensive shift of labour from sectors with low net product per man-year to sectors with high net pro-duct. (ii) It is probable that our capital figures, as computed, exaggerate the decrease during the War in the current produc-tion capacity of the capital.[1]

The low marginal capital–output ratio in the early post-war years can be plausibly explained as follows: (i) The capital in-crease in those years was accompanied by a very sharp rise in employment. (ii) The marginal productivity of capital was high, because the real capital volume per employed was lower than before the War. (iii) Simultaneously with the capital increase there was a rapid technological change. In 1946 the results of six to seven years of rapid development abroad were suddenly at our disposal.

It is more difficult to explain the high and rising capital–output

[1] Cf. p. 92.

ratio from 1948 onwards. It has been suggested that the investment structure may have had some effect, and that may be true.
But the main factors appear to be the following: (i) The rate of
increase in employment has been somewhat slower in 1948 than
earlier in the century, and substantially slower than in the first
two post-war years. (ii) Because of the high investment level in
post-war years, real capital per employed has risen rapidly
(from 12,000 1938 kroner in 1946 to 18,000 kroner in 1956). The
marginal productivity of capital has therefore dropped. (iii) The
decreasing demand pressure since 1950 has probably curbed the
production increase. (This is the factor that was originally suggested above as the *only* explanation, but which we rejected as
such.) (iv) Because the average age of the capital has been declining, its productivity has risen less than the capital volume,
as measured in this study.

The explanation of the post-war development given in the
preceding paragraphs contains quite different implications for
the future than the simple explanation originally advanced. If we
admit that the volume of production does not only depend on
the volume of capital, but assume more complicated production
functions, it cannot be taken for granted that the marginal
capital–output ratio will drop again to its former level of about
3·0. On the contrary, it is quite possible that in the future we
must again reckon with a ratio of the present order of 5·0 or
higher. Whether the one or the other will be the case is a question
of great importance for the future prospects of our economy.
With our present net investment rate (15–18 per cent per annum)
a marginal capital–output ratio of 5·0–6·0 corresponds to a rate
of growth for the national product of 2·5–3·6 per cent per annum. A marginal capital–output ratio of 3·0 will with the same
investments give a rate of growth of 5·0–6·0 per cent per annum.
The difference is so great that further attempts to investigate the
shape of the aggregate production function are well justified.

V. SOME EXPERIMENTS IN FITTING A PRODUCTION FUNCTION TO DATA

(a) *Selecting the form of the function*

Attempts to estimate relatively strongly aggregated production
functions have frequently been made. The earliest and the
majority of these experiments have concerned individual

manufacturing groups or manufacturing in general,[1] but some have also been applied to agriculture.[2] A few studies have adopted production functions for the whole national economy.[3]

Most of these studies have used functions of the Cobb–Douglas type or variations of this. In its original form this was written as an exponential function of the type.

$$Y = AC^{\alpha}L^{\beta} \qquad . \qquad . \qquad . \qquad (1)$$

where the magnitudes A, α, and β are constants, and where Y, C, and L denote the production volume, input of capital, and labour respectively. In the early studies by Cobb and Douglas it was assumed that the sum total of the exponents α and β equalled 1 (which is tantamount to assuming that the production law has *pari-passu* character). The function above can then be written somewhat more simply, namely as

$$Y = AC^{\alpha}L^{1-\alpha} \qquad . \qquad . \qquad . \qquad (2)$$

where there are only two constants α and A. In later works efforts have also been made to estimate the constants α and β freely, i.e. assuming that the sum total does not necessarily equal 1.

The Cobb–Douglas function in its original form does not take into consideration changing techniques. This has been done in some later studies, where attempts have been made to allow for the effect of technological improvements by introducing a trend factor, while maintaining the general form of the Cobb–Douglas function. In his attempt to estimate a production function for the overall U.S. economy in the period 1921–41, Tint-

---

[1] The most well-known research works are perhaps those done by C. W. Cobb, P. H. Douglas, and a number of his collaborators. Cf. for instance C. W. Cobb and P. H. Douglas, 'A Theory of Production', *American Economic Review*, Vol. 18. Supplement 1928. P. H. Douglas, *The theory of Wages*, New York, 1934. M. L. Handsaker and P. H. Douglas, 'The Theory of Marginal Productivity Tested by Data for Manufacturing in Victoria', *The Quarterly Journal of Economics*, Vol. 52 (1937/38). G. T. Gunn and P. H. Douglas, 'Further Measurement of Marginal Productivity', *The Quarterly Journal of Economics*, Vol. 54 (1939/40). M. Bronfenbremer and P. H. Douglas, 'Cross-section Studies in the Cobb–Douglas Function', *The Journal of Political Economy*, Vol. 47 (1939). G. T. Gunn and P. H. Douglas, 'The Production Function for American Manufacturing in 1919', *The American Economic Review*, Vol. 31 (1941).

[2] G. Tinter, 'A Note on the Derivation of Production Functions from Farm Records', *Econometrica*, Vol. 12 (1944).

[3] G. Tintner, 'Some Applications of Multivariate Analysis to Economic Data', *Journal of the American Statistical Association*, Vol. 41 (1946), pp. 496–500. J. Tinbergen, 'Zur Theorie der langfristigen Wirtschaftsentwicklung', *Weltwirtschaftliches Archiv*, 1942, p. 509.

ner[1] used a relation which is linear in the logarithms to Y, C, L and in the variable time. Tinbergen's earlier work involved a production function of the type

$$Y = \epsilon^t C^\alpha L^{1-\alpha} \qquad . \qquad . \qquad . \qquad (3)$$

V. E. Smith [2] has tried to estimate the constants in a production function for the Canadian automobile industry in the period 1918–30 by the formula

$$Y = AC^\alpha L^\beta (10^{ht + gt^2}) \qquad . \qquad . \qquad (4)$$

For our purpose it is natural to regard the net national product as a function of the production factors real capital, labour, and 'technique'. We shall assume that the shape of the functional relationship is such that the three factors of production enter into it symmetrically in the same manner as in production functions of the Cobb–Douglas type. The factor 'technique' is defined broadly so as to include the general level of technical knowledge, the efficiency of management and workers, the industrial structure, etc. So defined, the 'volume of technique' cannot be measured, however, and for our purpose we shall simply assume that it can be represented by an exponential function e^{ht}, where t denotes time and h the rate of growth of the 'volume of technique'. The plausibility of this assumption is, of course, debatable. It leads to the following formula for the production function of the overall economy

$$Y_t = AC^\alpha_t L^\beta_t e^{t\gamma} \, [3] \qquad . \qquad . \qquad (5)$$

which written in logarithmic form becomes

$$\log Y_t = \log A + \alpha \log C_t + \beta \log L_t + \gamma \log e \cdot t \qquad (6)$$

Here Y_t is the net national product in year t measured in 1938 kroner, C_t the real capital volume at the end of year t also measured in 1938 kroner, L_t employment in year t measured by number of man-years, and t the time measured with 1925 as

---

[1] G. Tinter, *loc. cit.*

[2] *V. E. Smith*, 'Nonlinearity in the Relation between Input and Output: The Canadian Automobile Industry 1918–1930', *Econometrica*, Vol. 13, 1945.

[3] We have $Y_t = AC^\alpha_t \, L^\beta_t \, (e^{ht})^\lambda$, where λ denotes the elasticity of net product with respect to the 'volume of technique'. Inserting the letter γ for $h \cdot \lambda$ we get the expression in formula (5) above. The elasticity λ cannot be estimated separately, since we have no direct estimates of the 'volume of technique' or its rate of growth h. The rate of growth in production resulting from improvements in 'technique', in which we are primarily interested, can, however, be ascertained by the estimate of γ which measures the combined effect of both h and λ.

base year. A, α, β, and γ are constants, the numerical value of which can be estimated on the basis of the available data.

A structural relationship of this type cannot be expected to hold exactly. We therefore choose to give it a stochastic formulation:

$$\log Y_t = \log A + \alpha \log C_t + \beta \log L_t + \gamma \log e \cdot t + u_t \quad (7)$$

where u_t is a stochastic residual with expectation zero and variance $\gamma_u{}^2$. If we assume that the variables are observed without measurement errors and that C_t and L_t are non-stochastic variables, the parameters A, α, β, and γ can be estimated by minimizing the sum of the square deviations on $\log Y_t$ in (7).

(b) *Computation results*

Estimates computed on the basis of observations for the periods 1900–39 and 1946–55 give the following numerical values for the constants in the production function:

est $A = \hat{A} = 2{\cdot}262$; est $\alpha = \hat{\alpha} = 0{\cdot}203$; est $\beta = \hat{\beta} = 0{\cdot}763$; est $\gamma = \hat{\gamma} = 0{\cdot}0181$

with dispersions for α, β, and γ of respectively

$$\hat{\delta}_\alpha = 0{\cdot}101 : \hat{\delta}_\beta = 0{\cdot}191 : \hat{\delta}_\gamma = 0{\cdot}0029.$$

If these estimates are used and the stochastic residual is disregarded the production function becomes

$$Y_t = 2{\cdot}262 \cdot C_t^{0{\cdot}203} \cdot L_t^{0{\cdot}763} \cdot e^{0{\cdot}0181 \cdot t} \qquad . \qquad . \qquad (8)$$

Formula (8) says: (i) A partial increase of the volume of real capital by 1 per cent will, *ceteris paribus*, raise the national product by 0·2 per cent. (ii) A partial increase of labour by 1 per cent will, *ceteris paribus*, raise the national product by 0·76 per cent. (iii) With constant capital volume and constant employment the national product will, as a result of gradually improving 'techniques', increase at the rate of approximately 1·8 per cent per annum.

The values for net national product for the years 1900–55 which can be derived from formula (8) and the available data on C and L on the whole fit in well with the actual observations. Table VI illustrates this, showing the magnitude of the percentage deviations (without regard to signs) between computed and actual values of the national product in the years under review.

As will be seen, the fit is particularly good for the post-war period, when the deviations apart from 1946 in no year exceed 2 per cent. For the inter-war period, when the production showed sharp short-run fluctuations, the deviations are notably larger.

TABLE VI

Comparison between Computed and Actual Figures for National Product

Numbers of observations (years) grouped according to the size of the percentage deviations between computed and estimated figures.

Period	Number of years in the period	Of which with percentage deviations				
		Less than 1%	1·0–2·9%	3·0–4·9%	5·0–6·9%	7% and more
1900–16	17	5	5	4	3	0
1916–39	23	5	8	3	2	5
1946–55	10	5	4	0	1	0
1900–55	50	15	17	7	6	5

As we already have seen, the estimates for the dispersion of the parameters in the production function are in some cases considerable. In particular, the dispersion is relatively large for the elasticity with respect to capital. If a rejection region of 0·05 is chosen we cannot reject the hypothesis $\alpha = 0$. The other parameters are, on the other hand, with this critical region significantly different from 0.

An impression of the reliability of the estimates may also be gained by studying their sensitivity to the choice of period. In the table below the results for the whole period 1900–55 are compared with estimates computed on the basis of data for some part-periods. (The figures in brackets give the estimated dispersions for some of the structural coefficients.)

Period	$\hat{A}$	$\hat{\alpha}$ $(\hat{\delta}_\alpha)$	$\hat{\beta}$ $(\hat{\delta}_\beta)$	$\hat{\gamma}$ $(\hat{\delta}_\gamma)$
1900–55 . . .	2·262	0·203 (0·101)	0·763 (0·191)	0·0181 (0·0029)
1917–55 . . .	6·085	0·282 (0·105)	0·513 (0·193)	0·0198 (0·0028)
1917–39 . . .	0·045	0·719 (0·795)	0·619 (0·288)	0·0118 (0·0169)
1922–39 . . .	0·057	0·622 (0·645)	0·390 (0·263)	0·0160 (0·0130)

Some of the parameters are found to depend strongly on which period the computations were made for. Another general feature is that the estimated dispersions are much bigger when the observations, for the post-war period are not included in the estimates.

We may add that insertion in (7) of the estimates for the periods 1917–39 and 1922–39 gives a very poor fit for the post-war years. The computed values for the net national product which these estimates give are far above the actual (largely because of the high values for $\hat{\alpha}$). On the other hand, the fit is affected only slightly if the estimates for 1900–55 are replaced with the estimates for the period 1917–55.

(c) *Conclusions*

The computations discussed in the foregoing can be judged from two rather different viewpoints. First, they may be regarded as experiments in macro-economic curve fitting. Second, the computations may be viewed as an attempt to determine the constants in a macro-economic structural relation.

From the first point of view the computations are an example of how it is possible to arrive at a comparatively simple macro-relation which gives a good fit for a relatively long period for an economy like the Norwegian. The actual development of three macro-economic variables (net national product, real capital volume, and employment volume) and time has been found to be such that a Cobb–Douglas function with a trend component gives a very good description of the actual course of events in the period 1900–55.

If the computations are interpreted as an attempt to determine the parameters in a production function, the results assume an entirely different meaning. For in that case the computation results are supposed to *explain* the growth of net national product in terms of capital input, labour input, and technique, considered as independent variables.

A necessary condition for this interpretation is that the shape we have chosen for the production function can be given an economic justification. In micro-analysis we are probably justified in regarding production functions of the Cobb–Douglas type as fairly well-founded hypotheses on the production laws. Whether one can expect to find stable production functions of equally simple shape in macro-analysis is an entirely different matter. Even more fundamentally, this is a question which concerns not only the shape of the function. It also raises the problem as to whether it is at all possible to explain production trends in macro-analysis merely by studying changes in macro-variables, without specifying, say, in which industries such changes occur. The basis for much of the macro-economic analysis, however, is presumably that it is possible to disregard such changes between factors in micro-analysis. On this basis it does not seem entirely unrealistic to reckon with a production function in macro-analysis of the type we have chosen.

There is little in our computation results to indicate that such a macro-type production function cannot be a useful hypothesis, rather the contrary. It is particularly interesting in this context that the production trend in the post-war period, which so obviously contradicts the idea of a constant marginal capital–output ratio, seems to have quite a natural explanation in the light of the production function estimated from the observations through the whole period 1900–55. Nevertheless, we would warn against placing too much confidence in the value of the parameters estimated, for several reasons. (i) Our choice of function shape is rather arbitrary. In this study the main reason for this choice is that a function shape of this type has to a great extent common usage in economic analyses. (ii) Particularly dubious is the assumption that technique, considered as a factor of production, can be represented by a trend component of such a simple time shape as the one we have used. (iii) The estimates on the value of the parameters are based on the assumption that the volume of employment and real capital can be regarded as two non-stochastic variables, and this is probably unrealistic. (iv) Substantial margins of error must be allowed for the observed variables, especially the employment data before 1930. Moreover, our capital data apply to capital in existence, while in the product function real capital in actual use is probably the relevant variable. (v) Finally, we may add to this list that the estimated dispersions for the constants are relatively large. This also applies to the estimates which were computed on the basis of the observations for the whole period 1900–55. However, having stated these qualifications, we shall in conclusion venture to discuss some implications which seem to follow from our estimates.

(d) *An economic interpretation of the computation results and their implications*

The most striking conclusion that can be drawn from our computation results is that the role of capital as a production-increasing factor appears to be considerably smaller than generally assumed. On the basis of (8) we can derive the following general formula for the relationship between the relative increase in national product, employment, capital, and technique (time):

$$\frac{dY_t}{Y_t} = \frac{0.76}{(0.191)} \frac{dL_t}{L_t} + \frac{0.20}{(0.101)} \frac{dC_t}{C_t} + \frac{0.0181}{(0.0029)} dt \qquad (9)$$

(Figures in brackets indicate estimated dispersions.) This means that: (i) An increase in labour by 1 per cent, with constant capital and with given technique, will raise the national product by 0.76 per cent. (ii) An increase in the capital by 1 per cent will, with constant labour and given technique, increase the national product by 0.20 per cent. (iii) The national product will have a tendency to grow at a rate of 1.81 per cent per annum even with unchanged labour and capital, simply as a result of gradual technical improvements.

If the formula holds, it permits us – for any period – to say something about the 'causes' of the percentage rise in the national product which has been achieved. For the period after 1948 employment has increased by an average of 0.6 per cent per annum and the real capital volume by 5.6 per cent per annum. According to the estimated production function, this warrants an annual rate of growth for the national product which may be computed thus:

Growth as a result of:
1. Rise in employment: 0.76 . 0.6 = 0.46 per cent per annum
2. Rise in capital: 0.20 . 5.6   = 1.12 ,,   ,,   ,,   ,,
3. Improved technique etc.:   1.81 ,,   ,,   ,,   ,,

Aggregate rate of growth   3.39 per cent per annum

The actual rate of growth in the period was virtually the same as indicated by the formula, viz. approx. 3.4 per cent per annum on average. Of this growth, only about one-third should therefore be attributable to the growth of capital.

This result should probably not be taken too literally, however. Even apart from the uncertainty connected with the constants in the product function (cf. the dispersion estimates), the interpretation of the trend component presents difficulties. In the foregoing we have assumed the trend component to represent 'technique' (in the widest sense) as special factor of production on line with labour and capital. It is certainly unrealistic, however, to assume that the rate of the technological progress is completely independent of the rate of increase in the capital volume. To put it differently, it is almost certain that the increase in the national product of 1·81 per cent per annum which has been ascribed to technique in the foregoing, would *not* have occurred without a simultaneous increase of the capital.

Even allowing for considerable margins of uncertainty for the parameters derived, they give a convincing explanation of the high and rising values which we found in Section IV for the marginal capital–output ratio for the years around 1948. If we transform the expression of the relative increments in formula (9), we get the following expression of the marginal capital–output ratio

$$\frac{dC_t}{dY_t} = \frac{1}{\frac{Y_t}{dC_t}\left(0{\cdot}76\,\frac{dL_t}{Lt} + 0{\cdot}0181\,dt\right) + 0{\cdot}20\,\frac{Y_t}{C_t}} \tag{10}$$

The formula states that the marginal capital–output ratio varies inversely with the rate of growth in labour (dL_t/L_t), and rises with the fraction of national product devoted to investment, e.g. the net investment ratio (dC_t/Y_t) and the size of the average capital–output ratio (C_t/Y_t). For the years after 1948 the net investment ratio has averaged approximately 17 per cent, the increase in labour approximately 0·6 per cent per annum, and the average capital–output ratio approximately 3·2. This should, according to (10) give a marginal capital–output ratio of 5·12. The actual figure was, as previously mentioned, 5·13. (The close agreement between the computed and the actual figure is, of course, only a reflection of the fact that our production function fits so well with the data for the period in question.) With a net investment ratio of the order of magnitude we had in the interwar period, about 10 per cent, and equal conditions otherwise, the value of the marginal capital–output ratio would have been approximately 3·45 according to the formula. This puts an entirely new light on the trend in recent years. The high marginal capital–output ratio after 1948 is in no way 'contradictory to the experience of earlier times', on the contrary, it seems to have a natural explanation in our high investment level.

If the effects of a capital increase on the national product are as slight as our estimates suggest, it means that the chances of speeding up the growth in the national product by expanding the scope of investments are smaller than hitherto assumed. A transformation of the formula above gives us the following expression of the net investment ratio (dC_t/Y_t) which is required to achieve a given rate of growth for the national product (dY_t/Y_t) when the increase in labour (dL_t/L_t) is given and when the average capital–output ratio (C_t/Y_t) is also given.

$$\frac{dC_t}{Y_t} = \frac{1}{0.20} \cdot \frac{C_t}{Y_t} \left(\frac{dY_t}{Y_t} - 0.76 \frac{dL_t}{L_t} - 0.0181dt \right) \qquad (11)$$

In the following table we have compiled rounded rates of growth for the national product derived from alternative assumptions for the net investment ratio and changes in employment. The table is based on an average capital–output ratio corresponding to the ratio in Norwegian economy today, namely approximately 3·40.

Net Investment Ratio (dC_t/Y_t)	Employment Increase Per cent per annum (dL_t/L_t)			
	0	0·5	1·0	1·5
	Rates of Growth for National Product Per cent per annum			
0	1·8	2·2	2·6	3·0
10	2·4	2·8	3·2	3·5
15	2·7	3·1	3·5	3·8
20	3·0	3·4	3·7	4·1
30	3·6	4·0	4·3	4·7

It is clear that the rate of growth of the national product is affected comparatively little by the level of investment. Without any increase in employment it is necessary to have as high investment ratio as 20 per cent in the next years to accomplish a 3 per cent growth per annum in the national product. If we reckon with an employment increase of, for example, 0·5 per cent per annum, a net investment ratio of 15 per cent (somewhat lower than the average in Norway in the last years) will give a growth in the national product of approximately 3·1 per cent per annum. To raise the rate of growth to 4 per cent would – if our computations are realistic – require a net investment ratio of no less than 30 per cent.

In light of the above, it appears that the rate of growth which can be attained in a society like the Norwegian depends to a much smaller extent than was hitherto believed on the investment policy followed. Whether the rate of investment within reasonable limits is high or low, the national product with constant employment will rise by 2–3 per cent per annum, largely because the technical factor alone automatically warrants a growth which here has been estimated at roughly 1·8 per cent per annum. The pace can be increased somewhat beyond this by maintaining a high investment level, but not very much.

If this is correct, it has obvious economic-policy implications. A stringent economic policy designed to maintain a high investment level becomes much harder to justify. One question which naturally arises in this connection is whether the trend factor here termed 'technique' in itself is an invariable or whether it can be influenced, for example by placing more emphasis on the education of efficient management, technicians, and workers. This is an interesting and important question. If the answer is positive, the low effect of investment suggested above gives a hint that a higher rate of growth could possibly be obtained, by releasing resources now devoted to investment for a greater effort in education and research, for example. However, to this the present study can provide no answer.

APPENDIX OF TABLES

TABLE I

Fixed Real Capital [1] by Type at the End of the Years 1899–1939 and 1945–1955

At constant (1938) prices. Millions of kroner

End of Year	Total Fixed Real Capital	Of which			
		Government Building and Construction	Building and Construction of Enterprises	Machinery, Tools, and Transport Equipment Excl. Ships	Ships and Boats
1899	7,250	1,052	5,351	472	375
1900	7,417	1,073	5,451	505	388
1901	7,583	1,093	5,551	532	407
1902	7,724	1,114	5,631	557	422
1903	7,840	1,131	5,695	578	436
1904	7,970	1,145	5,770	600	455
1905	8,075	1,156	5,835	622	462
1906	8,212	1,165	5,913	649	485
1907	8,395	1,174	6,024	689	508
1908	8,581	1,183	6,147	731	520
1909	8,746	1,195	6,260	770	521
1910	8,961	1,207	6,405	813	536
1911	9,239	1,224	6,580	860	575
1912	9,567	1,248	6,782	924	613
1913	9,905	1,278	6,994	991	642
1914	10,224	1,311	7,217	1,044	652
1915	10,550	1,336	7,460	1,077	677
1916	10,904	1,354	7,756	1,116	678
1917	11,098	1,370	8,026	1,145	557
1918	11,340	1,393	8,253	1,164	530
1919	11,745	1,424	8,507	1,228	586
1920	12,203	1,454	8,782	1,287	680
1921	12,403	1,506	8,909	1,278	710
1922	12,573	1,590	9,002	1,280	701
1923	12,804	1,671	9,136	1,300	697
1924	13,070	1,727	9,315	1,320	708
1925	13,351	1,769	9,470	1,341	771
1926	13,536	1,813	9,560	1,339	824
1927	13,736	1,856	9,674	1,354	852
1928	14,082	1,896	9,852	1,412	922
1929	14,500	1,939	10,037	1,500	1,024
1930	14,990	1,982	10,227	1,569	1,212
1931	15,317	2,030	10,368	1,599	1,320
1932	15,482	2,076	10,536	1,628	1,242
1933	15,662	2,116	10,702	1,651	1,193
1934	15,926	2,160	10,911	1,694	1,161
1935	16,319	2,214	11,165	1,773	1,167
1936	16,851	2,280	11,481	1,899	1,191
1937	17,564	2,365	11,814	2,058	1,327
1938	18,192	2,422	12,141	2,204	1,425
1939	18,874	2,492	12,528	2,360	1,494
1945	16,461	2,545	11,423	1,673	820
1946	17,157	2,614	11,781	1,788	974
1947	18,256	2,698	12,289	2,004	1,265
1948	19,311	2,796	12,802	2,240	1,473
1949	20,413	2,913	13,374	2,465	1,661
1950	21,587	3,040	14,006	2,744	1,797
1951	22,760	3;159	14,631	3,070	1,900
1952	24,051	3,287	15,327	3,483	1,954
1953	25,435	3,444	16,055	3,879	2,057
1954	26,868	3,636	16,776	4,337	2,119
1955	28,284	3,839	17,477	4,719	2,249

[1] Structures and equipment only.

114

TABLE II

Fixed Real Capital [1] by Industry and by Types of Assets at the End of the Years 1899, 1939, and 1953

At constant (1938) prices. Millions of kroner

Industry, Type of Asset	1899	1939	1953
Agriculture and forestry	1,112	2,090	2,382
Building and construction	1,014	1,880	2,043
Machinery	92	188	301
Transport equipment	6	22	38
Fishing	108	282	280
Fishermen's sheds, piers, etc.	23	49	42
Boats	60	185	185
Equipment	25	48	53
Whaling (boats)	5	70	105
Mining and manufacturing	555	2,552	4,067
Building and construction	332	1,277	1,902
Machinery, etc..	215	1,236	2,100
Transport equipment	8	39	65
Electricity and gas	30	1,100	2,083
Building and construction	21	900	1,718
Machinery, etc..	9	200	365
Business buildings (buildings)	454	930	1,250
Dwellings (buildings)	3,062	6,200	7,289
Shipping (ships)	310	1,239	1,767
Railway transport	378	964	1,343
Railroad construction	355	843	1,223
Rolling stock	23	121	120
Tramways, etc.	17	98	95
Tramway, etc., construction	14	79	75
Rolling stock	3	19	20
Road transport (transport equipment)	5	133	232
Air transport (aircraft)	—	3	20
Communication (building and communication installations)	46	220	348
Wholesale and retail trade	50	198	336
Transport equipment	8	50	86
Other equipment	42	148	250
Harbour construction	30	150	165
General government building and construction	1,052	2,492	3,444
Highways and bridges	540	1,320	1,771
Other building and construction	512	1,172	1,673
Other industries	36	153	229
Transport equipment	—	3	9
Other equipment	36	150	220
Total fixed real capital	7,250	18,874	25,435
Of which:			
Building and construction of enterprises	5,351	12,528	16,055
Government building and construction	1,052	2,492	3,444
Ships and boats	375	1,494	2,057
Transport equipment excl. ships	53	390	590
Machinery and other equipment	419	1,970	3,289

[1] Structures and equipment only.

TABLE III

Total Fixed Real Capital [1] and Net Domestic Product at Constant (1938) Prices, and Total Employment in Thousands of Man-years 1900–39 and 1946–55

Year	Total Fixed Real Capital	Net Domestic Product	Total Employment	Average Capital–Output Ratio	Real Capital per Man-year
	Millions of kroner	Millions of kroner	Thousands of Man-years		Kroner
	1	2	3	4 = 1 ÷ 2	5 = 1 ÷ 3
1900	7,417	1,821	977	4·07	7,592
1901	7,583	1,860	987	4·08	7,683
1902	7,724	1,882	993	4·10	7,778
1903	7,840	1,858	996	4·22	7,871
1904	7,970	1,850	999	4·31	7,978
1905	8,075	1,860	1,002	4·34	8,059
1906	8,212	1,931	1,005	4·25	8,171
1907	8,395	2,019	1,008	4·16	8,328
1908	8,581	2,085	1,013	4·12	8,471
1909	8,746	2,119	1,023	4·13	8,549
1910	8,961	2,213	1,027	4·05	8,725
1911	9,239	2,302	1,041	4·01	8,875
1912	9,567	2,406	1,055	3·98	9,068
1913	9,905	2,528	1,071	3·92	9,248
1914	10,224	2,589	1,090	3·95	9,380
1915	10,550	2,726	1,107	3·87	9,530
1916	10,904	2,870	1,124	3·80	9,701
1917	11,098	2,605	1,142	4·26	9,718
1918	11,340	2,455	1,161	4·62	9,767
1919	11,745	3,084	1,178	3·81	9,970
1920	12,203	3,171	1,202	3·85	10,152
1921	12,403	2,734	1,107	4·54	11,054
1922	12,573	3,037	1,122	4·14	11,206
1923	12,804	3,127	1,179	4·10	10,860
1924	13,070	3,099	1,201	4·22	10,883
1925	13,351	3,245	1,173	4·11	11,382
1926	13,536	3,241	1,097	4·18	12,339
1927	13,736	3,380	1,096	4·06	12,533
1928	14,082	3,573	1,151	3·94	12,235
1929	14,500	3,888	1,188	3·73	12,205
1930	14,990	4,196	1,187	3·57	12,628
1931	15,317	3,791	1,153	4·04	13,284
1932	15,482	3,999	1,178	3·87	13,143
1933	15,662	4,093	1,192	3·83	13,139
1934	15,926	4,253	1,213	3·74	13,129
1935	16,319	4,480	1,240	3·64	13,160
1936	16,851	4,808	1,276	3·51	13,206
1937	17,564	5,012	1,309	3·50	13,418
1938	18,192	5,102	1,330	3·57	13,678
1939	18,874	5,353	1,358	3·53	13,898
1946	17,157	5,555	1,394	3·09	12,308
1947	18,256	6,311	1,441	2·89	12,669
1948	19,311	6,567	1,467	2·94	13,164
1949	20,413	6,772	1,489	3·01	13,709
1950	21,587	7,073	1,499	3·05	14,401
1951	22,760	7,322	1,509	3·11	15,083
1952	24,051	7,629	1,522	3·15	15,802
1953	25,435	7,812	1,522	3·26	16,712
1954	26,868	7,915	1,537	3·39	17,481
1955	28,284	8,323	1,534	3·40	18,438

[1] Structures and equipment only.

TABLE IV
Fixed Real Capital [1] by Type for Selected Years
Current prices. Millions of kroner

End of Year	Total Fixed Real Capital	Of which			
		Government Building and Construction	Building and Construction of Enterprises	Machinery, Tools, and Transport Equipment Excl. Ships and Boats	Ships and Boats
1900	3,456	456	2,382	332	286
1905	3,559	484	2,398	352	325
1910	4,291	552	2,914	463	362
1915	6,855	770	4,566	778	741
1920	25,629	2,771	17,248	3,051	2,559
1925	17,108	2,142	11,932	1,962	1,072
1930	12,209	1,548	8,243	1,337	1,081
1935	12,800	1,656	8,675	1,509	960
1939	19,588	2,656	12,804	2,464	1,664
1946	32,802	5,113	21,830	3,506	2,353
1950	51,154	7,053	30,939	6,495	6,667
1955	90,763	12,753	52,169	13,874	11,967

[1] Structures and equipment only.

TABLE V
National Wealth of Norway at the End of the Year 1953
Millions of kroner at current prices

	Total [1]	Of which [1] Public [7]
A. *Enterprises* . . . . total	89,700	9,767
I. Reproducible assets . . . . . total	86,655	9,767
1. Structures . . . . . total	45,977	8,203
(a) Dwellings [2]	22,013	..
(b) Agricultural	5,413	..
(c) Other	18,551	8,203
2. Equipment . . . . . total	21,078	1,564
(a) Agricultural	831	..
(b) Other	20,247	1,564
3. Inventories [3] . . . . . total	19,600	..
(a) Livestock	1,300	..
(b) Other agricultural	800	..
(c) Other	7,500	..
(d) Standing timber	10,000	..
II. Non-reproducible assets, land . . . total	3,045	..
(a) Agricultural	3,045	..
(b) Forest	..	..
(c) Other	..	..
B. *Government* [4] . . . . . . total	10,642	
I. Reproducible assets . . . . . total	10,642	
1. Structures [5]	10,642	
2. Equipment	..	
3. Inventories	..	
II. Non-reproducible assets, land . . . total	..	
C. *Consumer durables* . . . . . total	550	
1. Passenger cars and other vehicles [6] . . .	550	
2. Other	..	
D. *Foreign assets* . . . . . . total	−1,370	
1. Monetary metals	185	
2. Other net foreign assets	−1,555	
Total	99,522	

[1] .. Not available; not included in totals.
[2] All dwellings.
[3] Livestock and standing timber included.
[4] Only general government (military assets not included). For the distinction between general government and government enterprises and public corporations (which are entered under A. Enterprises, column public) see – *A System of National Accounts and Supporting Tables*, United Nations, pp. 11, 12.
[5] Roads, bridges, and public schools included.
[6] Only privately owned cars, wholly or partly in use for private consumption.
[7] Only government enterprises and public corporations, for a further explanation see [4].

THE PREPARATION OF A NATIONAL BALANCE SHEET: EXPERIENCE IN THE NETHERLANDS

By the Division of National Accounts of the Netherlands Central Bureau of Statistics

INTRODUCTION

THE compilation of national wealth estimates and of national balance sheets has always been an integral part of the work programme in national accounting of the Netherlands Central Bureau of Statistics. However, as will appear from this report, the national balance sheets have not yet reached the same stage of statistical development as the work on national accounts. In this connection, it may be pointed out that national balance sheets should be based on a fairly detailed set of sector balance sheets and detailed sub-classifications of the components if they are intended to be useful for purposes of economic analysis. Hence, the basic sources of information from which the estimates must be derived should be well developed and should meet the standards required.

At present, however, the data available for the compilation of the national balance sheet do not quite meet these requirements. For example, surveys of consumers' finances have not been conducted in the Netherlands, and the statistics of the tax on personal wealth do not provide a breakdown by types of assets. In the field of financial statistics, there is little information on the breakdown of bank deposits and other claims by type of holders. Statistics derived from the corporate income-tax system are not very helpful for the evaluation of national wealth, because statistical compilations relate only to profits and certain other data, and not to the corporate balance sheets. Available inventory statistics, derived from various surveys, cover certain sectors only, accounting for not more than about 20 per cent of the total value of all inventories. No comprehensive statistical information is available on foreign investments in the Netherlands, or on Netherlands investments abroad. For all these reasons the preparation of national balance sheets encounters many difficulties. However, a number of sources of information exist which permit the preparation of the estimates by a variety of methods.

The need for national wealth estimates and national balance sheets has arisen from applications in economic analysis and from the requirements of economic policy. Some of the uses are listed below. Their importance has varied with the changes in economic conditions and the problems faced by the Government.

(a) One of the most important statistical uses is the need for a picture of the structure of the national economy that can be used in connection with the system of national accounts, so as to provide, among other things, a background for the analysis of current transactions.

(b) Since financial institutions (life-insurance companies, social insurance funds and pension funds, savings banks, etc.) have always held a substantial share of total government debt, mortgages, etc., the need arises to present data on the position of these institutions in relation to other groups of holders, e.g. households and commercial banks.

(c) The economic recovery programme, after the devastation caused by the War, required measures of changes in the total stock of capital goods, by main sectors and by main types.

(d) For analysis of inflationary and deflationary tendencies, information is needed on changes in primary and secondary liquidities by main sectors and by broad categories, i.e. corporations and unincorporated enterprises, financial institutions and intermediaries, households, etc.

(e) Estimates of the average value of fixed assets per person employed by main branches of industry are needed in connection with the country's industrialization programme.

(f) The estimates are used to calculate the ratio between the public debt and the national wealth, the size of the publicly owned industries in relation to the private enterprise sector, the composition of private wealth, etc.

Although estimates of total national wealth were made for some years in the nineteenth century, and also for several years after 1900, they were not sufficiently detailed by sectors to be useful for the analysis of economic growth. In 1947 a first attempt was made to draw up a national balance sheet in its present form, based on the concepts of the national accounts. Later it was possible to publish a detailed set of balance sheets, by sector, for 1948 and 1949 and estimates of the consolidated national balance sheet in current and constant prices for the years 1938 and 1946–52.[1]

I. BASIC CONCEPTS AND DEFINITIONS

1. *The national balance sheet and the national accounts*

In the Netherlands the national accounts developed out of national income and national product estimates. Purely financial transactions remained in the background, because it was assumed that monetary and credit transactions were less important than changes in the current demand for goods and services, in expenditure on fixed assets, and in similar 'physical' flows which have an immediate impact upon the volume of employment. In recent years more attention has been paid to changes in claims and liabilities as factors influencing economic conditions. Hence, the system of national accounts is intended to include balance sheets at the beginning and end of the accounting period. The changes in balance-sheet items, which may be obtained from a comparison of successive balance sheets, are divided into increases and decreases due to transactions, including capital transfers, and changes due to price fluctuations (including revaluations of assets). These transactions can be presented in the form of a system of accounts which, on the one hand, is linked with the existing system of current accounts and, on the other hand, with the balance sheets.

As has been mentioned above, the system of national balance sheets at present used by the Bureau was published for the first time in 1947. With only minor modifications, this system is still in use. It has been presented in a summary form in Appendix I to this paper. In this system of national balance sheets the following sectors are distinguished:

(i) business enterprises, including public enterprises;
(ii) government (national and local authorities);
(iii) banks and other financial intermediaries;
(iv) insurance funds, including public and private pension funds, social insurance funds and life-insurance;
(v) households and private non-profit institutions;
(vi) 'rest of the world'.

[1] See the bibliography in Appendix III, Nos. 8 and 14.

As in national accounting, the system of national balance sheets should be 'articulated', i.e. to each item there should correspond an opposite claim or liability on the balance sheet of another sector. This principle leads to a peculiar difficulty encountered in the preparation of national balance sheets: economic entities of one sector may require sub-classifications to which no comparable sub-classifications of other sectors correspond because the economic viewpoints of the various sectors are different. For instance, the distinction between primary and secondary liquidities is largely determined by the intentions of the holders of these claims; however, the distinction may very well be insignificant to the debtor. Therefore, when choosing appropriate sub-classifications, these and other differences must be taken into consideration. Secondly, the principles of valuation may be different for the various holders. For example, stock-holders will value the shares they own according to stock-market quotations, but in most cases this value will differ from the net worth of the corporation. This problem has been solved by allocating to the household sector the difference between the net worth of corporations and the market value of the shares. This is in conformity with the practice in the national accounts of allocating undistributed profits to the household sector.[1]

The system of the national balance sheet implies that capital transactions are classified as such in accordance with the treatment in the system of national accounts. For instance, since death duties are treated as capital transfers in the current accounts, they should consistently be treated as changes in balance-sheet items.

Capital goods are classified by main categories and by industry of use. The classifications adopted are those of the national accounts in the Netherlands. For certain capital-intensive industries a further sub-classification is needed. For instance, 'Transport and communications' is subdivided into sea-going shipping, inland navigation, railroads, street-cars and buses, other road-transport enterprises, air transport, post office, telephone and telegraph, etc.

The sector balance sheets record the stock of capital goods as well as claims and liabilities between sectors. The classification of claims and liabilities corresponds with the concepts and categories usually distinguished on the capital market as well as with

---

[1] See Appendix I, explanatory notes, No. 5.

the requirements of economic analysis, particularly of monetary analysis. Since discussions on methods of monetary analysis are still continuing in the Netherlands, modifications may be expected in the categories distinguished, particularly in short-term holdings by sectors. These developments may also affect the standards to be set up for various types of financial statistics. The main categories distinguished are indicated in Appendix I.

Annual estimates are not sufficient for the study of financial inter-relationships among the sectors of the economy. The analysis of current economic trends requires the preparation of quarterly estimates, and some writers have even suggested the use of monthly figures. Steps are now being taken to obtain quarterly balance-sheet data on a limited number of items for those sectors (banking, insurance, business enterprises) for which this type of information is considered indispensable.

2. *The concept of capital goods*

Capital goods are defined in accordance with the standards for capital formation in national accounting. Hence, patents, concessions, goodwill, works of art, collectors' items, etc., are not included in national wealth; nor are proved but unexplored mineral resources included.

In the national accounts, transactions in used assets and land are entered on a gross basis. The transfer costs, brokers' commissions, etc., are treated as a capital expenditure which is usually written off very rapidly. The treatment of these transactions in the national balance sheet should be consistent with this procedure.

In accordance with the present treatment in the national accounts for the Netherlands, public buildings, roads, parks, bridges, parking areas, subways, and thoroughfares are not included in the published estimates of the value of capital goods. Since it is proposed to adopt the definitions recommended by the United Nations, preliminary estimates of these items have been made and are included in Appendix II (B).

All outlay on military equipment is treated as government consumption expenditure; hence the stock of this equipment is not included in national wealth.

In accordance with international conventions for the estimates of capital formation, durable consumer goods in the hands of consumers or owned by private non-profit institutions are not included in national wealth. Here, too, a preliminary estimate has been made and is included in Appendix II (C).

Since outlay on small office equipment and small tools is usually treated as a current business cost, the stocks of such tools are not included with fixed assets, but with stocks of raw materials and semi-finished goods.

The value of work in process in the electrical and engineering industries is treated as part of the stocks of semi-finished goods.

3. *Valuation of assets and liabilities*

For the valuation of assets and liabilities, the principle is to estimate the present value of future net incomes and capital repayments. From this, two bases of valuation have been derived, which should, in principle, give the same results:

(a) capitalized net income;
(b) replacement value.

For financial claims, market quotations are in practice often available and can be considered to give the best approximation to the value mentioned under (a). For some claims, no market quotations are available; these can be valued by imputing the market quotation of similar claims. If this method cannot be used, as in the case with some claims between the Netherlands and the rest of the world, the estimates are obtained by a direct capitalization of the net income from these claims.

Capital goods, other than land, are valued at replacement cost net of depreciation, at prices prevailing at the balance-sheet date. The problems involved in determining the replacement value of the existing stock of capital goods on the basis of prevailing prices of new assets are difficult to handle; these problems have been solved by the application of various statistical methods, some examples of which will be given in Part II.

The valuation of capital goods on the basis of capitalized net returns has been used only for land. The most serious objection against this method is that actual returns represent the joint results of several factors of production. Hence, in order to apply the method it would be necessary to allocate the returns to the various factors of production. Only that part of total returns which is allocated to fixed capital should be capitalized. However, it is very difficult to establish satisfactory methods for valuing the income that should be imputed to each of the factors of production.

In principle, the Bureau does not estimate the value of capital goods on the basis of market prices. In monopoly conditions, for example, a favourable location of dwellings, market prices may differ from replacement costs. In the view of the Bureau, domestic monopoly gains do not form part of the (national) costs of the assets and are in principle inappropriate for estimates of national wealth. Market prices may also be affected by government regulations. For example, rent controls may have the effect of keeping prices of houses low. Or market prices may be high if the public expects a further decline in the purchasing power of money.

4. *Problems of allocation*

The preparation of sector balance sheets raises problems of allocation analogous to the treatment of the corresponding 'flows' in the national accounts.

For example, in the national accounts, decisions must be taken with respect to the imputation of income earned on the investments of life-insurance companies and pension funds. In the national accounting systems of the U.N. and O.E.E.C., such income is imputed to the household sector and included as a form of household saving which is transferred to the reserves of the life-insurance companies, etc. This treatment implies that in the national balance sheet the actuarial reserves of life-insurance companies, etc., appear as a liability of the insurance sector and as a financial claim of the households sector. However, in view of the special character of these reserves, a separate item 'insurance-funds wealth' is introduced in the national balance sheet of the Netherlands; this item also appears on the consolidated national balance sheet (Appendix I).

The treatment of the difference between the net worth of corporations and the value of shares has been discussed above in Section 1.

Co-operatives constitute another case in point. Benefits received by members are usually small and do not provide a reliable basis for valuing the assets of the co-operative. There is usually no market for the 'shares' in the co-operatives. In the case of producers' co-operatives, dividends usually include amounts corresponding to the margin between conventional and prevailing prices, and relate to quantities bought and sold rather than to the nominal value of the shares held. In the national-income calculations net profits are imputed to members, and therefore the entire 'net worth' of the co-operatives is imputed to the household sector. This method is consistent with the treatment of co-operatives in the national accounts.

Profits attributable to monopoly positions are included in the national income and affect the income distribution. However, in general, it is not possible to isolate the monopoly element; this is another reason why the capitalization method cannot be used.

In the case of unincorporated enterprises it is not possible to make a distinction between the assets and liabilities of the enterprise and those of the household. As a practical way out of this difficulty, the simplifying assumption has been made that the balance sheet for the enterprises as far as possible shows fixed assets only, while all financial claims and liabilities are recorded directly on the balance sheet of the household sector.[1]

II. PROBLEMS OF ESTIMATION

1. *Some notes on statistical measurement*

As explained in Part I, Section 3, the value of capital goods is generally estimated on the basis of replacement values. Land is an important exception to this rule, because in this case there is no replacement value. It could be argued that man-made improvements to land are replaceable, but very often it is impossible to separate these improvements from the original uncultivated land. It may be concluded that in the case of land, valuation on a replacement-cost basis is generally not possible, and therefore an attempt must be made to determine its value by capitalization of the net return at an assumed interest rate. Since the return is the result of the co-operation of several factors of production, it becomes necessary to determine the share of each factor, a problem explained briefly in Part II, Section 6.

In principle, various methods can be used to estimate the depreciated replacement value of capital goods. To apply some of these methods, information must be assembled on the age distribution and the length of life of the assets. A number of devices

---

[1] See Appendix I, explanatory notes, No. 5.

have been developed to estimate the lengths of life, depending on the type of basic data available – annual sales, age distribution of assets at one date, or at two dates, total stock at a certain date and cumulation over a series of preceding years, total stocks at two dates, and annual sales during the intermediate period.[1]

In accordance with the basic data which have been used, the following methods have been applied or examined to estimate the value of capital goods and the other items on the balance sheets:

(a) *Capitalization of known net income*

This method is used to make the estimates for agricultural land, and the items 3 and 6 of the table given in Appendix I, as well as for those foreign debts included in the items 11 and 16 for which no direct information was available. The difficult problem here is the choice of a capitalization factor.

(b) *Multiplication of the number of physical units by a known or estimated average price or value*

This method has been applied to estimate the values of capital goods (other than land) used in agriculture, horticulture and forestry, the fishing fleet, the merchant fleet, inland shipping, road transport, hotels, restaurants, cafés, etc., and of dwellings, bank and insurance office buildings, hospitals, cinemas, and the equipment of the liberal professions.

The units differ greatly. Prices of readily marketable goods have been used as well as more complex data, e.g. the estimated value of the investments per bed for hospitals or per seat for cinemas.

(c) *Cumulation of net changes in stocks*

This method is used only to estimate the value of inventories. This could be done on the assumption that in 1945, at the end of World War II, inventories were at zero. However, a whole series of consolidated national balance sheets for the years 1938 and 1946–52 was also computed by means of this method.[2]

A wider use of this method was not possible because the necessary breakdown of capital expenditures and depreciation between kinds of goods and branches of activity for a sufficient

---

[1] See Appendix III, Nos. 17, 18, 19, and 21.
[2] See Appendix III, No. 14.

period of years was not available. The uncertainties of this method arise from the price indices used, the choice of the periods of average economic length of life, and the errors in the available investment and depreciation figures, especially for the earlier years of longer periods.

(d) *Data from balance sheets, financial reports, expert findings, statistical publications*

This method is used for all capital goods not mentioned under (a), (b), and (c), and the items 2, 7–18, 20, 21, and 23 of the table given in Appendix I.

Balance sheets and financial statistics have been frequently used to ascertain and allocate the claims. The balance sheet of the Government will be discussed hereafter. The use of the balance sheet of electricity works will be mentioned in Section 4. Expert findings that have been used include, for example, the values of investments per man in the different branches of manufacturing industry.

Balance-sheet figures are also used, for retail trade and handicrafts, to estimate the values of structures and the value of the share of these industries in total inventories; estimates of the value of their equipment could be based on the results of inquiries. For wholesale trade, the estimates of all capital goods had to be computed from balance-sheet data; in this group the balance-sheet information was scarce. Balance-sheet data are also used to estimate the value of the capital goods of local authorities; municipal dwellings, however, which represent by far the largest item, are estimated by using method (b). For practically all the above-mentioned categories, for which balance-sheet figures are used, the balance-sheet values had to be adjusted to conform to the right standards. This required the use of price indexes and quantity relations. The age distributions of the stocks of capital goods could in these cases be estimated only on the basis of limited information and of general assumptions as to their growth.

(e) *Accounting for the residual item of a closed system*

This method is used for the items 5, 19, 22, 24, and 25 of the table given in Appendix I. Where the methods used result in estimates of gross replacement values, an additional computation of net values is required. The estimates of total depreciation are in some cases based on fairly accurate computations of the age distribution and the average length of economic life of the capital goods concerned. Examples of this will be found in the following paragraphs. Often, however, estimates based on expert information must be employed.

(f) *The census valuation method*

This has not yet been applied in the Netherlands because available census data do not include information on assets.

(g) *The estate multiplier method*

This has been used to prepare estimates of national wealth before the war. The method is not very accurate because differences in mortality rates of the various socio-economic population groups could not be taken into account.

(h) *Tax assessment data and other official values*

These were not found useful, mainly because basic data are collected for administrative purposes and are not suitable for statistical compilation.

As already mentioned, most financial claims and liabilities are estimated by means of balance-sheet data and available financial statistics, such as banking statistics, statistics of life-insurance companies, public and private pension funds, savings banks, the postal cheque and clearing service, etc. For most of these institutions, annual balance-sheet data are collected on a uniform basis. A serious omission is the absence so far of sub-classifications of depositors and debtors, consistent with the sectors used in national accounting, in the otherwise rather complete statistics of the commercial banks. However, for the government and insurance funds sectors and for the non-commercial banks, deposits and debts can be estimated independently, whereas the allocations to the other sectors can be based on the findings of banking experts.

For a number of years, the Ministry of Finance has published a State Balance Sheet as an appendix to the annual budget. The primary purpose of this balance sheet, which shows the assets and liabilities of the Central Government, is to give information supplementary to the budget. Its classifications therefore do not coincide with those of the national accounts. However, since the other concepts and definitions used do not differ greatly from the concepts of national accounting, it is a very useful source of information for the national balance sheet.

The assets include all short-term deposits and advances, including taxes payable, all long-term loans and advances, and investments in government enterprises. The assets of government enterprises – comprising the state-owned coal-mines and chemical works, the state railways, the postal, telegraph and telephone services, the postal cheque and clearing services, the Central Bank of the Netherlands, the Royal Dutch Airlines, and some minor enterprises – are estimated at depreciated replacement value. Real estate includes all public buildings, roads, bridges, etc., of the national government and all military equipment and stocks of materials. The method implies that depreciation of government assets is entered as a separate item on the government current account.

Liabilities include all long-term and short-term debts of the Government, domestic as well as foreign. Assets and liabilities (i.e. actuarial reserves) of the pension funds for government employees and of social-insurance funds are included, but only at a notional valuation.

Because of gradual improvements in methods of valuation and various changes in the presentation, the State Balance Sheets are not strictly comparable over time.

Although most balance-sheet items for local authorities are available, they have not yet been collected in the form of a balance sheet. Moreover, the valuations of capital goods given are not based on replacement costs. Classifications consistent with the system of national accounts had to be obtained from other sources.

2. *An estimate of the value of the Netherlands merchant fleet.*[1]

The value of the merchant fleet at 31 December 1952 is estimated on the basis of the following data:

(a) The age distribution of all ships at 31 December 1952 according to *Moorman's Jaarboek voor Scheepvaart en Scheepsbouw, 1953*, a shipping yearbook which gives the tonnage and the year of construction of all sea-going vessels under the Netherlands flag.

[1] See Appendix III, No. 18.

(b) The construction costs of five major types of ships (passenger ships, freighters with passenger accommodation, freighters, tankers, and coasters), per gross register ton as at 31 December 1952. This information has been supplied by experts in the Ministry of Transport and Waterways and in the shipbuilding industry.

(c) Depreciation rates of ships. This information is not immediately available, and therefore estimates had to be prepared by means of calculations of the average length of life of merchant ships.

The first method of estimating the average length of life is based on the identity:

$$B + T - A = E,$$

in which B = tonnage of ships at the beginning of the period;
T = tonnage of ships purchased during the period;
A = tonnage of ships sold to abroad and sold for scrap in the Netherlands and ships lost;
E = tonnage of ships at the end of the period.

If during the period considered $A = B$, or $T = E$, then it may be stated that under certain simplifying assumptions the average length of life of the ships is approximately equal to the length of the period considered. If the two identities are not fulfilled, then the average length of life may be estimated by multiplying the length of the period studied by the ratio $B:A$ or $E:T$. The average of the two figures found may be accepted as the final estimate.

The main statistics are shown in Table I.

TABLE I
Statistics of the Netherlands Merchant Fleet 1923–39
000's G.R.T.

Total tonnage 1 January 1923	.	.	.	2,390
Total tonnage 1 January 1939	.	.	.	2,630
Total tonnage 1 January 1940	.	.	.	2,752

Cumulative changes 1923–39					
Purchases	.	.	.	.	2,228
Withdrawals					
Wrecked	.	.	.	168	
Sold or scrapped	.	.	.	1,685	
					1,853

K

According to the figures in Table I:

$B = 2,390$, $A = 1,853$; average length of life $2,390/1,853 \times 17$
= 21·8 years.
$E = 2,752$, $T = 2,228$; average length of life $2,752/2,228 \times 17$
= 21·1 years.

If the year 1939, which marked the beginning of the War, is omitted, the averages are slightly higher, viz. 22·8 and 22·2 years.

The method cannot be very accurate, because the numbers of ships purchased and sold are small, and ships vary greatly as to type, equipment, size, and speed. All these factors affect the length of life. It is not possible to carry out computations for the major types separately because the numbers are too small.

TABLE II

Replacement Value of the Netherlands Merchant Fleet,
31 December 1952

	G.R.T. (000's tons)	Building Costs (guilders per ton)	Gross Replacement Value (million guilders)
Passenger ships . . .	971	1,960	1,904
Freighters with passenger accommodation . . .	787	1,226	965
Freighters	595	1,073	639
Tankers	499	828	413
Coasters	225	1,328	298
Total. . .	3,077		4,219

The method is based on the assumption that the oldest ships are sold first. This assumption is not essential for the second method of estimation, which for this reason appears to be more realistic. For this second method, all ships sold or scrapped during the period are classified by age groups. The mode of the resulting frequency distribution is supposed to be a good approximation to the economic length of life. Frequency distributions of lengths of life have been constructed separately for ships sold and scrapped, for the two categories combined, and for the periods 1923–30 and 1931–38, as well as for the entire period 1923–38. Because of the War losses in 1940–45, and the recovery thereafter, the data for the period 1948–53 cannot be used, since this period cannot be considered normal.

The results obtained by the two methods are, however, in close agreement. Hence, an economic length of life of twenty years is accepted as the final estimate. This figure is in line with the standard for the economic length of life for merchant ships mentioned in the literature, although the technical length of life is somewhat longer.

TABLE III

Estimate of the Value of the Netherlands Merchant Fleet, 31 December 1952

Construction Year	Tonnage G.R.T. (× 1,000)	Gross Replacement Value (million guilders)	Depreciation (%)	Net Value (million guilders)
1903–32	622	950	85	143
1933	2	3	80¾	1
1934	12	23	76½	5
1935	40	37	72¼	10
1936	57	55	68	17
1937	67	91	63¾	33
1938	183	261	59½	106
1939	226	294	55¼	131
1940	40	53	51	26
1941	78	113	46¾	60
1942	104	134	42½	77
1943	245	308	38¼	191
1944	228	271	34	179
1945	308	338	29¾	237
1946	125	226	25½	169
1947	80	131	21¼	103
1948	137	198	17	165
1949	141	212	12¾	185
1950	141	182	8½	166
1951	102	152	4¼	146
1952	139	187	0	187
Total	3,077	4,219	—	2,337

It is assumed that for the merchant fleet as a whole, depreciation rates are a constant percentage of the gross replacement value. A further simplifying assumption is that for the merchant fleet as a whole, major repairs, which materially lengthen the life of ships, are almost evenly distributed over the years.

The scrap value of a ship depends greatly on market conditions. As an average, it has been estimated that the scrap value of a ship represents 15 per cent. Hence, the maximum depreciation is 85 per cent. This percentage has been applied to all ships which on 31 December 1952 were more than twenty years old.

3. *An estimate of the value of all dwellings* [1]

The methods used to estimate the total value of all dwellings are similar to those used for valuing the merchant fleet. For the estimation of the average length of life of dwellings, only the first method of Part II, Section 2, could be used. (A period is calculated for which the stock of dwellings at the beginning of that period = number of dwellings demolished during that period; or the number of dwellings built during the period = stock of dwellings at the end of the period.)

The development of the stock of dwellings has been reconstructed as far back as 1830. Since the growth of the stock of dwellings is more gradual than that of ships, and since fluctuations in the volume of residential building are much less pronounced, it is believed that the results of this method are more accurate than the estimates obtained for the shipping fleet.

The figures of Table I indicate that over a period of 120 years, after allowing for the destruction caused by acts of war in 1940–45, the number of houses demolished was roughly equal to the existing stock in 1830. The number of houses built between 1830 and 1950 is approximately equal to the housing stock on 31 December 1950. The conclusion is drawn that the length of life of houses was approximately 120 years. Since the period of observation is very long, it is difficult to state whether the figure found is applicable to houses built in recent years. There are reasons to believe that in the near future housing standards may continue to rise, resulting in a higher rate of depreciation of existing houses. If this assumption is correct, then it would be justified to adopt a shorter length of life, e.g. 100 years instead of 120 years. Therefore the calculations have been based on an average length of life of 120 years for houses built in 1830–40, which declines gradually to 100 years for houses built in 1930. As in the case of ships, annual depreciation rates are assumed to be a constant percentage of replacement values.

The age distribution of houses on 31 December 1950 has been derived from annual construction data in previous years. The value of all houses is found by applying the depreciation rates to

---

[1] See Appendix III, No. 17.

this distribution. The results are summarized in the following table:

TABLE IV

Age Distribution, Average Age, and Depreciation of all Dwellings in the Netherlands on 31 December 1950

Period of Construction	Stock of Dwellings by Period of Construction (thousands) (1)	Average Age 31 December 1950 (years) (2)	Annual Depreciation (%) (3)	Accumulated Depreciation 31 December 1950, (thousands of dwelling units) (1) × (2) × (3)
1830–39	77	115	0·83	73·5
1840–49	68	105	0·85	60·7
1850–59	96	95	0·86	78·4
1860–69	116	85	0·88	86·8
1870–79	135	75	0·90	91·2
1880–89	125	65	0·92	74·8
1890–99	164	55	0·93	83·9
1900–09	189	45	0·95	80·8
1910–20	177	35	0·97	60·1
1921–30	455	25	0·98	111·5
1931–40	414	15	1·00	62·1
1941–50	214	5	1·00	10·7
1830–1950	2,230	—	—	874·5

The value of all dwelling units on 31 December 1950 is obtained on the basis of the replacement value, i.e. the average building cost, which amounted in 1950 to 10,500 guilders per dwelling unit. This leads to the following results:

			billion guilders
Gross replacement value	.	. (2,230,000 × f. 10,500)	23·4
Depreciation	. . .	. (874,500 × f. 10,500)	9·2
	Net value on 31 December 1950 .	. . .	14·2

4. *An evaluation of the fixed assets of electricity works* [1]

The study represents an attempt at an evaluation of the fixed assets of all electricity works in the Netherlands. The electricity works are all government owned, and comparable statistics based on detailed questionnaires are published annually by the Central Bureau of Statistics. However, the basis of valuation of the assets adopted by the electricity works is not, in general, in accordance with the concept of replacement value net of depreciation. The only exception, so far, is the annual report by the

---

[1] See Appendix III, No. 19.

electricity company of the province of Friesland, which has based its depreciation allowances and valuation methods on very much the same concepts as those used in national accounting. On the basis of the available information for the electricity company of Friesland, national totals may be obtained by means of various technical coefficients derived partly from data on the physical assets of all electricity works shown in the annual electricity statistics published by the Central Bureau of Statistics, and partly from the annual report of the electricity company in Friesland. This material also permits certain internal checks on the estimates obtained, because the totals so derived should agree with the totals published.

The detailed data on technical equipment published in the annual reports of the company of Friesland and in the national statistics permit the use of a number of factors for 'blowing up' the data for Friesland. Allowance had to be made for the fact that the average age of its equipment is less than the national average. Although it is not certain that the electricity company

TABLE V

Technical Ratios for the Netherlands and Friesland,
31 December 1952

Technical Unit	Weighting Standard	Fries-land	Nether-lands	Ratio
Steam generation	Capacity of boilers in megawatts	94·2	2,175	23·1
Generation of electric power	Capacity of turbo-generators in mega-watts	94·5	2,204	23·3
Feeding, distribution, and low-tension net-works; transformers	Number of consumers (× 1,000)	78·1	2,470	31·6
Meters and meter-ser-vice	Number of meters (× 1,000)	84·9	2,590	30·5

of Friesland is typical of the country as a whole, it is believed that the factors chosen for 'blowing up' have resulted in reasonably reliable estimates because of the satisfactory outcome of the checks on certain totals obtained.

Table V shows the technical ratios derived from available data for the Netherlands and the electricity company of the province of Friesland.

The figures of replacement values and original cost in Table

VI have been obtained by multiplying the data for Friesland by the ratios shown in Table V. In calculating the total depreciation percentages by groups of assets, account has been taken of the differences in age between equipment for the Netherlands as a whole and the equipment of the electricity company of Friesland. The original cost estimates for the Netherlands as a whole

TABLE VI

Estimated Value of Electricity Works in the Netherlands, 31 December 1952

Technical Unit	Gross Replacement Value (million guilders)	Total Depreciation (%)	Net Replacement Value (million guilders)	Original Cost (gross) (million guilders)
Central station:				
Steam generation .	455	56	200	245
Generation of electric power . .	285	60	115	160
General equipment	85	30	60	50
Total . .	825	55	375	455
Feeding, distribution, and low-tension networks; transformers	2,190	35	1,430	1,125
Meters and meter-service . . .	225	45	125	110
Other equipment .	260	42	150	135
Total value of all technical units .	3,500	40	2,080	1,825

(Table VI; 1,825 million guilders) can be checked against information from other sources on total original cost of electricity works in the Netherlands (1,880 million guilders).

5. *The value of fixed assets in agriculture* [1]

Capital goods in agriculture include the following assets:

(a) farm buildings, excluding farm dwellings;
(b) machinery and equipment, transport vehicles;
(c) livestock.

Stocks of fertilizers, fuels, etc., and standing crops are not included in the estimates. The calculations relate to agriculture and exclude horticulture.

[1] See Appendix III, No. 21.

As stated in Part I, the value of the fixed assets is estimated on the basis of replacement values minus depreciation. In general, the basic data are derived from surveys providing information on replacement values of farm buildings per hectare of farmland, for various types of farms. This information is supplied by the Ministry of Reconstruction and Housing. Data on accumulated depreciation are derived from information on the age distribution of farm buildings for a stratified sample of farms collected by the 'Landbouw Economisch Instituut' in 1955. The average life of farm buildings has been estimated at 125 years. The results of the calculations for the end of 1952 are as follows:

Type of Farm	Total Area (hectares)	Total Value (million guilders)
Arable farms	597,000	490
Pastoral farms	451,400	520
Mixed farms	1,181,100	2,120
Total . . .	2,229,500	3,130

The 'Landbouw Economisch Instituut' has published estimates of the replacement value of machinery and equipment as of 31 December 1952,[1] based on an inquiry carried out by the Central Bureau of Statistics in 1950.[2]

	Million guilders
Tractors	258
Tools and implements	1,418
Transport equipment	399
Engines, etc.	17
Total	2,092

The amount of machinery and equipment purchased in 1951 and 1952 has been derived from import statistics, etc. Rates of depreciation have been derived from information on the length of life and the age distribution of various types of machinery.

The value of livestock has been estimated on the basis of the annual census of agriculture of the Central Bureau of Statistics [3]

[1] *Landbouwciijfers 1953* (Statistics of Agriculture), p. 51, Landbouw-Economisch Instituut (in Dutch).

[2] *Census of Agriculture 1950*, II (in Dutch).

[3] 'Census of Agriculture of December 1952', published in *Statistics of Agriculture 1952* (in Dutch).

and average prices per animal. The results for 31 December 1952 are as follows:

Livestock	Number (thousands)	Value (million guilders)
Cows . . .	2,734	2,061
Pigs and hogs . . .	2,259	262
Horses . . .	241	204
Sheep . . .	383	38
Chickens . . .	15,709	63
Ducks . . .	337	1
Total . . .		2,629

The calculations of the total value of capital goods used in agriculture at 31 December 1952 may be summarized as follows:

	Billion guilders
(a) Farm buildings, excluding farm dwellings . .	3·1
(b) Machinery and equipment, tools, implements and transport vehicles	1·3
(c) Livestock	2·6
Total	7·0

6. Estimates of the value of agricultural land [1]

As has been explained in Part I, replacement values are accepted as the basis for estimating national wealth. Since in the case of land it is impossible to determine a replacement value, the capitalization method must be used, despite its theoretical and statistical disadvantages.

Because of government controls of prices and rents of farm land, actual transactions do not give the right valuations, nor can rents be used as a basis for determining the returns from land in the post-war period. Market prices of farm land are influenced by the great scarcity of land in the Netherlands, and by the desire of purchasers to protect themselves against a possible decline in the purchasing power of money. Hence, market prices cannot be used as a basis for estimating the total value of agricultural land.

In order to estimate the value of agricultural land, the net returns must be determined on the basis of available data about gross value of production less costs of fertilizers, seeds, fodder and other materials, fuels, depreciation allowances on farm buildings and equipment, paid wages and imputed wages for the farmer and the unpaid labour of members of his family. Since

[1] See Appendix III, No. 20.

the purpose of the study is to determine the value of farm land, excluding all buildings, an imputed interest for farm buildings and equipment should also be deducted. The calculations in this paragraph relate to land in agriculture and exclude horticulture.

The necessary data are derived from annual surveys of financial results of farms collected by the Landbouw-Economisch Instituut. These surveys relate to a number of farms under efficient management, producing under average or near-average conditions. The value of production and the operating costs are estimated on the basis of objective norms, which in principle are consistent with economic concepts. There norms are adhered to as strictly as possible.

In order to eliminate the effects of short-term fluctuations in returns, averages for a five-year period (1948–52) have been computed. The average returns have been capitalized assuming an interest rate of 3 per cent. However, alternative computations based on interest rates of 4 and 5 per cent, and on slightly higher rates for the imputed wages of the farmer, have also been made. The main results, based on an interest rate of 3 per cent and averages for the period 1948–52, are as follows:

Type of Farm	Average Net Return (per hectare in guilders)	Value of Farm Land (per hectare guilders)	Total Value (billion guilders)
Arable farms .	408	13,400	8·0
Pastoral farms .	223	7,300	3·3
Mixed farms [1] .	37	1,200	1·4
Netherlands [2] .	173	5,700	12·7

[1] This group includes the small-holdings in the less-fertile regions, which greatly reduces the average net returns per hectare for this type of farms.
[2] Weighted averages.

To assume slightly higher inputed wages for the farmer cannot greatly affect the results, as the following figures show:

Type of Farm	Entrepreneurial Wages: (imputed) (per hectare in guilders)	Net Returns per Hectare in guilders. Assumed increases in imputed entrepreneurial wages			
		0%	10%	20%	30%
Arable farms .	165	408	403	398	393
Pastoral farms .	366	223	218	213	208
Mixed farms .	647	37	30	23	16

III. FINAL REMARKS

The work on the national balance sheet in the Netherlands after the War was at first mainly confined to the formulation of concepts and the development of the system. In recent years more attention has been given to statistical problems. In the previous sections both subjects have been discussed. In this concluding section something will be said about the present situation and future expectations.

On theoretical concepts, the point of view of the Bureau has remained unchanged. The national balance sheet forms an integral part of the system of national accounts, and is therefore based upon the same concepts and definitions as the current accounts. The contemplated changes in the accounts – acceptance of international standards and extension of the system into financial flows – will therefore automatically influence the presentation of the national balance sheet.

The main statistical problems are the scarcity of basic data and the difficulties encountered in the interpretation of those which are available. In this respect, the valuation of capital goods presents especially serious problems. The balance-sheet valuations of capital goods of enterprises in the Netherlands are generally based not on the cost-accounting principles used in the national accounts, but on rather heterogeneous considerations. In general, it is difficult to use this material for the purposes of national accounting.

There is, however, a growing interest in enterprises in balance-sheet figures conforming to the standards of national accounting. There is a growing conviction that such figures are indispensable for sound cost accounting; the central government has introduced these methods for government enterprises, and some large private enterprises now use them. As material of this kind becomes available it will be possible to arrive at better estimates for certain branches. The example of the electricity works shows what is meant here and what can be achieved. In addition, it is proposed to include in current or newly planned statistics additional questions relating to the quantities and prices of capital goods.

The valuation problem is less serious for financial claims, since the valuations needed are either used in the available sources or can be derived from them. In this case, more basic data are available, while the planned development of a system of financial flows will tend to fill the main gaps. New statistics will include data about the financial items in the balance sheets of corporations; statistics of savings will provide the same kind of information for wage-earners and for non-corporate enterprises. When this information is available, the problem of including the financial claims of non-corporate enterprises in the household sector can be solved more satisfactorily.

It should be borne in mind that national balance-sheet items should give valuations of future returns and repayments; the problems connected with these valuations cannot be solved by merely collecting statistics; to a greater extent than in other fields of economic research, the statistician must base his estimates on expert opinion.

APPENDIX I

THE SYSTEM OF THE NATIONAL BALANCE SHEET

	Enterprises Assets	Enterprises Liab.	Banks Assets	Banks Liab.	Government Assets	Government Liab.	Insurance funds Assets	Insurance funds Liab.	Households Assets	Households Liab.	Rest of the world Assets	Rest of the world Liab.	Combined Bal. Sheet Assets	Combined Bal. Sheet Liab.	Consolidated Bal. Sheet Assets	Consolidated Bal. Sheet Liab.
1. Capital goods	a		a				a						Σa		Σa	
2. Shares		×	×	×	×		×	×	×		×		×	×		
3. Indirect investments	×		×				×		×			×	×	×		
4. Property rights		×			×		×		×				×	×		
5. Free property		×		×				×	×				×	×		
6. Direct investments	×	×	×						×		×	×	×	×		
7. Bonds	×	×	×	×		×	×				×	×	×	×		
8. Mortgage bonds	×	×	×	×			×				×	×	×	×		
9. Mortgages		×	×	×			×		×	×	×	×	×	×		
10. War-damage claims	×		×			×			×				×	×		
11. Long-term debts	×	×	×	×	×	×	×	×	×	×	×	×	×	×		
12. Treasury bills	×		×		×	×	×				×		×	×		
13. Savings banks				×					×				×	×		
14. Money	×		×	×	×		×				×		×	×		
15. Gold and foreign exchange			×								×	×	×	×		
16. Short-term debts	×	×	×	×	×	×	×	×	×	×	×	×	×	×		
17. Counterpart to coin and currency notes				×	×								×	×		
18. Deferred liabilities and advance payment	×	×	×	×	×	×	×	×	×	×	×	×	×	×		
19. Net worth of public corporations				×	×								×	×		
20. Participation in I.M.F. and I.B.R.D.					×							×	×	×		
21. Obligations to I.M.F. and I.B.R.D.						×					×		×	×		
22. Net government debt					b									−b		−b
23. Insurance-funds wealth								c						c		c
24. Private wealth										d				d		d
25. Foreign balance												e	e		e	
26. Balance total	×	×	×	.×	×	×	×	×	×	×	×	×	×	×		
27. National wealth													Σa +e	−b +c+d		

Explanatory notes

1. Capital goods. This item includes all fixed assets as well as stocks and dwellings. They are all included in the sector Enterprises. (See Part I, Section 3.)
2. Shares. Includes only the shares of Netherlands corporations. The shares of the Government corporations are not included (see item 19).
3. Indirect investments. These include foreign bonds and shares held by the Netherlands.
4. Property rights. These are the counter-items to item 1 for ownership of capital goods by the other domestic sectors (see item 6).
5. Free property. The net worth of incorporated enterprises, banks and insurance funds, as far as this is not specifically covered by the items 'shares' and 'net worth of public corporations', is allocated to the household sector. (See Part I, Section 1.) (This is analogous with the allocation of profit in the rating accounts.) For the Enterprise sector this item also includes the property rights of the Household sector. (See Part I, Section 4.)
6. Direct investment. Including the ownership of Netherlands capital goods by foreign countries and the reverse.
7. Bonds. All bonds issued by the Netherlands public authorities and by private institutions.
8. Mortgage bonds. Bonds issued by the Netherlands mortgage banks.
9. Mortgages. Mortgages on Netherlands capital goods. Mortgages between households are consolidated. Mortgages on foreign assets are included in long-term debts.

143

Explanatory notes (continued)

10. **War-damage claims.** All claims for war-damage on the Government and Netherlands insurance institutions.
11. **Long-term debts.** Includes all debts covering periods longer than the current period of one year which have not been given separately.
12. **Treasury bills.** Includes all transferable short-term paper issued on behalf of the Treasury.
13. **Savings banks.** Includes all savings deposits with banks.
14. **Money.** All Netherlands coin and fiduciary money, including credits with the Netherlands money-creating institutions.
15. **Gold and foreign exchange.** Includes all assets and liabilities comprised in the gold and exchange holdings of the Netherlands Central Bank.
16. **Short-term debts.** Includes all debts covering periods of one year or less which have not been given separately.
17. **Counterpart to coin and currency notes.** This book-item accounts for the inclusion of all money issued by the Government in the sector banks.
18. **Deferred liabilities and advance payments.** All payments deferred or advanced on current transactions.
19. **Net worth of public corporations.** This is the closing item of the balance sheet of public corporations.
20 and 21. **Participations in and obligations to I.M.F. and I.B.R.D.** These items relate to the International Monetary Fund and the International Bank for Reconstruction and Development.
22, 24 and 25. **Net public debt, private wealth, and foreign balance.** These are the closing items of the Government, Households, and Rest of the world sectors.
23. **Insurance Funds wealth.** This item gives the capital available and designed to meet the insurance obligations. It is not equal to actuarial reserves, as the government pension funds fall short of this standard.

APPENDIX II

NATIONAL WEALTH OF THE NETHERLANDS
ON 31 DECEMBER 1952

Billion guilders at current prices

	Undepreciated	Depreciated	$\dfrac{\text{Depreciated}}{\text{Undepreciated}}$ (%)
A. Enterprises . . . . . total	113·4	78·4	—
I. Reproducible assets . . . total	97·0	62·0	—
1. Structures . . . total	53·4	32·5	61
(a) Dwellings [1] . . .	30·1	18·3	61
(b) Agricultural . . .	5·1	3·1	61
(c) Other [2] . . .	18·2	11·1	61
2. Equipment . . total	33·0	18·9	57
(a) Agricultural [3] . .	2·8	1·5	53
(b) Other . . .	30·2	17·4	58
3. Inventories . . total	10·6	10·6	100
(a) Livestock . . .	2·6	2·6	100
(b) Standing timber . .	0·8	0·8	100
(c) Other agricultural [4] .	1·4	1·4	100
(d) Other . . .	5·8	5·8	100
II. Non-reproducible assets: land . total	16·4	16·4	100
(a) Agricultural . . .	13·1	13·1	100
(b) Forest	0·2	0·2	100
(c) Other	3·1	3·1	100
B. (Government) [5] . . . . total	(24·0)	(12·0)	(50)
I. Reproducible assets . . . total	..	..	..
1. Structures	..	..	..
2. Equipment	..	..	..
3. Inventories . . .	..	..	..
I. Non-reproducible assets: land . total	..	..	..
C. (Consumer durables) [5] . . total	(33·3)	(24·2)	(73)
1. Passenger cars and other vehicles .	0·3	0·2	45
2. Other	33·0	24·0	73
D. Foreign assets . . . . total	8·1	8·1	100
1. Monetary metals . . .	2·2	2·2	100
2. Other net foreign assets . .	5·9	5·9	100
Total (A + D)	121·5	86·5	—
(A + B + C + D) .	(178·8)	(122·7)	—

[1] All dwellings. [2] Land included; harbours of Amsterdam and Rotterdam included.
[3] Forestry included. [4] Sown seeds and growing crop included.
[5] Not included in the system of national balance sheets of the Netherlands; B. and C.2 are rough estimates.

APPENDIX III

BIBLIOGRAPHY

Abbr.: *S.E.O.* = *Statistische en Econometrische Onderzoekingen* (Statistical and Econometric Studies), quarterly published by the Netherlands Central Bureau of Statistics.

1. C. A. Verrijn Stuart, Ons Maatschappelijk vermogen voor 30 jaren en thans, bijdragen van het Statistisch Instituut, No. 2, 1888, p. 267.

2. W. A. Bonger, *Vermogen en inkomen in Nederland 1908–1913*, Amsterdam, 1914.

3. W. A. Bonger, *Vermogen en inkomen in Nederland gedurende den oorlogstijd (1913–1920)*, Amsterdam, 1923.

4. C. A. Verrijn Stuart, 'Volksvermögen und Volkseinkommen in den Niederlanden', *Bulletin de l'Institut International de Statistique*, T. 25, 1931, Livre 3, p. 461.

5. J. B. D. Derksen, 'Berekening van het nationale vermogen uit de aangiften voor de successiebelasting', *De Nederlandsche Conjunctuur*, mei 1939, p. 72, Central Bureau of Statistics.

6. J. B. D. Derksen, 'De samenstelling van het nationale vermogen', *De Nederlandsche Conjunctuur*, Augustus 1939, p. 123, Central Bureau of Statistics.

7. J. B. D. Derksen, *A System of National Book-keeping*, National Institute of Economic and Social Research, Occasional Papers X, Cambridge, 1946, p. 15.

8. Central Bureau of Statistics, 'Uitkomsten voor enige berekeningen betreffende het nationale vermogen in Nederland in 1938', *S.E.O.*, 1947, No. 3, p. 66.

9. Central Bureau of Statistics, 'Het nationale vermogen van Nederland en zijn verdeling eind 1947', *S.E.O.*, 1949, No. 1, p. 5.

10. Central Bureau of Statistics, 'Het verband tussen de nationale balans en het stelsel der nationale jaarrekeningen', *S.E.O.*, 1950, No. 3, p. 107.

11. F. S. Bray, 'A National Balance Sheet', *Accounting Research*, Vol. 2, No. 3, July 1951 (see *S.E.O.*, 1950, No. 3, p. 107).

12. Central Bureau of Statistics, *National Accounts of the Netherlands 1948–1949*, Netherlands Central Bureau of Statistics, 1952, p. 8: 'Part I, The National Wealth of the Netherlands'.

13. Central Bureau of Statistics, 'Gegevens betreffende de materiële schade veroorzaakt door de overstromingen in Februari 1953', *S.E.O.*, 1953, No. 2, p. 29.

14. Central Bureau of Statistics, 'De nationale balansen voor de jaren 1938 en 1946–1952', *S.E.O.*, 1954, No. 1, p. 3.

15. Central Bureau of Statistics, 'National Balance Sheets for the Years 1938 and 1946–1952', *Statistical Studies*, No. 3, 1954, p. 3.

16. Central Bureau of Statistics, 'Balanswaarde van en afschrijvingen op woningen', *S.E.O.*, 1954, No. 1, p. 11.

17. Central Bureau of Statistics, 'Balance Sheet Values and Depreciation Allowances for Dwellings', *Statistical Studies*, No. 3, 1954, p. 10.

18. Central Bureau of Statistics, 'De vermogenswaarde van de Nederlandse koopvaardijvloot', *S.E.O.*, 1955, No. 4, p. 151.

19. Central Bureau of Statistics, 'De vermogenswaarde der electriciteitsbedrijven in Nederland', *S.E.O.*, 1956, No. 4, p. 178.

20. A. P. H. Berkhuysen, 'Enkele statistische berekeningen betreffende de vermogenswaarde van de landbouwgronden in de nationale balans', *S.E.O.*, 1957, No. 1, p. 5.

21. Central Bureau of Statistics, 'Een vermogensopstelling der productiemiddelen in de landbouw op het einde van 1952', *S.E.O.*, 1957, No. 2, p. 77.

6

AN ESTIMATE OF THE NATIONAL CAPITAL ACCOUNT OF THE FEDERAL GERMAN REPUBLIC[1]

By Ferdinand Grünig

I. EARLIER ESTIMATES OF NATIONAL WEALTH

THE first very rough estimates of German national wealth date from before World War I, and are associated with the names of Steinmann-Bucher, Helfferich, and Ballod. According to their estimates, the national wealth immediately before World War I amounted to between 350 and 400 milliard[2] goldmark, which would make it around seven times the value of gross national product of the time, determined many years later. This is, however, a dubious comparison, since the methods of estimation of national wealth and national product were dissimilar. The estimate of national wealth was based on the fire-insurance values of real assets, to which were added the current commercial values of land and other public and private property not insured against fire; the calculation of national product, on the other hand, is based directly upon the value of goods and services originating in the process of production and distribution. National-wealth estimates for 1939 (compiled by Hunscha, Grotius, Nieschlag, Harmssen, and others) are no more illuminating in this respect. National wealth for that year, which they set at between 450 and 600 milliard DM, was five to six times the gross national product of the time, but conceptual differences make it impracticable to compare this result with the other estimates made before World War I.

II. PRINCIPAL CONSIDERATIONS UNDERLYING THE NEW ESTIMATES

In these circumstances the research group of the Deutsches Institut für Wirtschaftsforschung, Berlin, which had been appointed to consider questions of social accounting – including, besides myself, Dr. Krengel, Dr. Arndt, Dr. Seidler, and Mr.

---

[1] Summary of the report submitted to the 1957 Conference. The full report was published in German in *Sonderhefte des Deutschen Instituts für Wirtschaftsforschung*, Neue Folge, Nr. 41, Versuch einer Vermögensrechnung der Deutschen Bundesrepublik, Berlin, 1958. See also Nr. 42 in the same series.

[2] 1 milliard = thousand million.

Schimmler – decided to construct a capital account closely related to the income and expenditure account, and based on social-accounting results. The group approached its task by considering the most important sectors of the economy, housing, manufacturing, etc., first and by compiling, in the light of the information which this produced, a comprehensive account for all sectors afterwards. As far as practicable, data were to be drawn from existing records of stocks of physical assets for the different sectors. Assets would first be valued at their original cost, adjusted to 1950 prices, the fixed bench-mark year. From the resulting 'Neuwert' (which we shall translate by gross value) a second calculation, involving the deduction of the appropriate depreciation allowances, would give the 'Zeitwert' or net value of physical assets. The ratio of net value to gross value was called 'Gütegrad' or *net–gross ratio*, in accordance with the custom of the German Federal Railway System in the presentation of its balance sheet.

There is a twofold relationship between a capital account arrived at in this way and the income and expenditure account. In the first place, the sum of gross capital formation taken from annual gross national expenditure over a long period must give the gross value of the capital assets, after appropriate deductions have been made for worn-out assets which may have disappeared before the bench-mark year. In the second place, it can be assumed that there are definite functional relations between the gross value of capital assets and their current output, and the empirical determination of these relations must be one of the most important purposes of a capital account which is intended to correspond to the income and expenditure account.

III. METHODS OF COMPUTATION

1. *Housing*

Statistics for the total number of dwellings in the Federal Republic of Germany have been collected several times during the last three decades – i.e. in 1927, 1939, and 1950. The results of these counts, combined with official statistics on annual housing construction, enabled an estimate to be made of the age-distribution of existing dwellings. This, together with data on average building costs per dwelling, made it possible to transform physical data into values. After making adjustments for price, we arrived at the gross value of the stock of dwellings. For the next step in the calculation, certain assumptions had to be made on theoretically justifiable allowances for depreciation. In doing this, consideration was given to changes in the degree of utilization since construction of buildings in respect of the remainder of their expected life, and also in respect of the quality of each unit in terms of 'gross value'; account was also taken of the condition of the buildings, in view of the wide divergence in efforts at repair and maintenance.

To avoid complicating the calculation unnecessarily, Dr. Arndt, initially allowed for constant average rates of depreciation (1 per cent per annum of gross value) and of maintenance (0·75 per cent per annum of gross value). A depreciation rate of 1 per cent per annum of gross value corresponds to an average effective life for dwelling-houses of 100 years, which was found to apply approximately to conditions in Germany since the middle of last century. The maintenance rate of 0·75 per cent per annum of gross value accords with recent experience in Germany. Repairs at this level are not regarded in our estimates as investments (new building), but count as normal provision arising from the use of dwellings. Periods of particularly great wear and tear (through war damage, times of below-average repairs, etc.) or of unusually intensive reconstruction, were taken account of by special deductions from, or additions to, the 'net–gross ratio' of total construction. This way we can assess the net–gross ratio and the net value of different age groups of dwelling-houses year by year.

2. *Manufacturing*

Fixed capital assets of manufacturing, unlike those of the housing sector, could not be based on actual statistics of inventories, since such inventories have not hitherto been compiled, and in view of the diversity of industrial capital equipment and the difficulty of its valuation, it seems unlikely that they will be made in future. The data furnished in the balance sheets of joint-stock companies are of little assistance, since such accounts are concerned only with 'book values', and not with 'gross values' and 'net values', in the sense of our present study. Consequently, Dr. Krengel had to adopt other means to assess the magnitude of gross values and net values of West German manufacturing assets. He took as a starting-point annual gross capital formation in manufacturing; for the post-currency reform period (i.e.

after mid-1948) these could be ascertained from earlier studies of the DIW, supervised by Dr. Krengel himself. For the pre-war years there were statistics covering the whole of the former Germany, and these had to be adjusted to the boundaries of the present Federal Republic, and also for price changes. Gross capital formation for the remaining years was estimated from various other sources. The assumption of 'normal' average depreciation rates was an important factor in shaping the estimates. Unlike the housing sector, where we could use a single constant rate (1 per cent per annum) throughout, it proved more accurate in the case of manufacturing to assume different depreciation rates for buildings (2 per cent per annum throughout) and for equipment (3 per cent and, later in the period under review, 5 per cent per annum). In addition, war damage and postwar losses (dismantling) had to be allowed for by special depreciation allowances, and in the case of total losses the depreciation base had to be readjusted.

These depreciation rates correspond to an average effective life of fifty years for buildings, and of twenty to thirty-three years for equipment. For war losses the corresponding deductions were made from gross value. Working from the above assumptions and thus, to a certain extent, on an econometric model, it was possible to establish, year by year, the size and age structure of the total stock of capital assets. The next step was to calculate the net value of capital assets at constant prices. This was done by deducting depreciation allowances for part of the effective life which had already elapsed – a procedure which involved tiresome calculations (since each year has its own rates of depreciation), but which otherwise, as long as the model was adhered to, presented no methodological problems.

IV. ESTIMATES OF FIXED CAPITAL ASSETS OF THE FEDERAL REPUBLIC

There is no need to enter here into our methods of estimating fixed capital assets of the other large sectors of the economy, such as agriculture, power supply, transport, and public administration. Whereas we have continuous calculations of wealth for housing and manufacturing, our inquiries into other sectors have not yet been completed. Nevertheless, for the purpose of the present volume, and with many reservations, approximate estimates of capital assets have been prepared for specified bench-mark years, and these enable us to furnish a preliminary review of the size and development of total capital assets of the Federal Republic since 1913 (see the tables on p. 156–9).

1. *Gross values of fixed capital assets in the territory of the present-day Federal German Republic*

These were as follows:

1913	.	.	.	341 milliard DM
1929	.	.	.	401 ,, ,,
1939	.	.	.	476 ,, ,,

(All the results are shown at 1950 prices.)

This indicates a rise of nearly 40 per cent in twenty-six years, or an annual rate of increase of only 1·4 per cent. World War I and the subsequent inflation and later, in the early 1930s, the world economic crisis explain this slight rate of growth.

The destruction caused during World War II, later dismantling, and above all the completely inadequate replacement of assets made much greater inroads into West German capital assets. Their gross value dropped from 476 milliard DM in 1939 to 413 milliard DM in 1948, and thus stood only 3 per cent above the level of twenty years earlier.

The seven-year reconstruction period from 1948 (the year of the currency reform) to 1955 is the most interesting for the study of capital investment. In this relatively short time the growth in assets was greater than in any of the earlier periods investigated by us. The gross value of West German capital assets in these seven years rose from 413 milliard DM to 544 milliard DM, i.e. by about 30 per cent, and thus stood about 14 per cent above the 1939 level and 60 per cent above the 1913 level. But it had taken years to achieve this increase, so that the average annual rate of growth over the forty-two years from 1913 to 1955 works out at only a little more than 1 per cent.

2. *Net–gross ratio of capital assets*

The net–gross ratio provides information on the reductions in value which take place between the date of purchase of a capital asset and the chosen date of stock-taking. They are generally due to the annual decrease of the expected life of the asset; even if efficiency reflected in *annual* output remained the same, this diminishing life expectation until the asset is finally withdrawn from the process of production will necessarily lead to a diminishing expectation of *total* future output of the asset. In addition, with increasing age many assets also show a lower efficiency reflected in the diminishing annual output. This form of value depreciation can be taken care of by an equivalent reduction in the expected life of the asset by our estimating technique.

It may be demonstrated that when the rate of investment remains uniform, the capital stock will achieve a net–gross ratio of 50 per cent. On the other hand, a great expansion of investment sustained over many years results in much higher ratios, e.g. from 60 to 65 per cent. Net–gross ratios of 70 per cent and over are, however, rare, and indicate that there has been a multiple increase in annual investments in the course of the effective life of the equipment.

The net–gross ratio of the total stock of capital equipment in the total economy, which was 63 per cent in 1913, remained nearly unchanged until 1939. The events of the war and post-war years produced an abrupt drop to 51 per cent in 1948. This decrease can be explained by the low investment activity during those years and the other reductions caused by the War in the value of total capital equipment. Economic reconstruction caused the ratio to rise once more to 56 per cent in 1955.

In the individual economic sectors the net–gross ratio was subject to more violent fluctuations.

3. *Net values of capital assets*

According to our definition 'net-value = gross value × net–gross ratio'. The series for net value will therefore differ from those for gross values only by the net–gross-ratio factor. As long as this ratio does not alter, net values, although on a lower level, must follow a trend proportional to that of the corresponding gross values. On the other hand, rising ratios resulting from an expansion in investment activity cause net values to rise proportionately higher; conversely, when investments fall off, the net–gross ratios decline; in time of depression, therefore, net values lag behind the trend in gross values. Net value of West German capital assets rose from 215 milliard DM in 1913 to 299 milliard DM in 1939. The average annual rate of increase for these twenty-six years is just under 1·4 per cent, only very slightly different from the average rate of increase in gross values; this indicates that the net–gross ratio of capital assets also remained fairly stable in relation to movements in net assets in these twenty-six years. On the other hand, the falling-off between 1939 and 1948 due to the War was much more pronounced in net values than in gross values: gross values dropped by about 14 per cent and net values by about 30 per cent. The net–gross ratio of the total stock of capital equipment fell at the same time from about 63 to about 51 per cent. In the seven-year reconstruction period (1948–55), however, the net value of capital assets rose by no less than 45 per cent; the increase in gross values was only about 30 per cent. The net–gross ratio of capital assets rose in these years from 51 to 56 per cent.

All in all, the net value of the stock of West German capital increased from 215 milliard DM in 1913 to 306 milliard DM in 1955 – a rise of 42 per cent in forty-two years – while the corresponding increase in gross value amounted to 60 per cent. Here, too, the much lower increase in net value was accompanied by a considerable diminution in the net–gross ratio of capital assets: in 1913 it was 63 per cent, in 1955 only 56 per cent.

4. *Distribution of capital assets by industry*

The average share of the net values of capital assets over the forty-two years examined, is as follows:

Percentage Shares

Housing	35
Transport	18
Public administration, including military assets	15
Manufacturing	14
Agriculture	6·5
Supply of power	3·5
Other sectors	8
	100·0

With a few exceptions, the distribution of capital assets according to economic sectors has changed relatively little on balance in the course of the forty-two years under review. The chief exceptions are manufacturing and power supply, which, particularly during the seven-year reconstruction period (1948–55), increased their share of total capital assets of the economy substantially. In 1955 their shares were respectively 18 per cent and 5 per cent, an increase which was achieved at the expense of transport and, to a lesser extent, of the housing sector.

5. *Capital coefficients*

It is one of the chief objects to compare the results of a capital account based on social-accounting principles with current transactions. This can be done for the whole economy, and also for each of its sectors. A further problem to be considered is whether, in comparing capital assets with gross national product, it is more useful to start from the gross value or the net value of the capital assets, or else, better still, to calculate both coefficients, and then give preference to one or the other series according to the purpose of the inquiry. In order to distinguish the two coefficients, we suggest that the ratio of gross value of capital assets to gross national product should be called gross capital coefficient, and the ratio of net value of capital assets to gross national product should be called net capital coefficient. The gross capital coefficient relates size and technical capacity of capital assets (in so far as these are represented by gross value) to the current value of production. The net capital coefficient compares depreciated capital investment with current output.

The following is a summary of the trends of gross capital assets and gross national product – including the gross capital coefficient – for all bench-mark years.

The Trend of Gross and Net Capital Assets and of Gross National Product in the Federal Republic

	1913	1929	1939	1948	1950	1955
Milliard DM at 1950 Prices						
Gross capital assets . .	341	401	476	412	440	544
Net capital assets . .	215	245	299	212	226	306
Gross national product .	63	68	104	68	97	150
Ratios						
Gross capital coefficient .	5·4	5·9	4·6	6·1	4·5	3·6
Net capital coefficient .	3·4	3·6	2·9	3·1	2·3	2·0
Net–gross ratio of capital assets	63	61	63	51	51	56

It is noticeable that the gross capital coefficient has dropped steadily over the period – from 5·4 to 3·6. From this rough consideration the years 1948 and 1950, and to some extent, 1929 are

an exception to this trend, because in these years fixed capital
was under-utilized. The degree of under-utilization can be seen
by the deviation of the coefficient from its general trend. In 1955
capital equipment was overloaded, and the gross capital coefficient might have been 5 per cent greater than the actual one
with normal plant utilization, i.e. 3·8 instead of 3·6.

The declining trend of the gross capital coefficient is partly
attributable to the structural changes in capital assets: the increased importance of manufacturing and power supply as
compared with transport and housing. But the cause of this
decreasing trend must also be sought in the ever-increasing
rationalization of the production process; this appears to have
been more effective in reducing the capital coefficient than the influence exerted by the increasing capital content of the production process (measured by capital outlay per unit of labour employed), which by itself would have led to a higher capital
coefficient.

There is no need to enter into a similar examination of the development of the net capital coefficient. It can be arrived at, in a
pure mechanical way, by multiplying the gross capital coefficient and the net–gross ratio of capital assets. The capital coefficients in the various economic sectors vary. They fluctuate
from a coefficient of 12·5 for housing (with unrestricted rents, in
the case of rent-restricted dwellings the coefficient is considerably higher) to between 1·1 and 1·4 for manufacturing.

V. 'REPRODUCIBLE' WEALTH OF THE FEDERAL REPUBLIC

Besides fixed capital assets 'reproducible' wealth includes inventories, furniture, and other property of private households,
as well as wealth invested abroad or in foreign securities (including gold and foreign currency, after deduction of the appropriate liabilities due to foreign countries). We do not, however,
include the value of land, of mineral wealth, or of works of art.
Claims on foreign countries are commonly excluded from reproducible wealth, but it seems more appropriate to its function in
the production process (balance-of-payments surplus) to include
it.

As already indicated in the introduction, we are concerned
here not so much with an estimate of the value of private and
public property – measured in terms of some concept of value,
such as current commercial value, earning power, fire-insurance

values, etc. – but rather with an attempt to develop a new tool of economic analysis, i.e. a current capital account appropriate to the national product account. This being our intention, it is particularly important to supplement the estimates of fixed assets (which has been our sole concern until now) by a corresponding estimate of inventories and of the amount of claims against other countries (foreign balance). This is because the changes in these three items (capital assets, inventories, and the net foreign balance) appear in the income and expenditure account in the section entitled 'Disposal of gross national product'. On the other hand, the annual purchases of consumers' durables, etc., do not appear as formation of wealth in real assets in the national-product account, but are treated as 'private consumption', and are therefore separated from the process of (real) capital formation. This customary treatment of consumers' durables does not, of course, debar us from extending the system of social accounts in order to study the formation of wealth within private households in the context of the social accounts, as has already been done in several specialized inquiries; on the basis of such investigations we can seek, then, to estimate future demand for, e.g., household furniture. It will be seen that there are obvious relations between the size of this 'household wealth' and the growth of the national economy.

Total Reproducible Wealth of the Federal Republic
Summary Table

	1913	1929	1939	1948	1950	1955
Milliard DM at 1956 Prices						
Fixed capital assets, net value	214	245	299	212	226	306
Inventories . . .	19	20	31	23	27	42
Wealth of private households, net value . .	35	55	85	35	50	90
Wealth in gold and foreign securities (foreign balance)	24	.	6	.	.	.
Total reproducible wealth	292	320	421	270	303	438
Milliard DM at Current Prices						
Total reproducible wealth	133	237	245	305	303	530

The situation is different for non-reproducible wealth, and particularly land. Since this is neither produced nor consumed, the wealth it represents cannot enter into the national product

Capital Assets in the Federal Republic of Germany
Year's End [1]

	1913	1929	1939	1948	1950	1955
Gross value [2] Milliard DM at 1950 prices						
Agriculture . . .	29·0	30·9	31·5	28·4	30·0	33·2
(a) Equipment	6·5	8·0	9·7	7·7	8·8	11·5
(b) Buildings . . .	22·5	22·9	21·8	20·7	21·2	21·7
Manufacturing . . .	35·0	52·8	58·9	57·2	63·8	91·2
(a) Equipment	25·0	35·5	39·2	39·7	43·7	64·5
(b) Buildings . . .	10·0	17·3	19·7	17·5	20·1	26·7
Electricity, gas and water supply . . .	5·0	11·5	16·4	14·2	16·0	24·8
(a) Equipment	2·3	7·0	11·0	9·8	11·0	18·2
(b) Buildings . . .	2·7	4·5	5·4	4·4	5·0	6·6
Transport . . .	70·0	76·0	92·0	80·0	84·0	96·0
(a) Equipment	27·0	30·0	33·0	25·0	28·0	35·0
(b) Buildings . . .	43·0	46·0	59·0	55·0	56·0	61·0
Housing	118·5	130·0	146·0	130·0	138·0	168·0
(a) Equipment	—	—	—	—	—	—
(b) Buildings . . .	118·5	130·0	146·0	130·0	138·0	168·0
Public administration .	55·0	66·0	91·0	68·0	71·5	85·0
(a) Equipment .	8·0	11·0	15·0	11·0	11·9	15·0
(b) Buildings . . .	47·0	55·0	76·0	57·0	59·6	70·0
Other sectors of economy .	28·5	33·8	40·2	34·7	37·2	45·8
(a) Equipment .	6·7	10·0	14·1	12·3	13·6	16·8
(b) Buildings . . .	21·8	23·8	26·1	22·4	23·6	29·0
Economy as a whole .	341·0	401·0	476·0	412·5	440·5	544·0
(a) Equipment .	75·5	101·5	122·0	105·5	117·0	161·0
(b) Buildings . . .	265·5	299·5	354·0	307·0	323·5	383·0
Net value [3] Milliard DM at 1950 prices						
Agriculture . . .	21·7	18·2	19·0	13·4	13·6	18·8
(a) Equipment .	4·8	4·2	6·8	3·1	3·3	7·9
(b) Buildings . . .	16·9	14·0	12·2	10·3	10·3	10·9
Manufacturing . . .	20·0	28·0	32·7	32·2	36·5	55·9
(a) Equipment .	13·5	18·3	21·5	22·0	24·4	38·3
(b) Buildings . . .	6·5	9·7	11·2	10·2	12·1	17·6
Electricity, gas and water supply . . .	3·2	8·0	11·2	6·7	8·3	14·3
(a) Equipment .	1·6	5·1	7·8	4·5	5·6	10·3
(b) Buildings . . .	1·6	2·9	3·4	2·2	2·7	4·0
Transport . . .	39·0	44·0	54·5	38·0	40·5	48·5
(a) Equipment .	16·0	17·5	19·0	10·5	12·5	17·5
(b) Buildings . . .	23·0	26·5	35·5	27·5	28·0	31·0
Housing . . .	90·0	96·0	110·0	75·5	77·0	100·0
(a) Equipment .	—	—	—	—	—	—
(b) Buildings . . .	90·0	96·0	110·0	75·5	77·0	100·0
Public administration .	27·0	34·0	50·0	31·0	32·4	42·5
(a) Equipment .	4·0	5·5	8·0	5·0	5·0	7·5
(b) Buildings . . .	23·0	28·5	42·0	26·0	27·4	35·0
Other sectors of economy .	13·6	17·3	21·6	15·7	17·7	26·0
(a) Equipment .	3·1	5·9	8·9	5·9	6·7	10·0
(b) Buildings . . .	10·5	11·4	12·7	9·8	11·0	16·0

[1] 1948 Mid-year.   [2] Building cost or original cost value.   [3] See Note 1 p. 158.

Capital Assets in the Federal Republic of Germany—continued.

	1913	1929	1939	1948	1950	1955
Net value [1] in Milliard DM at 1950 prices (contd.)						
Economy as a whole . .	214·5	245·5	299·0	212·5	226·0	306·0
(a) Equipment . .	43·0	56·5	72·0	51·0	57·5	91·5
(b) Buildings . . .	171·5	189·0	227·0	161·5	168·5	214·5
Net–gross ratio in % [2]						
Agriculture . . .	74·8	58·9	60·3	47·2	45·3	56·6
(a) Equipment . .	73·8	52·5	70·1	40·3	37·5	68·7
(b) Buildings . . .	75·1	61·1	56·0	49·8	48·6	50·2
Manufacturing . . .	57·1	53·0	55·5	56·3	57·2	61·3
(a) Equipment . .	54·0	51·8	54·8	55·4	55·8	59·4
(b) Buildings . . .	65·0	56·1	56·9	58·3	60·2	65·9
Electricity, gas and water supply . . .	64·0	69·6	68·3	47·2	51·9	57·7
(a) Equipment . .	69·6	72·9	70·9	45·9	50·9	56·6
(b) Buildings . . .	59·3	64·4	63·0	50·0	54·0	60·6
Transport . . .	55·7	57·9	59·2	47·5	48·2	50·5
(a) Equipment . .	59·3	58·3	57·6	42·0	44·6	50·0
(b) Buildings . .	53·5	57·6	60·2	50·0	50·0	50·8
Housing	75·9	73·8	75·3	58·1	55·8	59·5
(a) Equipment . .	—	—	—	—	—	—
(b) Buildings . . .	75·9	73·8	75·3	58·1	55·8	59·5
Public administration .	49·1	51·5	54·9	45·6	45·3	50·0
(a) Equipment . .	50·0	50·0	53·3	45·5	42·0	50·0
(b) Buildings . .	48·9	51·8	55·3	45·6	46·0	50·0
Other sectors of economy .	47·7	51·2	53·7	45·2	47·6	57·8
(a) Equipment . .	46·3	59·0	63·1	48·0	49·3	59·5
(b) Buildings . . .	57·2	47·9	48·7	43·8	46·6	55·2
Economy a whole . .	62·9	61·2	62·8	51·5	51·3	56·3
(a) Equipment . .	57·0	55·7	59·0	48·3	49·1	56·8
(b) Buildings . . .	64·6	63·1	64·1	52·6	52·1	56·0
Percentage of gross value held by different sectors of the economy						
Agriculture . . .	8·5	7·7	6·6	6·9	6·8	6·1
(a) Equipment . .	8·6	7·9	8·0	7·3	7·5	7·2
(b) Buildings . . .	8·5	7·6	6·2	6·7	6·6	5·6
Manufacturing . . .	10·3	13·2	12·4	13·9	14·5	16·8
(a) Equipment . .	33·1	35·0	32·1	37·6	37·4	40·1
(b) Buildings . . .	3·8	5·8	5·6	5·7	6·2	7·0
Electricity, gas and water supply . . .	1·5	2·9	3·4	3·4	3·6	4·6
(a) Equipment . .	3·0	6·9	9·0	9·3	9·4	11·8
(b) Buildings . . .	1·0	1·5	1·5	1·4	1·5	1·7
Transport . . .	20·5	18·9	19·3	19·4	19·1	17·6
(a) Equipment . .	35·8	29·5	27·0	23·7	28·9	21·7
(b) Buildings . . .	16·2	15·4	16·7	17·9	17·3	15·9
Housing	34·8	32·4	30·7	31·5	31·3	30·9
(a) Equipment . .	—	—	—	—	—	—
(b) Buildings . . .	44·6	43·4	41·2	42·4	42·7	43·9

[1] Gross value minus depreciation, war damages, and taking account of valuation adjustments due to a surplus or deficit of maintenance costs.

[2] Ratio of net value to gross value.

Capital Assets in the Federal Republic of Germany—continued.

	1913	1929	1939	1948	1950	1955
Percentage of gross value held by different sectors of the economy (*contd.*)						
Public administration .	16·1	16·5	19·1	16·5	16·2	15·6
(a) Equipment . .	10·6	10·8	12·3	10·4	10·2	9·3
(b) Buildings . . .	17·7	18·4	21·5	18·6	18·4	18·3
Other sectors of economy .	8·3	8·4	8·5	8·4	8·5	8·4
(a) Equipment . .	8·9	9·9	11·6	11·7	11·6	10·4
(b) Buildings . . .	8·2	7·9	7·3	7·3	7·3	7·6
Economy as a whole . .	100·0	100·0	100·0	100·0	100·0	100·0
(a) Equipment . .	100·0	100·0	100·0	100·0	100·0	100·0
(b) Buildings . . .	100·0	100·0	100·0	100·0	100·0	100·0
Percentage of net value by different sectors of the economy						
Agriculture . . .	10·1	7·7	6·4	6·3	6·0	6·1
(a) Equipment . .	11·2	7·4	9·4	6·1	5·7	8·6
(b) Buildings . . .	9·9	7·4	5·4	6·4	6·1	5·1
Manufacturing . . .	9·3	13·2	10·9	15·1	16·2	18·3
(a) Equipment . .	31·4	32·4	29·9	43·1	42·5	41·9
(b) Buildings . . .	3·8	5·1	4·9	6·3	7·2	8·2
Electricity, gas and water supply . . .	1·5	2·9	3·8	3·2	3·7	4·7
(a) Equipment . .	3·7	9·0	10·8	8·8	9·7	11·3
(b) Buildings . . .	0·9	1·6	1·5	1·4	1·6	1·9
Transport . . .	18·2	18·9	18·2	17·9	17·9	15·8
(a) Equipment . .	37·2	31·0	26·4	20·6	21·7	19·1
(b) Buildings . . .	13·4	14·0	15·6	17·0	16·6	14·4
Housing	42·0	32·4	36·8	35·5	34·1	32·7
(a) Equipment . .	—	—	—	—	—	—
(b) Buildings . . .	52·5	50·8	48·5	46·7	45·7	46·6
Public administration .	12·6	16·5	16·7	14·6	14·3	13·9
(a) Equipment . .	9·3	9·7	11·1	9·8	8·7	8·2
(b) Buildings . . .	13·4	15·0	18·5	16·1	16·3	16·3
Other sectors of economy .	6·3	8·4	7·2	7·4	7·8	8·5
(a) Equipment .. .	7·2	10·5	12·4	11·6	11·7	10·9
(b) Buildings . . .	6·1	6·1	5·6	6·1	6·5	7·5
Economy as a whole . .	100·0	100·0	100·0	100·0	100·0	100·0
(a) Equipment . .	100·0	100·0	100·0	100·0	100·0	100·0
(b) Buildings . . .	100·0	100·0	100·0	100·0	100·0	100·0

account. Its value may amount to around 100 milliards DM at 1950 prices – which would have to be included in total national wealth, but not in the reproducible part of this wealth.

The total reproducible wealth of the Federal Republic is thus built up from the components shown in the table on p. 156. Apart from fixed capital assets the figures for these components are only rough estimates. Of the wealth of private households two-thirds may be durables and one-third semi-durables.

7

THE NATIONAL WEALTH OF YUGOSLAVIA AT THE END OF 1953

By Ivo Vinski

THE present paper contains a direct estimate of all physical assets located in the present territory of Yugoslavia, together with an estimate of net foreign assets, the figures relating to 31 December 1953. The main text of the paper contains a general review of the estimates. The estimates themselves are presented, in summary and in detail, in Appendix I. A survey of sources and methods, followed by notes on each item, appears in Appendix II.

I. HISTORICAL REVIEW

The first estimates of national wealth go back to the period prior to World War I. In 1896 Mulhall, in a survey of national-wealth data, estimated the total wealth of the Kingdom of Serbia at £211 million or £92 per head. During World War I a group of Serbian refugee economists prepared a study of the national income and wealth of Serbia (including Macedonia) at the period between the end of the Balkan War and the outbreak of World War I,[1] arriving at a total figure of national wealth of 11·8 billions of gold dinars (£470 million or £97 per head). These estimates were prepared in connection with the ascertainment of Serbia's war damages. In 1910–12 Avramović prepared a sample survey of 835 peasant farms in Serbia, containing also data regarding capital.[2] For the regions of Yugoslavia which until 1918 formed part of Hungary (within the Austro-Hungarian Empire) estimates by Fellner are available. From his study of national wealth of Austria and Hungary in 1910–12, he apportioned wealth between Hungary (Trianon borders) and the Succession states.[3] On the basis of Fellner's estimates the share of the Yugoslav regions (i.e. the provinces Vojvodina, Croatia, and Slavonia and the district of Rijeka) amounted in the years 1910–12 to 8 billion gold crowns (£340 million or £84 per head).

---

[1] Comité Central Serbe, *La Serbie economique 1914–1918*, Genève, 1918.
[2] Avramović, *Our Peasant Farming* (Naše seljaćko gazdinstvo), Beograd, 1928.
[3] Fellner, 'Die Verteilung des Volksvermögens und Volkseinkommens der Länder der Ungarischen Heiligen Krone zwischen dem heutigen Ungarn und den Successionsstaaten', *Metron*, Vol. III, No. 2, Ferrara, 1923.

For the territory of the newly created state of Yugoslavia, Gini prepared early in the 1920s an estimate of national wealth before World War I, arriving at a total of 30–35 billions of francs (£1,200–£1,400 million or £95–£105 per head).[1] In the late 1920s the Dresdner Bank published estimates of the national wealth of the territory of Yugoslavia in 1913/14 amounting to 27–28 billion marks (£1,325–£1,365 million or £93–£108 per head). As the source of these figures, the Dresdner Bank quotes Gini's estimates. For 1926, the Dresdner Bank figure for Yugoslavia's national wealth is as high as 38 billion marks (£1,860 million or £142 per head), quoting estimates prepared by Gourjou and Parkinson.[2] For the inter-war period, some data concerning fixed capital on farms are published in a sample survey by Dublić [3] and by Predavic [4] based on peasant farm-accounting records. In 1940 a survey of the composition of assets on sixty farms in Croatia was prepared; the results of this sample survey are published by Petrićević.[5] For fixed capital in railroad transport in 1926 an estimate was published by Milenković.[6] For fixed capital in manufacturing and electricity at the end of 1938 the Ministry of Industry and Commerce published an estimate, summarized from questionnaires submitted to nearly all establishments in this branch; but the results obtained are very unreliable, because inadequate attention was given to the concept of money value of capital.[7] New investment in mining is reported annually from 1931 until 1938 by the mining authorities.[8] For the territory of Croatia the present author published an estimate of new investment in the inter-war period.[9]

In the post-war period a comprehensive census of fixed capital was organized by the Central Planning Office in 1953, covering all the socialized sectors of the economy. In 1955 a similar census took place of health and social security institutions and of a

---

[1] Prepared in a report to the League of Nations (in the press). I am indebted to Professor Gini for his kindness in letting me have a copy of his manuscript.
[2] *Die wirtschaftlichen Kräfte der Welt*, Dresdner Bank, Berlin, 1930.
[3] Dubić, *A Contribution to the Study of Peasant Farming* (Prilog istraživanju seljaćkog gospodarstva), Križevci, 1933.
[4] Predavec, *The Village and the Peasants* (Selo i seljaci), Zagreb, 1934.
[5] Petrićević, *Untersuchungen über die Betriebsformen der Bauernbetriebe Kroatiens*, Aarau, Switzerland, 1942.
[6] Milenković, *The New Rail–Road Net* (Nova željeznička Mreža), Beograd 1926.
[7] Statistics of manufacturing, prepared by the Ministry of Industry and Commerce, Beograd, 1941.
[8] Published in current yearbooks of the Ministry of Forestry and Mines.
[9] *Investment in Croatia in the Inter-war Period*, Beograd, 1955.

considerable range of public utility institutions and enterprises. These censuses did not cover roads, streets, bridges, quays, schools, residential buildings, timber stands, the private sector of agriculture, etc. However, Dr. Vladimir Stipetić recently prepared a comprehensive estimate for Yugoslav agriculture in 1955 covering all physical assets (except dwellings, stocks on farms, and land) reckoned at undepreciated replacement value (livestock, of course, is evaluated by Dr. Stipetić at market prices received by farmers).[1] In addition, we had the opportunity of using unpublished data on fixed capital in agriculture, originating from a sample survey organized in 1953 for Croatia and in 1954 for Serbia.[2]

II. THE PRICE-LEVEL PROBLEM

The determination of an appropriate price level for the valuation of capital goods is a difficult problem in countries where a significant proportion of the stock of machinery, equipment, and parts is of foreign origin. A similar problem arises in countries whose heavy construction and other industries supplying capital goods do not enjoy the accumulated experience and skill of the older industrialized countries and have high relative production costs. In both cases it seems reasonable to apply foreign prices, with an appropriate conversion rate, to the evaluation of machinery and equipment.

In our wealth estimates for Yugoslavia all buildings and structures are valued at internal building prices prevailing in 1951/53. On the other hand, all machinery, equipment, and parts have been valued on the basis of Western European prices prevailing in 1952/53, applying a unified conversion rate of 540 dinars for 1 U.S. dollar. It is an awkward problem to reconcile such a major component as machinery and equipment, valued at Western European prices, with other wealth components valued at internal prices. In fact, the question is whether the conversion rate is appropriate or not. In the case of our estimate for Yugoslavia, however, we may verify the adequacy of this procedure as follows: building prices in Yugoslavia in 1953

[1] Stipetić, *Fixed Capital in the Yugoslav Agriculture* (in the press). Dr. Stipetić has very kindly permitted me to use estimates from his manuscript.
[2] I am indebted to the director of the Serbian Statistical Office D. Bjelogrlić and to Ing. Dorćić of the Institute of Agricultural Economics in Zagreb for permission to use these unpublished data. I also wish to thank Professor Bićanić for supplying the relevant information on prices of farm land.

were on average about 22 times 1938 prices for the same type of construction. Western European prices for machinery, vehicles, and other equipment ranged in 1952/53 between 1·8 and 2·4 times the 1938 level. The exchange rate for 1 U.S. dollar for the acquisition of foreign machinery and equipment amounted in 1938 to 55 dinars for 1 U.S. dollar. Taking into account a rise in prices on the Western European markets for machinery and equipment of 2·2 times on average, we arrive at the result that the purchasing power of 55 dinars devoted in 1938 to foreign equipment and machinery equals 1,188 dinars in 1953 (540 × 2·2 = 1,188). From this purchasing-power ratio there results an increase of 22 times during the period in question for machinery and equipment, i.e. just the same increase as the above-mentioned increase of internal building prices in the same period.

It must be emphasized that the ratio between prices of machinery and equipment actually produced in Yugoslavia and the corresponding Western European prices would yield a considerably higher conversion rate for 1953 than the above-mentioned rate of 540 dinars for 1 U.S. dollar. In subsequent years, however, prices of Yugoslav machinery and equipment decreased steadily, and further decreases in prices may be expected in the future, owing to an increase in productivity in these branches of Yugoslav industry.

In this national wealth estimate Western European prices for all machinery and equipment were applied, regardless of their origin. The valuation of these assets on the basis of the extraordinarily high production costs which prevailed in Yugoslavia in 1953 would not result in meaningful estimates of wealth. In addition, it must be borne in mind that for a certain volume of machinery and equipment included in the 1953 inventory, no corresponding production existed in Yugoslavia, and consequently no prices of home production could be established.

By this evaluation procedure a reasonable relation between machinery and equipment and buildings has been established. It must be emphasized, however, that we have used a market-price valuation for some major wealth components – land, live-stock, and growing stock in forests – which distorts this arrangement. In fact, substantial changes have taken place in the relation between prices of major wealth components in 1953 as compared with 1938. As mentioned above, building prices rose by about 22 times in the period under consideration, and about the

M

same increase was imputed in the evaluation of machinery and equipment. The rise in the price level for agricultural land in the same period amounts on average to only 6·5 times, for urban land as little as 4·5 times, for growing stock (stumpage prices) about 15–16 times, for livestock (market prices for live weight received by farmers) about 15–16 times. Some part of these differences may be attributed to the difference in the valuation basis. For buildings and structures, machinery and equipment a market-price valuation could not be conveniently applied, because factories, mines, and other assets of the socialized sector are not subject to sale.

III. THE CAPITAL–INCOME RATIO

Since comprehensive national wealth studies before 1953 are lacking, we are not in a position to ascertain the capital–income ratio for Yugoslavia in earlier periods.

In 1953 the national income of Yugoslavia at market prices, estimated in accordance with the western income concept, by the present author was 1,096 billion dinars.[1] If our depreciated national wealth estimate of 8,402 billion dinars at the end of 1953 as shown in Appendix I of this paper is applied to the above estimate of national income, we arrive at a ratio of 7·6. For reproducible tangible assets only (i.e. omitting land and net foreign assets) the ratio declines to 5·8.

According to recent researches of Mr. Colin Clark, the capital–income ratio in most countries is in the range of 2·5–4·0.[2] For these international comparisons Mr. Clark conceived capital as reproducible wealth for purposes of production (including business inventories but excluding consumers' stocks) and computed the national income at market prices. In order to compare the Yugoslav ratio with these estimates we excluded consumers' durables and non-durables, standing timber, and some minor items from the Yugoslav capital figure and arrived at a ratio of 4·5 for 1953.

One of the reasons for this relatively high ratio might be the considerable volume of uncompleted projects, amounting to roughly 5 per cent of total capital, in Yugoslavia at the end of

[1] *National Expenditure of Yugoslavia 1953–1954* (Upotreba narodnog dohotka Jugoslavije 1953–1954), Ekonomski pregled, Zagreb, No. 5/1956, English summary, p. 367.

[2] C. Clark, *The Conditions of Economic Progress*, 3rd edn., London, 1957, pp. 572–580.

1953. Besides, a proportion of these large-scale projects completed in recent years had not yielded a full income in 1953, mainly because of inadequate skill of the labour force and limited experience in management as compared with the older industrialized countries. A similarly high ratio appears to have prevailed in Germany and France in the period prior to World War I, as can be seen from the historical data prepared by Helfferich for Germany [1] and Colson for France.[2]

Available data in this field seem to indicate the following conclusions about the order of magnitude of the capital–income ratio in various stages of economic growth:

(1) In under-developed countries this ratio seems to be low, probably under 2·5, because labour is the main factor of production in these countries. In India, which forms a substantial part of the under-developed world, the ratio amounted to 1·8 in 1950, as is shown by the estimates of Mukherjee and Sastry (Chapter 13 of the present volume).

(2) In countries undergoing the process of accelerated basic industrialization the ratio may rise to over 4·0. This was the case in Germany and France over half a century ago, and was characteristic of Yugoslavia in 1953.

(3) In what are now advanced countries the ratio generally ranges between 2·5 and 3·5, the decline being caused by a more economical utilization of capital, increase of productivity, inventions, etc.

The marked constancy of the capital–income ratio in the United States from 1897 until 1929, as shown in Dr. Goldsmith's study,[3] seems, however, to disprove the above statement. Further research in this field might indicate that this phenomenon is attributable to specific conditions of economic growth in the United States, or it might indicate the need for a re-examination of the above statement.

IV. THE RATE OF GROWTH OF CAPITAL

Yugoslavia is a country with a relatively high investment level in the post-war period; the share of net investment in net

[1] K. Helfferich, *Deutschlands Volkswohlstand, 1888–1913*, Berlin, 1914.

[2] The historical data prepared by Colson for France are compared with contemporary estimates in the study by Divisia, Roy Dupin, *A la Recherche du Franc Perdu*, Vol. 3. *Fortune de la France*, Paris, 1957.

[3] R. Goldsmith, 'The Growth of Reproducible, Wealth of the United States of America from 1805 to 1950', *Income and Wealth Series II*, Cambridge, 1952.

national product in 1953 amounted to nearly 21 per cent. In this connection it may be of interest to ascertain the rate of growth of real capital.

According to the present author's study mentioned above (p. 164, footnote 1), gross investment in Yugoslavia amounted to 412·1 billion dinars in 1953. Depreciation of fixed capital in the various branches of industry amounted to 140·1 billion dinars. This depreciation total does not cover non-productive assets such as dwellings, wells, schools, public buildings, etc., for which we made a special estimate of imputed depreciation totalling 62 billion dinars. We thus arrive at total depreciation of 202 billion dinars. Subtracting this figure from the gross investment total of 412 billion dinars, we derive a net investment figure of 210 billion dinars in 1953.

Applying this net investment figure to the total of reproducible tangible assets (excluding consumers' durables and non-durables), amounting to 5,454 billion dinars at the beginning of 1953, we arrive at a net rate of growth of 3·9 per cent in 1953. In the light of the available information it might reasonably be assumed that the rate of growth of reproducible tangible wealth in 1954 did not differ substantially from the 3·9 per cent rate of growth achieved in 1953.

V. MAJOR COMPONENTS OF NATIONAL WEALTH

In the summary table, presented in Appendix I, national wealth is classified by industrial use of capital goods. The main item is land, comprising nearly one-quarter of total physical assets, notwithstanding the relatively low market prices for land.[1] Dwellings rank as the next item in our summary table, amounting to 15·1 per cent of total physical assets. Transport, agriculture, and manufacturing (including mining and electricity) rank nearly equal (excluding uncompleted projects) each branch comprises about one ninth of total physical assets.

The total of physical assets may be broken down in various ways. On the basis of our detailed breakdown of national wealth, presented in Appendix I, we have attempted to re-classify total physical assets from the point of view of their location in major economic areas.

[1] In relation to building prices, urban land prices are about 5 times lower in 1953 as compared with the 1938 level; prices of farm land are nearly 3 times lower in relation to crop prices.

TABLE I
Physical Assets by Type of Location

Area	Billion dinars	Percentage
TOTAL PHYSICAL ASSETS . . .	8,444	100·0
FARM AREA	3,890	46·1
Agricultural land 1,809		
Means of production . . . 915		
Rural dwellings, wells, and cisterns . 708		
Handicrafts and cottage industries . 13		
Commerce 47		
Education, health, and administration . 26		
Consumers' stocks 372		
FOREST AREA	813	9·6
Forest land 147		
Timber stands 606		
Other 60		
URBAN AND INDUSTRIAL AREA .	2,778	32·9
Urban land 87		
Residential buildings 591		
Public utilities 103		
Education, health, and administration . 251		
Manufacturing, mining, and construction 1,171		
Commerce 182		
Handicrafts 36		
Consumers' stocks 357		
REMAINDER		
(Transport and communication) [1] .	963	11·4

TABLE II
Physical Assets by Type of Ownership

Branch	Collective People's Ownership	Private Ownership
	Billion dinars	Billion dinars
TOTAL	4,056	4,388
Manufacturing and mining, construction, transport, and commerce . . .	2,366	3 [2]
Handicrafts and cottage industries . .	28	22
Dwellings and public utilities . .	352	1,132
Education, health, and government . .	270	6 [3]
Agriculture, including land . . .	359	2,365
Forestry and logging, including land . .	681	131
Consumers' stocks	—	729

[1] Transport in cities is excluded.
[2] Refers mainly to transport and commerce.
[3] Refers mainly to privately owned buildings actually used for public education.

The residual item of 963 billion dinars represents the transport and communication network, including rolling stock, etc., which could not be conveniently apportioned.

Finally, we present a breakdown of total physical assets by type of ownership (Table II).

Collective people's ownership, embracing roughly one-half of total physical assets, consists of public assets, such as roads, sea and river quays, public buildings, etc., and assets under 'social self-administration', such as factories, mines, etc., controlled by workers' councils. Assets of co-operative ownership are classified under collective people's ownership.

VI. AN INTERNATIONAL COMPARISON

In this section we present an attempt at a comparison of national wealth components among three countries at different levels of economic growth.

TABLE III
Percentage Composition of National Wealth Components

Branch	Nether-lands [1] 1949 (%)	Yugo-slavia 1953 (%)	India [2] 1950 (%)
Agriculture (including forestry and fishing)	19·9	48·4	63·1
Manufacturing, mining and construction	22·4	17·5	5·7
Handicrafts (including cottage industries)	0·2	0·8	2·2
Commerce	9·0	3·7	5·2
Transportation (including communication)	13·1	8·0	7·2
Dwellings	34·7	20·5	15·8
Other	0·7	1·1	0·8
TOTAL	100·0	100·0	100·0

[1] *National Accounts of the Netherlands* 1948–1949 prepared by the Division of Research and Co-ordination of the Netherlands Central Bureau of Statistics (The Hague, 1952).

[2] M. Mukherjee and N. S. R. Sastry, *An Estimate of the Tangible Wealth of India.* Ch. 13. p. 365 below.

In the table below we show the percentage composition of national wealth components for the economically advanced Netherlands, for under-developed India and for Yugoslavia, the latter ranking near the border-line between economically advanced and under-developed countries.

To make the above estimates comparable we excluded from the Indian and Yugoslav estimates public assets, such as schools, hospitals, roads, canals, etc., since these assets are not included in the Dutch estimate. From the Yugoslav estimate we also excluded consumers' durables and non-durables, because these assets are not covered by the Indian and Dutch estimates. Land is not shown separately, because it was apportioned among the respective branches.

The comparisons given above should be regarded as provisional, in particular because the Central Bureau of Statistics of the Netherlands is engaged in preparing a new wealth estimate using a revised approach for various items; the revised Dutch data were not available when this paper was completed.

APPENDIX I

NATIONAL WEALTH OF YUGOSLAVIA
AT THE END OF 1953

TABLE IV
Summary Table
Billions of dinars (1953 prices)

	Fixed Capital Replacement Value		Stocks	Uncompleted Projects	TOTAL	
	Undepreciated	Depreciated			Undepreciated	Depreciated
(1) Manufacturing, mining, and electricity	1,061	652	261	199	1,521	1,112
(2) Agriculture	1,107	714	195	6	1,308	915
(3) Forestry	688	656	8	1	697	665
(4) Transport	1,637	933	14	22	1,673	969
(5) Construction	57	35	24	1	82	60
(6) Commerce	100	62	166	1	267	229
(7) Handicrafts	85	34	16	0	101	50
(8) Dwellings	2,490	1,263	—	10	2,500	1,273
(9) Public utilities	207	113	—	2	209	115
(10) Health	120	74	—	5	125	79
(11) Education	244	128	—	29	273	157
(12) Government	72	38	—	2	74	40
(13) Consumers' stocks	—	—	729	—	729	729
TOTAL CAPITAL	7,868	4,702	1,413	278	9,559	6,393
(14) Land	—	—	—	—	2,051	2,051
TOTAL PHYSICAL ASSETS	—	—	—	—	11,610	8,444
(15) Net foreign assets	—	—	—	—	−42	−42
NATIONAL WEALTH	—	—	—	—	11,568	8,402

TABLE V
National Wealth by Industry and Type of Asset
Billions of dinars (1953 prices)

Branch	National Wealth	
	Undepre- ciated	Depre- ciated
(1) *Manufacturing, mining, and electricity.*	**1,521**	**1,112**
(1-a) Fixed capital	**1,061**	**652**
Electricity	188	121
Mining and metallurgy	236	157
Manufacturing	637	374
(1-b) Stocks	**261**	**261**
(1-c) Uncompleted projects	**199**	**199**
Electricity	59	59
Mining and metallurgy	87	87
Manufacturing	53	53
(2) *Agriculture and fishing*	**1,308**	**915**
(2-a) Livestock	**223**	**223**
Cattle	123	123
Horses	41	41
Sheep and goats	24	24
Pigs	22	22
Other	13	13
(2-b) Non-residential structures	**425**	**231**
Stables	334	190
Other	91	41
(2-c) Home processing of farm products	86	44
(2-d) Transportation equipment, machinery, and tools	**122**	**60**
Farm cars and harness	63	30
Tractors	15	8
Ploughs	8	4
Threshers, grain drills and other machinery for crops	18	9
Cutters and others implements for animal husbandry	4	2
Sprayers and other implements for vineyards and fruit trees	2	1
Tools	12	6
(2-e) Perennial plants	**147**	**66**
Orchards	51	33
Vineyards	95	33
Hopfields	1	0
(2-f) Land improvements	**144**	**137**
Flood control and improvement of river beds	87	87
Drainage	37	33
Irrigation	20	17
(2-g) Veterinary stations	4	2
(2-h) Stocks on farms	**138**	**138**
Cereals (stored)	48	48
Wine and brandy (stored)	25	25
Other farm products (stored)	52	52
Sown seeds	13	13
(2-i) Uncompleted projects	**6**	**6**
(2-j) Fishing	**13**	**8**
Vessels and nets for sea fishery	8	4
Fish ponds and inland-water fishery	5	4

TABLE V—continued.

National Wealth by Industry and Type of Asset
Billions of dinars (1953 prices)

Branch	National Wealth	
	Undepre-ciated	Depre-ciated
(3) *Forestry and logging*	**697**	**665**
(3-a) Timber stands	**606**	**606**
Coniferous trees	228	228
Oak-trees	101	101
Beech-trees	222	222
Other hardwood broad-leaved trees .	49	49
Softwood broad-leaved trees .	6	6
(3-b) Timber stocks at forest depots . . .	8	8
(3-c) Communication lines . . .	52	32
(3-d) Transportation equipment . .	10	5
(3-e) Foresters' and rangers' houses and other buildings	7	4
(3-f) Flood-control equipment . .	9	7
(3-g) Hunting guns and other equipment .	4	2
(3-h) Uncompleted projects . . .	1	1
(4) *Transportation and communication* . . .	**1,673**	**969**
(4-a) Railroad transportation . .	**762**	**374**
Rolling stock	226	97
Railway lines, bridges, tunnels, stations, etc.	536	277
(4-b) Maritime transport	**106**	**77**
Merchant marine	53	29
Quays and lighthouses . .	45	44
Warehouses, cranes, tractors, etc. .	8	4
(4-c) Inland-water transport . . .	28	17
(4-d) Road transport	**702**	**442**
Roads	625	389
Bridges	46	39
Rolling stock of public transport, including tram lines	26	12
Trucks and carts of private forwarding agents	5	2
(4-e) Air transport	2	1
(4-f) Postal, telephone and telegraph communication	37	22
(4-g) Stocks	14	14
(4-h) Uncompleted projects . . .	**22**	**22**
Railway lines	11	11
Roads	4	4
Vessels for merchant marine . .	5	5
Other	2	2
(5) *Construction*	**82**	**60**
(5-a) Fixed capital	57	35
(5-b) Stocks	24	24
(5-c) Uncompleted projects . .	1	1
(6) *Commerce and Hotels*	**267**	**229**
(6-a) Fixed Capital	**100**	**62**
Wholesale and retail trade . .	63	41
Hotels, restaurants, etc. . .	37	21
(6-b) Stocks	**166**	**166**
Wholesale trade . . .	90	90
Retail trade	73	73
Hotels, restaurants, etc. . .	3	3
(6-c) Uncompleted projects . .	1	1

TABLE V—*continued*.

National Wealth by Industry and Type of Asset
Billions of dinars at 1953 prices

Branch	National Wealth	
	Undepre-ciated	Depre-ciated
(7) *Handicrafts and Cottage Industries*	**101**	**50**
(7-a) Handicrafts	**47**	**24**
Establishments in the socialised sector	24	13
Small-scale handicrafts (private sector)	23	11
(7-b) Cottage industries other than home food processing	**38**	**10**
Looms, spindles, and distaffs	16	4
Water mills	18	4
Various small-scale industries of farm co-operatives	4	2
(7-c) Stocks	**16**	**16**
Handicraft establishments (socialized sector)	11	11
Handicrafts of the private sector	5	5
(8) *Residential Buildings*	**2,500**	**1,273**
(8-a) Rural dwellings	**1,218**	**682**
Brick-walled houses	392	306
Stone-walled houses	272	158
Wooden-walled houses	168	75
Adobe, wicker and daub walled, etc., houses	386	143
(8-b) Urban residential buildings	**1,238**	**557**
Luxurious construction	97	43
Good-quality construction	666	295
Poor-quality construction	341	150
Suburban dwellings of very poor quality	134	69
(8-c) Dwellings at factories and mines outside urban areas	34	24
(8-d) Uncompleted projects	10	10
(9) *Public utilities*	**209**	**115**
(9-a) Waterworks, sewage, market-halls, slaughter-houses, gas-pipes (excluding electricity)	66	40
(9-b) Streets and squares in urban areas	82	46
(9-c) Green areas in towns and outskirts	5	4
(9-d) Wells in urban and rural areas	34	14
(9-e) Cisterns private and public in rural and urban areas	20	9
(9-f) Uncompleted projects	2	2
(10) *Health and Social Security*	**125**	**79**
(10-a) Public Health institutions	**95**	**60**
Hospitals and clinics	65	41
Out-patient polyclinics	14	8
Natural health resorts	6	3
Institutes for medicine and hygiene	6	5
Pharmacies	1	1
Other	3	2
(10-b) Physicians' private surgeries	2	1
(10-c) Public Social security institutions	23	13
(10-d) Uncompleted projects	5	5
(11) *Education, research, and art*	**273**	**157**
(11-a) Elementary and eight-year schools	103	35
(11-b) Secondary and vocational schools	59	33
(11-c) Universities and colleges (excluding clinics and institutes of the Faculties of Medicine)	17	12

TABLE V—*continued.*

National Wealth by Industry and Type of Asset
Billions of dinars (1953 prices)

Branch	National Wealth Undepreciated	National Wealth Depreciated
(11) *Education, research, and art—continued*		
(11-d) Institutes, museums, and libraries	13	9
(11-e) Theatres, cinemas, cultural centres, etc.	11	7
(11-f) Social and political organizations	4	2
(11-g) Stadiums, athletic and other fields, mountain hostels, gymnasia, paddling, and other sports	19	13
(11-h) Rural co-operative cultural centres	18	17
(11-i) Uncompleted projects	29	29
(12) *Public Administration*	74	40
(12-a) Central and local government buildings	50	25
(12-b) Equipment of central and local government	13	7
(12-c) Building and equipment of banks and insurance institutions	9	6
(12-d) Uncompleted projects	2	2

Branch	National Wealth
(13) *Consumer durables and non-durables*	**729**
(13-a) Household furniture and appliances	**417**
Agricultural households	218
Non-agricultural households	199
(13-b) Clothing and footwear	**285**
Agricultural population	142
Non-agricultural population	143
(13-c) Fuel	**10**
Agricultural households	7
Non-agricultural households	3
(13-d) Food in non-agricultural households	5
(13-e) Passenger vehicles	**12**
Passenger cars	1
Motor cycles and bicycles	11
(14) *Land*	**2,051**
(14-a) Agricultural land	**1,809**
Arable land and gardens	1,212
Land under orchards	67
Land under vineyards	41
Meadows	299
Pastures	189
Land under fish-ponds	1
(14-b) Forest land	**147**
Land under forests	120
Agricultural enclaves in forest areas	27
(14-c) Urban and other land	**95**
Land under residential buildings	60
Other	35
(15) *Net foreign Assets*	**−42**
(15-a) Liabilities for foreign credits, loans, and for nationalized assets	−154
(15-b) Monetary gold and claims against foreign countries for reparations and other indemnities	+112

APPENDIX II

METHODS AND SOURCES

(1) *General approach*

In the tables of Appendix I the results of our national wealth estimates are presented, based on an inventory concept. We attempted to
estimate national wealth by direct measurement of physical assets on
the basis of census data, sampling surveys, or expert estimates. For
wealth measurement in Yugoslavia this method is more appropriate
than any indirect methods based on income-tax statistics or on
death-duty statistics, as roughly one-half of the total wealth of Yugoslavia is owned privately, the other half representing public or
socialized assets.

In our wealth estimate, inventory data are for 31 December 1953,
though some minor differences in date have been unavoidable. For
the major part of the socialized sector of the economy – manufacturing and mining, transportation and communication, commerce
and hotels, etc. – fixed capital census data refer to 31 December 1952
(all data of the post-war fixed-capital censuses are unpublished). On
the other hand, fixed-capital census data for health, social security,
and the major part of public-utility institutions or enterprises refer
to 31 December 1954. In order to adjust all these fixed-capital estimates to the end-of-1953 basis we added or subtracted from depreciated fixed-capital census figures, net investments in the prior or
subsequent year. For undepreciated fixed capital we added or subtracted from census figures new investments in tangible fixed capital
in the prior or subsequent year. New investment in fixed capital is
conceived in this context as gross investment in tangible reproducible
assets (excluding repairs and maintenance) in a given period minus
the total of undepreciated fixed capital actually dismantled or
scrapped during the period in question. In both specified procedures there might be an appreciable margin of error if carried
on for longer periods. For the purpose of our estimates, however,
the period involved in the census adjustment does not exceed
two years and the margin of error might be within reasonable
limits.

The estimate of national wealth covers, in principle at least, all
tangible assets situated on the present-day territory of Yugoslavia at
the end of 1953. We included the two districts Kopar and Buje which
in fact in 1953 still formed part of the Free State of Trieste under the
administration of the Yugoslav Army, but were incorporated in
Yugoslavia after the conclusion of an agreement in October 1954

between the United Kingdom, the United States, Yugoslavia, and Italy.

Of non-reproducible assets, we included only land. Other non-reproducible assets, such as subsoil stocks of minerals, are omitted owing to the difficulties of estimating them satisfactorily (underground installations, however, are included in our fixed capital estimates for mining). All kinds of intangibles, such as patents, goodwill, etc., are omitted from our wealth estimates. Historical monuments, churches, and works of art are not included owing to the difficulties of valuation.

Fixed capital is computed at both undepreciated and depreciated replacement value, on the basis of 1953 prices. Depreciation is conceived as an economic concept rather than an accounting concept. In practice, the following procedure was adopted for the socialized sector of the economy: the replacement value of the assets in question was estimated by experts on the basis of unified price lists, based in the case of buildings and structures on internal building costs prevailing in 1952/53; for machinery and equipment, Western European prices were applied on the basis of an unified conversion rate of 540 dinars for 1 U.S. dollar. The information on prices for machinery and equipment was based mainly on invoices and price lists from Western European manufacturers. At the same time, experts estimated the effective life still to be expected from the assets in question and applied it to the total effective life of this type of asset, as listed in a special manual. In this way depreciation for fixed capital was derived.

The above-mentioned price lists and tables of the effective life period for nearly all types of capital goods were prepared by special expert groups at the Yugoslav Central Planning Office for purposes of the 1953 and subsequent fixed-capital censuses.

This procedure of valuation was applied to the 1953/54 fixed-capital censuses, covering the socialised sector of the economy. Of public assets, only health and social-security institutions were covered by these censuses; all others – such as roads, quays, schools, public buildings, etc. – were excluded. The 1953/54 censuses covered about 31 per cent of the total of Yugoslavia's physical assets (or nearly two-thirds of total physical assets in collective people's ownership).

For the private sector of the economy, public assets other than health and social security institutions, consumers' stocks, and other assets not covered by the official censuses, various methods of estimation were used, as indicated in the comments on the corresponding items of this Appendix. These methods generally follow the methods of the official censuses, though in many cases a more simplified procedure was necessarily applied, based mainly on statistics of physical units. The valuation of these physical units was based in most cases on the above-mentioned unified price lists and tables of effective life period, as applied to the official 1953/54 fixed-capital censuses, in order to achieve consistency between the wealth estimates of the socialized sector of the economy and the estimates of the private sector, public assets, etc.

All items of fixed capital in our national-wealth estimate are valued at both undepreciated and depreciated replacement value, with the exception of livestock (horses, cattle, asses, and mules) and timber stands, which are estimated at average market prices prevailing in 1953.

All items of business stocks, except stocks on farms, are valued at cost prices, which are not likely to differ substantially from replacement value. Stocks on farms are valued at average ex-farm prices in 1953. Smaller species of livestock (sheep and goats, pigs, poultry, and beehives) are treated as farm business stocks and are included in column 'Stocks' in the summary table in Appendix I. Consumers' stocks of durables and semi-durables are valued at market prices for second-hand goods.

Uncompleted projects consist of uncompleted structures and machinery equipment and parts not yet installed but physically located at the place of their instalment. Machinery and equipment located at the inventory date at producers' factories are included in business inventories, with the exception of ships under construction, which have been treated as uncompleted projects in the branch of transport, although they were physically located in shipbuilding yards at the inventory date. Uncompleted projects are valued at 1953 replacement value, not taking into account any depreciation.

Land was valued at average market prices prevailing in 1953 for the various categories of agricultural land, urban land and land under forests.

(2) *Manufacturing, mining, and electricity*

(1-a) *Fixed capital.* This item is based, in general, on census data, though it was necessary to carry out a number of adjustments. Census data refer to 31 December 1952 and embrace a considerable part of the logging industries as well as dwellings, restaurants, out-patient and social security institutions, etc. for the accommodation of employees. In the field of electricity, the census of fixed capital did not cover a substantial part of the network, especially in rural areas. We present a summary of these adjustments below:

	Replacement value in billions of dinars at 1953 prices	
	Undepre-ciated	Depre-ciated
Fixed Capital at 31 December 1952 (not adjusted).	1,032	631
Adjustments:		
Less fixed capital engaged in logging . .	−14	− 6
Less land	− 7	− 7
Less dwellings, restaurants, etc. . .	−89	−66
Plus additions to electricity network not covered by census	+42	+28
Fixed capital at 31 December 1952 (adjusted) .	964	580
Increment of fixed capital in 1953 . . .	97	72
Fixed capital at 31 December 1953 . . .	1,061	652

The distribution of the above totals of fixed capital at 31 December 1953 by major industrial groups is as follows:

TABLE VI
Distribution of Fixed Capital by Certain Industry Groups

Fixed Capital – Replacement Value in Billions of Dinars at 1953 Prices

Major Industrial Group	Undepreciated			Depreciated		
	Produc-tive Assets	Dwell-ings, Restaur-ants, etc.	Total	Produc-tive Assets	Dwell-ings, Restaur-ants, etc.	Total
TOTAL . .	1,061	89	1,150	652	66	718
Electricity .	188	2	190	121	2	123
Mining and metallurgy .	236	40	276	157	25	182
Manufacturing	637	47	684	374	39	413

Electricity comprises power plants and network. Mining and metallurgy comprises coal-mining and gas production, petroleum industry, quarrying, metal-mining and non-metallic-mining, ferrous and non-ferrous basic-metal industries. Manufacturing covers all other branches enumerated in the Yugoslav statistical classification for industrial production.

(1-b) Stocks include raw materials, work in progress, and finished goods held by industrial enterprises and mines at 31 December 1953. These data were derived from the balance sheet of enterprises summarized by the National Bank. Work in progress in heavy construction industries is included, provided this machinery and equipment was physically located at inventory date at the producers' factory. The only exception is uncompleted ships, which are allocated to the item 'Uncompleted projects' in the transportation branch rather than to inventories of the shipbuilding industry.

(1-c) *Uncompleted projects.* This item includes all fixed capital in new industrial enterprises. In addition, it includes uncompleted buildings and structures (including building material) as well as machinery, equipment, and parts in existing factories, mines, etc., not installed at 31 December 1953. The figure of 198·5 billion dinars represents productive assets only; uncompleted dwellings, restaurants, etc., for accommodation of employees, amounting to 16·5 billion dinars, are not included. These items result partly from the fixed-capital census and partly from our estimates made in collaboration with experts.

(3) *Agriculture and fishing*

The main source for fixed capital in agriculture is a comprehensive study of Dr. Vladimir Stipetić, *Fixed Capital in Yugoslav Agriculture* (in the press). In addition, there are two important unpublished sources: A sample survey prepared in July 1954 by the Serbian Statistical Office covering 453 agricultural households in Serbia and a comprehensive inquiry of the Institute of Agricultural Economics in Zagreb on physical assets, production costs, etc., in 253 agricultural households in Croatia, prepared early in 1953. For the socialized sector of agriculture, embracing nearly one-eighth of total fixed capital in agriculture (excluding amelioration projects and dwellings) census data on fixed capital are available.

(2-a) *Livestock.* Horses, cattle, asses, and mules are treated as fixed capital; all other species are, for practical purposes, regarded as farm stocks. The estimate for livestock is derived from the study of Dr. Stipetić, where livestock numbers at 15 January 1955 are valued at average market prices received by farmers in 1955 (price data are weighted on the basis of marketed quantities). To arrive at an estimate for 1953 we adjusted the estimates of Dr. Stipetić for changes in livestock numbers, ascertained by census data, for changes in weight, derived from slaughtering statistics, and for changes in market prices received by farmers for live weight according to price statistics prepared by the Statistical Offices.

(2-b) *Non-residential structures.* Stables refer to buildings for horses, cattle, asses, and mules. Floor space of all stables in Yugoslavia, registered at the 1951 livestock census, amounts to 44·8 million square metres. Applying a conversion coefficient of 0·82 (that is the average coefficient for all types of rural residential buildings),

N

we arrive at 54·7 million square metres of building area. Assuming that the value of stables per square metre is 40 per cent lower than for rural dwellings, we arrive at an average price of 5·754 dinars per square metre of building area (for price of rural dwellings see item 8-a) or to a total undepreciated replacement value of 314·7 billions of dinars. This total is increased by 19 billions of dinars, due to relatively better quality stables in the socialized sector of agriculture. Depreciation of stables of the private sector is estimated at 44 per cent on the basis of the above-mentioned sample surveys for Croatia and Serbia. For the socialized sector depreciation was calculated at 37 per cent in the light of the 1953 fixed-capital census. In this way we arrived at a total remaining value of 189·9 billion of dinars. The average age of stables, weighted on the basis of floor space, amounts for 1953 to twenty-six years (derived from the sample surveys of Croatia and Serbia, raised to full coverage).

Maize baskets, barns, and other structures are computed from the sample surveys of Croatia and Serbia.

(2-c) *Home processing of farm products.* This item comprises home processing of food products only (home processing of other agricultural products is included in cottage industries; see item 7-b). Undepreciated replacement value of wine cellars, casks, drying sheds, distilling installations, etc., are derived from estimates of Dr. Stipetić. Depreciation has been calculated on the basis of the sample survey for Croatia and Serbia.

(2-d) *Transport equipment, machinery, and tools.* These items have been derived from detailed estimates provided by Dr. Stipetić. His computations refer to subsidized home prices for agricultural machinery. By comparison with import prices of the same type of machinery, we arrive at an exchange rate of about 540 dinars for 1 U.S. dollar, i.e. roughly at the same price level as the basis on which machinery and equipment in manufacturing and other industrial branches has been computed in our national wealth estimates. Depreciation for the private sector is derived from the above-mentioned sample surveys. For the socialized sector data from the 1953 fixed-capital census were applied.

(2-e) *Perennial plants* exclude land, which is computed separately. Sown seeds of lucerne and clover are included in farm stocks rather than in this item. The value of orchards is conceived as the value of timber stands of fruit-trees, valued at 1953 stumpage prices, plus investment costs as seedlings, etc. Timber stands of fruit-trees, valued in the same way as timber stands in forests, amount to 23·3 billion dinars. To the market value of timber stands we added 28·1 billions of dinars for estimated investment costs and arrived at the undepreciated total of 51·4 billions of dinars. Depreciation of orchards was

calculated on the basis of the estimated age composition of fruit-
trees, applying the ascertained depreciation of the above-mentioned
investment costs.

The value of vineyards was derived from estimates of Dr. Stipetić.
Depreciation was estimated in collaboration with experts.

(2-f) *Improvements to land* were ascertained from the data of an inventory of amelioration equipment prepared in 1955/56. Depreciation was reckoned on the assumption that a 20 per cent share of fixed
capital in irrigation projects and a 15 per cent share in drainage projects is subject to depreciation (pumps, water-gates, buildings, etc.),
the remainder having an essentially permanent character provided
adequate maintenance is undertaken.

(2-g) *Veterinary stations* have been estimated on the basis of data
prepared by Dr. Stipetić.

(2-h) *Stocks on farms.* This item consists of unprocessed and pro-
cessed agricultural products stored on farms and sown seeds at the
end of 1953, valued at average ex-farm prices prevailing in 1953. We
attempted to estimate stocks on farms both by the production and by
the expenditure approach. On the basis of the first approach we subtracted from production of major crops in 1953 all waste, sales, seeds,
and food consumption on farms, for people and livestock, from June
up to the end of 1953. The remainder represents stocks of maize,
wheat, hay, etc., as presented in the table in Appendix I.

The second method consists in deriving stocks from the expenditure approach. On the basis of detailed estimates of consumption of
food produced on farms, prepared for our study 'National Expenditure of Yugoslavia 1953-1954', we ascertained the volume of food
and livestock fodder consumed on farms in the first half of 1954,
which was necessarily taken from last year's stocks. Farm products,
stored on farms at 31 December 1953 for sale in the subsequent year,
were derived from a breakdown of National Bank statistics concerning purchases by commercial enterprises from farmers in the first
half of 1954. The results obtained by the expenditure approach con-
firmed reasonably well the stocks figures derived from the production
approach.

Sown seeds at 31 December 1953 represent seeds for winter crops,
mainly wheat and barley. We have also included one-third of the
value of sown lucerne seeds and one-fifth of the sown clover seeds in
soil.

(2-i) *Uncompleted projects* refer to structures of the socialised sector
and to uncompleted land-improvement projects. For the private
sector it was assumed that the construction of structures normally
does not extend over one season. On the other hand, gradual storing
of building materials on farms over longer periods is a frequent

phenomenon. Conceptually such stocks should be included in this item, but were disregarded owing to complete lack of information.

(2-j) *Fishing.* Fixed capital in sea fishery was estimated in collaboration with experts according to data on fishing crafts and nets, published in maritime statistics. Fish-ponds, occupying an area of nearly 7,000 hectares, were valued at 700,000 dinars per hectare on an average. Of the fixed capital we assumed that 40 per cent is subject to depreciation (buildings, gates, etc.), the remainder was considered as permanent. Fixed capital in inland-water fishery refers mainly to river fishery at Apatin on the Danube, as fixed capital in fishery at the Macedonian lakes is not significant.

(4) *Forestry and Logging*

(3-a) *Timber stands.* The volume of timber stands was valued at stumpage prices in 1953, assuming immediate sale of all timber for commercial purposes. An inventory of the volume of growing stock was taken in 1947 and is reported in the current forest statistics.

The distribution by type of the growing stock was estimated in collaboration with experts; scrub-woods are not taken into account.

TABLE VII
Valuation of Timber Stands by Type of Tree

Types of Tree	Net Timber Volume (million cubic metres)	Stumpage Price (dinars)	TOTAL (billions of dinars)
Total timber stands . . .	637	952	606
Coniferous trees	177	1,292	228
Pulpwood	45	900	41
Firewood	9	100	1
Sawlogs	92	1,800	165
Other roundwood . . .	31	700	21
Oak-trees	69	1,462	101
Sawlogs	25	2,500	62
Other roundwood . . .	17	1,700	29
Tanning and fuelwood . .	27	350	10
Beech-trees	345	643	222
Firewood	198	300	59
Pulpwood	38	650	25
Sawlogs	74	1,250	93
Veneer logs	6	4,000	24
Logs for sleepers . . .	20	800	16
Pit props	9	600	5
Other hardwood broad-leaved trees .	40	1,220	49
Softwood broad-leaved trees . .	6	983	6

(3-b) *Timber stocks at forest depots* at the end of 1953 were valued on the basis of inventory statistics. In the summary table in Appendix

I this item is classified as business stocks. It refers to logging enterprises only. Wood stored on farms is not included in this item; firewood on farms is included in consumers' perishables in item (13-c), technical wood on farms is omitted because there was no information.

(3-c, d, e) *Communication lines, transport equipment, and buildings* were valued mainly from data in the study of Ing. Surić *Forestry and Timber Industry* (Jubilee edition of the Union of Engineers and Technicians, Beograd, 1955).

(3-f) *Flood-control equipment.* The source is the same as for item (2-f). Depreciation was calculated only for wooden objects, as stone and concrete objects are of permanent character. This equipment is located mainly in the Karst, i.e. in deforested areas; for this reason they are included in this branch.

(5) *Transport and communication*

(4-a, b, c) *Railroad, maritime, and inland-water transport.* All assets, except quays, lighthouses, and winter ports, are derived from the 1953 fixed capital census (for railway rolling stock, however, some minor adjustments were introduced). Quays, lighthouses, and meteorological centres for maritime transport, as well as quays and winter ports for river transport, were not included in the official fixed-capital census in 1953. We have therefore prepared special estimates concerning these assets in collaboration with experts.

TABLE VIII
Valuation of Roads and Bridges

	Undepreciated Replacement Value	Depreciated Replacement Value
	(Billions of dinars at 1953 prices)	
Bridges – Total	46	39
27,200 m. permanent bridges over 7 m. latitude	27	25
24,000 m. permanent bridges 5–7 m. latitude	17	13
29,000 m. temporary bridges over 5 m. latitude	1	0
40,000 m. bridges under 5 m. latitude .	1	0
Roads – Total	625	389
3,040 km. asphalt, stone cube, and concrete roads	91	71
49,000 km. macadam roads . . .	441	265
129,000 km. earth roads	93	53

(4-d) *Road transport.* 'Rolling stock of public transport, including tram lines' was derived from the 1953 fixed capital census. This group includes, in addition to rolling stock, garages and repair shops of public-transport establishments. Vehicles belonging to commercial, manufacturing, construction, logging, and other enterprises, as well as to public utilities, government, etc., are not included in this item (which covers about 14 per cent of passenger cars and 22 per cent of the total number of trucks). This item includes tram and trolley lines.

Roads and bridges (other than railroad bridges) were not included in the 1953 fixed capital census. We have therefore prepared estimates as summarized in Table 8.

Depreciation of roads applies to the road surface only; sub-structure is treated as permanent and not subject to depreciation. Streets and squares in urban areas are included in item (9-b), and not here.

(4-e, f) *Air transport, postal, telephone, and telegraph communication.* For all these items, fixed capital was derived from the 1953 fixed-capital census except for aerodromes, which were not covered by that census. For buildings, structures, and equipment on civilian aerodromes we prepared separate estimates.

(4-g) *Stocks* were taken from balance sheets of all enterprises in question, summarized by the National Bank.

(6) *Construction*

(5-a) *Fixed capital* was derived from the 1953 fixed capital census, adjusted for net increments of fixed capital. To this item we added the value of vessels and machinery engaged in the construction of the Syrian port Lataquie.

(5-b) *Stocks.* The same source as for item (4-g).

(7) *Commerce and hotels*

(6-a) *Fixed capital.* The same source and procedure as for item (5-a). To this item we added restaurants, etc., of industrial enterprises (see item 1-a).

(6-b) *Stocks.* The same source as item (4-g). Government stockpiles (excluding military stockpiles) are included in wholesale trade stocks.

(8) *Handicrafts and cottage industries*

(7-a) *Handicrafts.* Data for fixed capital in the socialized sector were derived from the 1953 fixed-capital census. Fixed capital for the private sector was estimated in collaboration with experts.

(7-b) *Cottage industries other than food processing.* The value of looms, spindles, and distaffs in agricultural households was estimated from a sample survey for 453 agricultural households in Serbia. In collaboration with experts we raised the samples from the various regions of Serbia to full coverage of other regions in Yugoslavia, where similar conditions prevail in this respect. Water-mills were valued according to data of the number of water-mills and mill-stones.

(7-c) *Stocks*. For the socialized sector the same source as item (4-g). For the private sector estimates were prepared in collaboration with experts.

(9) *Residential buildings*

(8-a) *Rural dwellings*. The starting-point of our estimates are figures of the floor space volume, registered in all rural settlements of Yugoslavia on 15 January 1951. In collaboration with ethnographers and rural architects, we attempted to classify dwellings in each district by type of construction, applying 1953 construction prices to each type. For the purpose of ascertaining what sort of building material was used for walls we used a sample survey covering 32,389 rural households from all over Yugoslavia, which was prepared by the Statistical Office in 1955. We present a summary of these estimates.

TABLE IX
Valuation of Rural Dwellings

Building Material	Floor Space (mill. m.^{2})	Conversion Coefficient	Building Area (mill. m.^{2})	Price per m.^{2} (dinars)	Total (billions of dinars)
YUGOSLAVIA .	104·0	0·82	126·6	9,624	1,218
Brick houses .	27·7	0·80	35·1	11,190	392
Stone houses .	19·2	0·76	25·3	10,750	272
Wooden houses .	14·9	0·88	17·0	9,878	168
Adobe and wicker houses . .	42·2	0·86	49·2	7,841	386

To ascertain depreciation we adopted the following procedure. The useful lifetime of brick houses was assumed at 70–80 years, stone houses at 100 years, wooden houses (except oak) at 50 years, and

TABLE X
Depreciation of Rural Dwellings

Building Material	Undepreciated Replacement Value at 1953 Prices (billion dinars)	Depreciation (%)	Remaining Value at 1953 Prices (billion dinars)
TOTAL STOCK .	1,218·5	44	682
Brick houses .	392·8	22	306
Stone houses .	272·0	42	158
Wooden houses .	167·9	55	75
Adobe and wicker houses . .	385·8	63	143

adobe and wicker houses at 40–60 years. The average effective life of
the total stock of rural dwellings, weighted according to building
area, amounts to 66 years. The age composition of dwellings was
derived from a sample survey for 561 dwellings in Serbia prepared by
the Serbian Statistical Office and for 371 dwellings in Croatia prepared by the Institute of Agricultural Economics and the Central
Institute for Hygiene in Croatia. From these data we derived an
average age of the total stock of rural dwellings of 29 years. Applying
the average age to the effective life-time of the various types of farm-
houses we arrived at the result that the total stock of rural dwellings
in 1953 had depreciated by 44 per cent.

(8-b) *Urban residential buildings.* This category of buildings refers
to 346 settlements in Yugoslavia with about 4·2 million inhabitants
at the end of 1953. All the other 27,624 settlements are treated as
rural settlements with about 12·8 million inhabitants. Dwellings in
these rural settlements are included above in item (8-a).

In our estimate we started from census data of urban dwellings in
1950, providing detailed information of floor space, age-composition,
and equipment (but without any information about building area or
value of dwellings). We added to the census data the completions in
1950–53 and arrived at a total floor space of 43·3 million square
metres. To this figure we added 2·5 million square metres for commercial premises, public and other offices, etc., located in residential
buildings, as we aimed at estimating total urban residential buildings
rather than apartments. Using available statistics, we attempted to
classify residential buildings in four categories and then to value each
category at 1953 prices for residential buildings. We present below a
summary of this estimate:

TABLE XI.
Valuation of Urban Dwellings

Category	Floor Space (mill. m.²)	Conversion Coefficient	Building Area [1] (mill. m.²)	Price per m.² (dinars)	Total (billions of dinars)
TOTAL	45·8	0·60	76·0	16,280	1,238
Luxurious construction	2·1	0·50	4·2	23,000	97
Good-quality construction	20·0	0·55	36·4	18,300	666
Poor-quality construction	13·9	0·60	23·2	14,700	341
Suburban dwellings of very poor quality	9·8	0·80	12·2	11,000	134

[1] Building area is defined as total area covered by buildings exclusive of uncovered porches, terraces and steps, multiplied by the number of stories.

To ascertain depreciation we classified urban residential buildings in various age groups according to available census data, assuming a given useful length of life for each category. We now present in brief the results of this estimate.

TABLE XII

Depreciated Value of Urban Dwellings

Period of Construction	Undepre-ciated Replacement Value at 1953 Prices (billion dinars)	Useful Length of Life (years)	Average Age in 1953 (years)	Depre-ciation (%)	Nominal Depre-ciated Value at 1953 Prices (billion dinars)
TOTAL STOCK	1,238	83	41	48	640
Before 1918 .	610	90	63	70	183
1919–40 . .	460	73	25	34	303
1941–44 . .	31	73	11	15	26
1945–53 . .	137	80	5	6	128

From the above table a 48 per cent depreciation results for the whole stock of residential buildings in 1953. This estimate has been carried out, however, on the assumption of adequate repairs and maintenance. As repairs and maintenance of urban residential buildings were extremely poor between 1941 and 1953, the problem of adjusting the effective length of life still to be expected arises (resulting also in an increase of depreciation). To allow for inadequate repairs and maintenance during these 13 years, we assumed that the effective length of life of the total stock of urban residential buildings was reduced by 10 per cent. This means a reduction of the useful length of life from 83 to 75 years and an increase of depreciation from 48 to 55 per cent, resulting in a decrease of the depreciated value of the total stock of urban residential buildings at the end of 1953 from 640 to 557 billion of dinars. In fact, it is extremely difficult in practice to ascertain the acceleration of depreciation due to inadequate maintenance and repairs.

(10) *Public utilities*

(9-a) *Waterworks, sewage, etc.* This item comprises all types of public utilities with the exception of the electricity network and power plants (the latter are in item 1-a). Depreciated and undepreciated values of these assets were mainly derived from the fixed-capital census as taken in 1953 and 1955. For those assets which for one reason or another were not covered by the census, like sewage, etc., we prepared estimates in collaboration with experts.

(9-b) *Streets and squares in urban areas.* For this item we prepared estimates on the assumption that the sub-structure is of permanent character, only the surface being subject to depreciation. Total area of streets and squares in the 346 urban settlements amounts to 86·3 million square metres. This total was divided into three main categories – as was our estimate for roads – and evaluated at 1953 prices.

(9-c) *Green areas.* For this item we prepared estimates in collaboration with experts.

(9-d) *Wells and cisterns in urban and rural areas.* For these assets we prepared estimates according to a comprehensive census, prepared in 1949/50 by the sanitary authorities, covering all urban and rural settlements.

(11) *Health and social security*

(10-a, c) *Public health and social security institutions.* Data were derived from the 1955 fixed-capital census, though some minor adjustments had to be introduced. Clinics and institutes of Faculties of Medicine are included.

(10-b) *Physicians' private surgeries* were estimated in collaboration with experts. Dentists' surgeries are included.

(12) *Education, research, and art*

(11-a, b) *Elementary and secondary schools.* For elementary schools, eight-year schools, secondary and vocational schools, the basis of our estimates is the 1951 census of schools (except universities and colleges). These census data provide detailed information about floor space, age composition of school buildings, building materials, etc. Depreciation was ascertained by applying the average age of school buildings – amounting to 30 years for elementary and 24 years for secondary schools – to an assumed useful life of 45 years for elementary and 55 years for secondary schools.

(11-c) *Universities and colleges.* For these schools no census data are available. Our estimate is derived from the valuation of universities and colleges in Zagreb, prepared in our study *Investments in Croatia in the Inter-war Period* (Beograd, 1955) In this estimate we assumed that Zagreb accounts for about 30 per cent of all university and college institutions in Yugoslavia. Clinics and institutes of the Faculties of Medicine are included in item (10-a) rather than in this item.

(11-d, e, f, g, h, i). Figures for research institutes, theatres, cinemas, cultural centres, athletic fields, etc., are based on our estimates prepared in collaboration with experts. Inventories of museums, monuments, and other objects of art are excluded. Rural co-operative cultural centres are valued on the basis of data, published in *Co-operative Lexicon* (*Zadružni leksikon*), p. 223.

(13) *Public administration*

(12-a, b, c) *Central and local government buildings, vehicles, and equipment.* For public buildings and equipment no census data are available. We valued the buildings on the basis of the number of government employees (excluding health, education, and defence personnel), assuming a *per capita* floor space of 10 square metres. Passenger cars and other vehicles were estimated according to the number of cars, etc., published in current statistics.

(12-d) *Building and equipment of banks and insurance institutions.* This item was derived from fixed-capital census data.

(14) *Consumer durables and non-durables*

(13-a, b) *Household equipment, clothing, and footwear.* These items are valued at market prices for second-hand goods (i.e. taking into account the fact that these goods are used up to a certain extent). Our estimates are based on a sample survey for 453 agricultural house-holds in various regions of Serbia pr., Vojvodina, and Kosmet and Metohia. The sampling results for these regions were then applied to other regions of Yugoslavia, where similar conditions prevail. For Slovenia we applied sample results of Vojvodina, for Macedonia sample results of Kosmet and Metohia, for Croatia and Bosnia and Hercegovina combined sample results of Serbia, etc.

For non-agricultural households direct measurements are lacking. The Serbian Statistical Office took inventories in 1954 for over 200 non-agricultural households, but this material is not yet available. In our estimate we assumed, therefore, that the value of household furniture and appliances is about two-thirds higher than the level in agricultural households. For clothing and footwear we assumed that the value per head of the non-agricultural population is twice the value per head of the agricultural population.

(13-c, d) *Fuel and food.* This item was derived from an analysis of expenditure data, prepared in our study *National Expenditure of Yugoslavia 1953–1954* (p. 368 in the English summary). Food stored on farms for farmers' own use is included in Agriculture (see comments item 2-h).

(13-c) *Passenger vehicles* are valued according to current statistical data, though bicycles had to be estimated separately, as they are not compulsorily registered. Passenger vehicles held by business, government, and other institutions are not included, nor are farm carts.

(15) *Land*

(14-a) *Agricultural land* is estimated at current 1953 market prices on the basis of a sample survey prepared by the Institute of Agricultural Economics and additional information received from cadastres. We present a summary of our estimates.

Category	Area (in 000 hectares)	Price in 1953 per hectare (dinars)	TOTAL (billions of dinars)
TOTAL AGRICULTURAL AREA	14,251·1	126,930	1,808
Arable land and gardens .	7,283·0	166,500	1,212
Orchards	374·4	179,220	67
Vineyards	261·1	157,410	41
Meadows	1,892·1	157,910	299
Pastures	4,440·5	42,630	189

For orchards and vineyards we took into account only land under orchards and vineyards, as all improvements and plants are included in agriculture (see item 2-e, f). In practice, a market price hardly exists for this category of bare land; we have, therefore, imputed market prices for orchards ranging from 10 to 20 per cent below the corresponding market price for arable land in the region in question and for vineyards ranging from 25 to 30 per cent below the price for arable land.

Land under fish-ponds is added to agricultural land, valued on an average at 80,000 dinars per hectare. Land under marshes and reeds is excluded.

The computation of average prices for all agricultural land presents a difficult problem, since market prices of land vary greatly as a result not only of economic factors, such as fertility of soil, etc., but predominantly because of sociological and other factors.

(14-b) *Forest land.* The valuation of forest land encounters the same problem as land under orchards and vineyards. In our estimate we assumed that in 1953 land under forests accounts for one-eighth on average of the value of growing stock. In 1938 this proportion was estimated by experts at over one-third of growing stock; taking into account the rise in stumpage prices and average prices for agricultural land in 1953 as compared with 1938 (about 16 times for stumpage prices and 6·5 times for agricultural land), we arrived at the above-mentioned ratio of forest land to growing stock. In this way we reached an average price for land under forests amounting to roughly 20,000 dinars per hectare. Land under scrubs, karst, and other barren ground is not included.

(14-c) *Urban and other land.* As market prices for urban land, especially in the central parts of cities, are not representative, we attempted to value land under urban residential buildings (including courtyards) in proportion to the value of buildings. We ascertained in collaboration with experts that land under residential buildings (including courtyards) represented in 1938 in urban areas on average about 19 per cent of the total value of such real estate or roughly 24 per cent of the undepreciated value of buildings. Deflating the total of urban residential building to 1938 undepreciated value, we arrive at 55·9 billions of dinars at 1938 prices. Applying to this amount the above-mentioned ratio of 24 per cent, we derived the value of urban land under buildings at 1938 prices 13·4 billions of dinars. To arrive at 1953 prices for urban land we applied a conversion factor of 4·5. This factor was obtained from expert estimates (in the central parts of cities the rise of prices was about twice and even less, but in the outskirts it ranged from five to seven times).

For land under streets and squares as well as in green areas we applied an average price of 45 dinars per square metre, representing an increase of about 4·5 times as compared with 1938 prices.

Land under railroad lines and roads was valued on an average of 10 dinars per square metre, by analogy with prices for farm land and land under forests. Land under industrial and commercial establishments was valued at 20 dinars per square metre.

(16) *Net foreign assets*

In our valuation of net foreign assets we applied to all liabilities and claims a conversion rate of 540 dinars for 1 U.S. dollar. We adopted this exchange rate for the purpose of national-wealth estimates only. The reason we applied this exchange rate is that nearly all equipment, representing a substantial component of total national wealth, was computed in this estimate at West-European prices prevailing in 1952/53 converted by a unified exchange rate of 540 dinars for 1 U.S. dollar.

(15-a) *Liabilities for foreign credits, loans, and nationalized assets.* This item refers to actual liabilities of Yugoslavia in favour of the International Bank for Reconstruction and Development, the Export–Import Bank, and other foreign institutions at 31 December 1953. Yugoslav liabilities for nationalized assets are included.

(15-b) *Monetary gold and claims against foreign countries.* The stock of Yugoslavia's monetary gold, including her quota at the International Monetary Fund, is treated here as a claim against the rest of the world. Claims for reparations and other indemnities include those Yugoslav claims against foreign countries which were stipulated in agreements with foreign governments. Agreements concluded with foreign governments after 1953 were taken into account, because these claims existed *de facto* at 31 December 1953, and were for one reason or another realized in agreements after that date.

8

CANADA'S REPRODUCIBLE WEALTH

By Anthony Scott

I. SCOPE OF THE STUDY

1. *Introduction*

The estimates of the reproducible wealth of Canada presented in this paper are the result of an attempt to discover the orders of magnitude involved, and to investigate the available sources of information. It should be emphasized at the outset that the estimates are not official, though they lean heavily for support on data and estimates published by official bodies.

There is at the present time a programme in its early stages at the Dominion Bureau of Statistics which it is intended will produce an exhaustive appraisal of the statistical resources for the production of official estimates. My own estimates have been produced independently of this programme; the Bureau of Statistics, the Economics Branch of the Department of Trade and Commerce, and the Economic Research Department of the Bank of Canada must therefore be absolved of all responsibility for the interpretation and use of their published figures. At the same time, I wish to acknowledge the friendly co-operation and constructive interest in the project shown by members of these three organizations, particularly with respect to the estimates of fixed industrial capital.

Since the purpose of the project is, partly, to investigate the available sources of data, it may be as well to report here on my findings. In general, I believe that the raw materials now exist in sufficient detail to make possible, with some outside augmentation of official sources, a reasonably consistent periodic estimate of Canadian reproducible wealth. Detailed *inventory* estimates are already maintained by DBS for the calculation of the gross national expenditure. It seems to me that it would be valuable to strengthen them by census enumerations of inventories in the less-important industrial groups, such as forestry (operations in the woods), mining, construction, transport, and public utilities. Manufacturing, trade, and agriculture are already well served. *Fixed capital* estimates by industry and in aggregate can now be made fairly directly by the perpetual-inventory method using official expenditure figures. There are two important deficiencies, however. There are few price indexes of machinery and equipment, and an almost complete lack of knowledge of the service life and of the country of origin of assets used by the various industries. (Country-of-origin data are very helpful in determining which price index is most appropriate.) It should, given time, be possible to ascertain the country of origin of various types of asset by laborious consultation of the trade statistics; but this check cannot be applied to estimates for each industry. In the last analysis it will be necessary to survey the various industries directly to discover the types of assets used, their service life, and their country of origin. Information on *housing* construction is already of a fairly high order and is improving continually. *Consumer durable goods* are surveyed in the decennial census, and automobiles are counted in annual registrations. It would be possible, again given time, to check perpetual-inventory estimates against these physical counts.

In sum, it appears possible to measure the aggregate reproducible wealth using presently available sources. Certain industries, however, are very difficult to handle, and direct surveys will undoubtedly be necessary to reduce the amount of guessing to a minimum. This necessity will be even greater if it is desired to go behind the Canadian aggregate and produce estimates by industry; and materials scarcely exist at all for estimates by region.

2. *Concept and method of presentation*

The totals shown in this paper are estimates of the depreciated (net) stock of assets valued at 1949 prices. This price level is a convenient one for Canada, since most official constant-dollar series are based on the same year – for example, the gross national expenditure. The depreciated or net stock has been chosen to permit comparability with the estimates of other countries. A 1955 estimate is also presented in 1955 prices; but it is rather rough because the main estimates are a by-product of an investment-forecasting exercise for the Royal Commission on Canada's Economic Prospects which was for the most part undertaken in terms of 1949 prices.

I feel strongly that, in addition to its defects of coverage and lack of information, the total suffers by its neglect of natural resources and, to a lesser extent, land. Canada is a country that depends heavily upon the exploitation of depletable minerals and upon the management of replaceable resources, such as farm land, forests, and fisheries. The yearly changes in the known stocks of these resources are, from many points of view, even more important than the changes in man-made wealth. This is particularly so when the objective is to measure the *depreciated* stock. However, the statistical difficulties in the way of attaining wide coverage are presently almost insurmountable. There is some information available, in scattered sources, about the surface uses of land. Farm land is investigated in the decennial censuses and in provincial agricultural reports. The provincial governments have attempted, in varying elaboration, to measure their forest resources. And urban land can be investigated with the help of municipal planning reports, real-estate surveys, municipal assessment rolls and the compilations of provincial municipal affairs and land-taxation departments. To say the least, however, these sources do not present data on uniform bases, and a very large research effort is necessary to make use of them. There is some information on fisheries, but its evaluation has rarely been attempted.

When we come to underground resources, only suggestive global estimates exist. Further, no method has been worked out for adjusting the values annually to take account of new discoveries, and changed costs methods and markets. In nature, however, the problem of resource stock measurement is similar to that of inventory measurement and evaluation.

Because the data are so sketchy and non-homogeneous, and because the conceptual problems require a great deal of discussion and experiment, I have not presented a resource estimate, even of surface land, in the main estimates, but some rough calculations are appended in the notes. Natural resources remain a relatively unexplored area in Canadian statistics, and, I feel, deserve a fairly high priority in future statistical agendas.[1]

In the succeeding pages I will proceed by the following plan. First I present Table I, a summary table. Then, line by line the table is explained as to source and method. Alternative sources

---

[1] See Joseph Barnea, 'National Income, Capital Formation and Natural Resources', *Kyklos*, 1956, pp. 360–368; and the subsequent discussion in *Kyklos*, 1957, pp. 79–86, where Mr. Barnea attempts a measurement for petroleum and natural gas. See also my 'National Wealth and Natural Wealth', *Canadian Journal of Economics and Political Science*, August 1956, pp. 373–378.

O

of measurement are also mentioned. In the third part of the paper there are some brief comments on the findings.

TABLE I
Reproducible Wealth of Canada
Millions of dollars; depreciated (net) stock

Type of Asset	1947 (1949 prices)	1955 (1949 prices)	1955 (1955 prices)
Reproducible Assets			
1. Structures	24,010	35,210	47,210
(a) Private	18,450	26,452	35,362
(1) Dwellings . . .	9,340	12,632	16,649
(2) Other ('Industry') [1] . .	9,106	13,820	18,713
(b) Public	—	8,758	11,849
(1) Dwellings . . .	—	258	340
(2) Other civilian }			
(3) Military } . .	5,566	8,500	11,509
2. Equipment	11,481	22,605	26,511
(a) Private. . . .	10,671	21,875	25,597
(1) Producers' durables [1] .	5,250	10,950	13,907
(2) Consumers' durables .	5,421	10,925	11,690
(b) Public			
(1) Civilian . }			
(2) Military. } . . .	810	730	914
3. Livestock [1]	1,570	1,490	1,311
4. Inventories			
(a) Private [1] . . .	5,350	8,207	8,220
(b) Public			
(1) Civilian . }			
(2) Military. } . .	—	—	—
5. Monetary metals . . .	370	1,144	1,112
6. Net foreign assets	−7,300	−9,000	−11,100
7. Total Reproducible Assets . .	35,482	59,656	73,264
8. Total, Items 1–4 . . .	42,411	67,512	83,252
9. Total, Items 1–2 . . .	35,491	57,815	73,721
10. Total 'industrial assets' [1] . .	21,280	34,467	42,151

[1] Includes the reproducible capital of agriculture, fishing, forestry, mining, manufacturing, construction, transport, storage, communication, finance, trade, and private services industries.

Excludes public-services and community-services capital and housing.

II. NOTES, SOURCES, AND METHODS [1]
(Numbers refer to lines of Table I)
Reproducible Assets
1. *Structures*

All structures estimates are taken from Chapter VI of *Output, Labour and Capital in the Canadian Economy*, by William C. Hood and Anthony Scott, a study written for the Royal Commission on Canada's Economic Prospects. This study is also the source of the machinery and equipment estimates of the next section.

The sources and methods used are discussed in full in the study. In brief, they are the perpetual-inventory method applied to investment expenditure data collected since 1926 by the Department of Trade and Commerce and the Dominion Bureau of Statistics and from 1896 to 1926 by Kenneth Buckley in *Capital Formation in Canada, 1896–1930*. A discussion of these sources will be found by O. J. Firestone, 'Investment Forecasting in Canada', in the NBER volume *Short-term Economic Forecasting* and by Kenneth Buckley in the NBER volume *Problems of Capital Formation*, pp. 91–146. The problem of reconciling the earlier and later investment estimates is also discussed in the Hood–Scott study in Appendix C of Chapter VI. Most of the data on expenditure since 1926, and especially since 1945, have been collected by survey, and are published in a fine industrial classification. Therefore it has been possible to undertake the cumulation and depreciation for the assumed average service life of all assets used by each industry (distinguishing only between structures and machinery and equipment). The price indexes used are described in the Hood–Scott study. For structures, they are mainly synthetic series combining indexes of materials costs and wage-rates. In the exceptional case of dwellings, the index was slightly adjusted for changes in the productivity of construction workers; no other structures price index was so adjusted.

[1] Several acknowledgments are owed for assistance in preparation of these estimates. Mr. Wm. C. Hood in particular participated in the planning of the original 'industrial' capital estimates. Mr. D. H. Jones made useful comments on an earlier draft, and Mr. Christopher Saunders spotted a serious error. I have been assisted in locating data and making computations by Messrs Tom Wilson and Bruce Hurt; and assisted financially by the University of British Columbia Research Committee.

No original estimate is available of the same totals, by industry, in current values, nor at original cost, though an *aggregate* cumulation for all industry (that is, not the result of summing estimates for individual industry) was made at *original cost*; it is shown in the Royal Commission study as Table 6 B.7. An excerpt from this table is given below.

TABLE II

Industry; Net Stock Valued at Original Cost

Millions of dollars

	Structures	Machinery and Equipment	Total
1947	5,193	4,021	9,214
1948	5,694	4,849	10,543
1949	6,249	5,696	11,945
1950	6,898	6,516	13,413
1951	7,772	7,642	15,414
1952	8,958	8,814	17,772
1953	10,182	10,033	20,214
1954	11,311	10,900	22,211
1955	12,496	11,690	24,186

The last column of Table I gives some approximations to estimates in 1955 prices; it was obtained by multiplying the 1949-price estimate by the implicit price deflator for the gross national expenditure for 1955. In the case of dwellings the IPD was 131·8, and in the case of private and public structures it was 135·4.

(a) *Private*. Canadian investment expenditure data are not classified *in detail* as to ownership, though aggregative estimates are analysed as to 'public' and 'private' expenditures. Government investment in railways would be, for example, classified with the transport industry. Hence, using the perpetual-inventory method, it has not been possible to distinguish between publicly owned and privately owned capital. Instead, in the Hood–Scott study, a distinction was made between 'industrial' and 'social' capital. 'Industrial' capital includes all assets of the farming, lumbering, mining, trapping, fishing, manufacturing, transport, storage, communications, utilities, trade, finance, and private services industries. It excludes 'social capital', and assets of institutions and governments providing community and public services (i.e. it excludes such assets as churches, schools, hospitals, airports, public works, roads, and defence installations) and dwellings. For the most part, this distinction between industrial and social capital is maintained in the present report.

(1) *Dwellings*. This line in Table I shows all dwellings, public and private, for 1947, because it is difficult to distinguish publicly owned housing from privately owned, in value terms. In terms of 'housing units', Firestone estimates that in 1949 1·3 per cent of the stock was 'public'. That is, it was made up of war workers' and veterans' rental housing, residences and quarters for government employees and defence personnel, and 'emergency shelter units'. (A considerable portion of the remaining 98·7 per cent of the stock was, of course, financed in part with some type of government assistance.) It is impossible to tell what portion of this public stock still existed, in public ownership, by 1955. However, if we add the annual increments to the 1949 public stock, it would increase to almost 1·6 per cent of the total stock of units in 1955.

				Total Housing Stock Units	Public Units	Per cent
1949	.	.	.	3,125,000	41,000	1·3
1955	.	.	.	3,724,000	58,000	1·6

Many of these government-owned units are of substantial construction and because of their location, expensive to build. Obvious exceptions are 'emergency housing', and some low-cost construction. Since they are relatively new, the depreciation on them would be less than on that for the stock as a whole. The rate of growth of the public stock has also recently been greater than that of the total dwelling stock, as the above figures show. Therefore, it would appear that more than 1·6 per cent, perhaps as much as 2 per cent, of the total depreciated value of the dwelling stock in 1955 was publicly owned. I have used this estimate in the table, for 1955. (See Firestone, *Residential Real Estate in Canada*, 1951, Table 21; also Central Mortgage and Housing Corporation, *Canadian Housing Statistics*, Table 2.)

(2) *Other structures*. This line shows all structures owned by 'industry', whether privately or publicly owned. An analysis

by industry follows, taken from the Hood–Scott study, Table 6. B3:

TABLE III

	Millions of 1949 dollars	
	1947	1955
Agriculture	510	754
Resource industries	1,564	3,736
Primary manufacturing	796	1,062
Secondary manufacturing	1,688	2,358
Transport, storage, and communication . . .	2,957	3,033
Trade, services, and construction	1,591	2,878
Total Industry	9,106	13,821

In the table, 'Resource Industries' include forestry, fishing, mining, and the central electric-station industry. Items may not add to totals because of rounding.

There are few other sources of information on fixed capital of Canadian industry. A bibliography, along with his own estimates, is given by O. J. Firestone, 'Canada's Economic Development, 1867–1953, with Special Reference to Changes in the Country's National Product and National Wealth', published in *Income and Wealth Series VII*, Bowes & Bowes, London, 1958.[1] Balance-sheet asset totals, for tax-paying corporations, classified by industry, will be found in the Department of National Revenue's *Taxation Statistics*. Until recently, the Bank of Canada also presented condensations of the balance sheets of a large number of corporations in its *Statistical Summary*. For particular industries, estimates of fixed capital have been found, or are to be found, in *The Manufacturing Industries of Canada* (although its survey of capital employed was discontinued in 1943), and DBS publications on power facilities, livestock, grain, fisheries, flour mills, electric and steam railways, motor carriers, highways, etc. Some of these sources do not distinguish structures from fixed assets, such as equipment and land, but in others a distinction and even a classification is given. Estimates made with another object in mind are to be found in DBS *Canada's International Investment Position, 1926–1954*.

(b) *Public.* See the remarks above under 'private' structures.

(1) *Dwellings.* 1947 estimate is grouped with private dwellings above. For a discussion of the 1955 estimate, see (a) (1) above.

[1] See especially Table 74 and the notes on p. 321. Firestone's chief source was the manufacturing survey mentioned below.

(2) and (3). *Other civilian and military*. These lines show the Hood–Scott estimates for structures owned by the Government or by institutions. They are taken from Table 6. B.6, and can be analysed as follows:

TABLE IV

	Millions of 1949 dollars	
	1947	1955
Roads	1340	2197
Buildings	1682	2395
'Other engineering'	1268	1570
Institutions	1276	2340
Total public . . .	5566	8502

'Institutions' includes all schools, churches, hospitals, and universities, whether privately or publicly owned. 'Other Engineering' includes dams, canals, airports, etc.

2. Equipment

(a) *Private*. See the notes above on private as against public investment; the estimate given here covers 'industrial' equipment.

(1) *Producers' durables*. See the notes above on industrial structures; the same comments apply to the estimates of the net stock of machinery and equipment. Since the service life of equipment is shorter than that of structures, the sources of the data used for the perpetual-inventory method are more recent, and more reliable. This line shows all equipment owned by 'industry', whether privately or publicly owned. The following analysis of the totals, by industry, summarizes Table 3 of Appendix B of the Hood–Scott study:

TABLE V

	Millions of 1949 dollars	
	1947	1955
Agriculture	944	2,066
Resource industries	600	1,457
Primary manufacturing	614	1,346
Secondary manufacturing . . .	1,418	2,254
Transport, storage, and communication . .	1,116	2,205
Trade, services, and construction . .	559	1,618
Total industry . . .	5,251	10,946

Many of the sources given above for other private structures also contain estimates of producers' durables; often, however, they are grouped together as total fixed assets, sometimes with land. The 1955-price estimate was derived by multiplying by the gross national expenditure IPD of 125·2.

(2) *Consumers' durables.* This estimate is the total of three distinct computations: (i) passenger cars; (ii) furniture and other durable consumer goods, including appliances; (iii) clothing. Totals are shown in (iv).

(i) *Passenger cars.* There is a small overlap here with producers' durable goods, since some passenger cars are actually in business use. The extent of this overlap is not known. We have assumed here that 12 per cent of the annual expenditure on passenger cars is for business use. Consequently, taking into account the much shorter life of such business cars, we have reduced the stock by 6 per cent in order to obtain an estimate of the consumer-owned stock.

Since the concept of wealth sought is the stock net of depreciation, the usual figure used, the total of registrations in all Canadian licensing jurisdictions, had to be modified. The procedure used was based on the perpetual-inventory method: it produced some unexpected results. Starting with the total number of cars registered each year, the change in registration was subtracted from the number of new cars sold each year to yield an estimate of the number of cars scrapped each year. Next, investigating the average service life of cars, we counted back from 1947 to find how many years' sales were required to produce the number of cars registered in 1947. This number of years was used as the average service life of the cars which were scrapped in 1947. (It was surprisingly high, eighteen years, reflecting the low production and low scrappage rates from 1940 to 1946.) In years subsequent to 1947 the same procedure was followed: the average service lives were centred on their midyear, producing a series of service lives which was extrapolated in 1955. The reciprocal of the service life for each year was used as the straight-line depreciation rate for that year; this rate was applied to the gross stock (total registrations) of that year. The cumulated net investment figures (sales of new cars minus depreciation) produced the desired net stock figure. The net stock amounted to only one-sixth of the gross stock in 1947, but rose to one-half of the gross stock by 1955. This net stock was then multiplied by the average value in 1949, and adjusted for business ownership as discussed in the preceding paragraph.

Data on new sales were obtained from *Automobile Statistics for Canada*, 1931; *New Motor Vehicle Sales in Canada*, 1932–37; *Sales of Motor Vehicles and Motor Vehicle Financing in Canada*, 1935–39; and *New Motor Vehicle Sales and Motor Vehicle Financing*, 1946–55. The average 1949 value was also obtained from the last-named publication. The total registrations data were obtained from *Automobile Statistics for Canada*, 1931–40 and *The Motor Vehicle Industry*, 1943–55. A study of the *Canadian Automotive Industry* for the Royal Commission on Canada's Economic Prospects by the Sun Life Assurance Co. of Canada contains a section on scrappage rates and on business usage of passenger cars. The average-age figure of eighteen years used above is confirmed by this study 'for a recent year'.

(ii) *Other consumers' durables and furniture*. The perpetual-inventory method was used here on an expenditure series which includes: 'Automobiles (new) and net purchases of second-hand automobiles, household appliances and radios (including stoves and ranges, washing machines, vacuum cleaners, etc.), furniture and home furnishings, jewellery, silverware, watches and clocks. This is admittedly an incomplete description of durable consumer goods, since it has not been possible to date to include in the total a number of miscellaneous durable items such as dish-washing machines, bicycles, motor cycles, and durable sports equipment. Research designed to rectify this omission is now in progress' (*National Accounts, Income and Expenditure, 1926–50*). The same note appears in more recent numbers. Examination of the United States' income-tax work on service lives and depreciation rates, *Bulletin F*, Goldsmith's *Study of Saving in the United States, Volume III*, and works on consumer expenditure suggest that at the very least, furniture and automobiles should be dealt with separately from the other goods.

The *National Accounts'* consumer durable series described above is published from 1926 to 1955. The series on furniture (published in the *National Accounts* to 1950, extrapolated to 1955 on the basis of ratios to total expenditure) was subtracted from total durable goods, and the residue converted to 1949 prices using the household operation and furnishings indexes, reduced by the constant-dollar outlays on passenger cars from (i) above, and cumulated with an assumed service life of eleven years. The furniture outlays were deflated by the household operation and furniture indexes, and cumulated using an assumed service life of twenty years. Other information on particular consumers' durables can be obtained from DBS publications on the electrical-goods industries; and the 1951 census contains data on the number of homes with *one or more* appliances of given types. Using these sources, however, would leave unmeasured the stock of miscellaneous durables.

(iii) *Clothing*. This category consists of women's and children's and men's and boys' clothing and footwear, from the *National Accounts* expenditure series (extrapolated to 1955 on the basis of a ratio to total consumer outlays). A service life of two years was assumed; expenditures were deflated using the clothing and personal furnishings price indexes. The results are merely notional, since they are very sensitive to the assumed service life used.

(iv) *Total consumers' durables*. This total is not, of course, exhaustive; it includes only the items mentioned explicitly in the above paragraphs. The following table is stated in millions of 1949 dollars; the estimate in 1955 prices in Table I was obtained by using the GNE price deflator for durable goods for 1955 of 107·1.

TABLE VI (millions of 1949 dollars)

	Furniture	Passenger Cars	Clothing	Other Durables	Total Durables
1947	955	375	1,946	2,145	5,421
1948	1,037	510	1,842	2,381	5,770
1949	1,115	730	1,817	2,634	6,296
1950	1,196	1,160	1,803	2,886	7,046
1951	1,278	1,480	1,806	3,053	7,617
1952	1,365	1,780	1,889	3,312	8,346
1953	1,465	2,160	2,014	3,584	9,223
1954	1,566	2,440	2,138	3,791	9,935
1955	1,670	2,800	2,313	4,142	10,925

(b) *Public*. As above, this classification applies to government and institutions. The following analysis, from Table 6, Appendix B, of the Hood–Scott study of *Output, Labour and Capital in the Canadian Economy* is in millions of 1949 dollars:

TABLE VII
Millions of 1949 dollars

	1947	1955
Government	749	539
Institutions . . .	58	193
Total public . .	807	732

3. *Livestock*

This line summarizes the following estimates of livestock on farms (in millions of 1949 dollars):

TABLE VIII

1947	.	.	.	.	.	1,574
1948	.	.	.	.	.	1,483
1949	.	.	.	.	.	1,457
1950	.	.	.	.	.	1,434
1951	.	.	.	.	.	1,288
1952	.	.	.	.	.	1,378
1953	.	.	.	.	.	1,392
1954	.	.	.	.	.	1,437
1955	.	.	.	.	.	1,486

The source of data was the *Report on Livestock Surveys* for cattle, sheep, horses, hogs, and poultry for 1950 and 1955, and the *Canada Year Books*, 1948–55. Other animals were omitted. The estimates apply to 1 June each year. The 1949 values by which the physical counts were multiplied were the 1949 average price per head as given in the *Canada Year Book* 1951, p. 395. Further information will be found in *Progress and Prospects of Canadian Agriculture*, by W. M. Drummond and W. Mackenzie, a study for the Royal Commission on Canada's Economic Prospects. The 1955-price estimate was obtained by using the 1955 wholesale price index for livestock.

4. *Inventories*

(a) *Private.* This line summarizes estimates made by combining DBS estimates of *changes* in inventories (as published in the current and constant dollar tables of gross national expenditure in *National Accounts, Income and Expenditure* for various years) with estimates of the book value of inventory for the various industries. These latter estimates vary from published data for the main industries to informed guesses for the industries with small inventories. We consider in turn grain inventories on farms, grain in commercial channels, and business inventories.

(i) *Grain on farms.* This estimate applies to 1 July each year (millions of 1949 dollars):

TABLE IX

1947	.	.	.	.	.	.	120
1948	.	.	.	.	.	.	135
1949	.	.	.	.	.	.	158
1950	.	.	.	.	.	.	70
1951	.	.	.	.	.	.	118
1952	.	.	.	.	.	.	118
1953	.	.	.	.	.	.	324
1954	.	.	.	.	.	.	667
1955	.	.	.	.	.	.	326

The figures are based on the carry-over of grain on farms in the *Canada Year Book*, except for 1950 and 1955, which were obtained by subtracting from total grain carry-over data on grain in commercial channels as published in *Grain Trade of Canada*, 1949–50 and 1954–55. They were multiplied by the appropriate 1949 price for a representative grade of each grain as shown in the 'Prices' table of the *Grain Trade of Canada*. The price used was an average of the 1948/49 and the 1949/50 crop years. In the special case of wheat, the physical stock for each year was multiplied by a weighted average of 1949 prices, the weights being the quantities of each grade *inspected* during the year to which the stock applied (weights from *Grain Trade of Canada* tables on 'Grain Inspection').

(ii) *Grain in commercial channels.* This estimate is an annual average of last-week-in-month figures given in *Grain Trade of Canada* to 1954–55, and *Grain Statistics* for 1955 (in millions of 1949 dollars):

TABLE X

1947	.	.	.	.	.	279
1948	.	.	.	.	.	295
1949	.	.	.	.	.	352
1950	.	.	.	.	.	369
1951	.	.	.	.	.	467
1952	.	.	.	.	.	568
1953	.	.	.	.	.	744
1954	.	.	.	.	.	846
1955	.	.	.	.	.	839

Valuation procedures were identical to those used above for grain on farms. The 1955-price value was obtained by using a wholesale price index for grains.

(iii) *Business inventories*. This figure includes inventories held by government business enterprises but excludes stocks held by such non-business authorities as exist to maintain commodity prices. No precise estimate of the holdings of such authorities has been made.

Grain has already been dealt with. Butter and cheese stocks are the two chief commodities held by the Government. In 1955 there was a stock of 67·5 million pounds of butter in storage at 1 June; about 15 or 20 million pounds would appear to be the 'normal' amount in storage at this time. Hence we may judge that about 47 million pounds were surplus supplies in storage. By the same line of reasoning we may assume that about 15 million pounds of the stored stock of 31 million pounds of cheese were surplus; perhaps more. The wholesale price of butter and cheese were in the neighbourhood of 30 cents per pound; we may judge that the valuation of such stocks, outside manufacturing or trade ownership, was about 18 million dollars. This estimate, however, is very rough; it has not been used in the estimate of total inventories.

The next step was to obtain estimates of the book-value of inventories held in the various industrial sectors in 1951 (a year for which census estimates apply).

Forestry: *Taxation Statistics* was consulted to obtain the ratio of corporate inventories to profits and to fixed assets. Unfortunately, many logging corporations are also saw-millers, and the data must be adjusted to prevent overlapping the manufacturing estimates. An estimate of net income after wages and salaries was multiplied by the inventory–profit ratio, and the estimates of structures and machinery and equipment multiplied by the fixed-assets ratio. It might be possible, given time, to use unofficial trade association reports of various types of timber stocks.

Fishing: No estimate was made, since most inventories are held at the manufacturing stage.

Mining, quarrying, and oil wells: The published individual and aggregate balance-sheet inventories of gold, non-ferrous, and petroleum corporations were given wider coverage on the basis of their net income, and on the basis of their fixed assets. In this industry, like logging, most firms are in both the mining and the manufacturing industries, and adjustment to prevent double-counting is very hazardous. In recent years the commodity-statistics reports for various industries (by the DBS Industry and Merchandising Division) have shown stocks for some of the main minerals, but the count is not complete.

Manufacturing: The book-value of total inventory held was given in *The Manufacturing Industries of Canada*.

Transport, storage, and communication: The inventory figures of corporations in this sector were found in *Taxation Statistics* and the *Bank of Canada Statistical Summary*. This was checked against an estimate derived by the same method in the 1920s, and carried to the present on the basis of National Account investment-in-inventory estimates. The two methods did not agree well, and a compromise figure was chosen.

Public utilities: A similar procedure was followed to that used for transport, storage, and communications.

Construction: The statements of individual companies, and of those given in aggregate in the *Bank of Canada Statistical Summary* and *Taxation Statistics* were given wider coverage on the basis of net income.

Trade: The wholesale and retail figures given are those shown in the decennial census of distribution for 1951.

Services, finance, insurance, and real estate: Some corporate balance sheets were used, and the rather scattered findings were given wider coverage on the basis of net income.

These admittedly very rough procedures produced the following distribution of book-values of inventories in 1951:

TABLE XI

	Millions of Current Dollars	Per cent
Forestry, fishing, and mining	247	3·4
Manufacturing.	3,708	50·6
Construction	480	6·6
Transport, storage, communication, public utilities	102	1·4
Wholesale trade	1,240	16·9
Retail trade	1,480	20·2
Services, finance, insurance, real estate . .	64	0·9
Total business inventories . . .	7,321	100·0

This total is, in concept, similar to the book-value of inventories used to measure inventory investment in the gross national expenditure calculations (after deducting grain and farm inven-

tories). The GNE figures were therefore used to carry the above
total back to 1949. It was then necessary to convert this 1949
'book-value' estimate to 1949 prices, but information was not
available for this step; its absence gives our final figure a lower
level than it otherwise would have. The book-value for 1949 was
carried back to 1947 and forward to 1955 on the *National Accounts'* constant dollar investment in inventory figures; see also
the series given in Table 7:12 of the Hood–Scott study for the
Royal Commission on Canada's Economic Prospects.

(iv) *Summary*. The following results were obtained from the
three series of computations outlined above:

TABLE XII

	Millions of 1949 dollars	
	1947	1955
Grain on farms	120	326
Grain in commercial channels . . .	279	839
Business inventories	4,951	7,042
Total inventories . . .	5,350	8,207

The unavoidable roughness of the original book-value calculations, the omission of certain types of farm inventory, and the
difficulties of re-valuing business inventories in 1949 produce a
very wide margin of error in these estimates. They suggest an
order of magnitude, close to $9 billion in 1955, which may be
compared usefully with other types of wealth; but the distribution of magnitudes within this total requires further research.
(This order of magnitude agrees well with a check estimate computed by taking the total book-value of inventories in 1941 as
shown in *Public Investment and Capital Formation*, 1945, Table
76, and adding the change in inventory figures from the *National
Accounts* to 1951.)

The 1955-price estimate was derived by adding to our estimate
of the 1955 book value of business inventories, the re-valuation
of grain stocks mentioned in paragraph (ii) above:

Business inventories, 1955 book value .	7,875 millions
All grain inventories, 1955 prices . .	345 ,,
Total industrial inventories, 1955 prices	8,220 millions

(b) *Public*

(1) and (2) *Civilian and military*. Publicly owned industrial firms' inventories, grain held for the Wheat Board, government stocks of uranium, and similar inventories are supposed to be included within the total for industry just above. There are no consistent data on other inventories or supplies held by municipal, provincial, nor indeed national governments. The Department of National Defense nowadays gives no details on the stock of weapons or other materials held for it, although the first annual report of the Department of Defense Production gave the inventories of cloth and wool, strategic materials, and standard machine tools held by it as $48 million in 1951. Levels appear to have gradually fallen since then, and the 1955 book value is given as $36 million. The public accounts do not seem to reveal supplies held by the public works, post office, or northern affairs departments, to mention three of the largest.

5. *Monetary metals*

Gold is held by the Government's exchange fund account and by the Bank of Canada. The current value of these official holdings, in U.S. dollars, is stated for each month in the *Statistical Summary of the Bank of Canada*. The 1949-price estimate was derived as follows: the values for the last month of each year was multiplied by the ratio of the Canadian price of gold in 1949 to the American price ($39.90/35.00). Canadian gold stocks are held largely for international trade purposes; their value in this context, along with official holdings of U.S. dollars, is shown in the first table in the notes immediately below.

6. *Net foreign assets*

Table XIII, in billions of current dollars (except for the last three lines), is taken from *Canada's International Investment Position, 1926–1954*. The estimates for 1955 are preliminary (p).

It is impossible to distinguish private from public assets and indebtedness, since it is not known to what extent Canadian individuals or governments hold foreign government securities as

TABLE XIII
Billions of current dollars

	1947	1955
International liabilities:		
Total non-residents long-term investment in Canada.	−7·2	−13·2 p
Equity of non-residents in Canadian assets abroad .	−0·3	− 0·6 p
Canadian dollar holdings of non-residents .	−0·3	− 0·4 p
Canadian short-term assets of IMF and IBRD .	−0·3	− 0·2 p
Total gross liabilities	−8·1	−14·5 p
International assets:		
Total Canadian direct and portfolio investments abroad	1·4	2·8 p
Government of Canada loans and advances and subscriptions to IMF and IBRD . . .	2·2	2·0 p
Government of Canada holdings of gold . . .	0·3	1·1
Government of Canada holdings of foreign exchange (U.S. dollars)	0·2	0·8
Other Canadian short-term (non-commercial) assets abroad	—	0·3
Total gross assets	4·1	7·0
Net liabilities:		
Net international indebtedness	4·0	7·5
Less Net Government of Canada assets and gold and foreign exchange	2·3	3·6
Commercialized 'private and public international long-term indebtedness'	−6·3	−11·1
In 1949 Prices:		
GNE implicit price deflator (1949 = 100) . .	(86·0)	(123·3)
Commercialized private and public international long-term indebtedness, at 1949 prices . .	−7·3	−9·0
Non-commercialized Government of Canada loans and advances and subscriptions to IMF and IBRD	−2·6	−2·3
Official holdings of U.S. dollars . . .	0·4	0·6

assets. On the liability side of the above balance sheet, the following analysis is taken from the same source:

TABLE XIV

	Billions of current dollars	
	1947	1955
Government and municipal bonds held by non-residents.	1·5	1·9
Other non-resident investments	5·7	11·3
Total non-resident long-term investment in Canada .	7·2	13·2

7. *Natural Resources*

As explained in the first part of this study, the time is not yet right for an evaluation of Canada's natural resources. In principle, there are three ways the statistician can set about this task: (a) capitalization of the income from natural resources; (b) summation of balance-sheet evaluations; and (c) inventory techniques.

(a) *Capitalization.* Determination of the amount that buyers would pay for the right to exploit all resources requires a capitalization of the future net proceeds. Capitalization of present profits is not satisfactory, because profits are struck *after* royalties, etc., have been paid (and many taxes are actually royalties from this point of view) and *after* a wide variety of practices of accounting for depletion have been followed. What is required is the present value of expected future net proceeds before royalties and depletion allowances.

(b) *Summation of balance-sheet or market evaluations.* This procedure is valid only if either firms whose balance sheets show the assets, or organized markets, revalue them continually on the basis of transfer prices for *full* ownership. Agricultural land and crown-granted mineral rights are good examples; but valuations of the latter are very scarce, while farmers' accounts, where they exist at all, are rather unreliable. Forest, fish, and power resources are not usually the property of the exploiting companies.

(c) *Inventory techniques.* These involve multiplying estimates of the physical volume of each resource by the prices at the site (minus such outlays as are foreseeable excluding depreciation, depletion, and most income-taxes). In the case of mining and forestry, this is still likely to be a very difficult computation; in the case of petroleum and natural gas slightly less so.

Land values may be approached by approach (b) if we assume that taxable assessments have some consistent relationship to balance-sheet values. On the basis of an enumeration by the Canadian Tax Foundation and J. Harvey Perry (*Canadian Fiscal Facts* and *Taxation in Canada*) of the 1951 assessments and the taxing regulations in twelve large Canadian cities, we estimated that assessed land values amounted to about 27 per cent of total assessed real-estate values. We then found that total real-estate property taxes paid in these places amounted to about 16 per cent of our estimate of land value alone. If we assume that land assessments are equal to 100 per cent of market values, and that experience in other municipalities is the same as in the twelve in the sample, we can estimate the value of land in all municipalities. We may at least find the range within which the value probably lies if we assume that only 40 per cent of the land's market value is covered by assessments; i.e. that annual property taxes amount to about 8 per cent of land value alone. Separate calculations were necessary for rural municipalities (some of which are actually suburban).

	High	Low
	(millions)	
Metropolitan and urban municipalities . .	5,300	2,130
Rural municipalities	1,000	500
Total municipal land values . .	6,300	2,650

The Census of Canada, however, puts the 1951 value of occupied farm land and buildings at about $8 billion, a figure difficult to reconcile with the value for rural municipalities given above. About one-fifth of the $8 billion may be in buildings and improvements, and about one-third may be outside organized rural municipalities. Even then the discrepancy is significant, and a great deal of research will be necessary to remove it.

The value of forest land, according to the reasoning of paragraph (a) above, ought to be determined by the capitalization of future returns. We assume that stumpage value is about 10 per cent of the gross value of production in the woods (as measured by DBS). This figure can be defended on the basis of discussions of forest revenues in the New Brunswick, Newfoundland, and British Columbia inquiries into Forest policy, and in the Canadian Tax Foundation's *Forest Tenures and Taxes in Canada*. The capitalization of this annual stumpage in perpetuity at 5 per cent yields a present value of land of about $2 billion in 1953. Some of this, however, is included in the farmland valuation shown above.

The forest land calculations appear to be reasonably consistent with the following independent calculation of the value of the timber stock. We determined on an average value of 46 cents per cubic foot for cut timber in the woods. The forestry branch of the Department of Northern Affairs estimated that in

1953 there were accessible stands of 312,802 million cubic feet, which suggests that these stands might be worth $144 billion!

If we take a 10 per cent stumpage ratio, we find the upper limit of these stands' values to be about $14 billion. If we attempt to find a *market* value for these stands we must make allowance for the fact that some of them are presently immature, and that these will be exposed to hazards of fire, disease, and waste. We would guess that as much as 50 per cent should be deducted for these reasons, giving perhaps $7 billion as the value of forest stands.

The value of minerals and petroleum resources seems even more difficult to calculate. Rapidly changing rates of discovery and rapidly changing market prices obscure the picture. In addition, since most minerals in Canada are produced from land that has been claimed, then put into some type of tenure that is less complete than fee simple, there is no land-right valuation comparable to stumpage. This means in turn that it is impossible confidently to attribute any particular fraction of the net income from mineral enterprises to land, nor to discover a normal relation between the value of land and other property. In my opinion, this is a computation not worth attempting. However, we would suggest that some rough figure be obtained, then carefully kept up to date with increments and decrements measuring the values of new discoveries, depletion, and changes in market prices, as an adjunct to national-income estimates of net income.

We have, in summary: (billions of 1951 dollars):

Municipal land, average of high and low estimates	4·5
Forest land	2·0
Forests	7·0
Minerals, water power sites, etc. . . .	(?)

III. ANALYSIS OF FINDINGS

To make an economic analysis of these estimates is tempting, because Canada is a fast-growing economy with documented records which can be used to shed light on the process of economic development. But the reader is reminded that the wealth estimates presented here are tentative in the extreme; careful interpretation must wait for more detailed measurement of the stock.

For this reason, I have confined this section of my paper to comparing the rates of growth of the stock of wealth with the rates of growth of other economic variables: the labour force, the population, the gross national expenditure (GNE), and the gross domestic product (GDP) of industry. All values are measured at 1949 prices; the gross domestic product series is based for the most part on the Dominion Bureau of Statistics' indexes of industrial output for various industries, weighted by the gross domestic product at factor cost of each industry in 1949. The GDP for 'industry' excludes residential rents, military and government activity, and community services; it includes agriculture and business and professional services; its sources and methods of computation are described in Chapter 5 of the Hood–Scott study for the Royal Commission on Canada's Economic Prospects.

The following table summarizes these comparisons by presenting the ratios of various types of wealth to the flow variables, 1947 and 1955.

TABLE XV

Ratios of Wealth to Population, Labour, and Output
1949 dollars

Type of Wealth	Per Person		Per Member of Labour Force		Ratio to G.N.E.		Marginal Ratio to G.N.E. 1947–1955	Ratio to Industrial GDP	
	1947	1955	1947	1955	1947	1955		1947	1955
Total reproducible assets	2,832	3,831	7,180	10,739	2·32	2·76	3·86	2·98	3·63
Total structures, equipment, livestock, and inventories .	3,385	4,335	8,582	12,153	2·77	3·13	4·01	3·56	4·11
Total structures . .	1,917	2,261	4,858	6,338	1·57	1·63	1·79	2·01	2·14
Total equipment . .	905	1,452	2,294	4,069	0·74	1·05	1·78	0·96	1·38
Total inventories . .	427	527	1,082	1,477	0·35	0·38	0·46	0·45	0·50
Total 'industrial' structures and equipment .	1,146	1,590	2,906	4,459	0·94	1·14	2·11	1·20	1·51
Total 'industrial' structures, equipment, and inventories . .	1,573	2,118	3,988	5,936	1·29	1·53	1·65	1·65	2·01
Total consumers' durables	432	702	1,097	1,967	0·35	0·51	0·88	0·45	0·66
Total dwellings . .	745	828	1,890	2,320	0·61	0·60	0·53	0·78	0·78
Total consumers' durables and dwellings . .	1,177	1,530	2,987	4,287	0·96	1·11	1·40	1·23	1·44

It will be seen that all categories of wealth per person and per member of the labour force increased significantly between 1947 and 1955; but the increase was not so marked in the ratios to output. Indeed, the inventory-to-output ratio is approximately constant, as is that for dwellings-to-output. The industrial structures-to-output ratio (not shown) actually declines; only the rapid increase in government structures keeps the total structures-to-output ratio from decreasing. The marginal ratios reveal the great demands made by the economy, especially for social capital, in the process of growth. It must be remembered, however, that these are *marginal* ratios of *net* capital to *gross* output. In 1947 existing assets were heavily depreciated. By 1955, because of the enormous growth (some 63 per cent for items 1 to 4 in Table I), the average age of assets had declined rapidly. Hence the *net* stock had grown much more rapidly than the gross stock; that is, than the actual capacity. The large marginal ratios reflect, to a considerable extent, this reduction in average age of the stock.

These findings are therefore consistent with those of the Hood–Scott study for the Royal Commission on Canada's Economic Prospects. There it was argued on *a priori* grounds, and confirmed (with respect to the *gross* stock of fixed capital) on statistical grounds that the ratio of output to capital tends to remain fairly stable over long periods of time. However, since this proposition, analytically, depends upon knowledge of the ratio of saving to output (because it is saving that permits the capital formation), and since Canada has been heavily dependent on the saving of foreigners (see the high ratio of net foreign indebtedness to total assets in Table I), it is quite possible either that the capital–output ratio will change or that some other explanation lies behind the relatively small movements in the observed ratio. Certainly it is true that the importance of machinery and equipment, relative to structures, is increasing; it also seems that every worker is, while being equipped with more and more tools of production, at almost the same rate being equipped with consumer durables – and the dependants to use them.

For an independent estimate of incremental capital–population and capital–worker ratios, see D. C. MacGregor, 'Capital Requirements and Population Growth', a paper given at the 1957 annual meeting of the Canadian Political Science Association. Professor MacGregor's estimates are particularly oriented towards the measurement of social capital needed by provincial and municipal governments. Finally, the reader is referred to Table 29 of Book I of the Rowell–Sirois report, p. 116, where 'total capital investment' in 1920 and 1930 is shown, by industry.

9

PROBLEMS AND USES OF NATIONAL WEALTH ESTIMATES IN LATIN AMERICA

By Alexander Ganz

United Nations Economic Commission for Latin America [1]

I. ROLE AND IMPORTANCE OF ESTIMATES OF NATIONAL WEALTH IN LATIN AMERICA

INVESTMENT and capital accumulation are the main basis for economic development. In under-developed Latin American countries, whose main preoccupation is the acceleration of growth in *per capita* product and the narrowing of the gap in the standard of living of Latin America and the advanced industrialized countries, the study of capital formation, capital accumulation, investment needs, the role of foreign capital and the use of investment resources has been undoubtedly the most important economic theme of concern to government economic policy, academic study, as well as the work of international organizations such as ECLA.

In contrast with industrialized countries, where labour scarcity may be the most important factor limiting growth, in underdeveloped Latin American countries the shortage of capital in relation to development needs, the low level of capital per worker, as well as the problem of allocation of investment resources, are the most important limiting factors. The urgency of this question may be said to have come on the scene in full force in Latin America in the 1930s, coincident with the decline of world demand and prices for primary materials, and the decline in foreign investment. These factors had the effect of loosening ties with industrial countries and encouraging a change in the direction of resources. The fall in foreign exchange resources available for imports, and the corollary *de facto* protection of domestic manufacturing industry fostered the development of the Latin American industrial entrepreneur. Programmes of investment in basic social capital by Latin American Governments, as part of a newly developed counter-cyclical policy, enhanced growth and demand, and facilitated the development of industry.

---

[1] It should be noted that while this paper has been prepared on the basis of studies of the Economic Commission for Latin America (in which the author of this paper participated actively), the responsibility for the opinions expressed is exclusively that of the author.

While the beginnings of industrial growth and the acquisition of capital goods had occurred in the 1920s and even earlier in some countries, the dominance of export products in the shaping of economic policy, and the prevalence of low tariffs and a wide-open policy on imports, meant that domestic industry had a very difficult competitive position, the degree of utilization of industrial capital was low, and incentives and resources for industrial development were few. The world economic crisis of the 1930s was accompanied almost everywhere in Latin America by a change in governments, where exporter and foreign investment interests (geared to export of primary materials) were supplanted by domestic industrial entrepreneur and popular interests committed to fostering industrial development, protecting domestic industry, and expanding basic social capital in road transport, electric power and health, education and sanitation services, necessary for industrial development. This phase of economic growth relied heavily on the more intensive utilization of existing capital resources in manufacturing.

During World War II, Latin America was cut off from the traditional suppliers of manufactured goods and capital goods, at the same time that it became an expanded supplier of food and raw materials. Domestic manufacturing industry received a very strong stimulus, both in production of goods traditionally imported and in response to the expanded domestic demand arising from the expanded national income and its more equal distribution. Productive capacity was used very intensively. Machinery and equipment continued to be used for periods substantially beyond the usual estimated period of useful life. Internal relative price trends favoured manufacturing industry in this period as well as in the earlier period.

The accumulation of foreign-exchange resources, which could not be spent during the war, and the early post-war favourable trend in the terms of trade of exports, together with an exchange-control policy which favoured imports of capital goods and raw materials and intermediate products for industry, made possible a phenomenal era of investment in manufacturing industry in the early post-war years, Governments adopted economic development programmes geared to facilitate the expansion of manufacturing industry, including basic industries, such as iron and steel, chemicals, petroleum, machinery and equipment, as well as food processing and clothing.

With industrial development, investment and capital accumulation, and a relative transfer of man-power from primary-materials production activities to manufacturing, construction, transport, electricity, and communications services, as well as trade, government, professional and personal services, productivity (gross product per worker) and *per capita* product increased. The increase in *per capita* product was accompanied by an improvement in the equality of distribution of income arising from the relative shift of man-power, capital, and production to manufacturing and service activities. This expansion in *per capita* income and improvement in its distribution created a new and expanded level of domestic demand, fundamentally different from that existing heretofore. For the first time, a considerable number of Latin American countries had a sizeable domestic market. Increasingly, production has been geared to the domestic market. At the average *per capita* product level of $300, prevailing in 1956, the income elasticity of demand for food is already declining and that for manufactures and services is increasing. Thus, this growth in productivity and income has meant an accelerated demand for manufactures and services. One of the most striking effects has been the basic difference in the orientation of foreign capital in the post-war period; apart from unique cases, such as Venezuela and Peru, foreign capital is increasingly dedicated to manufacturing production for the domestic market as a means of obtaining access to a market within a tariff wall. The change in orientation of foreign capital from the production and export of primary materials to manufacturing for the local domestic market has meant that foreign capital has a greater and more fundamental interest in the expansion of the Latin American domestic market.

While the post-war years have represented a period of intense investment in manufacturing activity, not only to replace out-worn equipment, but to expand manufacturing capacity, investment in basic social capital in transport and energy lagged behind the rapidly growing demand and needs.

The rate of government investment in basic social capital in transport and energy, as well as in autonomous or mixed enterprises, has declined, partly as a consequence of the expanding burden of subsidies and transfer payments on government revenue resources, whose elasticity of growth was adversely affected by price inflation. In the earlier post-war years government economic policy, almost everywhere in Latin America, was committed to fostering industrialization and economic development, and ambitious investment programmes were adopted, financed in part by an implicit export tax deriving from exchange-control policy. This was feasible because of the post-war improvement in export terms of trade. Since 1950, the decline in export terms of trade and currency devaluation required to maintain production incentives for export products, and to price exports competitively in the world market, not only nullified indirect export taxes as a revenue source, but, in important instances, required the subsidization of exports. This became a serious drain on public revenues, especially in those countries which attempted to maintain a subsidized exchange rate for imports of industrial intermediate products and capital goods. At the same time, government transport and electric enterprises, with low, fixed rates, were adversely affected by post-war price inflation, which affected costs of operation, and which outran the tardy adjustment of utility rates. Operating deficits of government enterprises became an expanding charge on public revenues. Social-security programmes, adopted in the 1930s and early 1940s, without proper investment of contributions in inflation-proof assets, and without adequate actuarial estimation of benefit payments, are absorbing an expanding share of public revenue. Military expenditures expanded sharply with the adoption of 'continental defense' programmes after 1948, and have become an especially voracious consumer of public revenues.

The consequent decline in the rate of public investment has meant an increasing shortage of basic social capital in transport and energy, and this has recently become an important limiting factor in industrial development and the growth of industrial production.

While private foreign investment flowed readily into manufacturing enterprises, in which the rate of return compared more than favourably with that in industrialized countries, virtually no *new* foreign capital has gone into private electric-power production or railroad transport, since the traditional rate fixing in these activities concerned with the public interest precludes rates of return attractive to private foreign investment. Public international capital has filled a small part of the gap, especially in financing the equipment of electric power stations and the re-equipment of railroads.

The shortage of public investment in basic social capital has been further aggravated, in some important notable instances, by a misdirection of public investment resources. The backlog of needs for basic social capital, accumulated from the foreign-exchange shortage era of the 1930s and the cutting-off of imports during the war, were generally underestimated, and the series of present and prospective shortages was not well appreciated. This may be understandable, since the shortages themselves are a function of industrialization, economic growth and improvement in the standard of living, which are accompanied by an even more rapid growth in the need and demand for transport and energy. In addition, the basic social changes which have accompanied industrialization and the expansion of *per capita* income, especially urban growth, together with the shift in the centre of political power, added an element of urgency in the reduction of the backlog of social needs for hospitals, schools, water-works, housing, street paving, recreation facilities. Consequently, public investment resources were not always directed to economic projects having the first order of priority.

The shortage of basic social capital and the misdirection of public investment resources points vividly to the urgent need for a more complete and adequate information and analysis of capital formation, capital accumulation, the use of investment resources and their effect on growth and productivity if Latin American countries are to accomplish their goals of accelerated growth and expansion in *per capita* income. Such basic information is presently needed as a guide to economic policy, including questions of utilization of capital resources, needs for basic social capital, the degree of utilization of capital resources, productivity implications of alternative uses, role of foreign capital, capital needs and import limitations. In the work of ECLA, the study of investment and capital has proven to be useful in the analysis of the incidence of Government economic policy.

It should also be noted that Latin America has a significant saving and investment capacity, associated with its average *per capita* product of $300, in comparison with less than $100 for South-East Asia. Given optimum utilization of these resources, together with a margin of foreign capital that may be expected to be attracted to a developing and expanding market, the attainment of a satisfactory rate of growth is a real possibility.

Latin America today has an urgent need for good statistics on capital formation and the stock of capital. Where such adequate statistics have been developed, they have been immensely useful in the analysis of problems of economic development and as a guide to government investment policy, as will be shown, Nevertheless, the development of adequate statistics in this field has lagged behind needs. The consequent improvisation has led to some basic and costly errors of economic policy, as will be indicated.

Because of the importance of basic information on the stock of capital, the Economic Commission for Latin America has long been interested in estimating and analysing the stock of capital, and has long encouraged and aided work in this field in Latin America.[1]

In this paper, an attempt will be made to draw upon this experience to discuss:

(1) some significant conclusions based on the analysis of estimates of the stock of capital in some Latin American countries and in the region as a whole;

(2) problems of data, concept and method in the estimation of the stock of capital in Latin America;

(3) an evaluation of work done in the field of national-wealth estimation and analysis in Latin America.

II. SOME SIGNIFICANT CONCLUSIONS BASED ON THE ANALYSIS OF THE STOCK OF CAPITAL IN SOME LATIN AMERICAN COUNTRIES AND IN THE REGION AS A WHOLE

In the preceding section of this paper the role of investment and capital in the economic growth and structural change of Latin American economies in the last quarter century were dis-

[1] See *Economic Survey of Latin America, 1951–52, 1953, 1954, 1955, 1956*, United Nations Economic Commission for Latin America, Santiago, Chile; *Analysis and Projections of Economic Development:* I. *An Introduction to the Technique of Programming;* II. *The Economic Development of Brazil;* III. *The Economic Development of Colombia;* IV. *The Economic Development of Argentina* (unpublished); United Nations Economic Commission for Latin America, Santiago, Chile. *Fixed Reproducible Capital in Argentina, 1935–55*, Manuel Balboa and Alberto Fracchia, Argentine Government, United Nations Joint Study Group, United Nations Economic Commission for Latin America. *External Disequilibrium and the Economic Development of Latin America; The Case of Mexico*, United Nations Economic Commission for Latin America, Mexico City; *The Role of Economic Statistics in the Formulation of Economic Development Programs*, paper presented at the III Inter-American Statistical Conference, Quitandinha, Petropolis, Brazil, June 1955, by the United Nations Economic Commission for Latin America; *Selective Expansion of Agricultural Production in Latin America and its Relationship to Economic Development*, United Nations Economic Commission for Latin America, Santiago, Chile.

cussed. It was noted that the world economic crisis indirectly fostered Latin American industrialization through the loosening of foreign-trade and investment ties, decline in internal relative prices and relative importance of the primary materials export sectors, the protection of domestic industry, and the dedication of public economic policy and investment to industrialization, economic development, and the expansion of basic social capital. While the decline in export earnings and the terms of trade adversely affected capital-goods imports in the 1930s, tariff protection of domestic industry made it possible to use more intensively and more efficiently the industrial production capacity created in the 1920s and earlier. It was seen how World War II, and the cutting off of Latin America from traditional sources of import supply, together with the increase and more equal distribution of income which accompanied the structural change of the 1930s, had the effect of further stimulating industrial production and the more intensive use of industrial capacity, as well as basic social capital in electricity and transport. The use of war-accumulated export earnings and the post-war favourable export terms of trade to create a phenomenal era of investment in manufacturing industry, and to finance economic development programmes, was noted. The recent decline in the rate of public investment, parallel with the increasing shortage of basic capital in electricity and transport, and the restrictive effect on industrial production and economic growth, was seen. The increasingly serious problem of adequate and appropriate direction of public investment resources was touched on.

Attention will now be given to the presentation of some significant conclusions based on the analysis of estimates of the stock of capital in some Latin American countries and in the region as a whole.

1. Long-term increase in the productivity of capital, and change in economic structure of the labour force, capital, and production

The analysis of estimates of the stock of capital and capital formation in Latin American countries on the threshold of economic development and industrialization gives a basic insight to the understanding of the processes and patterns of economic development and economic growth. New long-term economic time series for Latin American countries, including

TABLE I

Gross Product, Fixed Reproducible Capital (at Depreciated Replacement Cost), and the Product–Capital Ratio in Latin America, 1925–56

(Millions of dollars at 1950 prices)

	Gross Domestic Product	Fixed Reproducible Capital	Product–Capital Ratio
1925	16,229	55,607	0·29
1926	16,172	57,237	0·28
1927	17,015	59,376	0·29
1928	18,578	61,906	0·30
1929	18,874	64,678	0·29
1930	17,409	66,663	0·26
1931	17,318	67,333	0·26
1932	17,221	67,348	0·26
1933	17,314	67,483	0·26
1934	19,527	68,147	0·29
1935	20,440	69,224	0·29
1936	21,589	70,048	0·31
1937	22,494	71,387	0·31
1938	22,920	73,562	0·31
1939	23,848	75,047	0·32
1940	24,174	76,253	0·32
1941	25,915	77,435	0·33
1942	25,920	78,429	0·33
1943	26,990	79,273	0·34
1944	29,311	80,393	0·36
1945	30,335	81,906	0·37
1946	32,870	83,932	0·39
1947	34,503	87,498	0·39
1948	36,448	91,786	0·40
1949	37,685	95,945	0·39
1950	39,791	100,598	0·40
1951	42,029	105,366	0·40
1952	42,907	108,407	0·40
1953	44,258	112,613	0·39
1954	47,071	117,272	0·40
1955	49,324	122,030	0·40
1956	50·858	126,987	0·40

Sources: Economic Survey of Latin America, 1951–52, 1954, 1956, United Nations Economic Commission for Latin America, Santiago, Chile; *Analysis and Projections of Economic Development;* I. *An Introduction to the Technique of Programming;* II. *The Economic Development of Brazil;* III. *The Economic Development of Colombia;* IV. *The Economic Development of Argentina* (unpublished), United Nations Economic Development for Latin America, Santiago, Chile. *Fixed Reproducible Capital in Argentina, 1935–55,* Manuel Balboa and Alberto Fracchia, Argentine Government – United Nations Study Group, United Nations Economic Commission for Latin America. *External Disequilibrium and the Economic Development of Latin America; The Case of Mexico,* Economic Commission for Latin America, Mexico City.

Note: In some cases, previously published series have been up-dated and revised, and new unpublished series have been used. For reference to concept and methods, see Parts III and IV of this Study.

TABLE II

Gross Product, Fixed Reproducible Capital, and the Product–
Capital Ratio in Latin America and Five Selected Countries,
1925–55

(Millions of dollars at 1950 prices)

Five-year Periods	Annual Averages					
	Latin America	Argentina	Brazil	Chile	Colombia	Mexico

A. *Gross Product*

1925–29	17,374	5,485	4,540	932	957	1,418
1930–34	17,758	5,277	4,898	921	1,135	1,584
1935–39	22,258	6,310	6,128	1,155	1,409	2,329
1940–44	26,462	7,287	7,198	1,372	1,639	3,199
1945–49	34,368	9,049	8,598	1,678	2,135	4,449
1950–54	43,211	10,024	11,337	1,998	2,697	6,031
1955	49,324	10,916	13,167	2,142	3,089	7,216

B. *Fixed Reproducible Capital*

1925–29	59,761	22,267	11,505	[2]	4,203	5,213
1930–34	67,395	25,440	12,364	2,310	4,675	5,674
1935–39	71,944	26,345	13,848	2,458	5,123	6,096
1940–44	78,357	27,481	15,841	2,626	5,839	6,886
1945–49	88,213	29,835	18,096	2,920	6,734	8,467
1950–54	108,851	34,534	23,348 [1]	3,377 [1]	7,840 [1]	11,477
1955	122,030	36,784	[2]	[2]	[2]	13,731

C. *Product–Capital Ratio*

1925–29	0·29	0·25	0·39	[2]	0·23	0·27
1930–34	0·26	0·21	0·40	0·40	0·24	0·28
1935–39	0·31	0·24	0·44	0·47	0·27	0·38
1940–44	0·34	0·27	0·45	0·52	0·28	0·46
1945–49	0·39	0·30	0·48	0·57	0·32	0·53
1950–54	0·40	0·29	0·49	0·59	0·34	0·53
1955	0·40	0·30	[2]	[2]	[2]	0·53

Sources: *Economic Survey of Latin America, 1951–52, 1954, 1956,* United Nations Economic Commission for Latin America, Santiago, Chile; *Analysis and Projections of Economic Development;* II. *An Introduction to the Technique of Programming;* II. *The Economic Development of Brazil;* III. *The Economic Development of Colombia;* IV. *The Economic Development of Argentina* (unpublished), United Nations Economic Development for Latin America, Santiago, Chile. *Fixed Reproducible Capital in Argentina, 1935–55,* Manuel Balboa and Alberto Fracchai, Argentine Government – United Nations Study Group, United Nations Economic Commission for Latin America. *External Disequilibrium and the Economic Development of Latin America; The Case of Mexico,* Economic Commission for Latin America, Mexico City.

Note: In some cases, previously published series have been up-dated and revised, and new unpublished series have been used. For reference to concept and methods, see Parts III and IV of this Study.

[1] Annual average calculated for years 1950–53.
[2] Not available.

reliable, homogeneous, and detailed data on the gross product, capital formation and the stock of capital, labour force, and trade and payments, and covering periods up to thirty years (fifty-five years in the case of Argentina), demonstrate that the

TABLE III

Gross Product Per Capita *in Latin America, 1925–56*

Years	Gross Domestic Product (Millions of dollars at 1950 prices)	Population (Millions of persons)	Gross Domestic Product *Per Capita* (Dollars at 1950 prices)
1925 . .	16,229	96·4	168
1926 . .	16,172	98·1	165
1927 . .	17,015	99·7	171
1928 . .	18,578	101·4	183
1929 . .	18,874	103·2	183
1930 . .	17,409	105·0	166
1931 . .	17,318	106·7	162
1932 . .	17,221	108·4	159
1933 . .	17,314	110·1	157
1934 . .	19,527	111·8	175
1935 . .	20,440	113·6	180
1936 . .	21,589	115·5	187
1937 . .	22,494	117·9	191
1938 . .	22,920	120·2	191
1939 . .	23,848	122·5	195
1940 . .	24,174	125·0	193
1941 . .	25,915	127·4	203
1942 . .	25,920	129·9	200
1943 . .	26,990	132·7	203
1944 . .	29,311	135·4	216
1945 . .	30,335	137·5	221
1946 . .	32,870	140·6	234
1947 . .	34,503	143·8	240
1948 . .	36,448	147·3	247
1949 . .	37,685	150·8	250
1950 . .	39,791	154·5	258
1951 . .	42,029	158·3	265
1952 . .	42,907	162·1	265
1953 . .	44,258	166·0	267
1954 . .	47,071	170·0	277
1955 . .	49,324	174·1	283
1956 . .	50,858	178·3	285

Source: See Note to Table I.

process of economic development and industrialization involves a broad and basic improvement in the efficiency of utilization (productivity) of investment and capital resources, as well as the increase in the efficiency of utilization of man-power resources. This may appear to be repeating the obvious, but the significance of this new body of data lies in the quantitative measure of this process and the new light it throws on the problem and cost of economic development.

For the region as a whole, the gross product per unit of capital, in the five-year period 1950–54, was almost 40 per cent greater than in the years 1925–29 (see Table I). The long-term

TABLE IV

Gross Product, Labour Force Composition and Productivity, by Economic Activity, in Latin America in 1940 and 1955

	Gross Product		Labour Force		Gross Product per Worker	
	1940	1955	1940	1955	1940	1955
	(Millions of dollars at 1950 prices)		(Thousands of persons)		(Dollars at 1950 prices)	
Total . . .	*24,174*	*49,324*	*44,300*	*59,900*	*546*	*823*
Agriculture . .	7,131	11,887	27,510	30,309	259	392
Mining . . .	894	2,220	443	599	2,018	3,706
Manufacturing and construction .	4,617	11,492	5,980	11,022	772	1,043
Government and other services .	11,531	23,725	10,366	17,970	1,112	1,320
	(Percentage distribution)		(Percentage distribution)		(Indices: Total = 100)	
Total . . .	*100·0*	*100·0*	*100·0*	*100·0*	*100*	*100*
Agriculture . .	29·5	24·1	62·1	50·6	47	48
Mining . . .	3·7	4·5	1·0	1·0	370	450
Manufacturing and construction .	19·1	23·3	13·5	18·4	141	127
Government and other services .	47·7	48·1	23·4	30·0	204	160

Sources: *The Selective Expansion of Agricultural Production in Latin America and its Relationship to Economic Development,* United Nations, ECLA, Santiago, Chile, 1955; *Economic Bulletin for Latin America, Vol. II, No. 1,* Santiago, Chile, February 1957, article entitled 'Charges in Employment Structure in Latin America, 1945–55'; *Economic Survey of Latin America, 1955,* op. cit. *Study on Manpower in Latin America,* United Nations ECLA, Santiago, Chile, 1957; 'The relationship between population growth, capital formation and employment opportunities in Underdeveloped Countries', by Dr. Raul Prebisch, paper presented at the World Population Conference, Rome, 1954.

improvement in the productivity of capital resources was experienced by at least four countries, Argentina, Brazil, Colombia, and Mexico, whose gross product and stock of capital represent approximately 70 per cent of that of Latin America as a whole (see Table II). For two of these countries – Argentina and Colombia – detailed long-term series on investment and capital,

Q

by economic sector, and by type of capital good, are available, and make possible a detailed analysis and interpretation which will be referred to later in this section. While much remains to be done to round out the statistical record, there appears to be no doubt as to the validity of this basic conclusion on the long-term improvement in the efficiency of utilization of investment and capital resources, in the economic growth of Latin America. It is now also possible from the new historical record to clarify the nature of the process.

As will be shown, the long-term increase in the overall productivity of capital derives from the change in the economc structure of production, man-power and capital, the heart of the process of economic development and industrialization. In effect, the relative transfer of investment and capital resources, as well as labour force, to industry, signifies a more productive use of capital as well as labour, and raises the level of productivity in the economy as a whole (see Tables III and IV).

2. *Significance with respect to problem and social cost of economic development*

It has long been recognized that a prerequisite for development and industrialization is the prior creation of basic social capital in transport, communications and energy, housing, commerce, and services, including government services, which have a low capital productivity. The low product–capital ratio in basic social capital is not principally a matter of internal relative prices (although this may be a contributing factor), but is related basically to the length of life of the capital good, and the annual cost and rate of return based on the average expected length of life.[1] Conversely, the high product–capital ratio in manufacturing is related to the relatively short length of life of machinery and equipment, and the annual cost and rate of return related to it.

Other factors involved in the long-term improvement in the gross product per unit of fixed reproducible capital (at depre-

---

[1] See for example, 'Theoretical Aspects of Quality Change, Capital Consumption and Net Capital Formation', Edward F. Denison, *Problems of Capital Formation, Studies in Income and Wealth*, Volume Nineteen, National Bureau of Economic Research, New York, 1957, pp. 236 and 237. As Denison states, '. . . long life is an undesirable property of a capital good if the investment per year of service is the same. If the cost of capital goods were proportionate to their lives, then the shorter the lives of capital goods the larger would tend to be total output per unit of net capital'.

ciated replacement cost) in Latin America, in the period 1925–56, include: (1) the fuller and more intensive utilization of basic social capital as well as agricultural and industrial production capacity, and economies of scale deriving from the growth and expansion of the market; (2) the effect of external terms of trade and export demand on imports of capital goods and, consequently, the level and composition of investment and capital; (3) the changing role of foreign capital; (4) the effect of the rate

TABLE V

Fixed Reproducible Capital in Latin America and Selected Countries by Economic Sector, 1950

	Latin America	Argentina	Brazil	Chile	Colombia	Mexico
	(Thousand millions of dollars)					
Total fixed reproducible capital . .	*100·6*	*33·0*	*21·3*	*3·2*	*7·5*	*10·3*
Agriculture . .	26·1	5·2	5·3	0·5	2·9	1·3
Industry . .	15·1	5·0	3·6	0·8	1·0	1·1
Transportation, electricity, and communications. .	11·6	4·7	3·2	0·5	0·7	1·2
Non-farm housing, trade, services, and government . .	47·8	18·1	9·2	1·4	2·9	6·7
	(Percentage distribution)					
Total . . .	*100*	*100*	*100*	*100*	*100*	*100*
Agriculture . .	26	16	25	16	39	13
Industry . .	15	15	17	25	13	11
Transportation, electricity, and communications. .	12	14	15	16	9	12
Non-farm housing, trade, services, and government . .	47	55	43	43	39	65

Source: See note to Table I.

of growth on the relative importance of depreciation in the investment effort; (5) the incidence of internal relative prices on the saving and investment capacity of the industrial sector; and (6) the greater efficiency of new capital goods replacing older similar goods – the benefits of technological progress.

Nevertheless, as will be shown, the main factor explaining the development process is the change in economic structure and the growth in the relative importance of investment and capital in those economic sectors which, by the nature of the type of capital, represent an increase in the overall efficiency in the utilization of investment and capital resources (see Tables V and VI).

It is now possible to show, on the basis of the record of economic history, that economic development requires a tremendous social force, as can be appreciated in an economy 'starting'

TABLE VI

Gross Product and the Product–Capital Ratio, by Economic Sector, in Latin America and Selected Countries, by Economic Sector, 1950

(Millions of dollars)

	Latin America	Argentina	Brazil	Chile	Colombia	Mexico
A. *Gross Domestic Product*						
Total . . .	39,791	9,887[1]	10,120	1,872	2,383	5,412
Agriculture . .	10,545	1,451	2,937	280	945	1,030
Industry . .	10,226	2,952	2,166	483	682	1,522
Transportation, electricity, and communications. .	2,348	1,037	866	140	175	261
Non-farm housing, trade, services, and government . .	16,672	3,861	4,151	969	581	2,599
B. *Product–Capital Ratio*						
Total . . .	0·40	0·30	0·48	0·59	0·32	0·53
Agriculture . .	0·40	0·28	0·55	0·53	0·32	0·78
Industry . .	0·68	0·59	0·61	0·63	0·68	1·40
Transportation, electricity, and communications. .	0·20	0·22	0·27	0·30	0·18	0·22
Non-farm housing, trade, services, and government . .	0·35	0·21	0·45	0·69	0·18	0·39

Source: See note to Table I.

[1] Total at market prices, economic sectors at factor cost.

with a product–capital ratio of 0·25. In effect, under-developed countries need more capital per unit of product than do developed countries; a comparable investment effort yields less. For a full appreciation of the social force required in the process of economic development, there must be added to this basic factor the vulnerability of economic growth of under-developed countries to fluctuations in the terms of trade of primary materials; internal relative prices and income distribution which may not favour an appropriate allocation of resources – especially investment resources; the small size of market, consonant with a low *per capita* product, which limits the economies from scale of operations; the susceptibility of capital-goods imports to fluctuations in trade and foreign-exchange earnings; and fluctuations in the rate of growth, which, when declining, have the effect of increasing the relative burden of depreciation in the overall investment effort.

3. *Factors contributing to the increase in the efficiency, utilization, and productivity of capital in Latin America in the last quarter century*

Despite the relatively greater social force required, and the factors of vulnerability and susceptibility referred to above, Latin America has, in fact, experienced a significant rate of growth in the *per capita* product in the last thirty years, deriving in substantial part from a broad improvement in the efficiency of utilization of investment and capital resources (productivity of capital), as will be shown. The basic factors in the increase in the efficiency of utilization of investment and capital resources was the broad change in the economic sector structure of capital. The increase in the relative importance of manufacturing productive capacity, with its higher capital productivity deriving from the characteristic type of capital good with its advance in technology and shorter life span, was the basic factor which contributed to the increase in the efficiency and productivity of capital in the economy as a whole. A number of important factors facilitated the change in the economic sector structure of capital, and other factors, independent of the change in structure, also contributed to the increase in the efficiency, utilization, and productivity of investment and capital resources. These include the following:

(1) The relative decline in export demand and relative prices for agricultural products and raw materials, during the 1930s and during the war, together with policies of import restriction and exchange control adopted by main Latin American governments, had the effect of improving internal relative prices for the manufacturing sector, as well as its saving and investment capacity. This factor, together with the decline in the relative importance of foreign investment in this period, facilitated the relative shift of

investment and manpower resources to manufacturing (see Table VII). Restriction of imports of luxury consumer goods and improvement in the distribution of income (which accompanied political changes that paralleled the decline in the economic importance of agricultural and raw-materials exports and foreign investment) tended to enhance saving and investment in manufacturing, and to create a new market for manufactured goods.

TABLE VII

Foreign Investment and Fixed Reproducible Capital in Latin America, 1929, 1940, 1950, 1955

(Thousands of millions of dollars at 1950 prices)

Year	Foreign Investment	Fixed Reproducible Capital	Foreign Investment as a Percentage of Fixed Reproducible Capital
1929 . .	16	65	25
1940 : .	13	76	17
1950 : .	11	101	11
1955 . .	15	122	12

Sources: *Inversiones Internacionales en América Latina*, Javier Marquez, Bank of Mexico, Mexico City, 1945; *The United States and Foreign Investment Problems*, Cleora Lewis, The Brookings Institution, Washington, 1948; *International Transactions of the United States, during the War, 1940–45*, U.S. Department of Commerce, Washington, D.C. 1948; *The Balance of Payments of the United States, 1946–48*, U.S. Department of Commerce, Washington, D.C., 1950, and other publications, 1950–57; *Foreign Capital in Latin America*, United Nations Department of Economic and Social Affairs, New York, 1955.
See also Table I.

(2) The decline in exports, terms of trade, and the outflow of foreign capital adversely affected import capacity, in the period 1930–45, and made its greatest impact on capital-goods imports, which were sharply reduced. This seriously affected the composition and level of investment and capital, in these years. The reverse occurred in the period 1945–55, and on a much larger scale; the post-war expansion of exports and improvement in the terms of trade resulted in a phenomenal expansion in capital-goods imports, and Latin American manufacturing capacity more than doubled in the post-war years, while the stock of fixed capital rose by more than one-half.

(3) The degree of utilization of productive capacity expanded significantly; this was especially true in manufacturing,

but also occurred in transport, energy, and communications, as well as government capital in public works and welfare services. This expanding degree of utilization, which enhanced capital productivity, derived from the protection of manufacturing activity already referred to, the increase in domestic demand, and economies deriving from the expanding scale of operation. In addition, partly as a counter-cyclical device, and partly as an overt effort to spur industrialization, governments expanded basic social capital in roads, streets, water-works, and schools, and this expansion of basic social capital favoured the expansion of manufacturing output. All these factors made it possible to use more fully the existing productive capacity accumulated in the 1920s and earlier.

(4) In an expanding economy the share of the gross product absorbed in off-setting depreciation of the stock of capital declines, as has been demonstrated by Robert Eisner and others. Under these conditions the relative burden of depreciation and replacement charges in the overall investment effort is reduced. A given investment effort – a given gross investment rate – signifies a greater net investment content and a larger growth in the stock of fixed capital. This, in effect, has been the experience of Latin America in the last twenty-five years.

(5) As has been demonstrated in the case of capital in manufacturing, railroads, and public utilities in the United States, new capital is more efficient and productive than old capital, in the sense of greater yield and product per unit cost of capital. The productivity of fixed reproducible capital in Latin America has benefited from this increased efficiency of new capital goods replacing older similar goods and, thereby, without the need for pioneering, has benefited from technological progress.

Since World War II, foreign capital in Latin America has again been expanding; this time, with the outstanding exception of petroleum investment in Venezuela, new foreign investment has gone predominantly into manufacturing enterprises, in most Latin American countries, and has thereby contributed to the introduction of modern technology in the form of more efficient and productive capital equipment. (For Latin America, this development signifies a fundamental change in the role of foreign capital, since the new emphasis on investment in manufacturing enterprises reflects the growing domestic market, and the now united interest in its growth and expansion.)

4. *Factors affecting adversely the efficiency, utilization, and productivity of fixed reproducible capital in Latin America*

Even with the overall long-term improvement in the efficiency, utilization, and productivity of capital in Latin America, it should be noted that the product per unit of capital in the region has remained static since 1948 and in some important countries (Argentina, for example) has fallen below the 1948 level. A number of problems have contributed to this circumstance, including the following factors:

(1) inefficient use of land resources;
(2) mis-utilization of public investment resources;
(3) decline in the rate of government resources available for public investment;
(4) incidence of inadequate growth of export earnings on capital-goods imports and the level and composition of investment;
(5) problems of minimum economic scale of operations confronting economies on the threshold of industrial production of consumers' durable goods, capital goods, and the more complex metals, machinery, and chemical products.

The following examples of inefficient use of land resources and mis-utilization of public investment resources may be cited:

(a) *Inefficient use of land resources.* As is discussed more fully in the section on 'Problems of data, concepts, and methods', the detailed and adequate measure of agricultural improvement, including valuation at depreciated replacement cost of land clearing and levelling and other soil improvements, buildings, installations and fencing, plantations and permanent crops, cultivated forests and cultivated pasture, as well as machinery, equipment, and cattle, is fundamental to the analysis of investment, capital, productivity, and economic growth in Latin America. For this reason, the estimation of investment and capital in agricultural improvements has been the subject of special attention in our studies of development, especially in the case of Argentina and Colombia.

In the study of agricultural development in Colombia it was possible to make a very detailed cross-section analysis of value added, man-power, and fixed reproducible capital by main types of agricultural production, providing estimates of labour, land, and capital productivity.[1] As may be seen in Table VIII, land, labour, and capital productivity (value added per worker, per unit of land, and per unit of capital) was consistently and substantially lower in cattle-raising than in the cultivation of crops. In effect, the data revealed a low level of efficiency in the utiliza-

TABLE VIII

Colombia; Productivity in the Utilization of Agricultural Land, Labour, and Capital Resources in 1953

	Agriculture			
	Total	Coffee	Other Crops	Cattle
Gross value of production (millions of pesos)	3,785·2	899·7	1,497·0	1,388·5
Value of materials and service inputs originating in non-agricultural sectors (millions of pesos) .	447·3	56·4	187·0	203·9
Gross product (*millions of pesos*) .	3,337·9	843·3	1,310·0	1,184·6
Labour force (thousands of persons)	2,214·6	335·9	822·3	1,056·4
Gross product per worker (*pesos*) .	1,507	2,511	1,593	1,121
Fixed reproducible capital, total (*millions of pesos*) [2] . .	8,236	1,092	1,334	5,810
Land improvements . . .	2,342	166	545	1,631
Plantations and cultivated pasture	687	312	123	252
Buildings, installations, and fencing	1,458	609	519	330
Stock of cattle	3,585	—	—	3,585
Machinery and equipment .	164	5	147	12
Product–capital ratio . . .	0·405	0·772	0·982	0·204
Area cultivated (millions of hectares)	29,770	831	2,069	26,870
Gross product per hectare (*pesos*) .	112·1	1,014·8	633·2	44·1

Source: *Economic Development of Colombia, op. cit.*, pp. 190–195.

tion of man-power, land, and capital resources in cattle-raising, in comparison with other types of agricultural production; cattle-raising in Colombia was, in fact, a capital-intensive activity. This analysis provided a useful quantification of what was recognized [3] as one of the most serious problems of Colombian agriculture – namely, the anti-economic distortion in land

[1] *Economic Development of Colombia, op. cit.*, pp. 187–195, 376–383.
[2] At depreciated replacement cost.
[3] *Economic Development of Colombia*, Lauchlin Currie and collaborators, International Bank for Reconstruction and Development, Washington, 1951.

use. The prevailing practice in 1953 was the use of the few fertile, temperate, level, plain regions surrounding principal cities in mountainous, tropical Colombia for extensive cattle exploitation. The needs of the urban population, in comparison, indicated the need for intensive use of these lands for dairy and truck-crop cultivation, and the raising of cattle in other regions. This distortion in land use, with its anti-economic incidence on land, labour, and capital productivity, derived from the misapplication of the land reform law of 1936, which was substantially evaded by the eviction of agricultural labourers from the best lands. The result has been a serious shortage in food production,[1] substantial dietary and nutritional deficiency, and high relative prices for food, in a country combining tropical, sub-tropical, and temperate zones, and capable of producing all kinds of food. The estimates of fixed, reproducible capital provide a quantitative tool for evaluating and projecting the effect of alternative policies and measures aimed at solving this inefficient use of basic resources and its adverse consequences.

The study of the economic development of Argentina also analyses the incidence of mis-utilization of land resources involved in the post-war decline by one-third in area cultivated to permanent crops, excluding feed crops, and the giving over of this land to extensive cattle-raising. In this case, contributing factors included low, fixed prices for agricultural crops, and an increasing shortage of farm workers, without a compensating increase in agricultural mechanization. This decline in area cultivated to crops has resulted in a serious fall in Argentine exports, foreign-exchange earnings, imports of raw materials as well as capital goods, and has been a main factor in the post-1948 economic stagnation. The programme for economic recovery aims at bringing back into cultivation a large part of this land, and raising more cattle on less land through the use of cultivated feed crops.

(b) *Mis-utilization of public investment resources.* As has been indicated, the expanding role of Latin American governments since the 1930s in fostering economic development and industrialization through public investment in basic social capital and other aspects of economic policy has been accompanied in recent years, in some countries, by problems of mis-direction and mis-utilization of public investment resources, in relation to

[1] See *Economic Development of Colombia, op. cit.,* pp. 137–141.

needs, as well as a decline in the rate of public investment. In a number of countries a large share of public investment resources is going to military, administrative, and costly social-welfare projects, while the functioning and growth of the economy is hampered and limited by increasingly severe shortages of basic social capital in energy, transport, and other essential public services. An interesting example, for which quantitative data on investment and capital are available, is the case of Argentina.[1]

Argentina's post-1948 economic stagnation derived, in great part, from a mis-utilization of basic resources of land, labour, and capital, which resulted in imbalance and distortions in the structure of production, investment, and employment, and an overall decline in labour productivity, land productivity, and capital productivity. The post-revolution economic recovery programme, adopted in 1956, is based on the possibility of a rapid short-term recovery of productivity in land, labour, and capital through an economic policy and investment programme calculated to correct these distortions in the structure of production, investment, and employment. Attention will here be given to one aspect of these distortions – namely, the post-war mis-utilization of public investment.

Despite the relatively large investment resources available to the Argentine Government at the end of World War II, basic social capital in electricity, railroads, roads, petroleum, and coal exploitation, as well as iron and steel production capacity, were seriously neglected. As a consequence, fixed reproducible capital in railroad installations and rolling stock, which had already been seriously neglected by their foreign owners in the 1930s and during the war, continued to decline. No net new road construction (in terms of depreciated replacement cost) was undertaken after 1943. Expansion of electric-power capacity was only a fraction of needs, and industrial production, whose electricity supply was severely rationed, was seriously hampered. The failure to develop petroleum and coal exploitation and iron and steel capacity in line with expanding needs placed an impossible burden on import requirements, and forced severe restriction of imports of raw materials and intermediate products for industrial

---

[1] See *Economic Development of Argentina, op. cit.; Fixed Reproducible Capital in Argentina, 1935–55, op. cit.*, and following section of this paper, 'Capital formation, fixed reproducible capital, and economic growth in Argentina, 1900–1955'.

TABLE IX

Argentina; Composition of Real Investment of the National Government

(Percentage distribution of total)

	Historical Period [1] (Fixed Reproducible Capital in 1948)	1945–46	1947–51	1952–55	Projected Distribution of Investment Based on Investment Programmes [2] to 1961
		Investment			
Total	100·0	100·0	100·0	100·0	100·0
A. Investment of an economic character	67·5	33·4	53·6	72·6	78·0
I. Transport . .	41·1	26·2	27·4	29·0	40·6
Roads . .	18·4	12·9	8·6	12·3	18·0
Railroads . .	11·9	3·6	7·2	8·8	14·1
River and maritime shipping .	8·2	5·8	8·8	4·7	5·7
Air transport .	1·7	3·9	2·1	1·2	0·8
Urban transport.	0·9	—	0·6	2·0	2·0
II. Energy and communications .	21·9	3·2	16·7	24·4	23·7
Petroleum and coal . .	14·9	—	4·9	8·6	8·9
Water, electricity, and communications .	7·0	3·2	11·8	15·8	14·8
III. Agriculture .	0·8	0·9	0·7	1·7	3·3
Research and experiment .	...	—	0·1	1·0	2·3
Silos and grain elevators .	...	0·9	0·5	0·7	0·5
Meat-packing plants . .	...	—	0·1	—	0·5
IV. Industry . .	3·7	0·7	1·8	6·2	7·1
Iron and steel .	...	—	0·5	2·1	5·6
Other . .	...	0·7	1·3	4·1	1·5
V. Contribution to regional development . .	...	2·4	7·0	11·3	3·3
B. Investment of a social character .	28·0	14·8	18·3	12·5	11·4
Housing and other buildings .	11·9	8·5	13·7	8·4	7·6
Health projects .	12·6	5·9	3·6	3·7	3·5
Other. .	3·5	0·4	1·0	0·4	0·3
C. Investment in national defence . .	2·1	50·7	23·5	9·7	6·0
D. Investment of an administrative character . . .	2·4	1·1	4·6	5·2	4·6

Source: Economic Development of Argentina, op. cit.

[1] The historical period is calculated on the basis of the Census of Government Property made in 1948, excluding land and inventories of raw materials and inter-

production, as well as imports of new capital goods and replacement parts. Both agriculture and industry were severely hindered by shortages of transport facilities.[1]

The post-war distortion in the composition of public investment in Argentina, and the neglect of basic social capital, may be seen in Table IX, which compares the percentage distribution of fixed reproducible capital, at depreciated replacement cost, in 1948, reflecting the composition of public investment in earlier decades with that in the years 1945–46, the period of the first five-year plan, 1947–51, the years 1952–55, and the present investment programme, to the year 1961. In a developing economy, priorities in public investment in basic social capital change, but, as may be seen, the changes in the composition of public investment in the years 1945–46 and 1947–51 were contrary to the development needs of the country. As may be seen whereas in the historical period public investment of an economic character had represented 67 per cent of total investment, this share fell to 33 per cent in 1945–46 and 54 per cent in 1947–51; the proportion in transport fell from 41 to 26 per cent and 27 per cent, respectively; that in roads fell from 18 to 13 per cent and 9 per cent; railroad investment fell from 12 to 3 per cent and 7 per cent; petroleum and coal were neglected; electricity investment was far below needs; and basic iron and steel investment was not undertaken until after 1950. On the other hand, investment in national defence rose to 51 per cent of all national government investment in 1945–46, and 23 per cent in the period of the first five-year plan, 1947–51. With the onset of economic stagnation, especially after 1951, a frantic effort was made to change the direction of public investment, as may be seen in the increased share dedicated to projects of an economic character in the period 1952–55. An appreciation of the distortions in the composition of public investment may also be obtained by comparing the composition of present and projected investment

---

mediate products. The percentage distribution of the depreciated replacement value of government property in 1948, as adjusted, is considered a valid measure of the channelling of investment in the historical period. Investment in national defence in this period is probably underestimated, because some items are probably included in buildings and river and maritime shipping. Similarly, the group 'Petroleum and coal' may include investment in other mining activity.

[2] The projected distribution of investment is based on estimated investment needs and investment programmes actually under way, in accordance with the evaluation of existing shortages and the needs of an expanding economy.

[1] See *Plan de restablecimiento económico*, Raúl Prebisch, Economic Adviser to the President of the Provisional Government, Buenos Aires, January 1956.

programmes of the Argentine Government (to 1961), based on a detailed examination of needs and the fixing of priorities.

5. *Future outlook for Latin American economic growth, capital requirements, and capital productivity*

We may ask what does the foregoing analysis imply with respect to the future outlook for Latin American economic growth, capital requirements, and capital productivity? Without pretending to sketch the future pattern of Latin American economic growth, some important elements which appear clearly in the picture may be noted. The immediate future will be an era of concentration on the solution of production-hampering shortages of basic social capital in transport and energy. In a number of important countries basic new progress has already been made. This, together with expanded iron and steel and other intermediate materials production, should facilitate the greater concentration of import capacity on new capital goods and intermediate products for expanding industry. Progress may be expected in the development of a regional multi-lateral payments system, and regional market, which will provide a solution to some problems of adequate size of market for economies of scale. With such a development, the composition of Latin American exports will change, favouring manufactures, and the region's ability to absorb new foreign capital, also favouring manufactures, will increase. Thus, after a continued pause in the level of the gross product per unit of capital, which has been stagnant since 1948, further progress may be expected.

6. *Hypothesis with respect to the differences in the rate of increase and in the level of the product–capital ratio and the rate of economic growth of Argentina and Colombia*

Since 1929, the rate of economic growth in Colombia has been spectacular, while that in Argentina, for example, has been low. Whereas Colombia experienced an annual rate of growth in the *per capita* gross product of 1·9 per cent in the period 1929–55, that in Argentina was only 0·5 per cent. In effect, Colombia experienced a greater rate of increase in product per unit of capital, as well as capital *per capita*, and achieved a higher absolute level of product per unit of capital (as may be seen in Table X), and, *in relative terms, experienced a more balanced rate of change* in the structure of investment and capital. While post-war distortions in the direction of resources contributed to this relative imbalance and low rate of growth in Argentina, detailed long-term data on the economic sector composition of fixed reproducible capital in Argentina and Colombia, as well as data on the structural composition of capital for a number of other Latin American countries for the year 1950, suggest that more basic factors were involved. The data suggest that *relative changes in* the structure of investment and capital, and in the level of the gross product per unit of capital, reflect the era in which capital accumulation began to accelerate, the nature of basic resources, and the level of technology in this era, as well as the social structure and the pattern of demand.

TABLE X

Relative Importance of Change in Fixed Reproducible Capital Per Capita *and Increase in the Product per Unit of Capital in the Increase in Gross Domestic Product* Per Capita *in Argentina and Colombia, from 1929 to 1955*

(Dollars at 1950 prices)

	Argentina	Colombia
Gross product per capita:		
1929	505	148
1955	571	244
Annual rate of change (in per cent)	*0·5*	*1·9*
Fixed reproducible capital per capita:		
1929	2,111	622
1955	1,925	683
Annual rate of change (in per cent)	*−0·3*	*0·4*
Product per unit of capital:		
1929	0·24	0·24
1955	0·30	0·36
Annual rate of change (in per cent)	*0·9*	*1·6*

Source : See notes to Table I.

To put the matter in its most elemental terms, the quality and condition of housing, schools, hospitals, streets, parks, sanitary services, theatres, and recreation facilities in Argentina are relatively high and compare favourably with that in cities of Western Europe and the United States. This is not the case with Colombia, which, on the other hand, has a basic iron and steel industry – a factor of industrial development which Argentina will not have until 1961. This example may be said to have the following implications.

Newly developing economies have a simpler problem in attaining balance in the structure of growth than do older economies, and have been able to incorporate newer and more efficient capital, and concentrate a relatively greater share of the investment effort in expanding capacity in agriculture, industry, energy, and transport, in comparison with housing and other public social services. Argentina, for example, whose *per capita* gross product in 1900 was already $330 (at 1950 prices), and whose basic capital structure was established by 1915, has an old capital structure in industry, transport, electricity, and agriculture. Argentina has not been able to scrap or replace old capital to install new capital, in great part because of the great burden involved in financing investment for replacement as well as new growth. Colombia, a newly developing economy, on the other hand, has no such burden, and new investment goes for modern, efficient equipment.

These factors affecting the relative change in the structural balance of fixed reproducible capital may, therefore, be an important element of explanation of differences in the rate of increase in product per unit of capital, as well as differences in their absolute level.

7. *Capital formation, fixed reproducible capital, and economic growth in Argentina, 1900–55* [1]

In the period 1900–29 Argentina experienced an extraordinary rate of development in its gross product, fixed reproducible capital, and population, which increased at the annual rate of 5·1, 4·9, and 3·3 per cent, respectively. This impressive rate of growth was related to the extraordinary expansion of exports and improvement in the external terms of trade (see Table XI), which, together with a massive inflow of foreign capital and a heavy programme of public works, made possible an extremely high rate of investment (see Tables XII and XIII). This involved not only investment in agriculture and industry but also in railroad transport, roads, shipping, electric power, residential housing, commerce, and public administrative, social and welfare services (see Tables XIV and XV). Between the periods 1900–4 and 1925–29, fixed reproducible capital in agriculture doubled, that in industry expanded three times as great, while that in transport, communications, electricity, housing, commerce, and

[1] Minor differences from the data in the paper (following) by Balboa and Fracchia derive from differences in classification and the inclusion of cattle stocks. In addition, in the calculation of a long-term series from 1900 there is a slight difference in the treatment of depreciation.

TABLE XI

Argentina: Exports, Effect of the Terms of Trade, and the Gross Product, 1900–55

(Five-year averages)

Periods	Exports	Effect of the Terms of Trade in Relation to 1950	Gross Domestic Product	Exports	Effect of the Terms of Trade in Relation to 1950
	Millions of pesos at 1950 prices			As a percentage of the gross product	
1900–4	2,915	318	10,756	27·1	3·0
1905–9	4,036	1,219	15,890	25·4	7·7
1910–14	4,480	1,313	19,896	22·5	6·6
1915–19	4,601	888	19,131	24·0	4·6
1920–24	6,393	− 346	25,491	25·1	−1·4
1925–29	7,913	1,998	33,184	23·8	6·0
1930–34	7,405	−1,337	33,863	21·9	−3·9
1935–39	7,397	602	39,754	19·1	1·5
1940–44	5,963	−1,024	45,908	13·0	−2·2
1945–49	5,900	1,339	57,009	10·3	2·3
1950–54	4,685	− 175	63,150	7·4	−0·3
1955	4,697	− 563	68,769	6·8	−0·8

Source: *Economic Development of Argentina*, Argentina Government–United Nations Joint Study Group, *op. cit.*

TABLE XII

Argentina: Public and Private Investment, National and Foreign Investment, as a Percentage of Gross Domestic Product

(Five-year averages)

Period	Total	Public	Private	National	Foreign
1900–4 .	25·9	2·9	23·0	14·1	11·8
1905–9 .	48·2	5·3	42·9	30·2	18·0
1910–14 .	42·2	4·7	37·5	21·4	20·8
1915–19 .	13·0	1·7	11·3	9·6	3·4
1920–24 .	26·4	2·1	24·3	22·8	3·6
1925–29 .	33·3	3·6	29·7	28·5	4·8
1930–34 .	22·2	3·7	18·5	19·0	3·2
1935–39 .	23·7	6·0	17·7	21·2	2·5
1940–44 .	18·2	4·6	13·6	16·7	1·5
1945–49 .	24·4	8·7	15·7	24·3	0·1
1950–54 .	22·5	7·9	14·6	21·8	0·7
1955 .	22·4	5·9	16·5	22·1	0·3

Source: See Table XI.

R

TABLE XIII

Argentina: Gross Fixed Domestic Investment, by Economic Sector, as a Percentage of Gross Domestic Product, by Economic Sector

Period	Total	Agri-culture	Manu-facturing, Mining, and Con-struction	Transport, Communi-cations, and Electricity	Housing, Commerce, Finance, and Personal Services	Govern-ment
1900–4	25·9	9·9	24·7	87·5	33·5	59·7
1905–9	48·2	18·4	24·8	237·7	57·2	142·6
1910–14	42·2	18·4	25·8	136·4	50·9	114·7
1915–19	13·0	13·6	11·4	19·5	12·5	22·4
1920–24	26·4	16·7	19·5	57·4	34·9	34·0
1925–29	33·3	22·5	23·0	88·7	34·7	71·6
1930–34	22·2	12·4	15·0	50·6	25·0	57·0
1935–39	23·7	14·6	15·7	97·9	18·4	39·1
1940–44	18·2	7·5	10·8	51·1	21·8	41·5
1945–49	24·4	13·3	18·5	54·9	25·1	48·1
1950–54	22·5	13·4	15·3	34·5	26·8	47·3
1955	22·4	13·6	14·3	42·7	26·8	41·5

Source: See Table XI.

TABLE XIV

Argentina: Percentage Distribution of Gross Fixed Domestic Investment, 1900–55

(Five-year averages)

Period	Total	Agri-culture	Manu-facturing, Mining, and Con-struction	Transport, Communi-cations, and Electricity	Housing, Commerce, Finance, and Personal Services	Govern-ment
1900–4	100·0	12·0	18·5	13·4	44·2	11·9
1905–9	100·0	10·0	12·8	23·7	40·0	13·5
1910–14	100·0	10·3	15·3	19·6	41·4	13·4
1915–19	100·0	30·4	14·9	10·6	33·3	10·8
1920–24	100·0	16·8	15·4	15·5	45·1	7·2
1925–29	100·0	16·3	16·0	21·5	35·1	11·1
1930–34	100·0	13·2	15·4	20·0	36·3	15·1
1935–39	100·0	14·1	16·9	34·8	24·3	9·9
1940–44	100·0	9·6	15·4	24·7	35·7	14·6
1945–49	100·0	9·5	21·9	21·8	31·2	15·6
1950–54	100·0	9·3	19·4	16·4	35·9	19·0
1955	100·0	9·8	18·3	19·8	35·7	16·4

Source: See Table XI; also *Fixed Reproducible Capital in Argentina, 1935–45*, Manuel Balboa and Alberto Fracchia, *op. cit.*

TABLE XV

Argentina: Fixed Reproducible Capital, by Economic Sector, 1900–55

(Millions of pesos at 1950 prices; five-year averages)

Period	Total	Agri-culture	Manu-facturing, Mining, and Con-struction	Transport, Communi-cations, and Electricity	Housing, Commerce, Finance, and Personal Services	Govern-ment
1900–4	44,606	12,850	4,001	7,795	16,137	3,823
1905–9	68,274	16,698	6,974	12,867	24,694	7,041
1910–14	102,131	19,574	11,286	19,633	39,709	11,929
1915–19	110,151	22,335	12,251	20,014	42,383	13,168
1920–24	116,354	25,493	12,996	19,212	45,687	12,966
1925–29	140,280	29,281	16,763	22,805	56,322	15,109
1930–34	160,275	31,490	19,891	25,656	63,895	19,343
1935–39	165,975	31,307	21,193	29,194	63,346	20,935
1940–44	173,130	31,067	22,428	30,067	64,545	25,023
1945–49	187,963	31,622	26,000	28,895	70,558	30,888
1950–54	217,566	33,048	33,294	29,038	81,216	40,970
1955	231,737	34,068	35,496	29,322	87,500	45,351

Source: See Tables XI and XIV.

TABLE XVI

Argentina: Gross Domestic Product, by Economic Sector, 1900–55

(Millions of pesos at 1950 prices; five-year averages)

Period	Gross Domestic Product at Market Price, Total	Gross Domestic Product, Total	Agri-culture	Manu-facturing, Mining, and Con-struction	Transport, Communi-cations, and Electricity	Housing, Commerce, Finance, and Personal Services	Govern-ment
				(At factor cost)			
1900–4	10,756	10,119	3,367	2,086	426	3,686	554
1905–9	15,890	14,949	4,155	3,944	762	5,362	726
1910–14	19,896	18,718	4,715	4,996	1,205	6,817	985
1915–19	19,131	17,999	5,586	3,235	1,359	6,618	1,201
1920–24	25,491	23,981	6,779	5,287	1,816	8,680	1,419
1925–29	33,184	31,218	8,010	7,694	2,680	11,120	1,714
1930–34	33,863	31,658	7,996	7,744	2,966	10,960	1,992
1935–39	39,754	37,406	9,080	10,120	3,352	12,477	2,377
1940–44	45,908	43,189	10,669	11,897	4,033	13,653	2,937
1945–49	57,009	53,630	9,940	16,427	5,510	17,265	4,488
1950–54	63,150	59,400	9,858	17,997	6,761	19,083	5,701
1955	68,769	64,661	11,165	19,729	7,157	20,500	6,110

Source: See Tables XI and XIV.

government services increased two-fold. This was an era of broad expansion in population, labour force, cultivated area, agricultural production, industrial production and capacity, and basic social capital in transport and electricity, as well as housing and public services. The expansion in fixed reproducible capital was accompanied by an almost parallel increase in the production of goods and services by economic sector (see Table XVI).

TABLE XVII

Argentina: Gross Domestic Product per Unit of Fixed Reproducible Capital, by Economic Sector, 1900–55

(Five-year averages)

Period	Total	Agri-culture	Manu-facturing, Mining, and Con-struction	Transport, Communi-cations, and Electricity	Housing, Commerce, Finance, and Personal Services	Govern-ment
1900–4	0·241	0·262	0·521	0·055	0·228	0·145
1905–9	0·233	0·249	0·566	0·059	0·217	0·103
1910–14	0·195	0·241	0·443	0·061	0·172	0·083
1915–19	0·174	0·250	0·264	0·068	0·156	0·091
1920–24	0·219	0·266	0·407	0·095	0·190	0·109
1925–29	0·237	0·274	0·459	0·118	0·197	0·113
1930–34	0·211	0·254	0·389	0·116	0·172	0·103
1935–39	0·240	0·290	0·478	0·115	0·197	0·114
1940–44	0·265	0·343	0·530	0·134	0·212	0·117
1945–49	0·303	0·314	0·632	0·191	0·245	0·145
1950–54	0·290	0·298	0·541	0·233	0·235	0·139
1955	0·297	0·328	0·556	0·244	0·234	0·135

Source: See Table XI.

Nevertheless, the social force required was also extraordinary, as may be appreciated in an economy with a gross product per unit of capital which ranged from 0·244 in the period 1900–4, to 0·237 in the period 1925–29 [1] (see Table XVII). The relatively low level of the product–capital ratio derived from the 'under-developed' structure of production and fixed reproducible capital (see Tables XVIII and XIX), limitations of the size of the economy on achieving economies of scale, and some degree of

[1] In the United States, for example, the long-term level of the product–capital ratio (comparing the similar concept used here, excluding consumers' durable goods, inventories, monetary metals, and foreign investment), is approximately 0·40. See 'The Growth of Reproducible Wealth in the United States, 1805 to 1950', Raymond Goldsmith, *Income and Wealth Series II, Income and Wealth of the United States*, International Association for Research in Income and Wealth, Cambridge, England, 1952; also *Financial Research and The Problems of The Day, Thirty-Seventh Annual Report*, National Bureau of Economic Research, Inc., New York, May 1957, Part III, Table 1, p. 34.

TABLE XVIII

*Argentina: Percentage Distribution of the Gross Product at
Factor Cost, by Economic Sector, 1900–55*

(Five-year averages)

Period	Total	Agri-culture	Manu-facturing, Mining, and Con-struction	Transport, Communi-cations, and Electricity	Housing, Commerce, Finance, and Personal Services	Govern-ment
1900–4	100·0	33·3	20·6	4·2	36·4	5·5
1905–9	100·0	27·8	26·4	5·1	35·9	4·8
1910–14	100·0	25·2	26·7	6·4	36·4	5·3
1915–19	100·0	31·0	18·0	7·5	36·8	6·7
1920–24	100·0	28·3	22·0	7·6	36·2	5·9
1925–29	100·0	25·7	24·6	8·6	35·6	5·5
1930–34	100·0	25·2	24·5	9·4	34·6	6·3
1935–39	100·0	24·3	27·0	9·0	33·3	6·4
1940–44	100·0	24·7	27·5	9·3	31·7	6·8
1945–49	100·0	18·5	30·6	10·3	32·2	8·4
1950–54	100·0	16·6	30·3	11·4	32·1	9·6
1955	100·0	17·3	30·5	11·1	31·7	9·4

Source: See Table XI.

TABLE XIX

*Argentina: Percentage Distribution of Fixed Reproducible
Capital, by Economic Sector, 1900–55*

(Five-year averages)

Period	Total	Agri-culture	Manu-facturing, Mining, and Con-struction	Transport, Communi-cations, and Electricity	Housing, Commerce, Finance, and Personal Services	Govern-ment
1900–4	100·0	28·8	9·0	17·5	36·1	8·6
1905–9	100·0	24·5	10·2	18·8	36·2	10·3
1910–14	100·0	19·2	11·0	19·2	38·9	11·7
1915–19	100·0	20·3	11·1	18·2	38·4	12·0
1920–24	100·0	21·9	11·2	16·5	39·3	11·1
1925–29	100·0	20·9	11·9	16·3	40·1	10·8
1930–34	100·0	19·6	12·4	16·0	39·9	12·1
1935–39	100·0	18·9	12·8	17·6	38·1	12·6
1940–44	100·0	17·9	13·0	17·4	37·3	14·4
1945–49	100·0	16·8	13·8	15·4	37·6	16·4
1950–54	100·0	15·2	15·3	13·3	37·4	18·8
1955	100·0	14·7	15·3	12·6	37·8	19·6

Source: See Table XI.

under-utilization of manufacturing capacity due to the low level of tariff protection and the wide-open policy on imports, in this period.

The low level of the product–capital ratio in the period 1900–4 to 1925–29 is also notable when, added to the high rate of investment, account is taken of the favourable effect of the accelerated rate of growth on the proportion of the total investment effort required for maintenance and replacement of depreciated capital.

TABLE XX

Argentina: Relative Importance of Depreciation and Net Investment in the Gross Fixed Domestic Investment Effort, 1900–55

Period	Gross Fixed Domestic Investment	Depreciation	Net Investment	Depreciation	Net Investment
	As a percentage of gross product			As a percentage of gross investment	
	(Five-year averages)				
1900–4	25·9	2·3	23·7	9	91
1905–9	48·2	7·9	40·3	16	84
1910–14	42·2	12·3	29·9	29	71
1915–19	13·0	16·1	−3·1	124	−24
1920–24	26·4	13·5	12·9	51	49
1925–29	33·3	15·7	17·6	47	53
1930–34	22·2	18·5	3·7	83	17
1935–39	23·7	18·2	5·5	77	23
1940–44	18·2	17·0	1·2	93	7
1945–49	24·4	14·5	9·9	59	41
1950–54	22·5	15·0	7·5	67	33
1955	22·4	14·2	8·2	63	37
	(Period averages)				
1900–29	31·4	12·6	18·8	40	60
1930–55	22·3	16·2	6·1	73	27

Source: See Table XI.

In effect, mainly because of the accelerated rate of growth in the period 1900–29, only 40 per cent of the total gross fixed domestic investment effort was absorbed by maintenance, replacement, and depreciation of existing fixed capital; 60 per cent of the total investment effort was dedicated to net new investment. Other factors involved include the relative high gross investment rate and the relatively low depreciation rate associated with the relatively long average length of useful life of the structural composition of capital in this period (see Table XX).

This appreciation of the social force required for economic development under the conditions of the Argentine economy in the period 1900–29 represents an interesting quantitative demonstration of the difficulty and great social cost of economic development.

In the period since 1929 the Argentine economy has experienced basic structural changes in the economic composition of production, capital, and labour force. Exports, terms of trade, and foreign capital have declined, and industrial development has advanced, favoured by a protectionist policy, internal relative prices, government economic policy in the 1930s, which expanded basic social capital, and heavy post-war imports of productive machinery and equipment for industry. With the process of economic development and structural change, the gross product per unit of capital expanded. Despite this, the rate of growth of capital lagged behind, and serious distortions developed in the economic sector allocation of capital, especially in the post-war years.

In contrast with the period 1900–29, which had experienced an even more rapid rate of growth in the stock of capital than in the population (with annual rates of increase of 4·9 and 3·3 per cent, respectively), in the period 1929–55, the rate of growth of capital lagged behind (with annual rates of growth of 1·5 per cent in capital and 1·9 per cent in population), so that the level of fixed reproducible capital *per capita* declined at an annual rate of 0·3 per cent in this latter period. The annual rate of growth of the *per capita* gross product, which was 1·7 per cent in the period 1900–29, declined to 0·5 per cent in the period 1929–55.

The decline in the rate of growth of the *per capita* gross product would have been greater but for the increase in the gross product per unit of capital, which rose from 0·24 in 1929 to a peak of 0·32 in 1948, and fell thereafter to 0·30 in 1955.

The expansion of capital productivity, from 1929 to 1948, derived from the basic changes in economic structure, the process of economic development and industrialization, benefits of economy of scale, fuller utilization of manufacturing capacity, and the increased efficiency of new capital.

Since 1948, the Argentine economy has stagnated, capital

productivity and the *per capita* gross product have fallen, and broad distortions have developed in the structure of production, employment, investment, and capital.

These distortions in the utilization of resources of land, labour, and capital involved: (1) inefficient utilization of land, and consequent decline in agricultural production and exports, and export earnings; (2) crippling of manufacturing production as a consequence of shortages of imported raw materials and capital goods; (3) failure adequately to maintain and expand basic social capital in transport and energy, and the consequent hindering of agricultural and industrial production; and (4) with industrial employment declining, the increasing absorption of the urban labour force in service activities, which experienced a severe decline in productivity. These distortions in the use of resources may be attributed to the following factors: the misutilization of public investment funds, alluded to earlier; the drain on public revenue deriving from increases in transfer payments, including expanding deficits of government enterprises affected by the economic stagnation and faulty price policy; the inappropriate economic policy with respect to agricultural prices and mechanization to offset the outflow of labour force; the insufficiency of import capacity to provide minimum needs for the functioning of the economy, due to failure to push earlier and more seriously the establishment of a domestic iron and steel industry, and production of oil and coal, so that import capacity could be dedicated to imports of other intermediate products and capital goods. In addition, the post-1948 stagnation has had the effect of increasing the depreciation and replacement burden on the gross product and minimizing the net new investment in the given total investment effort. Of the post-war net increase in capital, less than one-third went to directly productive activities; more than one-third has gone to government administrative, social, and military services; and the remainder has gone to housing, commerce and financial services, and personal services. The post-war dedication of one-third of investment resources to government administrative, social, and military services represents a calamitous mis-direction of the country's vital investment resources. While this had represented 15 per cent of total fixed reproducible capital in 1944, by 1948 the proportion had risen to 32 per cent. In fact, the *per capita* stock of capital in government administrative, social, and military services was the only category of increase in capital *per capita* in comparison with the pre-war period. In 1955 directly productive capital *per capita*, including that in agriculture, industry, transport, communications, and electricity, was 20 per cent below the level of 1929; that in transport, communications, and electricity has fallen by 30 per cent. While capital per worker in industry more than recovered the effect of the depression and the war, that in agriculture has not recovered the 1929 level. The fall in basic social capital *per capita* in transport, communications, and electricity has represented a basic structural error in the use of investment

TABLE XXI

Argentina: Gross Fixed Domestic Investment, by Economic Activity, 1900–55

(Millions of pesos at 1950 prices; five-year averages)

Period	Total	Agriculture	Manufacturing, Mining, and Construction	Transport, Communications, and Electricity	Housing, Commerce, Finance, and Personal Services	Government
1900–4	2,789	335	515	373	1,235	331
1905–9	7,658	764	980	1,812	3,066	1,036
1910–14	8,403	868	1,287	1,644	3,474	1,130
1915–19	2,490	757	370	265	829	269
1920–24	6,718	1,130	1,032	1,042	3,031	483
1925–29	11,046	1,806	1,772	2,378	3,863	1,227
1930–34	7,528	994	1,160	1,502	2,736	1,136
1935–39	9,422	1,325	1,592	3,283	2,293	929
1940–44	8,344	804	1,282	2,062	2,976	1,220
1945–49	13,891	1,318	3,046	3,027	4,340	2,160
1950–54	14,236	1,318	2,760	2,336	5,123	2,699
1955	15,427	1,515	2,818	3,054	5,504	2,536

Source: See Tables XI and XIV.

and capital resources, and has been one of the main limiting factors with respect to the growth in industrial production and the gross product as a whole. This shortage of basic social capital in transport and electricity has been accompanied by significant under-utilization of capital in some sectors of industry and agriculture due, in part, to the shortages of basic social capital.

8. *Capital formation, fixed reproducible capital, and economic growth in Colombia, 1925–53*

The study of the economic development of Colombia, in the period 1925–53, including new, homogeneous, detailed quantum

estimates of the gross product, investment, and fixed reproducible capital, by economic sector, and by type of capital good,
also demonstrates that the process of economic growth signifies
a broad improvement in the efficiency, productivity, and utilization of investment and capital, in addition to man-power. The
case of Colombia holds special interest, because it represents an
economy expanding from a gross product *per capita* level of
approximately $100 in 1925 to $300 in 1953; in the case of
Argentina, the gross product *per capita* rose from approximately
$330 in 1900 to almost $600 in 1956.[1]

In the period 1925–53 Colombia experienced an annual rate of
growth of 2 per cent in the *per capita* gross product. This reflected a significant process of economic development and industrialization, including changes in the economic structure
distribution of production, labour force, investment, and productive capacity, which was accompanied by a persistent improvement in the product–capital ratio. In 1925 production
capacity was mainly confined to agricultural improvements,
housing, and government administrative and social services,
which represented 84 per cent of the total stock of fixed reproducible capital. In the same year the stock of capital in manufacturing, mining, transport, and electricity comprised only
16 per cent of total productive capacity. From then to 1953 the
stock of capital in the economy as a whole doubled, but that
corresponding to the first group of sectors mentioned increased
by only 70 per cent, while that in the other sectors increased by
three-fold. In this way the stock of capital in agriculture, housing, and government administrative and social services declined
in relative importance, from 84 to 69 per cent, in comparison
with that in the economy as a whole. This represents not only a
quantitative change but also an important qualitative change in
the composition of fixed reproducible capital, with the increase
in the relative importance of those sectors which represent a
higher level of technology.

These important modifications in the distribution of the stock
of capital by economic activities were the result of divergent

[1] It should be noted that the conversion of Latin American gross product, investment, and fixed reproducible capital series from national currencies, expressed in prices of 1950, to U.S. dollars, expressed in prices of 1950, has been
made on the basis of purchasing-power parity rates of exchange, based on pre-
war, pre-exchange-control era, exchanges. For a discussion of the implications of
this method, see Part III-B of this paper, 'Problem of International Comparison of
Investment and Capital'.

trends in the investment rate for the various economic sectors. While the average overall investment rate stood at 26·1 per cent in the period 1925–29, at 16·1 per cent in the years 1930–44, and at 19·9 per cent in the period 1945–53, the investment rate for agriculture was barely 13·4, 12·8, and 12·3 per cent in each of the periods mentioned, respectively. So low a rate of gross fixed investment did no more than allow agriculture's stock of capital to be replaced and maintained, and, at the most, an exceedingly slow rate of increase to be achieved.

The reverse took place in the manufacturing, mining, transport, and energy sectors, where the investment coefficient was very high, and a substantial increase in the stock of capital of these activities thus became possible.

In the case of industry (manufacturing, mining, and construction), the investment rate attained the high level of 48 per cent in the period 1925–29. During the 1930s and the war years industrial investment was severely affected, first by the reduced capacity to import and then by the restriction of maritime transport and the difficulties of purchasing capital goods from the more highly developed countries. The investment rate underwent a considerable decline, falling to as low as 13 per cent, in this period. In the post-war years the investment rate in industry recovered, attaining an average of 24 per cent, whereby the stock of capital in industry more than doubled. This high industrial investment coefficient was vital to the rapid progress made by Colombia's economy.

In comparison with the sector just analysed, transport and energy investment attained substantially higher investment rates on account of the heavy public investment in these branches. During the period 1925–44 more than two-thirds of total investment in transport – including roads, railways, ports, oil-pipes, airports, and also rolling stock and railway equipment – were financed by the Government. During the post-war period, this outlay amounted to more than half the investment in the sectors mentioned, and represented more than 40 per cent of total public investment during the post-war period. Public investment in electric-power installations, and in other services, has also assumed considerable dimensions in recent years.

Public investment has played an important role in the economic development of Colombia, both in the provision of basic social capital, as well as an element of compensatory economic policy, increasing in relative importance in periods of economic contraction, and declining in relative importance in periods of economic expansion.

Fluctuations in export earnings and the terms of trade, and their effect on the import capacity, have also had a considerable incidence on the level and composition of investment and capital, by economic sectors, as well as by type of capital good. This is due to the low level of domestic production of productive machinery and equipment, whose supply depends mainly on imports.

This situation affects the different economic sectors in different ways. In the case of agriculture, for example, less than one-fifth of total investment comprises machinery and equipment, while the greater part consists of direct use of man-power in land clearing, maintenance, and improvement, as well as for the establishment of plantations and perennial crops. In the case of the manufacturing sector, on the contrary, the situation is quite different, since productive machinery and equipment represents a substantial part of all investment. In these circumstances the great sensitivity of imports of productive machinery and equipment to fluctuations in the import capacity has had powerful influence on the variation of the rate of investment in the industrial sector.

In addition, the proportion of machinery and equipment in total investment has a determining influence on the degree of technological advance which that investment represents, and also influences the product–capital ratio. During the years 1925–29 the proportion of productive machinery and equipment in total fixed domestic investment reached 36 per cent; afterwards, due to the contraction in the capacity to import, the proportion fell to 22 per cent in the period 1930–38 and to only 17 per cent in the years 1939–45. This accentuated decline explains, in good measure, apart from the saving and investment capacity of the country, the fall in the overall investment rate from 26 per cent in 1925–29 to 16 per cent in the years 1930–44. The substantial improvement in the import capacity in the post-war years favoured an increase in the proportion of machinery and equipment in total investment, which rose to 35 per cent in the years 1946–53.

A close parallel may be observed between the variations in the proportion mentioned and the economic sector distribution of investment (see tables which follow). Investment in machinery and equipment for the manufacturing sector represented approximately 15 per cent of total investment in the periods 1925–29 and 1946–53, and only 9 and 7 per cent, respectively, in the periods 1930–38 and 1939–45. Similarly, in the case of transport, investment in rolling stock comprised 8 per cent of total investment for the economy as a whole in the period 1925–29, and 9 per cent in the years 1946–53, while in the intermediate periods the proportion fell to 4 per cent.

As might be expected, these tendencies had an important effect on the composition of the stock of capital. The modifications in the stock of capital which took place in the period 1925–53 represent not only a change in economic structure but also basic qualitative differences.

The proportion of productive machinery and equipment in the total stock of capital in 1925 was only 13·2 per cent. After rising to 16·4 per cent in 1929, the incidence of the curtailment of the capacity to import resulted in a decline to 15·9 per cent in 1938 and 14·3 per cent in 1945. In the post-war period the proportion rose rapidly, so that in 1953 the share of productive machinery and equipment represented 19·5 per cent of the total stock of capital.

The role of industrial development may be clearly appreciated in a comparison of the share of capital in productive machinery and equipment represented by industry with that in the economy as a whole. This share rose from 5·6 per cent in 1925 to 8·7 per cent in 1953.

This expanding importance of investment in machinery and equipment, with respect to that in construction and improvements, has been an important element in obtaining an improved utilization and productivity of investment and capital resources.

Changes in the composition of production, labour force, and capital by economic activity have signified a broad improvement in the efficiency and utilization of productive resources. The expanding productivity of labour is reflected in the increase in the gross product per worker and that of capital in persistent improvement in the product–capital ratio. In addition, the level of capital per worker is one of the basic determining factors in the level of the gross product per worker.

While the principal element in the long-term increase in the productivity of the Colombian economy has been the relative transfer of resources of man-power and capital to activities representing a more advanced technology and higher level of productivity, this has not been all. To this must be added the improvement – in some cases substantial – in labour and capital productivity within each economic activity sector. These improvements, in the case of capital productivity, derive from economies of scale arising with the expansion of the market, fuller degree of utilization, and a greater efficiency of new capital.

9. *Investment priority: case of the Cauca Valley Authority of Colombia*

In 1955 and 1956 David Lillienthal, former Director of the Tennessee Valley Authority in the United States and the International Bank, participated in the creation of the Cauca Valley Authority, a regional development body set up by several of the departments (provinces) of Colombia for the purpose of organizing a gigantic hydro-electric and irrigation development. In supporting the work of the Authority, Lillienthal had in mind the role of the Tennessee Valley Authority in spurring the economic development of the south-east region of the United States. Upon close examination, however, it soon became apparent that the cases of the Cauca Valley and the Tennessee Valley were quite different, that the Cauca Valley project would have represented a serious diversion of public investment resources from higher investment priority projects and, subsequently, the Cauca Valley Authority closed shop.

Large public investment in the Tennessee Valley, especially in the 1930s, had served as an important investment outlet in a country suffering in the throes of a severe business cycle characterized by a contraction in private investment, which adversely affected total demand and employment. The TVA project was one of a large number of public-works projects undertaken with the primary purpose of stimulating the economy, by offsetting the fall in private investment and providing employment. The TVA project was also undertaken in one of the most economically backward and under-developed regions of the United States. Subsequently, this large investment in basic social capital, with its sizeable energy and water resources, made possible the expansion of war production through the establishment of a broad range of manufacturing enterprises and, thereby,

TABLE XXII

Colombia: Growth and Composition of the Production of Goods and Services, 1925–53

	Composition of Gross Product by Economic Activity			Annual Rate of Growth	
	1925	1945	1953	1925–53	1945–53
Total	100·0	100·0	100·0	4·6	5·9
Agriculture . . .	58·8	47·0	36·9	2·9	2·7
Mining . . .	1·5	3·7	3·7	8·1	5·7
Manufacturing . .	7·6	13·4	17·2	7·7	9·2
Artisan industry . .	2·9	3·1	3·8	5·6	8·4
Construction . .	2·6	6·1	4·8	7·0	2·7
Transport . . .	2·3	4·2	7·4	9·1	13·7
Energy, communications, and public services .	0·4	0·7	1·2	8·7	12·7
Government . .	5·7	5·5	6·9	5·4	8·9
Commerce, finance, and services . . .	8·7	10·2	12·9	6·1	9·0
Rental income . .	9·5	6·1	5·2	2·3	3·8

Source: Economic Development of Colombia, United Nations, *op. cit.*

TABLE XXIII

Colombia: Population Growth and Distribution, by Economic Activity

	Percentage Distribution			Annual Rate of Growth	
	1925	1945	1953	1925–53	1945–53
Total population . .	100·0	100·0	100·0	2·1	2·2
Active population .	37·2	35·9	34·0	1·6	1·5
Inactive population .	62·8	64·1	66·0	2·3	2·6
Urban population .	23·2	34·0	42·7	4·4	5·2
Rural population .	76·8	66·0	57·3	1·1	0·4
Active population . .	100·0	100·0	100·0	1·6	1·5
Agriculture . .	68·5	59·9	53·8	1·4	1·7
Mining . . .	1·6	2·1	2·0	2·5	0·6
(a) Mining proper .	0·4	0·5	0·5	0·3	—
(b) Artisan mining .	1·2	1·6	1·5	2·5	0·6
Manufacturing . .	3·4	5·2	6·4	4·1	4·2
Artisan industry .	7·9	7·3	8·5	2·1	3·5
Construction . .	1·8	2·7	3·6	4·3	5·1
Transport, communications, and energy.	16·8	2·5	3·2		4·9
Commerce and finances		5·8	6·4		2·8
Government . .		2·4	3·7		7·2
Services . . .		12·1	12·4		1·8

Source: See Table XXII.

significantly changed the economic structure of the region, as well as the productivity and efficiency of utilization of manpower resources.

Cauca Valley, on the other hand, is one of the most advanced and most rapidly developing regions of Colombia, combining a

TABLE XXIV

Colombia: Stock of Capital and Investment Rate by Economic Activity

	Stock of Capital (Millions of pesos at 1950 prices)			Investment Rate	
	1925	1945	1953	1925–29	1945–53
Total . . .	10,553	16,776	22,262	26·1	19·9
Agriculture .	4,287	7,008	7,924	13·4	12·3
Mining . .	206	360	483	24·3	10·0
Industry .	845	1,445	3,183	48·1	23·8
Transport .	620	1,748	2,723	321·2	61·5
Energy . .	[1]	208	424	609·1	199·4
Housing . .	1,823	2,624	3,521	18·0	45·1
Services . .	2,762	3,383	4,004	7·6	10·5

Source: See Table XXII.

[1] Not available.

TABLE XXV

Colombia: Participation of Public Investment in Total Investment, by Economic Activity

(Percentages)

	1925–29	1930–38	1939–44	1945–53
Total	29·4	27·1	36·4	21·9
Agriculture . . .	0·3	3·1	25·5	13·5
Industry . . .	—	—	4·6	7·1
Transport . . .	74·9	77·9	82·2	50·9
Energy	—	0·6	9·0	52·7
Others . . .	32·6	44·9	33·4	21·7

Source: See Table XXII.

booming manufacturing and distribution centre (Cali), a rich coffee- and tropical-fruit-growing region, and a potentially rich coal-mining area. Expansion of energy facilities, the development of coal-mining, the improvement of transportation facilities (both road, rail, and air), had already been programmed by the national government planning council, in projects which equated needs and priorities for the country as a whole with

TABLE XXVI

Colombia: Composition of Gross Fixed Investment, by Type of Investment and Activity

(Annual averages; millions of pesos at 1950 prices)

	1925–29	1930–38	1939–44	1945–53
Gross fixed investment . .	680	532	730	1,236
Machinery and equipment .	247	117	118	427
Agriculture . . .	22	15	12	23
Mining	20	14	18	24
Industry	103	49	50	181
Transports . . .	57	22	25	112
Communications and energy	23	8	3	12
Services . . .	22	9	11	76
Construction of buildings .	83	87	169	298
Urban housing . . .	38	51	112	156
Rural housing . . .	2	2	4	6
Factories . . .	17	5	12	81
Offices and commerce . .	2	3	10	18
Other	24	27	30	35
Other constructions and im- provements . . .	349	328	443	511
Agriculture . . .	150	184	247	273
Transports . . .	160	73	107	110
Other	39	71	89	128

Source: See Table XXII.

TABLE XXVII

Colombia: Stock of Capital, by Type of Capital and by Activity, 1925–53

(Millions of pesos at 1950 prices)

	1925	1929	1938	1945	1953
Stock of capital . . .	10,553	12,185	14,093	16,776	22,262
Cattle	1,609	1,760	2,205	2,833	3,076
Machinery and equipment .	1,384	1,996	2,232	2,393	4,335
Agriculture . . .	104	129	110	92	144
Mining	154	199	238	270	362
Manufacturing . . .	590	880	935	999	1,926
Transport . . .	122	330	375	421	1,094
Communications and energy	—	—	96	104	212
Services	414	459	478	507	596
Constructions and improve- ments	7,560	8,429	9,656	11,550	14,851
Agriculture . . .	2,574	2,777	3,351	4,083	4,704
Mining	52	66	80	90	121
Manufacturing . . .	255	313	313	446	1,257
Transport . . .	498	765	1,016	1,327	1,629
Communications and energy	—	—	96	104	212
Urban housing . . .	1,833	1,899	2,084	2,624	3,521
Services	2,348	2,609	2,716	2,876	3,407

Source: See Table XXII.

S

available resources for investment, and in the light of growth in consumer demand, export demand, and total investment requirements. On the basis of these criteria, it was clear that the Cauca Valley Project would have introduced a great imbalance in the absorption of investment resources, with respect to overall needs for energy, and with respect to a volume of agricultural production out of proportion with foreseeable demand. With respect to public investment resources of the national government, it became a question of either rejecting the request of the Cauca Valley Authority for important resources or shelving the projected expansion of basic iron and steel production facilities of the Paz del Rio Iron and Steel Company, an autonomous,

TABLE XXVIII

Colombia: Gross Product and Fixed Reproducible Capital per Worker and the Product–Capital Ratio, by Economic Activity, 1925, 1945, and 1953

Gross Product per Worker (pesos at 1950 prices)	Total	Agri-culture	Mining	Industry	Artisan Industry	Transport, Communi-cations, and Services	Other Services
1925 . .	874	750	800	1,930	325	. .	1,628
1945 . .	1,347	1,055	2,390	3,489	581	2,678	1,628
1953 . .	1,882	1,293	3,575	5,057	842	5,061	2,141
Stock of capital per worker (pesos at 1950 prices):							
1925 . .	4,213	2,497	5,150	2,986	. .	. .	. .
1945 . .	4,600	3,206	4,675	3,190	. .	21,733	7,143
1953 . .	5,406	3,577	6,038	5,201	. .	23,841	6,974
Product–capital ratio:							
1925 . .	0·21	0·30	0·16	0·27	. .	0·08 [1]	0·13 [2]
1945 . .	0·29	0·33	0·51	0·56	. .	0·12 [1]	0·23 [2]
1953 . .	0·35	0·36	0·59	0·51	. .	0·21 [1]	0·30 [2]

Source: See Table XXII.

[1] Transport only.
[2] Includes communications and public services, commerce, finances, housing, and other services.

government-financed, steel-producing enterprise. On the basis of criteria of optimum use of investment and capital resources, based on overall analysis of the structure of investment and fixed reproducible capital, in part, the national government denied the Cauca Valley Authority request for investment resources.

III. PROBLEMS OF DATA, CONCEPT, AND METHOD IN THE ESTIMATION OF THE STOCK OF FIXED REPRODUCIBLE CAPITAL IN LATIN AMERICA

In the preceding section of this paper attention was given to the insight on the processes and problems of economic growth in Latin America obtained through the analysis of newly developed information on fixed reproducible capital in Latin America. The basic characteristic of 'under-developedness' as signifying inefficient use of investment and capital resources, as well as man-power resources was indicated. The long-term trend of increase in the productivity of capital, deriving principally from the change in economic structure, the heart of the process of economic development and industrialization, was demonstrated.

The role of increased utilization of basic social capital as well as industrial production capacity, and economies of scale deriving from growth and expansion of markets was also noted. The effect of external terms of trade and export demand on imports of capital goods and, consequently, the level and composition of investment and capital was shown, and reference was made to the changing role of foreign investment.

The effect of the rate of growth on the relative importance of depreciation in the investment effort was seen. The incidence of internal relative prices on the saving and investment capacity of the individual economic sectors was mentioned. Problems of inefficient utilization of land resources were presented. The growing importance of adequate and appropriate use of public investment and capital resources was treated. A hypothesis explaining the differences in the level of the product–capital ratio in a number of Latin American countries was discussed. The present critical shortage of basic social capital in transport and energy, the lag in export growth behind import requirements, and the potential contribution of a Latin American multilateral payments system to the capacity to import, the ability to absorb foreign capital, and the problem of economy of scale and degree of utilization of productive capacity were stated.

The purpose of the present section of this paper is to present and discuss problems of data, concept, and method in the estimation of the stock of fixed reproducible capital in Latin America, based on the work experience of the Economic Commission for Latin America in this field.

1. *Problems of data concept and method*

. The research work experience of the Economic Commission for Latin America in the analysis of economic growth, capital formation, and wealth has favoured the basic concept and methods of Raymond Goldsmith's perpetual-inventory system, and has also followed, in general, the concepts and estimating criteria recommended by Edward Denison. Our work in the estimation of capital is based on the accumulation of depreciated investment, in constant prices, with the use of Census bench-mark data most often as a point of reference and not as an estimating bench-mark. The preference for these concepts and methods is related to the problems of data as well as the analytical purpose in mind, including the following factors:

(1) the relative abundance of reliable data availabilities for estimating investment in constant prices, by type of good and by economic sector;

(2) the scarcity, incompleteness, and unreliability of census data, as well as its susceptibility to broad variation in reporting original cost and replacement cost, on account of the general inflation of prices;

(3) the primary interest in analysing investment and capital data for implications with respect to the efficiency, degree of utilization, and productivity in the channelling of investment resources;

(4) the convenience of carrying out basic research in investment and capital as an integral part of national income work.

The following comments may be made with respect to these factors which have favoured our preference for the concepts and methods of Raymond Goldsmith's perpetual-inventory method and Edward Denison's recommendation for a system based integrally on the accumulation of depreciated investments which are derived from national income estimation.

(a) *Relative abundance of reliable data availabilities for estimating investment in constant prices, by type of good, and by economic sector*

Data availabilities for the estimation of investment and capital are such that these statistics could be among the best and most reliable statistics in the region.[1] Investment in Latin America,

[1] *Economic Survey of Latin America 1951–52*, pp. 30–5, 38–9, 48, 53, 64, 69, 76, United Nations Economic Commission for Latin America, Santiago, Chile, 1953; *The Role of Economic Statistics in the Formulation of Economic Development Programs*, paper presented at the III Inter-American Statistical Conference, Quit andinha, Petropolis, Brazil, June 1955.

even in such rapidly industrializing countries as Argentine and Brazil, is based in large part on imports of capital goods. Trade statistics, including quantum estimates, classified by industry of origin, as well as by final destination for consumption, investment, or intermediate product use, as well developed and available for long time spans. Production statistics, especially capital goods production comprising a relatively new activity, are readily available. Quantum residential construction data are also generally available, as is the case with non-residential building. In most countries data on government income and expenditures permits the division of expenditure accounts into components of current-account expenditures for goods and services, transfer payments and financial services, and investment expenditures.[1]

In addition, quantum data on specific types of public investment is frequently available. It has also been possible to estimate agricultural improvements.[2]

In addition, in some countries, especially those in which the greatest advances in the field of income and wealth have been made, the estimation of investment and capital is carried on integrally as part of the national-income estimation work.

We have already published detailed estimates of gross investment and fixed reproducible capital, by type of good and by economic sector, in constant prices, for Colombia for the period 1925–53.[3] The series on capital is integrally based on the series on gross investment, with census and census-type estimates used as points of reference, and in some cases as bench-marks – housing, electric power stations, railroads, shipping. Similar, more detailed and more comprehensive, estimates for Argentina have been prepared for the period 1900–55. Long-term series on gross investment have been prepared for all important countries of the region, with most series extending from 1925.

[1] See *Economic Survey for Latin America, 1955*, Part II, United Nations Economic Commission for Latin America, Santiago, Chile, 1956.

[2] See *Analisis y Proyecciones del Desarrollo Económico; III, El Desarrollo Económico de Colombia*, pp. 222–227, 376–381, United Nations Economic Commission for Latin America, Santiago, Chile, 1956.

Selective Expansion of Agricultural Production in Latin America and its Relationship to Economic Development, United Nations Economic Commission for Latin America, Santiago, Chile, 1955.

[3] *Economic Development of Colombia, op. cit.*

(b) *The scarcity, incompleteness, and unreliability of census data, as well as its susceptibility to broad variation in reporting original cost and replacement cost, on account of the general inflation of prices*

While census methods have improved considerably in Latin America, especially in the last decade, census data are still relatively scarce, covers only a part of the universe of economic sectors, and generally omits an important part of the universe of manufacturing activity – namely, handicraft, artisan, and small-scale industry, in establishments of less than five workers. Even where censuses report on the stock of equipment, in quantity terms, or by value assets, there is generally little or no information on average age, or condition and degree of maintenance. Exceptions to this, of course, apply mainly to important capital goods, such as improved agricultural land, tractors, textile spindles, petroleum-refining capacity, basic iron and steel capacity, motors and generators, passenger cars, trucks, locomotives and railroad rolling stock, ships, aeroplanes, housing, and buildings; but this is not equivalent to a measure of the universe, in contrast to data on production and imports of capital goods, and construction and improvements – main elements in the flow of goods estimation of gross investment. Census data on the value of assets and buildings also generally does not separate the value of land from the value of construction. Most important of all, however, is the effect of the general price inflation in Latin American countries in the last twenty years on the reliability of census data on the value of capital assets. Whether census questionnaires call for the reporting of original cost or replacement cost, it is very difficult to evaluate the significance of the resulting data without knowing the age of equipment, in economies in which prices have increased ten-fold or more in the last twenty years, where obsolescence covers a longer time span, major rebuilding and repairing of equipment is the general practice, and where the sharp susceptibility of the composition and level of investment to fluctuations in import capacity make for a discontinuous investment process.

Nevertheless, when census or census-type data are available or can be developed, they are clearly useful and of vital importance as an independent check on the validity of estimates of capital stock, and as a point of reference and element in the estimation process. In the last analysis it is incumbent on the estimator to reconcile and explain the difference between an estimate of fixed reproducible capital, based on the accumulation of depreciated investment, with a census figure; otherwise there is no assurance that the estimate reflects reality.

(c) *The primary interest in analysing investment and capital data for implications with respect to the efficiency, degree of utilization, and productivity in the channelling of investment resources*

As was indicated in the preceding section of this paper, a basic characteristic of 'under-developedness' signifies an inefficient use of investment and capital resources, and that the process of development itself involves an improvement in the efficiency, utilization, and productivity of investment and capital resources. It was noted that the level of efficiency and rate of improvement in the use of these resources was subject to the effects of export earnings and the terms of trade on capital-goods imports, the changing role of foreign investment, increased degree of utilization and economies of scale deriving from market growth, the impact of the rate of growth on the relative burden of depreciation, the incidence of internal relative prices on the saving and investment capacity of economic sectors, the efficiency in utilization of land resources, the role of public investment. Two basic factors limiting the rate of growth of Latin American countries at the present moment were discussed: the critical shortage of basic social capital in energy and transport and the lag in export growth behind import requirements.

It may be readily seen, therefore, that one of the primary interests in analysing investment and capital data lies in its usefulness in evaluating quantitatively the efficiency, utilization, and productivity of investment and capital resources, and the contributing factors involved. This is important not only in the analysis of long-term growth, as well as short-term problems of stagnation, deflation, disequilibrium, and distortion, but is also a principle basis for projecting short-term and long-term economic policy – especially investment policy.

For this purpose, the main interest is the analysis, in constant prices, of alternative resource input and the resultant, or expectant, alternative resource output. For this purpose, a useful operational concept of fixed reproducible capital is the one based on accumulation of depreciated investment, without adjustment for quality change. Improved quality and efficiency of capital goods, and the consequent contribution to productivity, is precisely one of the important elements to be revealed.

(d) *The convenience of carrying out basic research in investment and capital as an integral part of national income work*

The analysis of the process, problems, and perspectives of economic growth is best carried out on the basis of homogeneous, internally consistent, basic macro-economic statistics, including the gross product, by industry of origin and destination, and by consumption and investment composition, together with estimates of fixed reproducible capital based on the accumulation of depreciated investment data. This tends to ensure the validity and reliability of analysis of the growth in output as well as the growth in capital. The process of estimation itself thereby provides a useful check on the validity and reliability of the series.

2. *Problem of international comparison of investment and capital*

Latin America contains some 180 million people divided into twenty countries. The problem of inadequate size of market for economies of scale, despite the impressive rate of growth in the last quarter-century, is already pressing and limiting the economic growth of many countries of the region. The problems and possibilities of the development of a regional market are the subject of active study. These considerations highlight the urgent need for an adequately comparable body of statistics on the gross product, investment, and capital, since any consideration of the growth and structure of a regional market, its investment requirements, and trade potential must be made on the basis of a common denominator of the purchasing power of national currencies in a base year. In addition, the relative importance of comparative investment efforts is insufficiently known.

Available methods of comparing levels of gross product and investment, as well as the rate of investment, have serious shortcomings, however. The general use of exchange controls with multiple exchange rates, together with the broad inflation in prices, and their effect on relative costs and relative prices, makes the use of exchange rates, as a comparison factor, very inadequate, even when exchange rates are adjusted on the basis of parity criteria.[1]

Two examples touching two important aspects of the problem may be shown to illustrate the nature of the matter. Official statistics indicate a very high investment rate in Argentina in the last twenty years, and a very low investment rate for Chile. When, however, adjustments are made to express the Argentine investment rate in terms of 1946 prices, for example, in place of 1950 prices as shown in the accompanying table, the Argentine

Argentina: Gross Domestic Investment as a Percentage of Gross Domestic Product, 1935–45

Year	Calculated in prices of:	
	1950	1946
1935	21·0	16·2
36	20·4	15·7
37	23·3	18·0
38	29·3	22·6
39	22·3	17·2
1940	19·5	15·1
41	20·6	15·9
42	17·6	13·6
43	16·6	12·8
44	15·9	12·3
1945	14·8	11·4
46	21·8	16·8
47	31·7	24·5
48	30·7	23·7
49	22·5	17·4
1950	21·8	16·8
51	24·8	19·1
52	24·1	18·6
53	18·3	14·1
1954	21·3	16·4

Source: *Producto e Ingreso de la República Argentina, en el periodo 1935–54*, República Argentina, Poder Ejecutivo Nacional, Buenos Aires, 1955, pp. 125, 133, 136, 137, and 157.

investment rate is lower by one-fifth. This reflects the fact that the price of investment goods rose much more rapidly than the general level of prices in the early post-war years, a result of the great scarcity of capital goods and the existence of an active internal market for capital goods. Since 1950, with some advance towards the normalization of supply in relation to demand, the disparity in prices has been reduced.

[1] See *Economic Survey of Latin America, 1951–52, op. cit.*, p. 33.

In the case of Chile the investment rate, as reported in official statistics, seriously understates the real investment of the country, and makes difficult the understanding of how the country could have experienced a 55 per cent increase in the real gross product in the twelve-year period 1940–52. This understatement of investment derives, in part, from the valuation of imported capital goods at a subsidized exchange rate, which, in 1950, in effect valued imported capital goods at approximately one-third of their purchasing-power parity value. If an indicated adjustment is made to value of imported capital goods, as is shown in the accompanying table, the resultant investment rate is substantially higher in the post-war years (during the war, Chile had been cut off from normal sources of supply of imported capital goods, and for this period, and consequently, both methods of estimation yield similar results for the war years).

Chile: Gross Domestic Investment as a Percentage of Gross Domestic Product, 1940–52

(Prices of 1950)

	Based on Official statistics [1]	As adjusted by ECLA [2]
	(Annual averages)	
1940–42 . . .	9·8	9·9
1943–45 . . .	9·3	9·3
1946–48 . . .	10·9	12·5
1949–52 . . .	10·3	13·2

[1] *Cuentas Nacionales de Chile, 1940–54*, Corporación de Fomento de Chile, 1956, pp. 15 and 17.
[2] *Economic Survey of Latin America, 1954*, United Nations Economic Commission for Latin America, Santiago, Chile, 1955, pp. 24 and 26.

To these examples of problems of comparison arising from price inflation and exchange controls may be added the indicated serious underestimation of the level of *per capita* gross product, investment, and capital in Latin American countries. The conversion of Latin American gross product, investment, and fixed reproducible capital series from national currencies, expressed in prices of 1950, to U.S. dollars, expressed in prices of 1950 has been made on the basis of purchasing-power parity rates of exchange, based on pre-war, pre-exchange-control-era exchange rates. It is recognized that this method probably understates the level of *per capita* gross product, investment, and capital by one-fourth to one-third. As is demonstrated in the study of Gilbert and Kravis,[1] the use of United States prices for the valuation of consumption and investment for lesser-developed countries, in which food consumption has a greater relative importance, and in which relative prices for food are low, has the effect of raising the level of the *per capita* gross product by as much as one-third, in comparison with estimates derived by the use of exchange rates. In the case of Latin American countries, with one-third to one-half of total consumption expenditures devoted to food, in comparison with less than one-fourth for the United States, and with low relative prices for food, it is estimated that the use of parity exchange rates to express national currencies in dollars has the effect of substantially understating Latin American *per capita* product in comparison with that for the United States.

The effects of price inflation, exchange controls, and of a pattern of internal relative prices different from more developed countries on international comparative analyses indicate the urgent need to renew efforts to develop an adequate measure of the purchasing power of national currencies, by main types of production and products. National product, investment, and capital should be estimated on the basis of a standardized method of accounts, expressing the parameters in terms of national currency, as well as the currency of a base country of comparison. Care must be taken in the selection of a base year to minimize distortions arising from the selection of 'problem' years. It is obvious that no serious evaluation of requirements and demand for capital in the region as a whole, or for groups of countries in the region, can be made until these problems are adequately solved.

3. *Importance of adequately measuring land improvements*

Fixed reproducible capital in agriculture, especially in land improvements, continues to represent an important share of all fixed reproducible investment in Latin America. In addition, serious problems of inefficient use of land resources have arisen in a number of Latin American countries in recent years. Examples of inefficient land use have derived from faulty application of land-reform programmes, internal price policy, labour shortages insufficiently offset by farm mechanization, and mis-

---

[1] *An International Comparison of National Products and the Purchasing Power of Currencies*, Milton Gilbert and Irving B. Kravis, Paris, OEEC, 1954.

guided trade and domestic industry protection policy. The serious consequences have included the critical decline in export earnings and shortages of food for the domestic population. These examples highlight the need and importance of adequately measuring land improvements, for which annual depreciated investment data are not generally available. The method used in ECLA studies is based on Census-type estimates of the fixed reproducible capital in land in a base year, as well as in one or more historical years.[1] In effect, the depreciated base-year cost of land clearing and preparation, by type of use, the construction of irrigation and drainage works, fencing, rural housing, farm buildings and other installations, buildings and equipment for the primary preparation of agricultural products, perennial crops, permanent plantations, and cultivated forests is estimated, always excluding the original value of the land. As in the case of machinery and equipment, no attempt is made to adjust for the 'quality' of the land – differences in quality, thereby, are reflected, along with other factors, in the product per unit of capital in land improvements. This is not to say there is no interest in a quantification of differences in quality. On the contrary, the studies referred to reveal that great pains have been taken to measure and describe the character of land resources. Since the main interest centres, however, in analysing changes in the efficiency, utilization, and productivity of land resources, as well the factors contributing to these changes, it is not desirable to adjust the depreciated, replacement value of land improvements for quality, even if this were operationally possible.

4. *Treatment of obsolescence and estimated useful life of fixed reproducible capital*

The effect of the world economic crisis of the 1930s and World War II was to severely reduce the flow of imported capital goods to many Latin American countries. This factor combined with the still small domestic production of productive machinery and equipment, and the substantial economic growth experienced by Latin American countries in the last quarter century, has resulted in a chronic shortage of productive machinery and equipment. In these circumstances the practice has been to continue to use productive machinery and equipment long beyond the usual useful life, through substantial repairing and rebuild-

[1] See especially *El Desarrollo Económico de Colombia, op. cit.*, pp. 376–384.

ing, and to continue to use old, inefficient equipment, made obsolescent by age and wear, as well as the development of improved and more efficient techniques. In addition to the incidence on productivity involved in continuing to use antiquated machinery and equipment, there arises the problem of measurement of useful life, as well as the treatment of substantial repairs and maintenance. While attempts have been made to adequately adjust for these phenomena,[1] this remains one of the important problems of concept and method.

5. *Problem and importance of estimating inventories*

While it has been possible to develop reliable series on gross fixed investment and fixed reproducible capital, this is not the case with inventories and inventory changes. There are virtually no comprehensive, reliable series on inventories and inventory changes. At most, published series are partial and cover main agricultural grains and inventories of corporations.

This is a serious shortcoming, since partial data tend to indicate that the rate of inventory turnover is substantially lower in underdeveloped countries than in developed countries.[2]

This need to maintain relatively larger stocks of inventories arises from the relative importance of imports in total goods availabilities, the effect of transportation time and distance, less-integrated supplier–user relationships, lesser-developed internal transport and distribution systems, and uncertainty with respect to foreign-exchange availabilities. Partial data suggest that the value of inventories may represent as much as one-fourth to one-third the value of fixed capital in underdeveloped countries in comparison to 10 per cent for the United States. This heavier inventory load represents an important capital cost whose magnitude may be said to seriously affect the rate of economic growth. For this reason, this remains an important area for future serious research and measurement.

IV. PRESENT STATUS OF WORK IN THE FIELD OF NATIONAL-WEALTH ESTIMATION AND ANALYSIS IN LATIN AMERICA

Following is a brief summary of the present status of research and analysis work in the field of national-wealth estimation in

[1] See *Fixed Reproducible Capital in Argentina, 1935–55*, Manuel Balboa and Alberto Fracchia, United Nations Economic Commission for Latin America, Santiago, Chile, August 1957, pp. 7–9.

[2] See *El Desarrollo Económico de Colombia*, *op. cit.*, pp. 121–123.

Latin America, together with an abbreviated roster of Latin American economists working in this field.

1. *ECLA's work on Latin America as a whole*

In 1952 and 1953 basic data and analyses were prepared for seven countries (in varying stages of quality and detail) in order to have a preliminary estimate for the region as a whole. The seven countries – Argentina, Brazil, Chile, Colombia, Cuba, Mexico, and Venezuela – account for approximately 90 per cent of the gross product and wealth of the region as a whole. By-products of this work have appeared in the following ECLA publications:

> *Economic Survey of Latin America, 1951–52, 1953, 1954, 1955, 1956, op. cit.*
> *Analysis and Projections of Economic Development: I. An Introduction to the Technique of Programming, op. cit.*
> *Selective Expansion of Agricultural Production in Latin America and Its Relationship to Economic Development, op. cit.*

In 1954 and 1955 work on wealth estimates for Brazil and Colombia was substantially intensified, with significant improvement in detail and quality in connection with two major studies completed. It may be noted that, in connection with the study on Colombia, the wealth concept was refined to include careful estimates of land improvements, at depreciated replacement cost.

> *Economic Development of Brazil, op. cit.*
> *Economic Development of Colombia, op. cit.*

In 1956 and 1957 intensive work was carried on in the preparation of estimates of wealth for Argentina, Bolivia, Mexico, and Peru, in connection with major studies undertaken by separate teams in these countries.

> *Economic Development of Argentina, op. cit.*
> *Economic Development of Bolivia, op. cit.*
> *External Disequilibrium and the Economic Development of Latin America: The Case of Mexico, op. cit.*
> *Economic Development of Peru* (in preparation), United Nations Economic Commission for Latin America, Santiago, Chile.

In the remainder of 1957 and 1958 attention will be given to the refinement and extension of wealth estimates for the region as a whole, in connection with the study of the growth perspective of the region, trade perspectives, and capital requirements.

ECLA economists who have been working in this field include, in addition to the author: Manuel Balboa, Celso Furtado, Juan Noyola, Raul Prebisch, Hugo Trivelli, Victor Urquidi, Pedro Vuskovic, and Pierre Van der Meiren.

2. Work in Argentina

Alberto Fracchia, co-author, with Manuel Balboa, of *Fixed Reproducible Capital in Argentina, 1935–55*, op. cit.

Cesar Belaunde has prepared long-term estimates of capital formation, which are referred to in the *Economic Survey of Latin America, 1951–52*, op. cit.

3. Work in Brazil

Americo Barbosa, formerly with the Banco do Desenvolvimento Economico, prepared estimates used in *The Economic Development of Brazil*, op. cit.

4. Work in Chile

Ewald Hasche, of the Corporación de Fomento de la Producción, is author of the study referred to in *Economic Survey of Latin America*, op. cit. At the present time, new series are being prepared for the Chilean economy.

5. Work in Colombia

The ECLA group and its work benefited greatly from an earlier work prepared by *Jacques Torfs* and *Alberto Zuluaga* of the government economic programming council.

6. Work in Cuba

Regino Boti, Dean of the Economics School of the Universidad del Oriente, has made estimates of the wealth of Cuba.

7. Work in Venezuela

Bernardo Ferran has made some partial estimates of wealth of Venezuela.

FIXED REPRODUCIBLE CAPITAL IN ARGENTINA, 1935–55

By Manuel Balboa and Alberto Fracchia

I. INTRODUCTION

THE team which is carrying out studies on the national income of Argentina has for some time back been making various estimates of annual depreciation in order to determine income and net capital formation. It estimates annual depreciation, at replacement costs or in terms of prices of a base period, by applying amortization rates to gross investment for previous periods classified by categories of goods and according to their probable useful average life.

The publication of Raymond Goldsmith's studies on the Estimation of fixed reproducible capital stock in the United States and the ECLA studies on capital in the Latin American countries and on the Analysis and Projection of Economic Development prompted the national-income team of Argentina to apply a method of the perpetual-inventory type for the purpose of estimating fixed reproducible capital stock.

It was, however, on the occasion of the establishment of the Joint Argentine Government–United Nations Study Group, under the chairmanship of Dr. Raul Prebisch, Executive Secretary of ECLA, that it was specifically proposed to study the historic evolution of gross and net capital formation. During 1956 the Joint Study Group carried out the necessary compilations and analyses for estimating capital formation and annual investment from the beginning of the century.

It should be noted that the co-operation extended by the national-income group of Argentina in the preparation of the basic series of these estimates was very valuable and, in some cases, decisive. Likewise, background information already available, or recently prepared in ECLA for the studies of the Argentine economy, were used for some aspects. Nevertheless, the responsibility for the opinions expressed and for the estimates included in this report lies exclusively with its authors.

In this report the results obtained in these statistical studies are presented in summary form, including the estimated figures for the value of fixed reproducible capital for each year of the period 1935–55 and the gross investment series used for these estimates.

In the study of the analysis and projection of the Argentine economy prepared by ECLA, as explained in the report by Alexander Ganz,[1] an economic analysis of these series has been made and estimates are included for periods prior to 1935, largely obtained from the series of gross annual investment included here.

The conceptual and methodological aspects of this report are limited to showing the results of the application of the perpetual-inventory method to the specific case of determining the value of fixed reproducible capital in Argentina. There is no intention of embarking on a discussion of the conceptual bases of the various economic criteria which might be used for such an estimate. These are being critically reviewed at present from various distinct points of view. Stress will be laid here on certain conceptual or logical aspects of the method used which are of special interest for the particular case of Argentina or which are useful to consider in order to arrive at a fair appreciation of the estimated figures.

II. STATISTICAL DATA AVAILABLE IN ARGENTINA FOR ESTIMATING FIXED REPRODUCIBLE CAPITAL

Except for the very old studies by A. Bunge, based mainly on the 1914 census, there are no official or private estimates in Argentina relating to any of the various concepts of national capital or wealth for more recent years. The only known estimates are those prepared by ECLA and published in 1953. They refer to annual series for values, at 1950 prices, of capital invested in durable capital goods for the economy as a whole and by large economic sectors during the period 1945–52. They are estimates obtained by the accumulation of depreciated investment, and are linked, in part, to figures taken from the 1914 census.

Other data available in Argentina relating to the value of capital invested by sectors of activity are scarce. Indeed, a

---

[1] Paper 9 in this volume. It should be noted here that there are certain discrepancies between the figures presented in this paper and those given by Dr. Ganz. These are due to differences in classification. In the case of the agricultural sector, for example, Dr. Ganz includes inventories of livestock which have not been included in our estimates: and Dr. Ganz has used a narrower concept of Government than that implied in our definition of Public Works.

T

review of available statistics shows that only the following information exists:

(a) Industrial censuses for 1935 and 1946. These include data
on the value of investment in land and buildings, machinery, installations and tools, vehicles, furniture, and other
facilities; but, whereas the 1935 census gives book values,
the 1946 census published the value at 1946 market prices.

(b) Agricultural census for 1937. This contains data on the
quantities or units of all existing capital goods on farms,
but not information on their age, year of installation,
value, etc.

(c) Census of transport enterprises and vehicles for 1947, containing statistics on the rolling stock, their age and distribution by economic sectors, and the amount of investment in railways and shipping enterprises according to
book values.

(d) 1948 census and permanent register of state property,
listing the value of buildings, various public works and
other government-owned capital goods.

(e) Isolated data on the depreciated value of capital investment in certain sectors, such as large-scale public-service
enterprises and certain data on the number of buildings of
all types.

A critical analysis of all these sources and available data
clearly showed that it was not possible to arrive at an estimate of
fixed capital stock in respect to even a minimum of economic
sectors for a given year which could be used as a base for bringing the estimate up to date by any known method. It happens that
the census figures could have been used only as a basis for the
industrial sector, but the adjustments which have to be made in
these data are very complicated and would always leave a wide
margin of uncertainty as regards the final estimate.

On the other hand, in Argentina, as in many other Latin
American countries, there are almost complete statistics on industrial production by economic sectors and on imports and exports by categories of commodities, which can provide the basis
for a detailed analysis of the commodity flow and thus for the
flow of capital goods to be estimated, as is being done to determine annual gross investment in the studies of national product
and income. Accordingly, there is no doubt that the accumula-

tion of depreciated investment is the only adequate or feasible method of arriving at estimates of the value of fixed capital, although it will require the assumption of certain working hypotheses which cannot be fully verified in practice.

III. ESTIMATION OF FIXED REPRODUCIBLE CAPITAL BY THE ACCUMULATION OF DEPRECIATED INVESTMENT

There are two alternative ways of applying the general method of estimating the stock of capital by the accumulation of depreciated investment. One is to use as a base a census figure pertaining to the stock of capital for a given period and to bring the inventory up to date by the method described, or to interpolate the stock between census years after adjusting the results to render them comparable. The other alternative must be used when census data, either total or sectoral, are not available or not useful. The stock is then obtained by calculating directly the accumulation of depreciated investment.

In practice, it is apparent that combined solutions may be applied, or total or partial estimates obtained independently by either procedure may be checked. In the first case, it may be said that census data may be used as a check on, or as a methodological or statistical base for the estimates. In the second case, the estimate and the very definition of the concept of capital are identified with the operational estimation procedure, and the statistical value is determined mainly by the accuracy of the estimates of gross annual investment and by the hypotheses adopted with regard to the concept and the measurement of the value of annual capital consumption.

The method followed in Argentina is the second alternative of the perpetual inventory, i.e. as already pointed out, the estimates are not based on census data but on an accumulation of net annual investment. Only in the case of shipping, electric power stations, agricultural buildings, and improvements was a separate method used for estimating the value of fixed capital stock directly.

A brief explanation follows of the way in which the annual series of gross investment were estimated and of the method used in determining depreciation.

IV. ESTIMATE OF GROSS FIXED INVESTMENT

Broadly speaking, the gross capital formation series used in this study are, from the standpoint of definition and method of valuation, the same as those incorporated in the estimates of the domestic gross product. Discrepancies with the official data published are attributable to improved statistical methods or to the incorporation of series for new items.

Tables IV and V give the estimated figures by broad categories of goods. The method used for these estimates was as follows:

(a) *Machinery and motors.* Series for values at current prices were compiled by type of commodity. It was impossible to follow a single procedure for the conversion of these series to current 1950 prices; in some cases they were deflated by means of price indices for machinery with the most stable specifications possible, while in others, values at constant prices were determined by the direct application of unit values to the volume series. A third procedure was that of deflating some items by means of price indices or unit values for other sectors for which data were available.

Needless to say, no adjustment for changes in quality were made, except in so far as they may have been implicit in the process of deflation, which does not seem very likely.

(b) *Transport and communication equipment.* Annual gross investment was determined by a procedure similar to that adopted in the case of machinery and motors. Only for inland waterway and overseas shipping was direct valuation of the stock on the basis of tonnage and age considered desirable.

(c) *Other producers' durable goods.* The general procedure described above was followed.

(d) *Agricultural improvements and housing.* The stock of capital in rural housing was estimated directly on the basis of census statistics, the intermediate years being interpolated. Among other elements, data on the number of farms and the agricultural population were taken into account. A computation of annual gross investment as deduced from capital estimates was incorporated in Table

IV, merely for the sake of completing the series. Under this head are also included perennial crops, wire fencing, mills and other agricultural installations, annual investment in which was estimated in accordance with the general method adopted for the preceding sectors.

(e) *Private non-agricultural construction.* Annual basic series were available relating to the area covered by the new construction classified according to region and main purpose. Real values were determined through the application of 1950 prices, by type of building and by region.

(f) *Public works.* The series for values at current prices were deflated by a construction cost index. This index was worked out on the basis of wages and prices of the most important types of materials used. Obviously, this type of deflation is in the nature of an overall cost adjustment, which does not explicitly take into account changes in the structure or composition of the value series. Nor are fluctuations in the productivity of the building industry taken into consideration.

(g) *Repair costs.* The gross investment series in Table IV include costs of repairs of railways, trams, motor vehicles, and machinery. Conversion to 1950 prices was effected by means of a repair-costs index and an index of inputs of materials in the case of railways and trams. Expenditure under this head was included under capital formation, because it was considered to relate not so much to current conservation and maintenance costs as to major repairs aimed at partly or totally restoring the production capacity of the equipment concerned or prolonging its useful life.

In general terms, the conclusion might be reached that the basic series for annual gross investment at 1950 prices, estimated by means of the procedures described, reflect the quantum of capital goods, but do not allow for variations in quality, except in so far as the methods of deflation utilized may have implicitly taken this factor into account in specific lines. In all likelihood the tendency has largely been to consider 1950 goods and those belonging to earlier periods on the same level, as if they were similar in characteristics, 'quality', etc.

The estimation of capital formation through the flow of goods is essentially a problem of estimating the quantum of production deriving from the capital-goods industries and from foreign-trade activities. Consequently, in such estimates the same criterion must be adopted as is applied in measuring the production of other types of goods, despite the greater complexity presented by the capital goods sector (R. Stone, *Quantity and Price Indexes in National Accounts*, OEEC). From this point of view, the increase in 'productivity exclusively attributable' to an improvement in the quality of capital goods would tend to be reflected in the industries producing such goods and not in the industries utilizing them as primary factors.

In this field of economic analysis and national accounts, therefore, any progress that might be made in the development of independent standards of measurement for variations in the quality of capital goods would be useful. Meanwhile, in practice the only solution is to incorporate new goods by means of deflation in terms of prices for similar goods or other indices of a general nature.[1]

V. ESTIMATE OF CAPITAL CONSUMPTION

The value of annual capital consumption was estimated on the following basis: (a) the determination of the probable average life of groups of goods; (b) the assumption that the good concerned will be completely worn out by the last year of its probable life; and (c) the assumption that annual consumption will represent a constant proportion of the value of the good when new (straight-line depreciation).

Recent analysis and practical studies (those of E. D. Domar, E. Shiff, etc.) show that estimates of consumption and net capital formation may differ substantially according to the method of amortization utilized.

There are two different approaches to this subject. One takes into account the probable evolution of market prices for used capital goods and another derives from the system of valuation in terms of current production capacity of the good.

Certain empirical data seem to suggest that in the former case the value of the good tends to decline much more rapidly in the early than in the middle years of its useful life; as regards the

---

[1] If a strict analysis were to be attempted, it would be found that a considerable number of 'new' goods would appear and that the application of the 'production cost in the base year' formula might frequently lead, especially in the case of long-term series, to results that would be unsatisfactory as expressions of the quantum of the product or of the stock of capital.

second method, although no theory is applicable to the various types of good, it has been pointed out that, broadly speaking, production capacity is maintained or does not decrease rapidly during the early years of useful life, that the process of decline may later be intensified and that, lastly, capacity may still remain at a certain level up to the year in which the good is withdrawn from service. These divergent behaviour patterns seem logical, since market prices are bound to be influenced by obsolescence and by the cumulative production capacity which the good still retains, whereas the functions considered in the second case take into account only current production capacity in each period.

In the special case of Argentina, no data were available on prices of used capital goods, and there was a complete lack of analyses or experiments of a relatively general nature against which to check hypotheses on the evolution of production capacity. Consequently, it was decided to adopt the general hypothesis of straight-line amortization on the value of the good at base-year prices in order to determine year-by-year depreciation.

Average useful life of goods

Broadly speaking, in Argentina there are no statistical data on the installation and withdrawal of existing goods, nor are there any censuses or statistics on the stock of capital goods broken down by age groups, except in isolated cases. Thus, the 1946 census registered an average age of 15 years for trucks and 13 years for passenger cars; for inland waterway and overseas shipping, data are available for several years, and indicate average ages ranging from 13 to 21 years; and with respect to railway material, data for 1954 show an average age of 35 years for trucks and 37 years for locomotives.

In the accounting practice of private enterprises the following are the periods of useful life for capital goods commonly adopted:

Buildings	33–50 years
Industrial machinery . .	10 years
Motor cars and trucks . .	5–7 years
Installations and furniture .	10 years
Tools	4–5 years
Agricultural machinery . .	10 years
Farm carts and wagons .	10 years

Tax regulations generally allow for these, or in some cases shorter, amortization periods. However, the life-spans established in accounting practice or by fiscal legislation cannot be adopted for depreciation estimates in national accounts, since it has been proved that in reality capital goods remain in production for longer spells of time. Consequently, although probable average life could not be statistically determined, the various data mentioned were taken into account, as well as estimates made for some sectors by administrative departments and technical experts. As a working hypothesis for determining depreciation rates, the following average life, by types of capital goods, were finally established:

Average useful life of capital goods assumed in estimating depreciation rates for fixed capital in Argentina

I. *Construction and agricultural improvements*

    (1) Perennial crops (alfalfa, fruit-trees, olive-groves, vineyards, etc.) . . . . 5–50 years

    (2) Agricultural installations . . . 33 years

    (3) Public and private construction . . 50 years

II. *Machinery and equipment*

    (1) Industrial and agricultural machinery . 20 years

    (2) Tools . . . . 5 years

    (3) Containers . . . . . . 4 years

    (4) Other producers' durable goods . . 20 years

    (5) Transport and communication equipment—

        (a) Aeroplanes . . . . . 8 years

        (b) Truck and bus chassis . . . 10 years

        (c) Motor vehicles for passenger and goods transport . . . . . . 20 years

        (d) Carts . . . . . . 20 years

        (e) Railway rolling stock . . . . 33 years

        (f) Inland waterway and overseas shipping 33 years

        (g) Railway installations . . . . 50 years

        (h) Durable goods for communications . 33 years

    (6) Repairs in general . . . . 4 years

The amortization rates derived from these periods of average useful life by types of goods were applied in order to determine the annual stock of capital throughout the period 1935–55. It was thought, however, that the average life-span of goods must have varied in the course of the long interval that has to be taken into account. In all likelihood, before World War II, and especially during the years immediately preceding the depression of the thirties, capital goods were replaced more frequently. But such changes could not be estimated, and nothing is known of their possible influence on estimates of the stock of capital during the period 1935–55.

If these data for Argentina are compared with those relating to the average life of goods in the United States, according to the research carried out by Raymond Goldsmith, it can be seen that as a general rule capital goods remain in use for a longer period in Argentina, especially where vehicles and agricultural machinery are concerned, but that the average useful life of construction and private buildings is practically the same.

It is no easy matter to establish a standard of measurement for the depreciation of investment in repairs. A device sometimes adopted has been to incorporate it in the stock of goods and depreciate it at the same rate as is used for the principal good. But if the amortization period is prolonged because of repairs, it might be contended that up to a point expenditure on repairs ought not to be reckoned as capital, since a tendency to overestimate the value of the stock of capital would result. Again, it must also be borne in mind that these incorporated repair costs, because they relate to major repairs, differing from mere conservation and maintenance costs, produce, at the time when they are effected, an increase in the value and productive capacity of the good, which may afterwards disappear, independently of the useful life of the good concerned. It was therefore decided, as a provisional compromise, to allow an amortization period of four years for costs of this kind.

Lastly, it must be noted that these estimates make no special allowance for obsolescence and exceptional losses. As regards the former, in Argentina's case there is no practical way of including it under the system of work adopted, unless precise information should happen to be available as to goods withdrawn from service before the expiry of their established average useful life. With respect to exceptional losses, while some were substantial, such as those caused by earthquakes, which particularly affected fixed capital in the form of buildings, the necessary data were not available.

VI. ESTIMATES OF FIXED REPRODUCIBLE CAPITAL BY TYPES OF CAPITAL GOODS AND ECONOMIC SECTOR ALLOCATION

The method adopted in regard to existing sources of information in Argentina provides a direct estimate only of the stock of capital goods classified by industries of origin, or in other words, by categories of goods. A classification of that stock by the economic sectors to which the goods were allocated can be undertaken only in so far as the characteristics of the separate categories of goods clearly show that they are intended for a given sector.

For those other goods which may be utilized in more than one economic sector, all that can be done is to determine some probable distribution by economic sector of destination as indicated by several factors.

Table II shows the figures for the depreciated value of the stocks classified according to six categories of goods: (1) machinery and motors, (2) transport and communications equipment; (3) other producers' durable goods; (4) agricultural improvements and housing; (5) private non-agricultural construction; and (6) public works. These six series constitute the results of the aggregation of thirty-four partial series, twenty-nine of which were determined by the usual method of accumulating annual depreciated investment and five series, corresponding to shipping, agricultural housing and certain improvements, and the fixed capital of electric power stations, represent a direct estimate of the depreciated value, in terms of prices for the base year, of the invested fixed capital.

Table III includes estimates of the stock of capital goods classified according to four major economic sectors of destination: (1) agriculture; (2) manufacturing, mining, and construction; (3) transport, communications, electricity, trade, housing, and personal services; and (4) public works. The allocation of the thirty-four series to these four major economic sectors was facilitated to a considerable extent by the fact that the basic national statistics of production and imports are compiled in many cases according to the sectors for which the goods are intended. Yet there are categories which had to be classified according to their main sector of destination and others which had to be distributed, sometimes tentatively, among the various sectors, since they included goods used in all sectors. This applies to motor cars, trucks, and wagons. Fortunately, for these categories, as noted at the beginning of this report, there are statistics which indicate for each year the stock of vehicles in operation by sectors of activity. Distribution coefficients were established which were applied in order to interpolate or project for other years the distribution recorded for a given period.

It would seem that this allocation, according to the criterion of main utilization or destination, together with probable and sometimes rather tentative distribution by sectors, must fall within reasonable margins of approximation, since it has been possible to make use of series by relatively small groups of industries of origin and statistical indices on distribution for given periods, and since it is also to be expected that there is some offsetting compensation for possible errors.

It would be desirable to compare these allocations with census figures or other statistical data referring to the value of fixed capital. But this could be done only for the industrial sector, since the 1935 and 1946 census record data correspond to the book value (1935) and market value (1946) of the capital invested in this activity.

The census figures had to be adjusted so that they could be expressed in terms of 1950 prices and in order to eliminate the value of the land which is included in the data with the value of buildings. Although considerable information was available on deflation indices by sectors of goods and on criteria useful for separating the value of the land, the census figures adjusted to 1950 prices must obviously be taken as rough estimates, since serious difficulties arise when dealing with the 1935 book value, and the impression is given that the 1946 census values must not be subject to a standard and relatively strict criterion of valuation because of the complexity in practice of replying to the question in the census form of that year. Table I summarizes the results of this comparison.

It will be noted that the partial figures for each category show sizeable differences but that the totals indicate a surprising degree of similarity. Nevertheless, it would be illogical to infer from this single experiment final conclusions concerning the accuracy of the results obtained or the effectiveness of the method used as compared with the census results. Insufficient information is available for an appreciation to be made of the accuracy of the deflation and of the adjustments in the 1935 census figures, and, generally speaking, it is doubtful whether the 1946 census figures correspond strictly to a valuation in terms of the current prices for that year of fixed capital invested

TABLE I

Fixed Capital Invested in Mining, Manufacturing, and Construction Industries

(In millions of pesos at 1950 prices)

Category	Adjusted Census Figures		Figure Obtained by Accumulation of Annual Depreciated Investment	
	1935	1946	1935	1946
1. Machinery, installations, tools, etc. . . .	7,258	7,485	7,580	6,838
2. Vehicles and other transport equipment . . .	1,535	1,885	1,783	2,457
3. Buildings	7,556	7,043	7,074	7,780
Total . . .	16,349	16,413	16,437	17,075

in industry. Yet, despite all these shortcomings, this experiment may be regarded as a means of showing that the economic concepts used in taking the census coincide with those used in the procedure of accumulating depreciated investment, and it also indicates, to a certain extent, the probable margin of error of the method adopted for this estimate of fixed capital.

VII. CONCLUSIONS

This attempt to determine the depreciated value of the stock of capital goods in Argentina, its statistical and economic interpretation and the use made of these estimates in the analysis and projections leads to the following conclusions:

(1) The method adopted seems to offer a practical and reasonably acceptable procedure, despite the complexity of the subject, for estimating the value of fixed capital by categories of goods and by large economic sectors of allocation.

(2) It will be seen that the following aspects require further development: periodical censuses of the fixed reproducible capital stock; compilation of prices of new and used capi-

tal goods; and investigation of the possibilities of deriving some objective standards for taking into account the variations in quality and intensifying the study of the productive capacity in terms of the age of the producing equipment.

(3) Two different systems of depreciation seem to offer themselves: one based on the law of market prices of used capital goods, and the other based on the (current) consumption of capital during the period or in the variation of productive capacity. The former would be influenced, *inter alia*, by the obsolescence and by the residual productive capacity of the equipment, and the latter depends on the 'need for replacements to maintain initial productive capacity'. The first criterion is what we might term the 'market price' or 'economic value' criterion and is the one which E. F. Denison apparently advocates; the second is connected with physical replacement requirements and regards capital rather as a factor of productive capacity (E. D. Domar, R. Eisner, E. Schiff *et al.*)

(4) The method of estimation actually adopted (perpetual inventory) obviously has conceptual and operational advantages because it is inherent in the structure and concepts of national accounts.

(5) In the particular case of this, the estimates of the stock of capital embody the practical problems and critical observations made to the estimate of investment by the commodity flow method.

TABLE II

Fixed Reproducible Capital in Argentina, by Type of Capital Good, 1935–55

(Millions of pesos of 1950)

Year	Machinery and Equipment				Construction and Improvements				Total
	Machinery and Motors	Transport and Communications Equipment	Other Producers' Durable Goods	Sub-total	Agricultural Improvements and Housing	Private Non-agricultural Construction	Public Works	Sub-total	
1935	12,867·1	27,784·1	9,257·9	49,909·1	13,953·1	67,545·4	23,232·8	104,731·3	154,640·4
1936	12,776·8	27,523·7	9,263·0	49,563·5	13,989·4	67,003·4	24,583·3	105,576·1	155,139·6
1937	13,060·8	28,146·2	9,407·4	50,614·4	14,018·2	67,087·8	26,366·9	107,472·9	158,087·3
1938	13,474·1	28,893·5	9,656·3	52,023·9	14,172·7	67,331·1	28,454·4	109,958·2	161,982·1
1939	13,301·9	28,576·5	9,721·6	51,600·0	14,373·6	67,674·1	29,983·0	112,030·7	163,630·7
1940	12,993·7	27,982·2	9,636·9	50,612·8	14,384·8	67,713·2	31,161·8	113,259·8	163,872·6
1941	12,475·9	27,357·4	9,546·1	49,379·4	14,261·4	68,194·2	32,122·0	114,577·6	163,957·0
1942	11,914·9	26,332·3	9,204·2	47,451·4	14,394·2	68,941·5	32,801·9	116,137·6	163,589·0
1943	11,213·1	25,016·6	8,936·6	45,166·3	14,346·1	69,840·7	33,443·7	117,630·5	162,796·8
1944	10,624·4	23,672·5	8,656·7	42,953·6	14,475·9	71,117·9	34,676·9	120,270·7	163,224·3
1945	10,107·9	22,267·8	8,454·9	40,830·6	14,557·1	72,343·4	35,738·9	122,639·4	163,470·0
1946	10,019·0	22,012·7	8,403·2	40,434·9	14,674·8	74,120·8	36,627·3	125,422·9	165,857·8
1947	11,064·9	26,343·3	8,912·7	46,320·9	14,830·8	76,069·8	37,349·8	128,250·4	174,571·3
1948	13,014·2	27,689·5	9,533·8	50,237·5	15,014·9	78,406·8	39,285·7	132,707·4	182,944·9
1949	13,957·6	26,957·5	9,633·7	50,548·8	15,098·2	80,576·5	42,069·2	137,743·9	188,292·7
1950	14,778·6	26,046·0	9,716·0	50,540·6	15,324·9	83,335·5	44,568·6	143,229·0	193,769·6
1951	15,532·9	25,930·2	10,059·1	51,522·2	15,472·7	86,127·3	46,757·3	148,357·3	199,879·5
1952	16,240·2	25,243·5	10,192·7	51,676·4	15,590·6	88,533·9	47,919·8	152,044·3	203,720·7
1953	16,867·7	24,891·5	10,142·3	51,901·5	15,688·8	90,368·7	49,069·8	155,127·3	207,028·8
1954	17,439·9	24,571·4	10,299·2	52,310·5	15,809·6	92,457·4	50,755·9	159,022·9	211,333·4
1955	18,170·7	24,787·2	10,476·4	53,434·3	16,140·9	94,946·6	52,295·3	163,382·8	216,817·1

TABLE III

Fixed Reproducible Capital in Argentina, by Economic Sector,
1935–55

(Millions of pesos of 1950)

Year	Agriculture	Manufacturing, Mining, and Construction	Transport, Communications, Electricity, Commerce, Housing, and Personal Services	Public Works	Total
1935	20,186·7	16,436·4	94,784·5	23,232·8	154,640·4
1936	20,091·1	16,563·0	93,902·2	24,583·3	155,139·6
1937	20,351·4	17,218·2	94,150·8	26,366·9	158,087·3
1938	20,758·9	17,790·7	94,978·1	28,454·4	161,982·1
1939	20,789·1	17,877·4	94,981·1	29,983·0	163,630·6
1940	20,502·1	17,812·5	94,396·2	31,161·8	163,872·6
1941	19,895·2	17,686·4	94,253·4	32,122·0	163,957·0
1942	19,505·1	17,420·1	93,861·9	32,801·9	163,589·0
1943	18,899·6	17,042·6	93,410·9	33,443·7	162,796·8
1944	18,527·1	16,766·1	93,254·2	34,676·9	163,224·3
1945	18,157·3	16,556·8	93,017·0	35,738·9	163,470·0
1946	18,052·8	17,074·1	94,103·6	36,627·3	165,857·8
1947	18,806·4	19,963·2	98,451·9	37,349·8	174,571·3
1948	19,398·7	22,783·4	101,477·1	39,285·7	182,944·9
1949	19,341·0	23,996·2	102,886·3	42,069·2	188,292·7
1950	19,558·8	24,996·1	104,646·1	44,568·6	193,769·6
1951	19,814·4	26,312·1	106,995·7	46,757·3	199,879·5
1952	20,101·4	27,053·6	108,645·8	47,919·8	203,720·6
1953	20,368·0	27,525·9	110,065·1	49,069·8	207,028·8
1954	20,414·1	28,214·0	111,949·4	50,755·9	211,333·4
1955	20,919·0	29,163·9	114,438·9	52,295·3	216,817·1

TABLE IV

Gross Fixed Investment in Argentina, by Type of Capital Good, 1915–55

(Millions of pesos of 1950)

Year	Machinery and Motors Excluding Repairs	Machinery and Motors Including Repairs	Transport and Communications Equipment Excluding Repairs	Transport and Communications Equipment Including Repairs	Other Producers' Durable Goods	Sub-total Excluding Repairs	Sub-total Including Repairs	Agricultural Improvements and Housing	Private Non-agricultural Construction	Public Works	Sub-total	Total Excluding Repairs	Total Including Repairs
1915	397·2	…	378·0	…	316·7	1,091·9	…	665·8	867·9	567·8	2,101·5	3,193·4	…
1916	425·9	…	341·8	…	370·7	1,138·4	…	570·3	729·9	439·9	1,740·1	2,878·5	…
1917	271·0	…	377·6	…	239·6	888·2	…	563·8	575·8	224·9	1,364·5	2,252·7	…
1918	281·1	…	309·0	…	196·3	786·4	…	607·8	711·0	171·0	1,489·8	2,276·2	…
1919	376·4	…	302·4	…	344·8	1,023·6	…	561·2	835·4	163·5	1,560·1	2,583·7	…
1920	653·5	…	563·6	…	597·0	1,814·1	…	923·2	1,800·6	275·2	2,999·0	4,813·1	…
1921	799·5	…	715·4	…	692·7	2,207·6	…	665·1	2,070·9	449·2	3,185·2	5,392·8	…
1922	592·5	…	1,181·0	…	553·7	2,327·2	…	730·1	2,757·6	490·8	3,978·5	6,305·7	…
1923	994·4	…	1,332·4	…	686·2	3,013·0	…	751·1	4,152·7	735·1	5,638·9	8,651·9	…
1924	1,367·3	…	1,705·3	…	755·5	3,828·1	…	719·4	3,985·0	744·9	5,449·3	9,277·4	…
1925	1,318·6	…	2,030·1	…	826·6	4,175·3	…	909·1	3,625·5	604·0	5,138·6	9,313·9	…
1926	1,524·0	…	2,118·0	…	955·6	4,597·6	…	781·2	3,041·5	795·9	4,618·6	9,216·2	…
1927	1,324·1	…	2,514·5	…	960·5	4,799·1	…	865·7	3,390·3	1,504·9	5,760·9	10,560·0	…
1928	1,539·5	…	3,627·8	…	879·7	6,047·0	…	885·9	3,976·9	1,615·3	6,478·1	12,525·1	…
1929	1,821·9	…	3,869·3	…	837·2	6,528·4	…	853·6	4,969·1	1,957·5	7,780·2	14,308·6	…
1930	1,369·0	…	2,575·2	…	856·3	4,800·5	…	804·6	4,425·7	2,037·4	7,267·7	12,068·2	…
1931	638·5	693·5	1,094·0	1,572·1	573·7	2,306·2	2,839·3	690·6	2,976·5	961·1	4,628·2	6,934·4	7,467·5
1932	443·6	498·6	391·4	839·5	404·3	1,239·3	1,742·4	713·4	2,097·9	732·6	3,543·9	4,783·2	5,286·3
1933	481·2	536·2	564·8	997·7	453·9	1,499·9	1,987·8	668·6	2,008·8	1,221·8	3,899·2	5,399·1	5,887·0
1934	527·5	582·5	1,148·8	1,553·8	471·4	2,147·7	2,607·7	699·5	2,603·5	1,833·9	5,136·9	7,284·6	7,744·6
1935	723·0	779·0	1,318·5	1,738·2	675·5	2,717·0	3,192·7	771·3	1,991·0	1,630·6	4,392·9	7,109·9	7,585·6
1936	809·1	878·5	1,432·5	1,916·5	693·0	2,934·6	3,488·0	694·7	1,725·0	2,076·2	4,495·9	7,430·5	7,983·9
1937	1,188·2	1,271·1	2,300·8	2,849·8	873·5	4,362·5	4,994·4	753·1	2,367·0	2,545·3	5,665·4	10,027·9	10,659·8
1938	1,356·7	1,449·4	2,481·6	3,083·6	1,007·2	4,845·5	5,540·2	735·6	2,554·0	2,894·5	6,184·1	11,029·6	11,724·3
1939	825·8	928·3	1,486·9	2,142·3	859·9	3,172·6	3,930·5	854·0	2,685·0	2,387·4	5,926·4	9,099·0	9,856·9
1940	720·7	818·0	1,275·1	1,935·1	713·8	2,709·6	3,466·9	702·9	2,414·0	2,078·8	5,195·7	7,905·3	8,662·6
1941	509·0	599·2	1,303·6	1,970·4	665·3	2,477·9	3,234·9	668·0	2,883·0	1,897·4	5,448·4	7,926·3	8,683·3
1942	472·8	558·9	894·1	1,628·0	406·8	1,773·7	2,593·7	694·5	3,185·0	1,651·4	5,530·6	7,304·3	8,124·3
1943	317·1	405·2	590·3	1,392·1	427·4	1,334·8	2,224·7	659·2	3,378·0	1,641·1	5,678·6	7,013·4	7,903·3
1944	387·4	472·7	500·7	1,377·5	386·1	1,274·2	2,236·3	763·3	3,800·0	2,261·2	6,824·5	8,098·7	9,060·8
1945	416·8	503·4	495·0	1,333·1	452·3	1,364·1	2,288·8	768·8	3,800·0	2,130·5	6,699·3	8,063·4	8,988·1
1946	795·5	886·5	1,666·7	2,454·5	587·5	3,049·7	3,926·5	829·4	4,403·0	1,993·8	7,226·2	10,275·9	11,152·7
1947	1,890·0	1,987·0	6,206·6	7,054·5	1,134·9	9,231·5	10,176·4	881·3	4,637·0	1,859·5	7,377·8	16,609·3	17,554·2
1948	2,833·9	2,914·0	3,388·9	4,238·5	1,299·1	7,521·9	8,451·6	960·1	5,091·0	3,105·2	9,156·3	16,678·2	17,607·9
1949	1,873·8	1,959·5	1,281·7	2,146·3	844·1	3,999·6	4,949·9	858·2	4,998·0	3,793·1	9,800·3	13,860·3	14,810·6
1950	1,733·3	1,836·1	1,031·0	1,856·2	849·2	3,613·5	4,541·5	883·0	5,659·0	3,552·5	10,335·1	13,948·6	14,876·6
1951	1,674·2	1,786·6	1,764·3	2,596·5	1,127·8	4,566·3	5,510·9	916·4	5,776·0	2,591·9	10,244·9	14,811·2	15,755·8
1952	1,674·5	1,787·5	1,169·1	2,044·5	945·1	3,788·7	4,777·1	903·9	5,478·0	2,627·1	8,973·8	12,762·5	15,750·9
1953	1,677·1	1,784·4	1,519·6	2,412·5	742·3	3,939·0	4,939·2	936·9	5,478·0	2,591·9	8,553·0	12,492·0	13,492·2
1954	1,692·0	1,807·7	1,584·6	2,493·7	926·4	4,203·2	…	901·0	5,377·?	2,627·1	…	…	…

TABLE V

Some Partial Long-term Series on Gross Fixed Investment in Argentina, 1885–1915

(Millions of pesos of 1950)

Year	Public Works	Private Non-agricultural Construction	Durable Goods for Communications	Railroad and Inter-urban Transport Equipment	
				Ways and Installations	Rolling Stock
1885	238·6	907·6	..	696·1	..
1886	226·8	935·1	..	295·2	..
1887	279·3	962·7	..	273·6	..
1888	302·5	996·2	..	922·5	..
1889	326·0	1,029·6	..	1,332·7	..
1890	221·1	1,064·3	..	2,323·0	..
1891	198·1	1,100·7	..	1,083·1	..
1892	226·8	1,136·9	..	198·2	..
1893	221·1	1,174·8	..	195·8	..
1894	232·5	1,215·4	..	107·8	..
1895	285·0	1,247·4	..	106·0	..
1896	415·6	1,283·6	..	358·2	..
1897	243·6	1,334·8	..	347·7	..
1898	518·9	1,373·7	..	217·6	..
1899	372·4	1,411·4	..	96·8	..
1900	288·6	1,452·1	..	126·5	..
1901	273·3	1,441·0	..	269·1	..
1902	205·9	1,322·1	5·8	245·2	16·7
1903	284·2	1,284·2	15·0	271·4	49·2
1904	675·6	1,400·5	13·1	497·3	113·7
1905	1,353·9	2,260·2	22·7	876·1	288·2
1906	905·8	2,852·2	37·9	1,444·0	371·0
1907	744·5	4,079·7	49·5	1,858·4	545·5
1908	705·9	3,982·2	40·9	1,119·1	261·2
1909	1,654·6	3,952·6	52·6	1,055·0	425·3
1910	1,593·4	5,034·0	68·8	1,190·6	498·7
1911	1,527·1	4,993·5	77·7	1,275·0	439·3
1912	1,084·5	3,836·4	72·0	678·5	380·9
1913	883·0	3,844·4	127·2	776·3	465·6
1914	807·6	1,692·4	87·8	378·0	282·2
1915	567·8	867·9	37·1	76·1	39·3

U

TABLE VI

Depreciation of Fixed Reproducible Capital in Argentina, by Type of Capital Good, 1935–55

(Millions of pesos of 1950)

Year	Machinery and Equipment				Constructions and Improvements				Total
	Machinery and Motors	Transport and Communications Equipment	Other Producers' Durable Goods	Sub-total	Agricultural Improvements and Housing	Private Non-agricultural Construction	Public Works	Sub-total	
1935	956·8	2,156·8	661·2	3,774·8	821·4	2,245·2	697·9	3,764·5	7,539·3
1936	968·8	2,177·0	687·9	3,833·7	731·4	2,267·0	725·7	3,724·1	7,557·8
1937	987·1	2,227·3	729·1	3,943·5	796·3	2,282·6	761·7	3,840·6	7,784·1
1938	1,036·1	2,336·3	758·3	4,130·7	654·1	2,310·7	807·0	3,771·8	7,902·5
1939	1,100·5	2,459·3	794·6	4,354·4	725·1	2,342·0	858·8	3,925·9	8,280·3
1940	1,126·2	2,529·4	798·5	4,454·1	745·7	2,374·9	900·0	4,020·6	8,474·7
1941	1,117·0	2,595·1	756·1	4,468·2	845·4	2,402·0	937·2	4,184·6	8,652·8
1942	1,119·9	2,653·2	748·8	4,521·9	614·7	2,437·7	971·2	4,023·6	8,545·5
1943	1,107·0	2,707·7	695·0	4,509·7	761·3	2,478·8	999·6	4,239·7	8,749·4
1944	1,061·4	2,721·6	665·2	4,448·2	687·5	2,522·8	1,028·0	4,238·3	8,686·5
1945	1,019·9	2,737·8	654·1	4,411·8	736·6	2,574·5	1,068·5	4,379·6	8,791·4
1946	973·4	2,709·5	639·2	4,322·1	769·7	2,625·6	1,105·4	4,500·7	8,822·8
1947	941·1	2,724·0	625·4	4,290·5	779·3	2,688·0	1,137·0	4,604·3	8,894·8
1948	964·7	2,892·3	678·0	4,535·0	840·0	2,754·0	1,169·3	4,763·3	9,298·3
1949	1,016·1	2,878·3	744·2	4,638·6	847·9	2,828·3	1,221·0	4,897·2	9,535·8
1950	1,015·1	2,767·7	766·9	4,549·7	725·3	2,900·0	1,293·7	4,919·0	9,468·7
1951	1,032·3	2,712·4	784·7	4,529·4	831·6	2,984·2	1,363·8	5,179·6	9,709·0
1952	1,080·2	2,731·2	811·5	4,622·9	860·0	3,071·4	1,429·4	5,360·8	9,983·7
1953	1,156·9	2,764·5	792·7	4,714·1	906·7	3,154·2	1,477·1	5,538·0	10,252·1
1954	1,235·5	2,813·3	769·3	4,818·1	940·1	3,228·3	1,523·9	5,692·3	10,510·4
1955	1,310·3	2,831·9	777·2	4,919·4	769·3	3,306·8	1,574·6	5,650·7	10,570·1

CAPITAL ACCUMULATION AND ECONOMIC GROWTH IN SOUTH AFRICA

By D. G. Franzsen and J. J. D. Willers

I. CAPITAL ACCUMULATION DURING THE PRE-UNION PERIOD

THE economic growth of a country can only be intrepreted in a historical context. In the case of South Africa, an investigation of the past growth of the Nation's capital stock calls for explicit recognition of the role played by two major structural changes, viz. (1) the advent, during the seventies and eighties of the last century, of the diamond and gold mining industries, and (2) the final achievement, in 1910, of the goal of the political and economic unification of the country. Two principal sub-periods may accordingly be distinguished in a survey of the capital accumulation process during the recent past, viz. (1) the development from 1870 until the formation of the Union of South Africa in 1910, and (2) the post-Union period.

Before 1910, there were four different colonial governments operating in the territory thereafter known as the Union of South Africa, and this lack of unity in the political and economic field resulted in a paucity of comparable information about economic trends. Much more is known about economic tendencies during the post-Union period, and hence this paper is mainly concerned with the post-1910 era. In this section a few general observations will nevertheless be made about, firstly, the role of the mineral discoveries in stimulating capital formation during the forty-year period, 1870–1910 – the *Gründerzeit* of modern capitalism in South Africa – and, secondly, the approximate order of magnitude of capital accumulation in the main sectors of the pre-Union economy.

Until the time of the discovery of diamonds (1867) and, subsequently, of gold (1886), South Africa was a typical example of a geographically isolated, pre-industrial society, with little scope for the production of surpluses and hence for the formation of capital. Apart from land, the most important possession of the European and non-European sections of the population was livestock. Moreover, the majority of the non-Europeans lived under tribal conditions, thereby escaping contact with the market economy.

The mineral discoveries changed South Africa's economic climate overnight. Not only was a vast amount of capital required for the opening up of the mines, but also for the removal of formidable physical bottlenecks, such as the total lack of modern transport facilities and communications in the inland regions where the minerals were located. Furthermore, the combination of capital and labour in the changed environment called for a complete readjustment of human values, in that it implied, among others, the willing acceptance, especially in the case of the tribal natives employed on the mines and elsewhere, of an entirely different way of life.

Chronologically, the diamond industry was in the van of South Africa's mineral development, but, not being a capital intensive industry, its own contribution to capital accumulation, in a physical sense, was limited, although its secondary influence in this regard was considerable. Thus, for example, it supplied the economic incentive for the construction of a railway network linking Kimberley, the 'diamond city', with the principal harbours. In the financial sphere, too, its influence was considerable, as it provided a formerly capital-starved country with a source of easily won wealth, and also attracted foreign risk capital to the South African capital market. The role of the latter factor was especially significant from the nineties onwards, and, fortunately for South Africa, its development of diamond and gold deposits took place at a time that Europe, and, more especially, the United Kingdom, were still in a position to undertake heavy overseas investments.

The opening up during the eighties of what eventually proved to be the world's largest gold-mining industry was the decisive factor in the consolidation of the gains accruing from the period of feverish development initiated by the diamond industry. The influence of gold on the country's subsequent economic growth is briefly summarized below.

In the first place, the mining of gold broadened the economic base of a country whose prosperity was formerly dependent on the fortunes of agriculture and diamonds. It should be borne in mind that the diamond industry, as a producer of a luxury commodity, was extremely sensitive to cyclical changes. Gold, on the other hand, exerted a stabilizing influence on the country's rate of growth, in that the continuous annual increase in the output of the industry, as well as the stability of its price,[1] tended to dampen the effect of cyclical fluctuations, and at the same time reinforced the upward secular trend of real income. This, in turn, reacted favourably on the level of domestic savings and capital formation. It cannot be denied, however, that the mining industry introduced the familiar elements of financial instability and overspeculation into the South African capital market, but the recurring financial crises did not impair the steady expansion of the South African gold output, which, from 1886 to 1909 with the exception of the years of the Anglo-Boer War (1899–1902), presented a remarkable picture of sustained growth.

Secondly, as gold is a unique example of a commodity enjoying an infinite elasticity of demand at the ruling price, its preponderance in South Africa's export trade during the latter part of the pre-Union period helped to solve the transfer problem usually encountered when an undiversified economy develops its natural resources at a rapid rate. The sale of gold abroad provided foreign exchange, not only for the importation of capital goods required for development purposes, but also for an increasing volume of imported consumer goods, the demand for which was rising as a result of the increase in the national income and general living standards.

Thirdly, the gold industry, like the diamond industry before it, stimulated capital investment in other fields, such as, for example, transport, communications, and urban development. Unlike the diamond industry, however, its direct contribution to capital formation was very substantial, as the mining of gold under the conditions obtaining in South Africa called for an industry with a high capital–output ratio. During the first few years after the discovery of gold on the Witwatersrand, mine operators confined their efforts to the exploitation of outcrops, but soon it became necessary to mine at greater depth. Deep-level mining demanded the outlay of large sums on shafts and specialized equipment. Moreover, gold could only be extracted profitably from the low-grade ore mined on the Rand by chemical treatment in expensive plants. The capital outlay required in order to bring a new mine to the production stage

[1] The price of gold in the United Kingdom remained at £4·24773 per fine ounce throughout the period 1884–1909.

amounted to about £1–£3 million during this early period, and as small-scale undertakings were not in a position to raise the necessary funds, the tendency towards financial consolidation, which was also apparent in the case of the diamond industry, soon made its appearance.

The changes in the size and composition of the nation's capital stock since 1870 can be illustrated by data culled from official and other sources, but unfortunately the available data do not enable one to construct a balance sheet of the economy in 1870. Nevertheless, it is obvious that in the then existing pastoral economy non-farming assets were of minor importance. By 1909, however, mining and ancillary developments in the private and public sectors of the economy had shifted the balance of power from the farming to the non-farming industries. The trends of capital accumulation in the principal industrial categories are set out below under five headings.

(i) *Farming.* It is estimated that the share of farming assets in the total capital stock declined from what must have been the very high 1870 percentage figure to about 30 per cent at the close of the pre-Union period. As pastoral production was still predominant in 1909, it is further estimated that about three-fourths of the total farming assets (valued at about £136 million) existing at that date was represented by livestock. The changes since 1870 in the value of the different kinds of livestock are shown in Table I.

TABLE I

Value of Livestock, in Current Prices, for Selected Years
(1870–1909)

(£ million)

Year	Cattle	Woolled Sheep	Non-woolled Sheep	Goats	Pigs	Ost-riches	Mules and Asses	Horses	Poultry	TOTAL
1870	5	5	1	1	—	1	1	2	—	16
1875	11	15	2	3	—	1	1	6	1	40
1891	18	14	2	3	1	4	1	8	1	52
1895	18	12	3	3	1	4	1	8	1	51
1899	24	24	6	6	1	7	2	13	2	85
1904	30	13	5	7	1	9	3	8	2	78
1909	33	15	5	4	2	19	3	11	3	95

(ii) *Mining.* The stake of the mining industry in the capital stock of the private sector is estimated at about one-sixth in 1909, as against virtually nothing in 1870. It should be borne in mind, however, that the total amount of money poured into this industry far exceeded the value of the reproducible assets employed for mining purposes. Accordingly, the concept of reproducible capital does not provide an adequate measure of the accumulation of capital required for the opening up of the various mining properties. By far the greatest portion of the initial capital raised by the various diamond companies, for example, was devoted to the purchase of mining properties and rights.

From the available evidence it would appear that the gross fixed capital formation of the diamond industry until the end of the seventies amounted to only about £1 million. During the eighties the same observation applied to the gold-mines, but the introduction, at the end of this decade, of the deep-level gold-mining techniques, referred to above, marked the beginning of the capital-intensive phase of this industry. During the two decades 1890–99 and 1900–9, gross capital formation in the mining industry amounted to £21 million and £31 million, respectively, as against the very low figure of about £3–£5 million for the eighties. The depreciated original cost of mining assets at the end of 1909 is estimated at £53 million.

(iii) *Manufacturing.* Manufacturing industry was still in its infancy during the pre-Union period, as is borne out by the low figures for reproducible capital employed in this field in 1904, when the first official Census data were collected. The relevant figures are shown in Table II.

TABLE II

Book Value of Buildings and Improvements, Machinery and Equipment of Manufacturing Industry in the Four Colonies, 1904 [1]

Colony	Buildings and Improvements	Machinery and Equipment
Cape	3·9	2·2
Transvaal	1·2	1·9
Natal	1·3	1·4
Orange Free State . . .	0·1	0·2
Total . . .	6·5	5·7

[1] The census covered private and public establishments, although the role of the latter was negligible during this early period. Furthermore, the generation of electric power and the building industry were also covered by the 1904 census. According to a census taken in the Cape Colony for the year 1891, the value of buildings and improvements and machinery and equipment amounted to £1·3 million and £1·6 million respectively.

The number of persons employed in manufacturing in 1904 was about 75,000, while the most important industrial category was the manufacture of food and drink, i.e. grain mills, bakeries, breweries, and distillers. During this period, manufacturing activity was mainly confined to the so-called 'sheltered' industries, whose further development was to a large extent determined by the rate of growth of the population. Already during this early phase, however, the capital and current requirements of the gold-mining industry for such commodities as explosives fostered local manufacturing development.

(iv) *Building and construction.* The economic expansion of South Africa greatly stimulated urban growth, especially in the mining areas. This is reflected in the figures relating to the municipal valuation of fixed property, i.e. land and improvements, which are set out in Table III.

TABLE III

Municipal Valuation of Fixed Property [1]

(£ million)

Year	Cape Colony	Transvaal		Natal		Orange Free State
		Johannes-burg	Other Muni-cipalities	Durban	Other Muni-cipalities	
1891	..	3	..	2	..	..
1894	18	5	..	..	..	..
1899	30	22	..	..	..	..
1904	55	39	..	..	..	..
1909	57	37	8	8	6	7

.. Not available.

[1] Broadly speaking, the ratio of land to improvements in the various centres varied from 30 to 35 per cent.

(v) *The public sector.* No less than one-third of the total capital assets existing at the end of 1909 must be classified as falling under the 'public sector'. By far the most important single item in this category was the assets of the state-owned railways and harbours system.

The building of a railway network proved to be a very expensive undertaking, not only on account of the great distances between the inland areas where the mines were situated and the nearest harbours, but also on account of topographical factors.

In 1909 the depreciated original cost of railways and harbours assets already amounted to no less than £85 million.

The combined capital outlay of the Railways and Harbours Administrations operating in the different colonies is set out in Table IV.

TABLE IV

Gross Capital Formation – Railways and Harbours

Decade	£ million
1870–79	9
1880–89	12
1890–99	39
1900–9.	43

II. CAPITAL ACCUMULATION DURING THE POST-UNION PERIOD

1. *Methods of calculation*

Before discussing capital accumulation during the post-Union period, a few comments on the methods of calculation are called for. The sources of the data are specified in Appendix II. The capital stock figures refer to reproducible assets, although estimates of the value of land, sub-soil wealth, and consumer durables [1] are given in Appendix III.[2]

Annual capital expenditure data were not available for the period prior to 1910, and, accordingly, the computation of a net capital stock series for the whole period, 1910–55, required, firstly, an estimate of the reproducible wealth existing at the beginning of the year 1910, and, secondly, an estimate of the net additions to this initial figure from 1910 onwards. The first step in the calculations was the determination of capital stock in terms of depreciated original cost (or book value) in the benchmark year, 1909. This entailed direct and detailed computations of the value of the stocks of the different types of capital goods employed in the various industries, such as mining, agriculture, manufacturing industry, etc.

The second step was the calculation of the gross capital-

---

[1] Motor vehicles only; a survey of the other items has not yet been undertaken.

[2] Transfer costs on immovable property have not been included in the capital-stock figures discussed in the present paper, although estimates of this item are given in the Gross and Net Capital Formation Tables in Appendix I (see Tables IV and V). For this reason, therefore, the net capital formation figures obtained as the difference between successive net capital stock data, valued at original cost (see Table I, Appendix I), will differ from the net capital formation figures appearing in the final columns of Tables IV and V in the same Appendix.

expenditure figures, in current prices, for each year during the period under review; finally, *net* capital stock figures from 1910 onwards were derived by adding, for example in the case of the initial year 1910, the gross capital expenditure of 1910 to the written-down capital stock figure of 1909 (obtained by means of direct investigation, as mentioned above), and then depreciating [1] the resulting total in accordance with the reducing-balance method. Similar calculations were undertaken for all subsequent years. Thus, in general, for any specific year, the initial net capital stock *plus* gross capital formation in prices of that year *minus* depreciation at pre-determined rates will yield the terminal net value of the capital stock.

Three capital-stock series are distinguished in Appendix I, viz. (a) capital stock, at depreciated original cost; (b) depreciated capital stock, in 1938 prices, and, finally, (c) depreciated capital stock, in current prices. Series (a) was derived in accordance with the statistical process outlined in the foregoing paragraph.

In the case of series (b), two sub-classes of the official Wholesale Price Index, namely, 'Metals' and 'Building Materials', were used as deflators. As mentioned above, no information about the annual capital expenditure on fixed assets was available for the pre-Union period, and hence, as the first step in the calculations, the net capital stock for the bench-mark year 1909 was expressed in 1938 prices by dividing the 1909 values, in terms of depreciated original cost, by the relevant price indexes for 1909 (base: 1938 = 100) – a procedure which rests, of course, on far-reaching assumptions. The present authors are confident, however, that future research will provide answers to this and other similar problems encountered in the attempt to trace capital accumulation back to the year 1910.

The next step in the derivation of series (b) was the expression of the annual gross capital expenditure series in terms of 1938 prices by means of the deflators already mentioned. As in the case of series (a), the method of deriving the net capital stock figures in 1938 prices was, firstly, that of adding, in each specific year, the deflated gross capital expenditure to the written-down value of the capital stock existing at the beginning of the year, and, secondly, depreciating the total thus obtained at the same rates as those utilized in the calculation of series (a).

---

[1] At rates set out in Table V in the text.

In the case of inventories, the book values were taken to represent both the cost and the market (or current) price of the goods. The general wholesale price index for the last quarter of each year was used to derive the value of inventories at base-year prices. The value, in 1938 prices, of the livestock component of the inventory series was obtained by multiplying the number of each type of livestock at the end of each year by the respective average price ruling during the year 1938.

For series (c), annual values, in current prices, of the capital stock were obtained by multiplying the net value, in 1938 prices, of the various types of assets (i.e. series (b)) by each year's price index.

The methods used in the calculation of gross capital formation and depreciation allowances for the different industrial categories were largely determined by the nature of the basic data. The sources of information on the Public Sector (including Public Corporations), as well as industries such as building and

TABLE V

Annual Rates of Depreciation

	Buildings	Other Construction	Machinery, Plant, and Equipment
	(%)	(%)	(%)
I. *Public Authorities*			
1. Union Government			
(a) South African Railways and Harbours . . .	1	1	1
(b) Other government enterprises	1¼	1¼	10
(c) General government . .	2	—	—
2. Provincial administrations. .	2	—	10 [2]
3. Local authorities			
(a) Trading departments . .	2	2	10
(b) Non-trading departments .	2	—	10 [2]
II. *Public Corporations* . . .	2	2	10
III. *Private Business Enterprises*			
1. Residential building . . .	2	—	—
2. Farming	1¼	1¼	10
3. Mining	3	3	6¼
4. Manufacturing. . . .	2	2	12½
5. Commercial and service establishments, banks and other financial institutions and professional persons . . .	2	—	10

[1] Actual depreciation taken from the Auditor-General's Annual Reports.
[2] In respect of heavy machinery for road-building.

mining, were in such a form that the actual expenditure on capital assets could be ascertained, also for the earlier years of the period under review. Although the expenditure method is useful for an investigation of this early period, it should be mentioned that the improvement in basic statistics since World War II will in due course make it possible to check the results obtained thus far by applying the commodity-flow method.

The work done for the purpose of this paper on the measurement of capital consumption is very limited in scope. The calculations were based on the national capital stock, valued at original cost, and hence further research will have to be undertaken in future in order to refine the estimates of the value of the capital stock at replacement cost.

Except in the case of the South African Railways and Harbours,[1] the reducing-balance method of calculating depreciation was used.[2]

The rates of depreciation employed in the present calculations are given in Table V.

2. *The pattern of growth of the national capital stock*

Since 1910, a great expansion has occurred in the range and size of South Africa's overall capital requirements, mainly as a result of the diversification of the economy. The most important single factor in this development was the growth of manufacturing industry,[3] whose capital assets, in 1938 prices, increased from a mere £22 million, in 1909, to no less than £352 million, in 1955. In percentage terms, its share in the total reproducible assets of the economy rose from about 4 per cent, in 1909, to 16 per cent in 1955, while that of mining declined from 13 to 10 per cent, and that of the railways from 20 to 12 per cent.

---

[1] The Railways and Harbours Administration calculates the average lives of the various types of assets, and hence the straight-line method can be applied.

[2] Owing to limitations of the basic information, it was not possible to determine the age structure of reproducible assets existing in 1910.

[3] The expansion of manufacturing industry was stimulated, among other things, by the two world wars, which restricted the normal flow of imported goods into the local market, thereby encouraging the establishment of local plants; by the policy of protection – although of a relatively mild character – adopted in the twenties; by the availability of cheap electric power as a result of the establishment of a number of integrated power plants serving large regions; by the emergence, during the past three decades, of modern heavy industries – a development which was made possible by the presence of ample deposits of iron ore and other important base minerals, as well as virtually unlimited quantities of cheap coal; and by the growth in size and purchasing power of the internal market.

The growth of manufacturing industry was also associated with an expansion of urban centres,[1] which, in turn, gave rise to a great increase in capital expenditure on residential buildings and other structures and municipal amenities. The greater relative expansion of the secondary and tertiary industries, as compared with primary industries, lessened the dependence of the economy on mining and agriculture, which were the main sources of wealth in the pre-1910 period. Thus the share of the two latter industries in the real geographical income of the Union declined from about 44 per cent in 1910, to 27 per cent in 1955.

Other general factors which helped to sustain the upward secular trend in production, employment and capital accumulation since 1910 were the rapid growth of the labour force; the contra-cyclical influence of the Union's built-in stabilizer, viz. the gold-mining industry, especially during the thirties —when the increase in the price of gold greatly stimulated expansion in this and other allied industries; the capital inflow from abroad; and, finally, the shift of unemployed or under-employed workers from rural areas to more productive work in urban centres.[2]

(a) *The rate of growth of the capital stock.* Over the period 1910–55 the average annual rate of growth of the Union's capital stock, valued in current prices, amounted to 5·9 per cent. The influence of changes in (1) the size of the Union's population, (2) the prices of capital goods, and (3) the real capital stock *per capita*, on the aggregate value of the capital stock is shown in Table VI. It is seen that, in real terms, the latter increased at an average annual rate of 3·1 per cent during 1909–55.

The relationship between the rates of growth of the *real* capital stock and the Union's population is made more explicit in Table VII. As shown by the data cited in Table VI, the Union's population has grown very rapidly since 1910, the average annual rate of growth over the period 1909–55 being 1·9 per cent. Accordingly, a correspondingly high rate of increase in the real capital stock was called for in order to maintain the existing relationship between capital and population.

[1] The percentages of the European and non-European sections of the population living in urban areas were 78·4 and 32·9 per cent, respectively, in 1951, as against 51·6 and 17·4 per cent in 1911.

[2] This applied especially to the so-called 'migrant' workers from the native tribal villages, where, in particular, a large measure of disguised unemployment existed as a result of the limited scope for division of labour in a peasant society.

In point of fact, however, capital formation during this period was such that it did not only lead to a broadening of the capital stock, but also enabled production processes generally to become more capital intensive. Thus the data set out in Table VII show that total capital stock *per capita* (in 1938 prices) increased from £94, in the 1909–18 decade, to £133 in the 1944–53 decade.

TABLE VI

Changes in Population, Prices, and Capital Stock

(Average annual percentage changes)

Decade	Popula-tion	Prices	Capital Stock Per Capita (1938 Prices)	Total Capital Stock (Current Prices)	Total Capital Stock (1938 Prices)
1909–18	1·8	10·3	−0·5	11·8	1·3
1914–23	1·6	2·7	−0·7	3·6	0·9
1919–28	1·9	−7·2	1·3	−4·2	3·2
1924–33	2·2	−3·2	0·9	−0·1	3·2
1929–38	2·0	0·3	2·0	4·4	4·1
1934–43	1·8	7·5	1·7	11·3	3·5
1939–48	1·8	7·0	0·9	9·9	2·7
1944–55 [1]	1·9	4·2	2·6	9·0	4·6
1909–55	1·9	2·7	1·2	5·9	3·1

Since the thirties a contributory factor in the expansion of the capital stock was the persistent labour shortage, as this factor led to more mechanisation, especially in such industries as farming and mining.

(b) *The relation between capital stock and real income.* Over the period 1918–55,[2] the real [3] domestic or geographical income of the Union increased at an average annual rate of 4·4 per cent, as against 3·8 per cent in the case of the real capital stock. The annual changes since 1918 in the relation between these two magnitudes (i.e. the 'capital coefficient') are set out in Table VIII.

Table VIII shows four capital coefficient series; the first two columns give coefficients based on total and fixed capital stock figures of *all* industries, while the last two columns show these coefficients after excluding capital stock in the form of residential buildings from the all-industry totals.

[1] Twelve-year period.

[2] At the present time geographical figures of the Union are only available on an annual basis since 1918.

[3] Due to the lack of appropriate indexes, the official retail price index was used to deflate the geographical income figures.

TABLE VII

The Relation between Capital Stock and Population

(Geometric averages for overlapping decades)

Decade	Capital Stock (in 1938 prices)				Population of the Union		Capital Stock *Per Capita* (in 1938 prices)			
	Total		Fixed				Total		Fixed	
	£ million	Percentage change from decade to decade	£ million	Percentage change from decade to decade	Thousands	Percentage change from decade to decade	£	Percentage change from decade to decade	£	Percentage change from decade to decade
1909–18	589		436		6,261		94		70	
1914–23	619	5·1	460	5·5	6,763	8·0	92	—2·1	68	—2·9
1919–28	692	11·8	502	9·1	7,400	9·4	94	2·2	68	—
1924–33	822	18·8	599	19·3	8,262	11·6	100	6·4	72	5·9
1929–38	987	20·1	739	23·4	9,153	10·8	108	8·0	81	12·5
1934–43	1,187	20·3	916	24·0	10,063	9·9	118	9·3	91	12·3
1939–48	1,356	14·2	1,057	14·7	10,999	9·3	123	4·2	96	5·5
1944–53	1,607	18·5	1,255	19·4	12,074	9·8	133	8·1	104	8·3
1909–18 to 1944–53 (decade average)		15·5		16·5		9·8		5·2		5·9

TABLE VIII
Capital Coefficients of the Union, 1918–55

Year	Reproducible Capital Stock Including Residential Buildings		Reproducible Capital Stock Excluding Residential Buildings	
	Total Capital Stock	Fixed Capital Stock	Total Capital Stock	Fixed Capital Stock
1918 . .	3·5	2·6	3·3	2·3
1919 . .	3·2	2·4	2·9	2·1
1920 . .	4·0	2·9	3·7	2·6
1921 . .	4·4	3·2	4·2	2·9
1922 . .	3·7	2·7	3·4	2·4
1923 . .	3·3	2·4	3·1	2·1
1924 . .	3·3	2·4	3·1	2·2
1925 . .	3·4	2·4	3·1	2·2
1926 . .	3·3	2·4	3·1	2·1
1927 . .	3·2	2·3	3·0	2·1
1928 . .	3·3	2·4	3·0	2·1
1929 . .	3·5	2·5	3·3	2·3
1930 . .	3·8	2·7	3·5	2·4
1931 . .	4·0	2·9	3·7	2·6
1932 . .	3·8	2·9	3·6	2·6
1933 . .	3·3	2·5	3·1	2·3
1934 . .	3·1	2·4	2·9	2·1
1935 . .	3·1	2·3	2·8	2·1
1936 . .	3·0	2·3	2·8	2·0
1937 . .	3·0	2·3	2·8	2·1
1938 . .	3·2	2·5	3·0	2·2
1939 . .	3·1	2·4	2·9	2·2
1940 . .	3·0	2·3	2·7	2·1
1941 . .	2·8	2·2	2·6	2·0
1942 . .	2·8	2·2	2·5	1·9
1943 . .	2·7	2·1	2·5	1·9
1944 . .	2·6	2·1	2·4	1·8
1945 . .	2·6	2·0	2·3	1·8
1946 . .	2·6	2·0	2·4	1·8
1947 . .	2·7	2·0	2·4	1·8
1948 . .	2·7	2·1	2·7	1·9
1949 . .	2·7	2·1	2·4	1·8
1950 . .	2·5	1·9	2·2	1·7
1951 . .	2·5	1·9	2·3	1·7
1952 . .	2·6	2·1	2·3	1·8
1953 . .	2·6	2·1	2·3	1·8
1954 . .	2·5	2·1	2·3	1·8
1955 . .	2·6	2·1	2·4	1·9

	Arithmetic Averages for Overlapping Decades			
	Total Assets	Fixed Assets	Total Assets	Fixed Assets
1919–28 .	3·5	2·5	3·3	2·3
1924–33 .	3·5	2·5	3·3	2·3
1929–38 .	3·4	2·5	3·2	2·3
1934–43 .	3·0	2·3	2·8	2·1
1939–48 .	2·8	2·1	2·5	1·9
1944–55 [1] .	2·6	2·0	2·4	1·8

[1] Twelve-year period.

The data for overlapping decades since 1919 do not reveal a tendency towards a 'deepening of capital', i.e. that more capital was utilized per unit of output. This, in turn, indicates that the changes in the structural relationships of the economy tended to divert a greater proportion of the available capital assets into the less capital-intensive industries, i.e. secondary and tertiary industries, as compared with the capital-intensive industries, such as, for example, railway transportation and public utilities.

The capital coefficients attained their peak during the world depression on account of the under-utilization of the then existing capital stock. Since then, however, a state of near-full, and, more recently, of over-full employment, has prevailed in the Union's economy. Moreover, mainly as a result of war conditions, which interfered with the normal flow of goods destined for capital works, a serious backlog developed in the provision of new facilities in a number of sectors, especially basic industries, such as railway transport, electric-power generation, and public utilities generally. To the extent that their capacity had been under-utilized previously, the new situation naturally led to a lowering of the capital coefficients in these sectors.[1]

(c) *Capital coefficients of individual industries*. Although it is particularly difficult to obtain reliable estimates of capital coefficients for individual industries, the figures given in Table IX below do permit the drawing of broad conclusions.

While all the coefficients given above show a tendency to decline, it is most noticeable in the case of the South African Railways and Harbours and Agriculture, both based on the total capital stock. As regards the former, this was brought about by the fuller utilization of the existing permanent way and rolling stock, while in the latter case it was due to the relative decline of inventories (i.e. livestock) in the agricultural field.

It will also be noted that of the three major industrial categories distinguished in Table IX, Agriculture had the highest capital–output ratio, followed by Mining and Manufacturing industry. In view of the declining importance of Agriculture, and, to a lesser extent, Mining, in the total capital stock, and the

[1] This is, of course, the reverse of the situation which existed in the pre-Union period, when indivisible items, such as railway lines, had to be constructed ahead of the existing demand for their services, thus causing an unavoidable under-utilization of these resources.

X

increase in the percentage share of Manufacturing, it may be expected that the trend towards a lower overall capital–output ratio will continue.

TABLE IX

Capital Coefficients of Individual Industries

(Arithmetic averages for overlapping decades)

Decade	Agriculture		Mining		Manufacturing		South African Railways and Harbours
	Total Capital Stock	Fixed Capital Stock	Total Capital Stock	Fixed Capital Stock	Total Capital Stock	Fixed Capital Stock	Total Capital Stock
1919–23	5·4	2·3	2·1	2·0	1·8	1·2	7·5
1924–33	6·3	2·9	1·8	1·8	1·8	1·1	7·1
1929–38	6·5	3·2	1·7	1·6	1·8	1·1	6·6
1934–43	5·5	2·9	1·6	1·5	1·7	1·0	5·9
1939–48	4·8	2·6	1·8	1·7	1·6	0·9	5·4
1944–45	3·5	2·1	2·0	1·9	1·6	0·9	4·5

(d) *The composition of the capital stock.* Mention has been made above of the changes in the Union's capital structure as a result of the industrialization process since 1910. Details of the changes in the percentage distribution, by industry, of the reproducible capital stock are given in Table X. Manufacturing industry's share in the total stock exceeded that of mining since the 1939–48 decade. Although the recent growth of manufacturing was more rapid than that of mining, it is nevertheless remarkable that the gold-mining industry, which is based on wasting assets, and which acted as a pioneer in the modern development of the economy in the last century, continued to experience steady secular expansion.[1]

Attention must also be drawn to the substantial percentage

---

[1] Pessimistic forecasts about the future of the industry were dispelled from time to time by geological surveys which revealed the existence of other areas where gold could be mined on a profitable basis. During the twenties the original mining area on the Central and Western Rand was expanded by the addition of the goldfields on the 'Far East Rand', while ultra-deep mining (i.e. depths more than 7,500 feet) was resorted to in the older mines. Since the thirties, further new goldfields have been opened up in three other areas in Transvaal and in the Orange Free State. As in the pre-Union period, the opening up of new fields stimulated vast capital investment in ancillary activities, e.g. transportation, urban development, public utilities, etc. During recent years, the lives of many gold-mines have also been extended by the exploitation of a valuable by-product viz. uranium.

share of the public sector (excluding public corporations) in the national capital stock. According to the available data, it would appear that this share remained practically stationary at about one-third during the period under review. The capital assets of

TABLE X

Percentage Distribution of Reproducible Stock, in 1938 Prices, by Industries

Decade	Agri-culture	Min-ing	Manufac-turing [1]	Resi-dential Build-ings [2]	Other Private	Total Private	South African Railways and Harbours	Other Public	Total Public	Grand Total
				A. *Total Assets*						
1909–18	27	13	5		23	68	19	13	32	100
1914–23	28	12	6		22	68	19	13	32	100
1919–28	29	11	6		22	68	18	14	32	100
1924–33	28	10	7	11	12	68	17	15	32	100
1929–38	26	10	8	12	12	68	16	16	32	100
1934–43	22	11	10	12	12	67	15	18	33	100
1939–48	21	10	11	13	12	67	14	19	33	100
1944–55 [3]	19	10	13	13	12	67	13	20	33	100
				B. *Fixed Assets*						
1909–18	15	16	5		22	58	25	17	42	100
1914–23	16	16	5		21	58	24	18	42	100
1919–28	17	14	6		20	57	24	19	43	100
1924–33	17	13	6	15	6	57	23	20	43	100
1929–38	17	12	7	16	6	58	20	22	42	100
1934–43	15	13	7	16	7	58	19	23	42	100
1939–48	15	12	8	16	7	58	17	25	42	100
1944–45 [3]	15	11	11	16	7	60	15	25	40	100

[1] Including Public Corporations.

[2] It is noteworthy that the percentage share of residential buildings in the Union's total capital stock is lower than similar figures for other Western countries. The reasons for this are, among others, that: (1) for technical reasons, European farm-houses were included under the heading 'Agriculture' in this table, and (2) municipal returns, which were the main source on residential buildings in the present study, cover dwellings of non-Europeans living in the urban areas, but not those of non-Europeans in rural and tribal areas. Almost three-fourths of the Natives, and a substantial portion of the Coloured and Asiatic population groups, live in non-urban areas. Unfortunately, however, it was not possible to include an estimate of the value of these rural dwellings in the present calculations, as that would have entailed extensive field surveys.

[3] Twelve-year period.

the South African Railways and Harbours Administration (a government enterprise, as mentioned earlier) used to form the main component of the public sector's reproducible capital, but as a result of the establishment and expansion of other public projects, it no longer dominates the capital formation of this sector.

A further breakdown of the capital stock, viz. by type of assets, is given in Table XI. Since 1909 the percentage share of machinery and equipment in the total remained more or less the same, but that of inventories declined.[4]

[4] One reason for this is the decline in the share of agricultural inventories (i.e. livestock) in all agricultural assets, viz. from 59 per cent in 1909–18, to 39 per cent in 1944–53.

(e) *Additions to the capital stock.* The data set out in Table XII show a high ratio of gross domestic capital formation to gross national expenditure since 1910. The table also illustrates

TABLE XI

Percentage Distribution of Capital Assets in 1938 Prices by Type of Asset

Decade	Buildings and Structures	Machinery and Equipment	Inventories	Total
1909–18 . .	57	17	26	100
1914–23 . .	58	16	26	100
1919–28 . .	58	15	27	100
1924–33 . .	58	15	27	100
1929–38 . .	60	15	25	100
1934–43 . .	61	16	23	100
1939–48 . .	62	16	22	100
1944–55 [1] . .	61	18	21	100

TABLE XII

Consumption, Domestic Capital Formation, and the Balance on Current Account (in Current Prices)

(Annual averages for decades)

Decade	Con-sumption	Gross Domestic Capital Formation	Total Domestic Expenditure	Balance on Current Account	Gross National Product at Market Prices
A. £ Million					
1919–28	203	46	249	− 7	242
1924–33	228	40	268	− 3	265
1929–38	261	57	318	− 1	317
1946–55	1,021	364	1,385	−88	1,297
B. Percentage Distribution					
1919–28	84	19	103	− 3	100
1924–33	86	15	101	− 1	100
1929–38	82	18	100	− 0	100
1946–55	79	28	107	− 7	100

balance on current account in the Union's national accounts. It is seen that throughout this period [2] domestic expenditure, or the contribution of the foreign sector, as measured by the

[1] Twelve-year period.
[2] The figures do not cover the war period 1939–45, as no estimates of the balance on current account are available for these years.

total available supply, exceeded the gross national expenditure, thus allowing consumers, entrepreneurs, and government authorities additional latitude for the satisfaction of their current requirements over and above the limits imposed by the size of the nation's own productive efforts.

The relationship between gross and net capital formation, on the one hand, and the gross and net national product, on the other, is shown in Table XIII.

TABLE XIII

Domestic Capital Formation as a Percentage of National Product for Overlapping Decades

Decade	Gross Capital Formation as Percentage of Gross National Product		Net Capital Formation as Percentage of Net National Product	
	Current Prices	1938 Prices	Current Prices	1938 Prices
1919–28 . .	18·8	18·7	13·3	12·1
1924–33 . .	15·1	17·4	8·7	10·8
1929–38 . .	18·0	19·1	11·9	12·7
1934–43 . .	17·6	15·1	12·2	8·9
1939–48 . .	19·7	13·7	15·2	8·0
1944–55 [1] . .	26·6	17·7	21·9	12·2

[1] Twelve-year period.

The percentage share of the Union's Gross Capital Formation in the Gross National Product amounted to 16·9 per cent over the period 1919–55, and 17·7 per cent during the post-war period (1944–55). It follows, therefore, that during the period under review the Union offered attractive investment opportunities, not only for the employment of capital in the exploitation of previously untapped natural resources but also for the expansion of existing material assets as a result of rapid population growth.

APPENDIX I

TABLES

TABLE I
Capital Stock at Depreciated Original Cost
(£ million)

Year	Agriculture	Mining	Manufacturing [1]	Residential Buildings	Other Private	Total Private	South African Railways and Harbours	Other Public	Total Public	Total Private and Public	Inventories	GRAND TOTAL
1909	41	47	13	67		168	82	56	138	306	149	455
1910	44	50	14	69		177	83	60	143	320	153	473
1911	46	56	17	71		190	86	62	148	338	158	496
1912	48	58	18	73		197	88	66	154	351	170	521
1913	51	61	18	75		205	92	68	160	365	173	538
1914	55	61	19	77		212	96	70	166	378	153	531
1915	58	61	20	77		216	99	72	171	387	145	532
1916	58	62	23	77		220	100	73	173	393	158	551
1917	59	63	25	79		226	100	74	174	400	167	567
1918	61	64	28	79		232	100	77	177	409	206	615
1919	65	65	30	81		241	103	80	183	424	233	657
1920	72	68	32	86		258	109	84	193	451	266	717
1921	77	70	34	90		271	114	89	203	474	227	701
1922	79	70	37	61	32	279	117	93	210	489	185	674
1923	82	71	38	64	33	288	120	98	218	506	200	706
1924	88	75	38	67	33	301	127	102	229	530	215	745
1925	93	76	39	69	34	311	132	108	240	551	221	772
1926	97	76	41	74	35	323	138	113	251	574	222	796
1927	102	76	44	77	35	334	143	119	262	596	231	827
1928	106	77	46	82	37	348	148	124	272	620	241	861
1929	113	77	47	88	39	364	153	130	283	647	243	890
1930	115	78	48	93	40	374	158	135	293	667	221	888
1931	117	79	48	97	40	381	160	141	301	682	192	874
1932	118	78	49	99	40	384	160	146	306	690	161	851
1933	118	80	51	101	40	390	160	150	310	700	181	881
1934	121	84	53	106	42	406	162	156	318	724	213	937
1935	125	92	60	113	45	435	164	165	329	764	225	989
1936	128	100	67	120	50	465	171	176	347	812	243	1,055
1937	133	110	71	128	56	498	178	190	368	866	269	1,135
1938	138	120	76	137	62	533	190	206	396	929	284	1,213
1939	142	127	80	147	67	563	197	225	422	985	293	1,278
1940	146	130	83	153	70	582	201	240	441	1,023	310	1,333
1941	150	133	86	159	72	600	202	252	454	1,054	343	1,397
1942	152	133	90	161	74	610	205	259	464	1,074	369	1,443
1943	156	130	95	161	74	616	207	269	476	1,092	399	1,491
1944	162	131	105	167	75	640	212	279	491	1,131	421	1,552
1945	169	132	119	176	79	675	221	292	513	1,188	435	1,623
1946	180	136	132	192	83	723	233	315	548	1,271	529	1,800
1947	196	145	150	215	92	798	248	344	592	1,390	637	2,027
1948	224	158	181	243	103	909	267	382	649	1,558	707	2,265
1949	252	176	219	272	120	1,039	296	422	718	1,757	727	2,484
1950	275	204	255	297	137	1,168	316	462	778	1,946	779	2,725
1951	309	237	299	330	158	1,333	331	505	836	2,169	971	3,140
1952	339	287	353	375	190	1,544	356	559	915	2,459	1,025	3,484
1953	370	333	430	420	222	1,775	399	616	1,015	2,790	1,028	3,818
1954	404	380	502	467	252	2,005	434	679	1,113	3,118	1,070	4,188
1955	440	416	556	520	281	2,213	465	748	1,213	3,426	1,153	4,579

[1] Including public corporations.

TABLE II

Depreciated Capital Stock in 1938 Prices

(£ million)

Year	Agriculture	Mining	Manufacturing[1]	Residential Buildings	Other Private	Total Private	South African Railways and Harbours	Other Public	Total Public	Total Private and Public	Inventories	GRAND TOTAL
1909	53	60	17	87		217	105	63	168	385	149	534
1910	56	64	19	89		228	107	66	173	401	152	553
1911	59	65	20	92		236	107	69	176	412	160	572
1912	62	74	22	94		252	109	73	182	434	167	601
1913	65	76	22	96		259	112	77	189	448	161	609
1914	69	76	22	98		265	115	79	194	459	157	616
1915	71	75	22	98		266	115	80	195	461	147	608
1916	71	74	23	97		265	114	81	195	460	146	606
1917	71	73	24	95		263	112	80	192	455	139	594
1918	71	71	24	93		259	110	81	191	450	151	601
1919	72	70	24	93		259	109	82	191	450	147	597
1920	75	69	24	93		261	110	83	193	454	163	617
1921	77	69	25	94		265	111	86	197	462	183	645
1922	79	68	26	66	30	269	111	88	199	468	176	644
1923	81	69	27	68	31	276	114	92	206	482	184	666
1924	85	72	28	71	32	288	117	97	214	502	194	696
1925	91	73	29	73	32	298	121	102	223	521	205	726
1926	95	73	32	77	33	310	126	107	233	543	209	752
1927	99	74	34	81	34	322	130	112	242	564	221	785
1928	106	75	37	86	36	340	135	119	254	594	231	825
1929	113	76	39	93	38	359	140	124	264	623	247	870
1930	116	77	40	98	39	370	144	131	275	645	249	894
1931	118	79	40	103	40	380	145	139	284	664	236	900
1932	119	79	43	106	41	388	146	145	291	679	222	901
1933	121	81	45	109	42	398	145	150	295	693	216	909
1934	126	86	48	115	44	419	147	158	305	724	233	957
1935	129	96	56	123	49	453	150	168	318	771	249	1,020
1936	135	107	64	132	55	493	157	181	338	831	268	1,099
1937	140	116	69	140	61	526	163	195	358	884	279	1,163
1938	143	126	73	148	66	556	174	212	386	942	288	1,230
1939	147	132	75	158	71	583	181	230	411	994	292	1,286
1940	149	133	76	162	72	592	181	240	421	1,013	289	1,302
1941	151	133	76	164	72	596	181	246	427	1,023	286	1,309
1942	151	130	77	164	71	593	179	250	429	1,022	268	1,290
1943	151	127	77	163	70	588	179	254	433	1,021	262	1,283
1944	153	125	81	165	70	594	179	258	437	1,031	269	1,300
1945	156	124	86	168	71	605	181	264	445	1,050	273	1,323
1946	161	124	92	176	72	625	187	275	462	1,087	323	1,410
1947	168	126	100	187	76	657	192	289	481	1,138	369	1,507
1948	180	131	112	199	80	702	199	307	506	1,208	390	1,598
1949	191	138	129	211	86	755	210	325	535	1,290	387	1,677
1950	199	147	143	221	93	803	215	340	555	1,358	381	1,739
1951	211	157	155	231	98	852	218	355	573	1,425	405	1,830
1952	217	170	168	243	107	905	222	369	591	1,496	378	1,874
1953	226	184	192	257	117	976	233	388	621	1,597	374	1,971
1954	237	199	216	272	127	1,051	243	409	652	1,703	383	2,086
1955	247	209	231	289	135	1,111	251	431	682	1,793	400	2,193

[1] Including public corporations.

TABLE III
Depreciated Capital Stock in Current Prices
(£ million)

Year	Agriculture	Mining	Manufacturing¹	Residential Buildings	Other Private	Total Private	South African Railways and Harbours	Other Public	Total Public	Total Private and Public	Inventories	GRAND TOTAL
1909	41	47	13	68		169	82	49	131	300	149	449
1910	44	50	15	69		178	83	51	134½	312	153	465
1911	47	51	16	73		187	84	55	139½	326	158	484
1912	48	57	17	72		194	84	56	140	334	170	504
1913	53	62	18	78		211	91	63	154	365	173	538
1914	62	68	20	87		237	102	71	173	410	153	563
1915	79	83	24	109		295	127	89	216	511	145	656
1916	100	104	32	137		373	161	114	275	648	158	806
1917	135	139	46	179		499	213	152	365	864	167	1,031
1918	161	161	54	211		587	249	184	433	1,020	206	1,226
1919	145	141	48	189		523	220	166	386	909	233	1,142
1920	167	153	53	207		580	245	184	429	1,009	266	1,275
1921	139	125	45	170		479	201	155	356	835	227	1,062
1922	101	87	33	84	38	343	142	112	254	597	185	782
1923	96	81	32	80	37	326	134	109	243	569	200	769
1924	95	81	31	80	36	323	131	109	240	563	215	778
1925	96	76	30	76	34	312	126	107	233	545	221	766
1926	96	74	33	78	34	315	128	109	237	552	222	774
1927	98	73	34	80	34	319	129	111	240	559	231	790
1928	99	70	35	80	34	318	126	111	237	555	241	796
1929	104	70	36	85	35	330	129	114	243	573	243	816
1930	107	71	37	91	36	342	133	121	254	596	221	817
1931	102	69	35	90	35	331	126	121	247	578	192	770
1932	95	63	34	85	33	310	117	116	233	543	161	704
1933	101	68	38	91	35	333	121	126	247	580	181	761
1934	107	73	41	98	37	356	125	134	259	615	213	828
1935	110	82	48	104	42	386	128	143	271	657	225	882
1936	116	91	55	113	47	422	134	155	289	711	243	954
1937	139	114	68	138	60	519	161	192	353	872	269	1,141
1938	143	126	73	148	66	556	174	212	386	942	284	1,226
1939	147	133	75	159	71	585	182	231	413	998	293	1,291
1940	192	170	97	207	92	758	232	307	539	1,297	310	1,607
1941	230	201	116	250	110	907	275	375	650	1,557	343	1,900
1942	256	221	131	279	121	1,008	304	425	729	1,737	369	2,106
1943	268	226	137	290	125	1,046	318	452	770	1,816	399	2,215
1944	272	223	145	295	125	1,060	320	460	780	1,840	421	2,261
1945	273	217	150	294	124	1,058	317	461	778	1,836	435	2,271
1946	280	215	160	306	125	1,086	325	477	802	1,888	529	2,417
1947	320	240	191	357	145	1,253	366	551	917	2,170	637	2,807
1948	363	264	226	401	161	1,415	401	619	1,020	2,435	707	3,142
1949	399	288	270	441	180	1,578	439	679	1,118	2,696	727	3,423
1950	441	325	316	489	206	1,777	476	752	1,228	3,005	779	3,784
1951	555	413	408	608	258	2,242	574	934	1,508	3,750	971	4,721
1952	674	528	521	754	332	2,809	689	1,145	1,834	4,643	1,025	5,668
1953	634	517	539	722	329	2,741	654	1,090	1,744	4,485	1,028	5,513
1954	643	539	586	737	344	2,849	659	1,109	1,768	4,617	1,070	5,687
1955	697	589	651	815	381	3,133	708	1,215	1,923	5,056	1,153	6,209

¹ Including public corporations.

TABLE IV
Gross and Net Capital Formation (Union Total) – by Type of Asset
(£ million)

Year	Building and Construction			Machinery, Plant, and Equipment			Change in Inventories	Transfer Costs	Total		
	Gross	Depreciation	Net	Gross	Depreciation	Net			Gross	Depreciation	Net
1910	13·8	3·6	10·2	8·3	5·2	3·1	3·9	0·3	26·3	8·8	17·5
1911	15·9	3·7	12·2	10·9	5·5	5·4	6·4	0·5	33·7	9·2	24·5
1912	15·5	3·8	11·7	8·1	5·7	2·4	7·0	0·5	31·1	9·5	21·6
1913	15·7	4·1	11·6	7·6	6·0	1·6	1·8	0·6	25·7	10·1	15·6
1914	15·2	4·1	11·1	8·3	6·1	2·2	−5·4	0·3	18·4	10·2	8·2
1915	11·4	4·2	7·2	7·0	6·2	0·8	−5·7	0·3	13·0	10·4	2·6
1916	9·4	4·6	4·8	8·3	6·3	2·0	4·8	0·5	23·0	10·9	12·1
1917	9·7	4·6	5·1	8·8	6·4	2·4	0·6	0·5	19·6	11·0	8·6
1918	10·9	4·7	6·2	9·3	6·9	2·4	17·3	0·6	38·1	11·6	26·5
1919	15·7	5·0	10·7	11·8	7·4	4·4	19·4	1·2	48·1	12·4	35·7
1920	22·0	5·5	16·5	17·8	7·9	9·9	30·4	1·4	71·6	13·4	58·2
1921	21·4	5·8	15·6	16·4	8·7	7·7	−14·2	0·8	24·4	14·5	9·9
1922	18·6	6·0	12·6	10·7	8·9	1·8	−11·8	0·7	18·2	14·9	3·3
1923	22·0	6·0	16·0	10·7	9·3	1·4	11·1	0·8	44·6	15·3	29·3
1924	25·2	6·4	18·8	14·2	9·5	4·7	9·4	0·9	49·7	15·9	33·8
1925	23·6	6·7	16·9	14·0	10·1	3·9	8·3	0·9	46·8	16·8	30·0
1926	26·1	7·1	19·0	15·1	10·6	4·5	7·7	1·1	50·0	17·7	32·3
1927	25·1	7·2	17·9	14·6	10·7	3·9	7·1	1·0	47·8	17·9	29·9
1928	27·0	7·4	19·6	15·9	10·9	5·0	10·9	1·2	55·0	18·3	36·7
1929	29·2	7·9	21·3	16·0	11·4	4·6	4·6	1·1	50·9	19·3	31·6
1930	28·9	8·2	20·7	12·3	11·5	0·8	−0·8	0·7	33·9	19·7	14·2
1931	24·4	8·3	16·1	9·6	11·3	−1·7	−14·8	0·7	19·9	19·6	0·3
1932	19·2	8·4	10·8	8·1	11·2	−3·1	−24·3	0·4	3·4	19·6	−16·2
1933	19·3	8·7	10·6	10·8	11·5	−0·7	10·0	0·6	40·7	20·2	20·5
1934	27·9	8·9	19·0	17·1	11·8	5·3	10·4	1·0	56·4	20·7	35·7
1935	37·6	9·3	28·3	24·2	12·8	11·4	14·5	1·0	77·3	22·1	55·2
1936	45·4	9·9	35·5	27·2	14·1	13·1	18·6	1·2	92·4	24·0	68·4
1937	51·8	10·6	41·2	29·0	15·4	13·6	17·7	1·2	99·7	26·0	73·7
1938	57·3	11·4	45·9	33·2	16·5	16·7	3·7	1·2	95·4	27·9	67·5
1939	57·8	12·1	45·7	27·7	17·6	10·1	10·4	1·0	96·9	29·7	67·2
1940	45·8	12·4	33·4	22·4	18·1	4·3	14·0	1·0	83·2	30·5	52·7
1941	41·3	13·0	28·3	21·6	18·8	2·8	16·9	1·4	81·2	31·8	49·4
1942	33·3	13·2	20·1	18·6	19·1	−0·5	2·2	1·8	55·9	32·3	23·6
1943	31·9	13·5	18·4	19·4	19·2	0·2	4·3	2·5	58·1	32·7	25·4
1944	43·3	13·9	29·4	29·3	20·0	9·3	8·7	3·4	84·7	33·9	50·8
1945	53·3	14·4	38·9	39·7	21·8	17·9	8·2	3·9	105·1	36·2	68·9
1946	74·7	15·4	59·3	48·1	24·1	24·0	79·6	5·2	207·6	39·5	168·1
1947	98·8	16·5	82·3	65·1	27·9	37·2	94·4	5·5	263·8	44·4	219·4
1948	120·8	18·0	102·8	99·1	34·2	64·9	66·0	5·6	291·5	52·2	239·3
1949	137·9	19·7	118·2	122·5	41·4	81·1	12·5	4·0	276·9	61·1	215·8
1950	142·1	21·9	120·2	116·2	47·8	68·4	35·3	4·2	297·8	69·7	228·1
1951	167·1	24·2	142·9	136·5	55·9	80·6	149·0	6·1	458·7	80·1	378·6
1952	216·3	27·2	189·1	165·6	65·4	100·2	7·5	6·3	395·7	92·6	303·1
1953	236·7	30·4	206·3	202·0	77·4	124·6	−13·2	6·8	432·3	107·8	324·5
1954	240·7	33·8	206·9	211·6	88·6	123·0	29·3	8·1	489·7	122·4	367·3
1955	249·6	37·2	212·4	196·7	99·2	97·5	72·7	8·2	527·2	136·4	390·8

TABLE V
Gross and Net Capital Formation (Union Total) – by Sector
(£ million)

Year	Public Authorities			Public Corporations			Private Businesses			Transfer Costs	Total		
	Gross	Depreciation	Net	Gross	Depreciation	Net	Gross	Depreciation	Net		Gross	Depreciation	Net
1910	6·2	1·8	4·4	—	—	—	19·8	7·0	12·8	0·3	26·3	8·8	17·5
1911	6·7	1·8	4·9	0·1	—	0·1	26·4	7·4	19·0	0·5	33·7	9·2	24·5
1912	8·3	1·9	6·4	0·1	—	0·1	22·2	7·6	14·6	0·5	31·1	9·5	21·6
1913	9·0	2·1	6·9	0·1	—	0·1	16·0	8·0	8·0	0·6	25·7	10·1	15·6
1914	8·4	2·1	6·3	0·1	—	0·1	9·6	8·1	1·5	0·3	18·4	10·2	8·2
1915	5·6	2·1	3·5	—	—	—	7·1	8·3	-1·2	0·3	13·0	10·4	2·6
1916	4·2	2·2	2·0	—	—	—	18·3	8·7	9·6	0·5	23·0	10·9	12·1
1917	3·9	2·3	1·6	0·1	—	0·1	15·1	8·7	6·4	0·5	19·6	11·0	8·6
1918	5·6	2·4	3·2	0·1	—	0·1	31·8	9·2	22·6	0·6	38·1	11·6	26·5
1919	10·1	2·6	7·5	0·1	—	0·1	36·7	9·8	26·9	1·2	48·1	12·4	35·7
1920	14·5	2·9	11·6	0·2	—	0·2	55·5	10·5	45·0	1·4	71·6	13·4	58·2
1921	13·2	3·1	10·1	0·3	—	0·3	10·1	11·4	-1·3	0·8	24·4	14·5	9·9
1922	9·0	3·3	5·7	0·5	—	0·5	8·0	11·6	-3·6	0·7	18·2	14·9	3·3
1923	10·7	3·4	7·3	0·2	—	0·2	32·9	11·9	21·0	0·8	44·6	15·3	29·3
1924	14·8	3·5	11·3	0·2	0·1	0·1	33·8	12·3	21·5	0·9	49·7	15·9	33·8
1925	15·2	3·9	11·3	0·9	0·2	0·7	29·8	12·7	17·1	0·9	46·8	16·8	30·0
1926	15·5	4·1	11·4	1·0	0·3	0·7	32·4	13·3	19·1	1·1	50·0	17·7	32·3
1927	15·4	4·1	11·3	1·2	0·3	0·9	30·2	13·5	16·7	1·0	47·8	17·9	29·9
1928	14·6	4·2	10·4	0·9	0·4	0·5	38·3	13·7	24·6	1·2	55·0	18·3	36·7
1929	15·4	4·5	10·9	0·6	0·4	0·2	33·8	14·4	19·4	1·1	50·9	19·3	31·6
1930	15·2	4·8	10·4	1·5	0·4	1·1	16·5	14·5	2·0	0·7	33·9	19·7	14·2
1931	12·4	4·9	7·5	0·6	0·4	0·2	6·2	14·3	-8·1	0·7	19·9	19·6	0·3
1932	8·7	5·1	3·6	2·0	0·5	1·5	-7·7	14·0	-21·7	0·4	3·4	19·6	-16·2
1933	9·0	5·2	3·8	2·6	0·6	2·0	28·5	14·4	14·1	0·6	40·7	20·2	20·5
1934	13·5	5·2	8·3	2·3	0·7	1·6	39·6	14·8	24·8	1·0	56·4	20·7	35·7
1935	18·1	5·5	12·6	3·4	0·9	2·5	54·8	15·7	39·1	1·0	77·3	22·1	55·2
1936	23·9	5·8	18·1	3·3	1·1	2·2	64·0	17·1	46·9	1·2	92·4	24·0	68·4
1937	28·8	6·2	22·6	2·9	1·2	1·7	66·8	18·6	48·2	1·2	99·7	26·0	73·7
1938	36·6	6·8	29·8	3·5	1·3	2·2	54·1	19·8	34·3	1·2	95·4	27·9	67·5
1939	32·9	7·3	25·6	2·3	1·3	1·0	60·7	21·1	39·6	1·0	96·9	29·7	67·2
1940	27·4	7·6	19·8	2·3	1·3	1·0	52·5	21·6	30·9	1·0	83·2	30·5	52·7
1941	21·6	8·0	13·6	3·0	1·5	1·5	55·2	22·3	32·9	1·4	81·2	31·8	49·4
1942	19·3	8·3	11·0	4·8	1·7	3·1	30·0	22·3	7·7	1·8	55·9	32·3	23·6
1943	20·2	8·4	11·8	5·2	1·9	3·3	30·2	22·4	7·8	2·5	58·1	32·7	25·4
1944	25·0	8·7	16·3	2·5	1·9	0·6	53·8	23·3	30·5	3·4	84·7	33·9	50·8
1945	31·7	9·0	22·7	1·8	1·9	-0·1	67·7	25·3	42·4	3·9	105·1	36·2	68·9
1946	42·2	9·7	32·5	3·5	1·9	1·6	156·7	27·9	128·8	5·2	207·6	39·5	168·1
1947	58·0	10·6	47·4	6·0	2·1	3·9	194·3	31·7	162·6	5·5	263·8	44·4	219·4
1948	74·3	12·0	62·3	11·8	2·8	9·0	199·8	37·4	162·4	5·6	291·5	52·2	239·3
1949	87·6	13·5	74·1	17·6	3·7	13·9	167·7	43·9	123·8	4·0	276·9	61·1	215·8
1950	72·8	14·8	58·0	19·5	4·8	14·7	201·3	50·1	151·2	4·2	297·8	69·7	228·1
1951	74·4	16·3	58·1	22·6	5·8	16·8	355·6	58·0	297·6	6·1	458·7	80·1	378·6
1952	102·0	18·2	83·8	30·4	7·4	23·0	257·0	67·0	190·0	6·3	395·7	92·6	303·1
1953	121·5	20·2	101·3	49·6	10·5	39·1	254·4	77·1	177·3	6·8	432·3	107·8	324·5
1954	121·0	22·5	98·5	40·7	12·8	27·9	319·9	87·1	232·8	8·1	489·7	122·4	367·3
1955	126·6	24·6	102·0	31·0	14·1	16·9	361·4	97·7	263·7	8·2	527·2	136·4	390·8

TABLE VI
National Product and Expenditure
(£ million)

Year	Gross National Product at Factor Cost (1)	Con-sumption Expendi-ture (2)	Gross Domestic Capital Forma-tion (3)	Balance on Current Account (4)	Gross National Expenditure at Market Prices ((2) + (3) + (4)) (5)	*Less* Indirect Tax *Plus* Subsidies (6)	Gross National Expendi-ture at Factor Cost ((5) + (6)) (7)
1918	176	145	38	4	187	−11	176
1919	214	160	48	20	228	−14	214
1920	219	202	72	−39	235	−16	219
1921	189	188	24	− 6	206	−17	189
1922	192	194	18	− 6	206	−14	192
1923	211	182	45	− 1	226	−15	211
1924	222	194	50	− 6	238	−16	222
1925	232	207	47	− 5	249	−17	232
1926	241	224	50	−15	259	−18	241
1927	258	236	48	− 6	278	−20	258
1928	270	244	55	− 8	291	−21	270
1929	264	248	51	−14	285	−21	264
1930	249	242	34	− 7	269	−20	249
1931	230	231	20	− 3	248	−18	230
1932	232	232	3	17	252	−20	232
1933	258	217	41	20	278	−20	258
1934	290	250	56	5	311	−21	290
1935	315	258	77	3	338	−23	315
1936	348	288	92	− 8	372	−24	348
1937	373	314	100	−14	400	−27	373
1938	389	328	95	− 6	417	−28	389
1939	420	..	97	..	447	−27	420
1940	460	..	83	..	487	−27	460
1941	507	..	81	..	538	−31	507
1942	554	..	56	..	589	−35	554
1943	600	..	58	..	636	−36	600
1944	644	..	85	..	682	−38	644
1945	686	..	105	..	736	−50	686
1946	730	645	208	−65	788	−58	730
1947	803	762	264	−156	870	−67	803
1948	886	843	291	−178	956	−70	886
1949	978	883	277	−118	1,042	−64	978
1950	1,153	929	298	− 9	1,218	−65	1,153
1951	1,283	1,010	459	−115	1,354	−71	1,283
1952	1,387	1,143	396	−74	1,465	−78	1,387
1953	1,533	1,260	432	−70	1,622	−89	1,533
1954	1,668	1,322	490	−45	1,767	−99	1,668
1955	1,778	1,412	527	−51	1,888	−110	1,778

APPENDIX II

NOTES ON SOURCES OF INFORMATION ABOUT CAPITAL ACCUMULATION

The notes on the different sources of information are grouped below under three main headings, viz. (a) Public Authorities, (b) Public Corporations, and (c) Private Business Enterprises.

(a) PUBLIC AUTHORITIES

(i) *Union Government*

South African Railways and Harbours. Data from the *Annual Report of the Controller and Auditor-General on the S.A. Railways Accounts* and the *Estimates of Expenditure*. Figures adjusted to exclude purchases of land and existing assets. For the period 1910–51, financial-year figures adjusted to calendar years. From 1952 onwards expenditure on calendar year basis estimated by the South African Railways and Harbours Administration directly.

Other government enterprises. Included hereunder are the Department of Posts, Telegraphs and Telephones, the South African Mint, the Government Printing Works, the Government Alluvial Diggings, the Government Garage, the Government Guano Islands, and the State Saw Mills. Information from the *Annual Report of the Controller and Auditor-General on the Appropriation and Miscellaneous Accounts (exclusive of Railways and Harbours) and the Finance Statements*, and directly from the enterprises concerned. Adjusted from financial to calendar years.

General government. Data from the *Annual Report* mentioned above. Includes capital expenditure from extra-budgetary funds, such as the South African Native Trust and other Native Councils and the National Parks Board, as well as the expenditure on houses built by the National Housing and Planning Commission for its own account; excludes expenditure on machinery and equipment and changes in inventories. Figures adjusted from financial to calendar years.

(ii) *Provincial administrations*

Information extracted from *Annual Reports* of the various Provincial Auditors. Includes the expenditure of the National Road Fund; excludes changes in inventories and expenditure on machinery and equipment, but includes expenditure on heavy machinery for road building.

(iii) *Local authorities*

Fixed Assets. 1922–55. Based on returns of capital expenditure submitted by local authorities under Statistics Act, 1914. Excludes expenditure on equipment by non-trading departments, but includes expenditure on heavy machinery for road building; includes expenditure on housing financed by the National Housing and Planning Commission.

Original statistics adjusted (a) by exclusion of purchases of land and existing assets (adjustment based on accounts of four largest municipalities); (b) from financial to calendar years.

Allocation between construction and equipment estimated by reference to accounts of four largest municipalities.

1910–21. Based on trend shown by four largest municipalities only.

Inventories. Comprehensive information available only from 1948. Estimates for earlier years based on accounts of four largest municipalities.

(b) PUBLIC CORPORATIONS

The following organizations are included hereunder: Electricity Supply Commission, South African Iron and Steel Industrial Corporation, South African Coal, Oil, and Gas Corporation, Phosphate Development Corporation, Klipfontein Organic Products, South African Broadcasting Corporation, Rand Water Board, South African Reserve Bank, Land and Agricultural Bank of South Africa, Industrial Development Corporation, Fisheries Development Corporation.

Data from *Annual Reports* published by the various organizations listed above, supplemented by additional information obtained directly from the enterprises concerned and adjusted to calendar years where necessary.

(c) PRIVATE BUSINESS ENTERPRISES
(i) *Farming*

Fixed Assets. 1949–55. Data from annual *Agricultural Census.*

1910–48. Census figures for construction extrapolated back to 1910 by means of a weighted index of: (a) net farm income; (b) value of construction in rural areas, and (c) value of fencing material used. Expenditure on machinery and implements (excluding motor vehicles) estimated from import, export, and local production figures. Motor vehicles estimated from: (a) the number of new registrations of passenger cars and commercial vehicles; (b) average price of each type of vehicle, and (c) percentage of vehicles belonging to farmers in 1936/37, 1946/47, and 1949/50. Fifty per cent of cost of passenger cars allocated to farming operations.

Livestock. Numbers of various types of livestock on farms from annual *Agricultural Census.* Prices for recent years obtained from the Division of Economics and Markets of the Department of Agriculture and extrapolated back to 1910 by means of the various meat-price indexes.

Other farm inventories ignored. Inventories held by Agricultural Control Boards included under item (vi).

All figures adjusted to calendar years.

(ii) *Mining*

Data from the table on 'Statistics of Capital' in the *Annual Report of the Government Mining Engineer*, adjusted to exclude Public Corporations with ancillary mining activities.

Excludes expenditure on mineral rights, options, and/or prospecting agreements over property and general prospecting work and boreholes.

(iii) *Manufacturing*

Fixed Assets. Information from *Population Census* of 1911 and annual *Census of Industrial Establishments* since 1915/16. All figures adjusted from financial to calendar years.

1910–48. As the figures supplied in returns refer to book values, depreciation allowances were added back so as to obtain gross values. Seventy per cent of land and buildings taken to represent buildings.

1949–55. Based on actual expenditure on new capital assets.

Inventories. See item (vi).

(iv) *Building construction*

Estimates based on annual and monthly data collected by the Bureau of Census and Statistics on the value of building plans passed and buildings completed in urban areas; figures adjusted to a 'work done' basis in accordance with an estimated construction period for the various types of buildings.

The Census Bureau's figures exclude farm and mine buildings. To exclude industrial and public buildings (which would otherwise be duplicated, as they are already accounted for in the returns of the Public Sector and the Manufacturing Census) an adjustment was made for the period 1910–46, based on information for later years.

Includes additions and alterations to existing structures, and a 2 per cent adjustment to take account of architects' and other fees.

A breakdown by type of building, i.e. residential and non-residental, was only possible since 1922.

(v) *Equipment of commercial and service establishments: banks and other financial institutions and professional persons*

1947–55. Based on the book value of equipment of commercial and service establishments in 1947 (from Distribution Census 1946/47), marked up to include other organizations, and extrapolated to 1955 by means of a sample of public companies. Depreciation at 10 per cent per annum added to net change in book values.

1910–47. Estimates based on the assumption that the expenditure of Commercial and Service establishments, etc., on equipment, constitutes a fixed percentage of the combined outlay of agriculture, mining, and manufacturing on fixed assets.

(vi) *Manufacturing and commercial inventories*

1910–38. In the absence of direct information, total investment in inventories (excluding farm inventories) taken as 40 per cent of the year-to-year change in national income over the years 1919–38, with arbitrary adjustments for the depression years 1930–33. Figures for 1910–18 estimated from import figures and the relationship between national income and imports during 1918–29 (excluding 1920); no national-income series is available for the whole period 1910–17.

Manufacturing component of the overall inventory total based on the relationship between manufacturing inventories and the gross value of output of manufacturing for 1938–53.

1939–55. Estimates of the calendar year changes *since 1952* in both commercial and manufacturing inventories based on bench-mark data extracted from the *Census of Distribution and Service Establishments*, 1946/47 and 1951/52, and the *Census of Industrial Establishments*, 1948/49 to 1951/52, and sample data compiled by the South African Reserve Bank on a monthly basis.

Financial year estimates for the years *1938 to 1951* derived from (a) the above-mentioned bench-mark figures and (b) sample data compiled by the Reserve Bank on an annual basis. Financial year figures adjusted to calendar years on the basis of the half-yearly import figures.

Includes inventories held by Agricultural Control Boards for their own account.

(vii) *Transfer costs*

Includes indirect tax (viz. transfer duty) and ¾ per cent of the value of immovable property transferred for conveyancers' fees and stamp duties.

APPENDIX III

SUMMARY TABLE OF NATIONAL WEALTH
(£ million)

	Estimate [1] [2]			
	Current Value		Base Price (1938) Value	
Type of Asset	Latest Year 1955	Comparison Year 1945	Latest Year 1955	Comparison Year 1945
(1)	(2)	(3)	(4)	(5)
I. *Reproducible Assets*				
1. Structures				
(a) Private				
(1) Dwellings	629	239	223	136
(2) Other	1,501	570	532	326
(b) Public [3]				
(1) Dwellings	79	22	30	12
(2) Other civilian	1,579	656	558	376
(3) Military	..	..	..	..
2. Equipment				
(a) Private				
(1) Producer durables	790	208	280	119
(2) Consumer durables [4]	188	..	67	..
b) Public [3]				
(1) Civilian	479	141	170	81
(2) Military	..	..	..	..
3. Livestock	398	213	126	128
4. Inventories				
(a) Private	693	200	251	131
(b) Public	62	22	23	14
(1) Civilian	..	..	..	..
(2) Military	..	..	..	..
5. Monetary metals	75	206	43	171
6. Net foreign assets				
(a) Private	..	..	..	..
(b) Public	..	..	..	..
II. *Non-reproducible Assets*				
1. Land				
(a) Private				
(1) Agricultural	1,182	498	224	226
(2) Other	899	288	150	144
(b) Public	329	102	55	51
2. Subsoil assets				
(a) Private	..	..	..	..
(b) Public	..	..	..	..

[1] All figures refer to net value, i.e. after allowing for accumulated depreciation.
[2] Assets for which no estimates are available, are indicated by the sign ...
[3] I.e. central and local governments and government-owned or controlled corporations and institutions.
[4] Passenger cars only.

12

THE NATIONAL WEALTH OF AUSTRALIA

By J. M. Garland and R. W. Goldsmith [1]

I. PREVIOUS ESTIMATES

AUSTRALIA made a promising beginning half a century ago in estimating its own wealth. One of its earliest and most enterprising statisticians, T. A. Coghlan, is credited with estimates of private wealth extending from 1813 to 1903.[2] Another statistician, A. M. Laughton, estimated the private wealth of Australia in 1911 at £A1,031 million,[3] and in 1918 G. H. Knibbs, Commonwealth Statistician, published a distinguished survey of the private wealth of Australia, based on the results of the war census of 1915, supplemented by inventory and devolution estimates.[4] The war census questionnaire of 1915 contained a schedule of questions relating to the approximate value of real and personal property held by persons either on their own account or on account of other persons or companies. A special return was obtained from all Australian companies. Wealth and income were classified to give a frequency relationship and a 'plutoprosodic' graph with multiple contours was drawn, for males and females. The devolution estimates were based on probate returns and an average rate of devolution, which emerges from an elaborate argument. However, the outcome of these calculations was not satisfactory, and Knibbs turned to the inventory method, using the war census totals, and other collections of data which he had available, and which gave him reasonably adequate results. His final estimate is shown below:

Private Wealth of Australia, June 1915

	£ million
Land and improvements . . .	1,106
Other assets	514
Total	1,620

---

[1] The authors wish to acknowledge the help they were given by many people in Australia, both within the Commonwealth Government and the Commonwealth Bank and outside. They wish in particular to acknowledge the assistance of Mr. R. H. Scott and his colleagues in the Economic Department of the Commonwealth Bank of Australia.

[2] *Official Year Book of the Commonwealth of Australia*, No. 26, 1933, p. 490.

[3] Mentioned by Knibbs, see below.

[4] *The Private Wealth of Australia and its Growth, together with a Report of the War Census of 1915.*

According to these estimates, land and improvements represented 68 per cent of the total, and private wealth was about six times net income.

Knibbs suggested at the conclusion of his survey that an inventory estimate of wealth should be made every five years, and that the quinquennial inventory estimates should be supplemented by a decennial inventory of wealth. C. H. Wickens, as Commonwealth Statistician, continued the inventory estimates and, using Knibbs' classification and methods, periodically published estimates of private wealth.[1] By 1929 aggregate private wealth had risen to £3,351 million, while the percentage of land and improvements remained virtually unchanged at 67 per cent.[2] It is of interest to note the concept which these figures cover. 'They represent the estimated value of the private wealth of Australia at 30th June, 1929, and include values for property in Australia owned by absentees. Property outside Australia owned by Australian residents is, of course, not included, and no account is taken of immaterial wealth such as title deeds, mortgage deeds, debentures, etc., the estimate being based entirely on the material private wealth itself, without regard to the individual titles thereto. Communal wealth in the property of Commonwealth and State Governments, and of local governing bodies, is not included, nor has any allowance been made for the interests of private investors by way of loans in such property.'[3]

After 1929 comes a gap. The earlier rate of progress was not maintained and there was no decennial inventory. A national register was taken in 1939 which included some wealth questions, but the tabulation of the returns was never fully completed. Land and buildings amounted, so we were informed, to a value of about £A1,700 million.

Virtually the only work done in the last quarter-century are the summary estimates of aggregate reproducible tangible assets for 1942, 1949, and 1953 made by the Queensland Bureau of Industry, and their more detailed estimates, also including land, for 1952/53 for Queensland alone.[4] The last of these estimates is of particular interest, since it is closer in its method to the approach taken in this paper than any of the earlier attempts.

---

[1] *Official Year Book, op. cit.,* p. 492.   [2] *Ibid.*   [3] *Ibid.*
[4] *Economic News,* May 1950 (unsigned but probably attributable to Mr. Colin Clark); September and November/December 1955 by R. E. Dyne and O. M. May.

II. SCOPE AND METHOD OF PRESENT ESTIMATES

The reason why the Commonwealth Statistician discontinued his estimates of Australian wealth is fairly clear. The statistics were not sufficiently comprehensive, and valuations were unreliable. These difficulties persist, and the methods which must be used to obtain any comprehensive figures of Australian wealth could perhaps fairly be described as somewhat adventurous. Census information which could be used for wealth estimation is very limited, and official inventories are scattered. Valuation involves a number of difficulties conceptual, statistical and practical, and methods of valuation have to be adapted to the information which is available. However, there is no need to labour the basic difficulties of wealth estimates, particularly in a country where little previous work has been done.

The concept of national wealth which has been used for this paper involves some addition to that used previously by the Commonwealth Statistician. We have included 'communal wealth', in the form of an estimate of the value of public works, and have also made some attempt to allow for international assets and liabilities.

Broadly, our concept of national wealth corresponds to the concept of net worth in a consolidated national balance sheet, with the proviso that no account is taken of the minor intangible assets, such as the value of patents and goodwill, which might theoretically be included in the national balance sheet. Our estimates, therefore, cover tangible assets, both reproducible and non-reproducible, and net foreign assets. In that respect they may be said to be close to international usage.

The specific items for which values are shown are:

1. Reproducible tangible assets –

    (a) Buildings –
        (i) Dwellings
        (ii) Other
    (b) Motor vehicles –
        (i) Cars
        (ii) Other
    (c) Equipment –
        (i) Agricultural
        (ii) Non-agricultural

    (d) Livestock
    (e) Inventories –
        (i) Farm
        (ii) Non-farm
    (f) Public works
    (g) Consumer durables

2. Coin bullion –
    (a) Silver and copper coin

3. Non-reproducible tangible assets –
    (a) Unimproved land value
    (b) Invisible and other non-structural improvements to
       land

4. Net foreign assets –
    (a) International assets
    (b) International liabilities

It has not proved possible to follow, consistently, one principle of valuation for all types of assets. Value of unimproved land has been estimated on the basis of current market prices, and livestock and inventories are, so far as is possible, also related to the market. For reproducible tangible assets, the basis of valuation is an estimated replacement cost conceived as price adjusted depreciated original (historical) cost. The use of different methods involves some difficulties, and throughout the paper problems of valuation are constantly recurring. These are mentioned where relevant, but some general preliminary observations may be offered here:

(1) It has been necessary to rely very heavily on index numbers for converting to current values. Price-index numbers are a particularly acute problem in Australia, and little more can be said than that we are aware that many problems have been ignored. Technically Australian price-index numbers are probably no better and no worse than in most other countries, and it is just as inappropriate in Australia as elsewhere to use index numbers for purposes for which they were not designed. We have endeavoured to avoid this misapplication, where possible, and have devised some composite indexes for particular uses, but it should be emphasized that the valuations of tangible assets in base-period prices are no better than the price

indexes on which they are based, and the indexes which have been used, we must admit, are often quite rough.

(2) The fact that land values are based on the market while other assets are on a replacement-cost basis does open up some possibility of duplication, particularly in relation to public works. In Australia, over the years, public-works projects have often involved relatively high capital outlays, and in some cases current charges are not adequate to cover running costs and depreciation. Current losses on public works would, on our method, not show themselves in any reduction of the value of the works, but there could be a capital increment to land values as a result of the virtual subsidy from current works operations. This could lead to some duplication, but what the scale of this duplication is we have no means of estimating.

(3) We have been very much concerned about the general problem of valuation of Australian land. The land valuations which find their way into Australian statistics are, we believe, very conservative, and it has been necessary to make arbitrary adjustments to them. The degree of under-valuation varies, and an accurate adjustment would involve extensive inquiries in all States. The difficulties are referred to in more detail in Section IV, but it may perhaps be mentioned at this stage that our estimate of total land values has been taken as high as we think is reasonable, having regard to all the difficulties. Nevertheless, it could still be conservative.

(4) This deficiency, however, is in one sense balanced by the gap which has been left in our estimation of Australia's international liabilities. We have found it extremely difficult to correct the figure of Australia's foreign liabilities for price changes and other differences between book and market values. This is mainly because of deficiencies in the price indexes and uncertainties about the interpretation of the figures collected from companies with overseas affiliations. We have, therefore, preferred to use the official figures, without correcting for price changes. In this respect our figure for total Australian wealth has been overstated, as it understates the value of foreign direct investments.

III. REPRODUCIBLE TANGIBLE ASSETS

1. *Methods of estimation*

The method adopted for estimating the stocks of reproducible tangible assets was, in most cases, to sum the depreciated values of annual expenditures on the various assets for the period of the life ascribed to them, and to convert these values to an estimate of replacement cost.

We had, in fact, little choice. The statistics which we had seemed inadequate, in most cases, to support any other method. But the method has the virtue of ensuring uniformity of valuation, even if the basis of the valuation is itself not ideal.

What was involved was, first, the conversion of annual expenditures in current prices to constant prices; secondly, the calculation of annual depreciation charges and the calculation and summation of the depreciated values of the annual expenditures; and, finally, the conversion of the sums of the depreciated annual expenditures back into prices ruling at the end of the years for which the stock estimates were required. The difficulties inherent in this method, apart from the inadequacy of basic data, are the lack of homogeneity within the expenditure aggregates with which it is necessary to work, together with all the difficulties and problems associated with price-index numbers.

The necessity for aggregation at the expense of homogeneity makes the choice of depreciation rates difficult and, in the result, somewhat arbitrary. It was also difficult to choose the basis for calculating depreciation, and we therefore decided to calculate depreciation on both a straight-line and declining-balance basis for nearly all assets; the only exceptions were consumer durables and motor vehicles, for which it seemed apparent that straight-line depreciation would be inappropriate.

The life finally attributed to each type of asset was chosen somewhat arbitrarily. Little information was available. Generally, the lives chosen were a matter of judgment based on general knowledge and experience in the United Kingdom and the United States of America. Another somewhat arbitrary choice was made for the remaining balance, which it was necessary to write off in the declining-balance calculation of depreciation. This remaining balance was arbitrarily set at a fairly low proportion, so that the implied annual rates of depreciation on the declining-balance basis are fairly high.

The following schedule shows the length of life attributed to each type of asset, the percentage of the original cost finally written off, and the annual rate of depreciation implied in the straight-line and the declining-balance calculation of depreciation.

Depreciation Schedule

Type of Asset	Assumed Life	In Declining-balance Calculation	In Declining-balance Calculation	In Straight-line Depreciation
		Percentage of Original Cost Finally Written Off	Annual Rate of Depreciation (%)	
Consumer durables . .	12 yrs.	4	22½	—
Dwellings . .	70 ,,	5	4	1 3/7
Other structures . .	50 ,,	6	5½	2
Motor vehicles:				
Cars	15 ,,	8	15	—
Commercial vehicles .	10 ,,	10	20	—
Producer durables . .	20 ,,	9	11½	5
Public works . . .	40 ,,	5	7¼	2½

Exceptions to the use of the method described above applied to the estimates of livestock values, farm inventories, and non-farm inventories. In these cases it was possible to make direct estimates of the values of the stocks. Statistics of livestock numbers and quantities of farm inventories, and also of prices for these items, were available. For non-farm inventories, estimates of book values were available for a large sample of private industry, and these were blown-up to obtain a total.

2. Sources of data

The main primary sources for the expenditure series for the period from 1938/39 to 1955/56 were the estimates shown in the Commonwealth Statistician's White Papers on National Income and Expenditure.[1] For the period from 1948/49 to 1955/56 the White Paper for 1955/56 was used. Figures for 1946/47 and 1947/48 were taken from the White Paper for 1954/55. For the period from 1938/39 to 1945/46 the White Paper for 1950/51

[1] Estimates prepared in the Commonwealth Bureau of Census and Statistics for presentation annually with Budget papers for the Commonwealth; issued by the Commonwealth Government Printer.

was used, this being the last year in which complete estimates for the war period were given. It was necessary to make some adjustments to the figures shown in the 1950/51 White Paper. For instance, expenditure on motor vehicles was not divided, in the White Paper, between cars and commercial vehicles. Adjustments were also required for expenditure on dwellings and public works which, as then given, included some maintenance expenditure.

The main primary source for the period from 1928/29 to 1938/39 was a paper (unfortunately available only in mimeographed form) presented to the Australian and New Zealand Association for the Advancement of Science in 1939 by Dr. (now Sir) Roland Wilson under the title 'Public and Private Investment in Australia'.

Prior to 1928/29, only estimates of expenditure on building and public works were required. For building, use was made of statistics of permits issued for new buildings by local government authorities as published by State Statisticians. These figures covered the period to the beginning of the century and were checked with census data for the years 1911, 1921, and 1933. Use was also made over this period of the annual reports on building operations of the Sydney Metropolitan Water, Sewerage, and Drainage Board. These basic sources were used to estimate annual expenditures on building. Estimates of expenditure on building prior to the turn of the century were taken from a monograph by N. G. Butlin.[1] For expenditure on public works prior to 1928/29, figures from 1919/20 were taken from a note by W. A. Sinclair.[2] For the period prior to 1919/20 back to the beginning of the century, the primary source used was the Commonwealth Statistician's *Finance Bulletins* for those years.

For some items, other sources were drawn upon than the main ones mentioned above. In the case of expenditure on agricultural equipment, recourse was had to the Commonwealth Statistician's *Production and Oversea Trade Bulletins*. The Commonwealth Statistician's publications were also exploited for the basic information underlying the estimates for the value of non-farm inventories and of livestock, supplemented in the latter case by information published by the Statisticians for in-

---

[1] *Private Capital Formation in Australia, Estimates 1861–1900, 1955.*
[2] 'Public Capital Formation in Australia, 1919/20–1929/30', *The Economic Record*, November 1955.

dividual States. The information used for the estimates of the value of farm inventories was taken from reports of the National Council of Wool-Selling Brokers and the Australian Wheat Board and from the Commonwealth Statistician's Production Bulletins. In all these cases the information in the primary sources was used as a basis for estimating expenditure or stocks.

The main price indexes used for conversion of the expenditure series in current prices to constant prices were the Commonwealth Statistician's 'C' series index (of retail prices), wholesale-price index, and average weekly earnings index (the latter linked to the nominal male wage index wherever necessary); the Commonwealth Bank's import price indexes; and a construction cost index obtained by linking together the best indexes available for the several periods for which information was required. Although these were, in the main, of unofficial character, they appear reasonable when compared with the nearest approach in the official indexes to what was sought.

The same indexes were also used for the conversion of the wealth estimates from constant prices to replacement cost. For this purpose also, additional information was required for livestock and farm inventories; this was taken mainly from the Commonwealth Statistician's publications.

Additional notes on the primary sources of data, where they were not sufficient in themselves for our requirements, are given in an appendix.

3. *Quality of data*

It is very difficult to assess the quality of the data. Of the expenditure series, the figures from the Commonwealth Statistician's estimates of national income and expenditure, covering the period from 1938/39 to 1955/56, can be accepted with a reasonable degree of reliance. Most of the figures for the preceding decade might also be accepted without much reservation, although they would probably be less accurate than those for the later period. Prior to 1928/29, however, the reliability of the figures lessens, except, in the case of expenditure on public works, back to 1919/20, although not beyond that point.

Nevertheless, as the accuracy of the expenditure series becomes more questionable, so does their influence on the final results become less. The depreciated value of annual expenditures in the first quarter of the century, for instance, still remaining in the estimates of stocks of assets after World War II is relatively small; the levels of expenditure in the last two decades overshadow those of the earlier periods; and it is unlikely that the errors in the expenditure series used for the earlier periods covered would have much, if any, significant effect on the wealth estimates for the period from 1946/47 on.

The price indexes are, perhaps, more questionable than the expenditure series. Except in the case of motor vehicles, none of them is wholly appropriate, and in many cases it was necessary to use some of them in combination to take account of the influences involved. Nevertheless, they are, probably, a reasonably reliable measure of changes in prices over the long run, and it was the long run which was involved.

4. *The estimates*

The resulting estimates of the stocks of reproducible tangible assets are shown in the following tables. The estimates resulting from calculating depreciation on both a straight-line and declining-balance basis are shown and, in both cases, the figures are presented in constant and current prices. The constant-price estimates are in terms of average 1936/37–1938/39 prices, and the current-price estimates are in terms of prices at the end of the years shown.

These estimates are given for each of the years from 1946/47 to 1955/56 in the case of straight-line depreciation, but estimates for the intervening years are omitted for the declining-balance calculations. However, it is probable that the year-to-year changes in the stock of assets are less reliable and have much less significance than the change over longer periods; perhaps no less than the change over a decade or a considerable fraction of it should be considered in interpretation.

IV. NON-REPRODUCIBLE TANGIBLE ASSETS

Land is the most important item in this group of assets. Valuation of land in Australia presents some complex problems, particularly for country land. The complexity is not surprising. Land value is essentially the capitalization of a residual product – an arbitrary multiplication, so to speak, of a net uncertainty. In a country which depends for a very important part of its rural production on export markets, the level of export prices must, over a long period, have an important influence on rural

TABLE I

Stocks of Reproducible Tangible Assets at Depreciated Replacement Cost
Constant (1936/37—1938/39) Prices (£A million)

End of Fiscal Year	1946/47 Declining-balance Depreciation	1946/47	1947/48	1948/49	1949/50	1950/51	1951/52	1952/53	1953/54	1954/55	1955/56	1955/56 Declining-balance Depreciation
					Straight-line Depreciation							
Consumer durables [1]	206	206	232	255	281	323	347	357	377	401	424	424
Dwellings	366	585	589	598	611	631	655	674	695	720	744	504
Other structures	205	323	322	324	326	331	337	335	347	355	369	241
Cars [1]	39	39	47	63	94	124	150	160	180	214	240	240
Other vehicles [1]	18	18	23	31	45	64	78	81	85	92	99	99
Agricultural equipment	46	62	64	67	74	83	96	102	109	117	125	95
Non-farm equipment	182	262	261	268	279	298	319	334	359	382	405	305
Livestock	228	228	238	246	254	262	261	268	275	281	289	289
Farm inventories	13	13	23	21	25	23	18	20	32	32	37	37
Non-farm inventories	377	377	422	428	426	428	487	425	436	461	452	452
Public works	509	868	883	910	954	1,019	1,081	1,141	1,200	1,261	1,320	900
Total straight-line depreciation	—	2,981	3,104	3,211	3,369	3,586	3,829	3,897	4,095	4,316	4,504	—
				Declining-balance Depreciation								
Total declining-balance depreciation [1]	2,189	—	2,313	2,403	2,576	2,785	3,011	3,074	3,242	3,431	—	3,586

[1] Declining-balance Depreciation.

TABLE II

Stocks of Reproducible Tangible Assets at Depreciated Replacement Cost
Current (End Year) Prices (£A million)

End of fiscal year	1946/47 Declining-balance Depreciation	1946/47	1947/48	1948/49	1949/50	1950/51	1951/52	1952/53	1953/54	1954/55	1955/56	1955/56 Declining-balance Depreciation
					Straight-line Depreciation							
Consumer durables [1]	272	272	334	403	486	669	864	925	988	1,075	1,208	1,208
Dwellings	820	1,310	1,502	1,680	1,906	2,309	2,699	2,979	3,162	3,456	3,735	2,530
Other structures	459	724	821	910	1,017	1,211	1,388	1,486	1,579	1,704	1,852	1,210
Cars [1]	87	87	96	132	210	327	453	520	520	621	744	744
Other vehicles [1]	30	30	42	62	99	161	211	223	235	254	297	297
Agricultural equipment	95	128	149	165	206	282	346	379	405	455	514	390
Non-farm equipment	375	540	608	659	778	1,013	1,148	1,242	1,335	1,486	1,665	1,254
Livestock	288	288	357	411	482	771	804	745	802	883	915	915
Farm inventories	45	45	108	77	112	103	79	84	117	112	118	118
Non-farm inventories	550	550	700	800	920	1,160	1,540	1,370	1,420	1,585	1,655	1,655
Public works	870	1,484	1,634	1,829	2,223	2,986	3,762	4,073	4,296	4,747	5,425	3,699
Total straight-line depreciation	—	5,458	6,351	7,128	8,439	10,992	13,294	13,987	14,859	16,378	18,128	—
					Declining-balance Depreciation							
Total declining-balance depreciation	3,891	—	4,605	5,188	6,279	8,348	10,208	10,741	11,447	12,653	—	14,020

[1] Declining-balance Depreciation.

land values, and where, as in the case of Australia, export prices fluctuate fairly widely, the determination of residual product, and therefore of value, becomes extremely uncertain. In addition, it is clear that changes in general interest rates will eventually affect the capitalization rate for land and the level of land values. It may be observed of the period 1947/56 that export prices have risen substantially and helped to force up rural land values; while interest rates, and rural costs, have also risen, and have tended to exert a contrary influence on land values.

Land valuation in Australia is based very largely on current sales, the market reflection of value. Turnover of properties, while it varies to some extent cyclically, is relatively small. The market must be regarded as sporadic and discontinuous, and the test of a few sales cannot be treated as very reliable evidence of value. To a certain extent it is possible to check the evidence of sales by calculating a 'productive' value, but even so, the basis of valuation is not very reliable, certainly not in the short run.

In addition, there is a considerable diversity of tenures in the Australian system of land holdings. Some land is held on freehold tenure, while at the other extreme, particularly in the pastoral areas, land is held under lease from the Crown, with varying conditions of resumption and reappraisement. In between there are other types of leases, conditional purchases, etc., with a wide range and variety of conditions. Clearly, any attempt to value these leases must reduce them to a common-tenure basis, but it is extremely difficult to be certain in the figures we have used that variations due to differences in tenure have, in fact, been excluded. In particular, we cannot be certain that even when they are ostensibly on a freehold basis, valuations have not been reduced by the capitalized value of the lease-hold rentals. The States, it may be observed, have revenue from leasehold rentals of about £A8 million p.a. A similar problem, of course, occurs where land is subject to an established land tax, and in fact it is difficult to escape the conclusion that Australian land values, especially in metropolitan areas, have been reduced by the incidence of land taxes.

Valuation data in Australia are extremely uneven in quality. Probably the most competent valuations, in a technical sense, were made by officers of the Commonwealth Land Tax Department. Unfortunately the valuations which have been made covered only estates in land greater than an exemption limit, which varied from £A5,000 unimproved value in 1946 to £A8,750 in 1952. After 1952 the tax was discontinued. The Commonwealth Land Tax valuations are therefore not particularly helpful for our purpose. In the States there are some very competent valuing authorities, but they cover mainly the metropolitan and non-country areas. To obtain total figures for each State we must aggregate the local valuations, but the local valuations (except where State valuers are operating) are often very conservative. It is a common practice to undervalue rateable land, and make the necessary adjustments in the rate applied to the land, in order to keep argument with rate-payers to a minimum. The figures of local land valuations, therefore, require heavy adjustments. Generally, we are informed, local valuation is on a freehold basis. Estimates have also been made of the amount of land which is exempt from local rates and therefore is not included in the valuation statistics; but the value of all land included in public reserves, forests, and roads has been excluded from the estimates.

Land-value totals are available for all the States, but have to be adjusted to bring them up to June 1956. The latest date for which complete figures are available is June 1954, and in June 1954, in fact, most of the valuations were lagging well behind the rise in the market. The lag varies from State to State, and the dispersion around the average seems fairly wide. A reasonable estimate of the lag, for the whole of Australia, would be about two years. Even if we apply the 1954 figures to 1952, however, it still seems to be necessary to make some adjustment for 'undervaluation'. Our procedure, therefore, is to add to this notional 1952 land-values total a rough percentage to bring it to the 1952 market, and then write up the total values by the estimated increase in value from 1952 to 1956. Our information is defective, but it is suggested that a reasonable estimate of the 'undervaluation' in 1952 would be 30 per cent, and that the increase in land values from 1952 to 1956 would be of the order of 25 per cent. This gives a total value for land in Australia as at June 1956, including rateable and exempt land, of about £A3,000 million.

For 1947 the problem is no less difficult. During the war the normal process of local valuation was suspended and a system of land-sales control operated from 1942 until September 1949.

This meant that during that period the official valuations were held, to an uncertain but a substantial extent, below the normal market level. We assume that, for our purposes, the degree of under-valuation of land values prevailing in June 1945 (before the post-war revaluations commenced) can be taken as about 30 per cent. We therefore commence with rateable values, add an allowance for exempt values, add 30 per cent for under-valuation, and thus obtain a total land value for 1945 of £A1,230 million. This seems a defensible figure for June 1945 in relation to 1956. If we took a corresponding figure in 1950 of say £A1,700 million, and for June 1952 of £A2,400 million, then the progression of values would be as follows:

1945–1950	.	.	.	+ 38 per cent
1950–1952	.	.	.	+ 40 „ „
1952–1956	.	.	.	+ 25 „ „

This seems to be reasonable in the light of what information there is about the movement of land values. The movement from 1945 to 1947 was relatively small. We then obtain the picture shown in Table III.

TABLE III

Australian Unimproved Land Values

(£A million)

	1945	1947	1950	1952	1956
Rateable values	856				1,637
Exempt values	90				178
	946				1,815
Allowance for valuation lag	} 284				} 1,185
Allowance for undervaluation					
Total unimproved value	1,230	1,280	1,700	2,400	3,000

These figures give us Australian land values on an 'unimproved' basis which is, in effect, what the market value of the land would be if the improvements (if any) had not been made. They thus exclude the value of all dwellings and other structures which have been estimated separately. In addition, they exclude a number of other improvement expenditures: all non-structural improvements, and in particular what are known in Australia as 'invisible' improvements, such as clearing and timber treatment, pest and weed eradication, pasture improvements and water and drainage improvements. To our estimate of unimproved land, therefore, it is necessary to add the value of invisible and other non-structural improvements. Unfortunately, there is no information on which an estimate of invisible improvements can be based. The problem is complicated, of course, by the fact that a considerable part of the expenditure on these improvements would be written off in the year in which it was incurred, and even on a strict accounting basis the expenditure each year would be only partly capitalized. However, it is assumed that for 1956 the value of invisible, etc., improvements would be about £A600 million. This would represent somewhat less than half the unimproved value of country land in Australia in 1956. Arbitrary (but relatively somewhat smaller) amounts have also been allowed for earlier years as shown in Table IV. It should be observed also that this item is not, strictly, non-reproducible, but it is retained under this heading, because of its intimate association with land value.

TABLE IV

Australian Land Values, Including Invisible Improvements
(£A million)

	1945	1947	1950	1952	1956
Total unimproved value. .	1,230	1,280	1,700	2,400	3,000
Invisible, etc., improvements .	250	260	325	480	600
	1,480	1,540	2,025	2,880	3,600

A separate estimate was made of country land value in 1947 and 1956. From the rateable values it is possible, roughly, to separate country lands (including some town lands incorporated in country areas). An addition must be made for exempt values, and an allowance for valuation lag somewhat above the average. The allowance for under-valuation should also be considerably larger for country than for non-country lands, since State valuations cover a large part of the metropolitan areas. Invisible, etc., improvements are assumed to relate wholly to country land, being absorbed into unimproved value in non-country areas. We then assign a proportion of the value of dwellings and other structures to country areas, on a population basis, assuming the average value of country dwellings to be about 10 per cent below the average value of all dwellings.

TABLE V
Value of Country Land
(£A million)

	June 1947	June 1956
Rateable values	470	676
Exempt values	25	34
Allowance for valuation lag . . . }	165	690
Allowance for undervaluation . . .		
Unimproved value	660	1,400
Invisible, etc., improvements . . .	260	600
Country proportion of dwellings . .	360	700
Country proportion of other structures . .	210	400
Improved value	1,490	3,100

This total may be compared with the only other estimate known to us made by Mr. H. G. Collins of the Commonwealth Bank. Mr. Collins' unpublished estimate of Australian country land at June 1956 is based on unit values (per sheep area, per acre of wheat land, etc.) applied to the total numbers of sheep, etc., and acres under cultivation. This, together with an estimated value of buildings, gives him a total of £A3,400 million, which suggests that our calculations may be conservative. Both methods, however, lean very heavily on judgments and arbitrary estimates, and in both of them the margin of error would be large.

For non-country land this leaves us with the following results:

TABLE VI
Value of Non-Country Land
(£A million)

	June 1947	June 1956
Unimproved value	620	1,600
Dwellings	950	3,035
Other structures	514	1,452
Improved value . . .	2,084	6,087

Our results, for Australian country land, show the relation of unimproved to improved value at 45 per cent in 1956. For all Australian land the relation is 33 per cent. The relation of total improved land value to total tangible private assets on a straight-line basis is 56 per cent. This compares with the 1929 figure of

z

68 per cent, and is a significant indication, despite all the statistical uncertainties, of the change in the structure of Australian wealth.

Other non-reproducible tangible assets cannot be included. There is some information available about subsoil assets, but nothing which would enable us to make any adequate additions to our calculations. They have therefore been excluded.

V. INTERNATIONAL ASSETS AND LIABILITIES

It is again a matter of some complexity to estimate Australia's net holding of foreign assets. The statistical information which is available is defective, although considerable improvements have recently been made. The figures for government debt are reasonably good; there is a fair amount of useful information on company assets and liabilities; but individual holdings present considerable difficulties. In particular, it is possible that some overseas holdings of Australian land escape statistical attention. Problems of valuation recur continuously throughout this section, and no consistent principle can be applied in view of the nature of the available data.

Australian public-authority securities domiciled abroad are known accurately, although no information is available about the extent of Australian holdings of these securities. Government securities redeemable in Australia are analysed between the different holders at the end of each June, on a face-value basis, and a reasonably good figure is available for foreign holders.[1] This is supplemented by a survey of nominee holdings of public authority securities on account of overseas residents.[2]

The usual kind of information is available about monetary gold and foreign-exchange holdings, but holdings of exchange other than by official and banking institutions are not known, and Australian currency holdings can be given only for overseas banks. This omission is probably not serious.

The official Australian balance of payments estimates [3] show a fairly full analysis of capital items, although there is a substantial residual item in some years covering errors and omissions, and short-term capital movements. In particular, the

[1] Commonwealth Bank of Australia, *Statistical Bulletin*, October 1956.
[2] Commonwealth Bureau of Census and Statistics, Canberra, *Survey of Companies with Oversea Affiliations*, 1947/48–1954/55.
[3] Commonwealth Bureau of Census and Statistics, *The Australian Balance of Payments 1951/52* and supplementary documents to 1955/56.

phenomenon of 'leads and lags' sometimes shows itself in a very conspicuous form, but this loses in importance if we are interested in decadal or longer movements. The capital items in the balance-of-payments statistics draw on information provided by the 'Ticket' system, which is a complete classification by the Australian banks of their transactions in foreign exchange, and also on the Commonwealth Statistician's annual survey of companies in Australia with overseas affiliations.[1]

The information on direct and portfolio investment has been obtained from surveys which have been conducted each year since 1948. They provide aggregates of the face value of paid-up capital, debentures, etc., with separate figures of 'direct' holdings, inter-company accounts between associate companies, net assets of branches and annual figures of undistributed profits of subsidiaries from 1947/48 for Australian subsidiaries and from 1952/53 for overseas subsidiaries. In the surveys investment is regarded as 'direct' when there is ownership of 25 per cent or more of a company's Ordinary Shares (or voting stock) by one company or number of companies incorporated in one country, or ownership of 50 per cent or more of a company's Ordinary Shares (or voting stock) by individuals or companies in one country. The term 'subsidiary' is applied to all companies in which there is 'direct' holding, irrespective of the degree of control, if any, which is actually exercised.

The figure for direct investment in Australian companies at June 1947 represents the 'direct' oversea holdings of paid-up capital, etc., in Australian companies, inter-company balances owing by Australian subsidiaries to oversea parent or associate companies, and the book value of net assets in Australia of branches of oversea companies. No allowance has been made for the reserves of Australian subsidiary companies at that date. The annual movement in these items, together with the undistributed profits of Australian subsidiary companies accruing to oversea parent companies and certain adjusting items, have been added to direct investment in the base year to give direct investment as at the end of June in each of the subsequent years. A similar procedure was followed in calculating direct investment abroad by Australian companies, except that undistributed profits of overseas subsidiaries have been included only

[1] Commonwealth Bureau of Census and Statistics, *Survey of Companies with Oversea Affiliations*, 1947/48–1954/55.

TABLE VII

Australian Foreign Liabilities

(£A million)

	1947	1948	1949	1950	As at 30 June 1951	1952	1953	1954	1955	1956
1. Foreign holdings of Australian currency [1]	4	3	6	52	48	12	5	4	4	4
2. Foreign holdings of public authority debt.	566	557	545	545	528	604	614	621	639	664 [4]
(i) Overseas issues	566	557	545	545	528	551	567	578	600	627
(ii) In Australia	n.a.	n.a.	n.a.	n.a.	n.a.	53	47	43	39	37 [4]
3. Other liabilities	239	275	315	389	451	538	565	630	724	806 [4]
Direct investment [2]	210	243	282	352	413	494	518	582	668	743 [4]
Portfolio investment	29	32	33	37	38	44	47	48	56	63 [4]
4. Total [3]	809	835	866	986	1,027	1,154	1,184	1,255	1,367	1,474 [4]

[1] Overseas banks only.

[2] Excludes undistributed profits of subsidiaries prior to 30 June 1947.

[3] Apart from the omissions referred to above, this total excludes investment in real estate, trade claims, and borrowing by individuals and unincorporated businesses.

[4] Estimated.

TABLE VIII
Australian Foreign Assets
(£ million)

	1947	1948	1949	1950	As at 30 June 1951	1952	1953	1954	1955	1956
1. Monetary gold[1]	30	27	27	39	44	50	50	57	62	73
2. Foreign exchange[1]	170	254	419	590	760	322	512	513	366	282
3. Other assets	23	25	28	30	33	35	42	46	55	64[5]
(i) Direct investment[2]	20	22	26	28	31	33	40	45	53	62[5]
(ii) Portfolio investment[3]	3	3	2	2	2	2	2	1	2	2[5]
4. Total[4]	223	306	474	659	837	407	604	616	483	419[5]

[1] Holdings of official and banking institutions only. Foreign-exchange item includes British Government Securities held by Central Bank.
[2] Excludes undistributed profits of subsidiaries prior to 30 June 1952.
[3] Excludes portfolio investments by individuals.
[4] Apart from the omissions referred to above, this total excludes investment in real estate, trade claims, and loans to individuals and unincorporated businesses.
[5] Estimated.

from 1952/53. Portfolio investment in each case has been taken as the difference between the total face value of paid-up capital, etc., and 'direct' holdings of such capital.

We have given careful consideration to the possibility of revaluing Australia's overseas assets and liabilities at current prices. There are, of course, no suitable indexes, and experiments in devising an appropriate index have not been encouraging. Moreover, some, perhaps a large proportion, of Australia's overseas liabilities would be fixed in money terms representing, for example, loans, debentures, and current accounts, but we have no means of deciding what proportion is 'fixed'. A distinction must be made, in this respect, between companies with United States and with United Kingdom affiliations; in practice, we would expect to find very different patterns of capital formation. In addition, a considerable number of Australian companies have revalued their assets during the last decade and made corresponding adjustments in their capital structure. It would be surprising if the same is not true of the overseas companies, and therefore much of the asset revaluation may in fact have already been taken into the figures.

All these difficulties and uncertainties lie in the path of revaluation. It seems clear, however, that both Australian assets and liabilities should be increased. The addition to assets would be small, while the addition to liabilities could be substantial. Any estimate which would be at all convincing would require much fuller investigation than we have been able to give to it. Even after further investigation, however, a doubt must persist whether the new total would be very meaningful in the context of exchange control and supervision over the outflow of capital.

VI. NATIONAL WEALTH – AGGREGATE ESTIMATES

It is now possible to bring together our estimates for reproducible and non-reproducible tangible assets, together with coin and net foreign assets, which we show in Table IX, for the years 1947 and 1956.

For 1947 National Wealth was £A6,432 million; in 1956 the corresponding total had risen to £A20,709 million. These estimates are expressed in current prices and based on straight-line depreciation (except for vehicles and consumer durables), and it should be recalled that there are various minor omissions from the total, noted in previous sections and in the Appendix.

If the alternative declining-balance depreciation estimates for structures and producer durables had been used, the estimates for 1956 would have been about 8 per cent lower, with declining-balance rates equivalent to twice straight-line rates, but about

TABLE IX
Australian Current Prices (1947–56); Straight-line-depreciated Replacement Cost
(£A million)

	June 1947	June 1956
Reproducible Tangible Assets		
1. Consumer durables	272	1,208
2. Buildings –		
Dwellings	1,310	3,735
Other	724	1,852
3. Vehicles –		
Cars	87	744
Other	30	297
4. Equipment –		
Agricultural	128	514
Non-agricultural	540	1,665
5. Livestock	288	915
6. Inventories –		
Farm	45	118
Non-farm	550	1,655
7. Public works	1,484	5,425
8. Total	5,458	18,128
Coin Bullion		
9. Silver and copper coin	20	35
Non-reproducible Tangible Assets		
10. Unimproved land values	1,280	3,000
11. Invisible, etc., improvements	260	600
12. Total	1,540	3,600
Net Foreign Assets		
13. Foreign assets	223	419
14. Foreign liabilities	809	1,474
15. Total (net)	− 586	−1,054
National wealth	6,432	20,709

18 per cent lower with the higher rates, suggested on p. 329 as representing probably the shortest lives, and hence the lowest wealth estimates that can be defended. The difference is considerably larger, as Table XII shows, for the five types of reproducible assets, to which the alternative declining-balance

method can be applied,[1] but is reduced in its effect on total national wealth by the weight of inventories, livestock and land which are not affected by this choice of methods. Table XII also indicates that it makes more difference for the 1947 estimates whether straight-line or declining-balance depreciation is used.

VII. NATIONAL WEALTH – SOME INTERPRETATIONS [2]

We turn now from statistics to interpretation. The brief remarks which follow on a few economic aspects of the estimates of Australian national wealth are, however, called interpretation by courtesy only. They are presented here as an indication that we have an interest in these figures which extends beyond mere compilation, and with the idea that they might throw some light, however inadequate, on the problems of Australian economic growth.

1. *The growth of national wealth*

Together with an analysis of the structure of national wealth and a study of wealth–output ratios, measurement of the long-term rate of growth of real (deflated) wealth, particularly reproducible tangible wealth, is probably the most important function of national wealth estimates. In the case of Australia this function is unfortunately gravely hampered by the absence of estimates between 1929 and 1947 and, more still, by the basic differences between the methods of the estimates for 1929 and earlier years, on the one hand, and for the last decade, on the other. Nevertheless, with judicious use of the available data some idea can be obtained of the rate of growth of wealth over the past half-century, and tentative generalizations can be ventured about periods of more or less rapid growth.

The figures on which we can place a substantial degree of confidence, notwithstanding the numerous reservations in detail

[1] For vehicles and consumer durables even Tables I and II use declining-balance depreciation.

[2] Throughout Section VII we are using, so far as estimates of reproducible tangible wealth for 1947 and 1956 are concerned, the figures employing straight-line depreciation for structures and for equipment except motor vehicles. This has been done partly because the use of straight-line depreciation at the rates indicated on p. 329 yields results which appear to be more in conformity with whatever bench-marks are available than the estimates using declining-balance depreciation. (This argument loses weight, as Table XII indicates, if the declining-balance estimates are recalculated using somewhat lower rates, for instance, rates equal to twice the straight-line rates underlying the estimates of Tables I and II.)

that have been mentioned in previous sections, are unfortunately limited to the last decade. This is hardly long enough to enable us to speak about long-term trends. For that period the estimates indicate an average annual rate of growth of real (deflated) total wealth of 4·0 per cent and a slightly higher rate – 4·6 per cent – for reproducible tangible assets (straight-line depreciation) alone. If these figures are adjusted for the substantial increase in population we obtain per head rates of growth of 1·6 per cent for total wealth and of 2·2 per cent for reproducible tangible wealth. The latter rate is, of course, much more significant, if only because of the acute conceptual and statistical difficulties of deflating values of land and foreign assets and liabilities.

While we cannot make an entirely satisfactory adjustment for growth of net foreign indebtedness, we know that the proportion of Australia's national wealth held by foreigners is small enough – the statistics show it to be in the neighbourhood of 5 per cent in 1956, and it certainly is less than 10 per cent – that its increase during the past decade is not likely to reduce the rate of growth of domestically owned wealth substantially below the figures for total wealth.

The last decade has been a period of sustained prosperity and expansion. Export prices rose by about 90 per cent from 1947 to 1956. Population increased by 24 per cent over the period, assisted by an immigration equal to 12 per cent of the population of 1946. There was also an increase in interest rates, bank overdraft rates rising from $4\frac{1}{2}$ to $5\frac{1}{2}$ per cent and the yield on long-term government securities increasing from $3\frac{1}{4}$ to about 5 per cent, but this rise, as could be expected in such a situation, did not inhibit a rapid increase in real wealth. There was no major setback during the decade, but the annual rates of growth of reproducible tangible wealth showed considerable year-to-year fluctuations, particularly when adjusted for the much smoother growth in population. They varied between increases of less than 2 per cent and about 7 per cent before adjustment for population growth; but on a per-head basis between a small negative fraction and a maximum of slightly more than 4 per cent. The fluctuations were, however, erratic, with no long runs of years of rapid or slow growth. The general configuration is convex – the top being reached in 1950/51 and 1951/52 with about $6\frac{1}{2}$ per cent a year (almost 4 per cent per head), and somewhat lower averages for the two three-year periods at the beginning and the end of the period (slightly over 4 and almost 5 per cent respectively for aggregates, $1\frac{1}{2}$ and $2\frac{1}{2}$ per cent for per-head figures).

This rate of increase should be considered against the background of movements in earlier periods. The difficulty is that estimates of national wealth for earlier decades are quite different in method. However, the differences do not seem to be sufficiently large to make broad comparisons impossible, and we feel that we can hazard some generalizations about long-term average movements in earlier periods.

(a) Between 1890 and 1903 private wealth – the only aggregate for which estimates are available – probably declined if allowance is made for price changes and population growth. The absolute aggregate figures, as estimated by Coghlan,[1] show a small decrease from £A1,019 million to £A982 million. This may have been offset by the slight price decline which is indicated in the available indices – Melbourne wholesale prices (building-material prices, however, increased by about 10 per cent) and cost of construction. Meanwhile, population increased by about 25 per cent. Hence it is difficult to see (unless the relation between Coghlan's estimates for 1890 and 1903 in current values is much farther off the truth than we have reason to assume) how real private wealth per head can have helped declining substantially during this period. Though the proportion of public to private wealth may well have increased, the relative size of these two components is such – one to three in 1903 [2] – that this movement could only have mitigated but not offset the indicated decline in private real wealth per head. For total real wealth per head the annual decline may have been as large as 1 per cent.

There are three pieces of evidence that confirm the likelihood of a decline in real national wealth per head between 1890 and 1903, two direct, the other indirect. First, this period witnessed a serious and long drawn out depression.[3] Secondly, real income per head of the population declined. The decline amounted to about one-eighth if Clark's estimates are accepted.[4] In the face of this decline a growth in real wealth per head would imply an

---

[1] *Official Yearbook* 1933, p. 490.   [2] See Table XIV.

[3] See, e.g., E. A. Shann, *Economic History of Australia*, Chapter XIX.

[4] *The Conditions of Economic Progress*, 3rd ed. It is assumed that the 1891 figure for New South Wales can be regarded as representative for Australia as a whole.

increase in the capital–output ratio of a size which is difficult to accept. Thirdly, domestic net capital formation in the decade 1891–1900 was probably negative.[1]

In assessing the significance of the decline in per-head real wealth between 1890 and 1903 account should also be taken of the probable decline in Australia's net foreign indebtedness. Domestically owned wealth, therefore, declined less than total national wealth.

(b) From 1903 to 1915 the Australian economy was in a relatively quiet phase of growth. Export prices rose by little more than 10 per cent to the outbreak of war, while retail prices increased about 25 per cent. Population grew by 26 per cent over the period. Interest rates were rising. At the turn of the century yields on government securities were about 3 per cent, but in 1915 they reached about $4\frac{1}{2}$ per cent. It was a situation which was particularly discouraging to the growth of rural land values.

From 1903 to 1915 total real wealth per head appears to have changed little, the increase of 30 per cent in current values being largely offset by price increases. Reproducible tangible assets alone appear to have fared a little better, the per-head average in current prices advancing by almost 40 per cent and thus leaving some, though not a wide, margin for an increase in deflated values. Such a small rise is not much out of line with the trend of real national income per head, which increased by only 5 per cent between 1901–3 and 1915–16.[1]

(c) After 1915 the rate of growth quickened. Export prices more than doubled from 1915 to 1924 and in 1929 were about 50 per cent above 1915. Retail prices were 33 per cent higher, and population rose by nearly 30 per cent.

There is little doubt that real wealth per head rose between 1915 and 1929, but the size of the increase can be estimated only approximately. The estimates show advances in wealth per head of 60 per cent for the aggregate and 70 per cent for reproducible tangible assets. The increase in real reproducible wealth per head, therefore, may have been of the order of 10–15 per cent, or

---

[1] Butlin (*op. cit.*, p. 9) gives only figures for gross capital formation excluding maintenance. It is, however, almost certain from the low level of these figures – less than one-half of the preceding decade and less than even during the decade 1871–80 – that net domestic capital formation was negative, for the entire decade possibly by as much as £100 million.

[2] Clark, *loc. cit.*

about 1·0 per cent a year. Such rates are not out of line with the indicated rates of growth of real national income per head of 1·8 per cent.[1]

(d) For the period 1929–47 our main problem is a statistical one, to build a bridge between the estimates of 1929, the last of the Coghlan–Knibbs–Wickens series, which is essentially of the synthetic Census type, and that of 1947, the start of our own effort following for reproducible assets the much more flexible and controllable perpetual-inventory method.

As a starting-point we have the 1929 estimate, in current prices, of about £A4,350 million for total wealth and of about £A3,300 million for reproducible assets. These estimates are equivalent to £A690 and £A520 per head for total and reproducible wealth compared to values of £A930 and £A720 respectively, again in current prices, for 1947. The increase is about 35 per cent for both definitions. In the interval wholesale prices rose nearly 40 per cent (building materials alone over 90 per cent); retail prices about 15 per cent; Clark's national-income deflator about 50 per cent; and a combined index of construction costs and durable goods prices about 80 per cent. There would thus seem to be little doubt that the current values of average wealth per head rose considerably less than the relevant price indices, but the diversity of the indices gives some idea of the difficulties and risks of deflation. If we use the probably most appropriate index, that of capital-goods prices, the decline in real reproducible wealth per head is of the order of not less than 25 per cent. Even the substantially lower national-income deflator would yield a decline by about 10 per cent.

Another approach to linking the 1929 and 1947 figures for reproducible wealth is to start from Dyne and May's 1929 estimate because it specifically includes public reproducible wealth and excludes land, both of which have to be roughly allowed for in starting from Wickens' estimates used in Table X; and because it is much closer to a perpetual-inventory estimate than Wickens'. This estimate is just under £A3,000 million in current prices.[2] On the assumption that the 1929 price level for capital goods was about 7 per cent lower than that of 1936/39 – an assumption based on the available data on building costs and durable goods prices – this estimate yields an average per head

[1] Clark, *loc. cit.*
[2] *Economic News*, Vol. 24, 11/12 (November/December 1955), p. 8.

TABLE X
The Growth of Australia's National Wealth

Year	Current Values			Constant (1936/39) Prices
	Total National Wealth (1)	Domestic Wealth (2)	Reproducible Tangible Wealth (3)	Reproducible Tangible Wealth (4)
I. *Aggregates (£A million)*				
1903	1,309	964	900	1,800
1915	2,137	1,730	1,550	2,300
1921	2,823	2,326		
1929	4,350		3,300	3,400
1947	7,018	6,432	5,458	2,981
1956	21,763	20,709	18,128	4,504
II. *Per Head Values (£A)*				
1903	330	245	230	460
1915	430	350	315	470
1921	520	425		
1929	690		520	530
1947	930	850	720	395
1956	2,310	2,198	1,920	475

Note: Figures between 1929 and 1947 are not comparable.

SECTION I

Col. 1. 1903–21   Benham, *The Prosperity of Australia*, p. 83. Benham used Knibb's figures for private wealth and added his own estimates for public wealth (*op. cit.*, p. 58).

1929   Wickens' estimates of private wealth (*Year Book of the Commonwealth of Australia*, 1933, p. 492) plus rough estimate of public wealth based on Benham's ratio for 1921 and 1923.

1947, 1956   From Table IX.

Col. 2. 1901–21   Benham, *op. cit.*, p. 83. Figures are derived by subtracting external indebtedness from national wealth, hence do not make allowance for foreign assets or for foreign equity investments in Australia.

1947, 1956   Obtained by deducting net foreign investment in Australia (Table IX) from total national wealth.

Col. 3. 1903–29   Obtained by adding a very rough estimate for public land to the estimates of private land of Table XIV and deducting the sum from Col. 1. The resulting figures are slightly above the independent estimates of reproducible tangible assets of Dyne and May (*Economic News*, November, December 1955, p. 8) for 1915 (£A1,483 million), but considerably above this estimate for 1929 (£A2,993 million). For discussion of comparability with estimates for 1947 and 1956, see text.

1947, 1956   From Table IX. Figures (as those for 1903–29) include consumer durables.

Col. 4. 1903–29   Obtained by dividing Col. 3 by a very rough index of building costs, durable goods prices and wholesale prices weighted by the approximate share of structures, producer and consumer durable goods, and inventories in reproducible tangible wealth.

1947, 1956   From Table I.

SECTION II

Cols. 1–4. 1903–56   Obtained by dividing figures of Section I by year-end estimate of total population, usually derived by averaging official year-end estimates.

value in 1936/39 prices of £A450, which compares with £A395 in 1947, a decline of 12 per cent or 0·7 per cent a year. This is probably the minimum decline that can be squared with the material now available. Our judgment, however, is that this figure still somewhat overstates the decline, if any, in real reproducible wealth per head between 1929 and 1947 that would be found to have occurred in that period if consistent, comprehensive, and trustworthy figures were available.

This judgment takes into account the circumstances of the period we are considering. The period covers the Great Depression, and World War II, with all the waste and interruption to accumulation which they entailed. The thirties was a period of relatively low capital formation, of low capital imports and of high unemployment. Income and savings recovered after 1940, but much of the wealth which the savings represented was blown off through the cannon's mouth. Any judgment about the growth of wealth over the period must give considerable weight to these factors.

We thus end up with the following rough picture of the trend of real reproducible wealth per head:

(a) 1890–1903: A substantial decline, possibly by as much as 1 per cent per year
(b) 1903–15: No substantial change
(c) 1915–29: Some increase, possibly about 1 per cent per year
(d) 1929–47: A small decline – say ½ per cent a year – with a possibility of no significant change
(e) 1947–56: A sharp increase averaging 2 per cent per year
(f) 1890–1956: An average increase of ¼ to ½ – and possibly as much as ¾ per cent per year,[1] a figure of limited significance because of wide variations among sub-periods, and the statistical shortcomings, particularly the weak link between 1929 and 1947.

Since the proportion of national wealth represented by net foreign investment in Australia has decreased over the period as a whole, the rates of growth of domestically owned wealth

[1] This may be compared with Clark's estimate of a total increase in real national income per head of 67 per cent between 1891 and 1952/53, or 0·8 per cent a year.

would be slightly higher than indicated above for the entire period and most sub-periods.

2. *Gross v. net wealth*

For some purposes figures on the gross stock of durable assets are wanted instead of, or to supplement, net stock data, particularly for the measurement of capacity which is sometimes regarded as moving more closely with the gross than the net stock of structures and equipment. Indeed, the closer durable

TABLE XI

Distribution of Gross and Net Stock of Reproducible Tangible Wealth at Current Values

	1947		1956	
	Gross (1)	Net (2)	Gross (3)	Net (4)
1. Dwellings	24·0	24·0	21·4	20·6
2. Other structures	12·2	13·3	11·4	10·2
3. Public works	29·4	27·2	31·0	30·0
4. Producer durables	15·3	12·3	12·5	12·0
5. Commercial motor vehicles	0·9	0·5	2·1	1·6
6. Passenger cars	3·1	1·6	4·2	4·1
7. Consumer durables	6·6	5·0	8·6	6·7
8. Livestock	2·8	5·3	3·0	5·1
9. Inventories	5·7	10·8	5·8	9·7
10. Total	100·0	100·0	100·0	100·0

Sources: Cols. 1 and 3. Table XIII.
„ 2 and 4. Table I.

assets are (or are regarded to be) to the famous 'one hoss shay' in their utility emission the most appropriate is the gross stock as an indicator of capacity, provided the original expenditure figures are deflated for price changes in equipment of equal productive power. Gross stock figures in constant prices are obtained easily by summing expenditures over the number of years corresponding to the expected useful life of the asset under consideration, and figures in current prices are derived by multiplying the base price estimates by appropriate price indices. The estimates can be slightly refined by assuming that assets of a given type acquired during one year are retired in accordance with a stipulated distribution rather than in one single year. This refinement has not been applied in Tables XI and XIII.[1]

[1] It can be shown that estimates using a retirement distribution will be slightly below those omitting it, but that the difference is not likely to exceed 10 per cent.

TABLE XII
Alternative Estimates of Stock of Selected Reproducible Tangible Assets at Depreciated Replacement Cost
(1936/39 Values: £A million)

Item	June, 1947			June, 1956		
	Straight Line	Declining Balance		Straight Line	Declining Balance	
		A[1]	B[2]		A[1]	B[2]
	(1)	(2)	(3)	(4)	(5)	(6)
Dwellings	585	500	366	744	640	504
Other private structures . .	323	260	205	369	310	241
Public works . .	868	710	509	1,320	1,130	900
Agricultural equipment .	62	50	46	125	100	95
Other equipment . .	262	210	182	405	335	305
Total . . .	2,100	1,730	1,308	2,963	2,515	2,045

[1] Twice straight-line rates.
[2] Rates (higher than A) shown in schedule on p. 329.
Source: Cols. 1 and 4. From Table I.
   ,, 2 and 5. Obtained by applying twice straight-line rates to annual deflated estimates of expenditure underlying Table I.
   ,, 3 and 6. From Table I.

TABLE XIII
Gross Stock of Reproducible Tangible Assets

	Absolute Figures (£A million)				Distribution			
	1936/39 Values		Current Values		1936/39 Values		Current Values	
	1947 (1)	1956 (2)	1947 (3)	1956 (4)	1947 (5)	1956 (6)	1947 (7)	1956 (8)
1. Dwellings . . .	1,127	1,300	2,525	6,525	20·1	17·2	24·0	21·4
2. Other private structures .	573	691	1,285	3,470	10·2	9·2	12·2	11·4
3. Public works . .	1,794	2,303	3,070	9,465	32·0	30·5	29·4	31·0
4. Producer durables .	774	925	1,595	3,800	13·8	12·3	15·3	12·5
5. Commercial motor vehicles . . .	53	216	90	650	0·9	2·9	0·9	2·1
6. Passenger cars .	145	410	320	1,270	2·6	5·4	3·1	4·2
7. Consumer durables .	521	922	690	2,630	9·3	12·2	6·6	8·6
8. Livestock [1] . .	228	289	288	915	4·1	3·8	2·8	3·0
9. Inventories [1] .	390	489	595	1,773	7·0	6·5	5·7	5·8
10. Total	5,605	7,545	10,458	30,498	100·0	100·0	100·0	100·0

[1] Identical with net stock.

Source: Cols. 1 and 2. Lines 1–7 derived by cumulating capital expenditures in 1936–39 prices for the number of years corresponding to the assumed length of life as shown on p. 329.
            Lines 8 and 9 from Table I.
Cols. 3 and 4. Lines 1–7. Values of columns 1 and 2 respectively multiplied by mid-year price indices of respective types of durable goods. The indices are the same as used to deflate current expenditures (see Section III).
            Lines 8 and 9 from Table II.

The gross stock of reproducible assets is, of course, considerably higher than the net stock. Excluding inventories and livestock, for which both concepts coincide, the difference is almost 95 per cent in 1947, but less than 70 per cent in 1956.[1] The reduction in the relative excess of gross over net stock indicates a lowering of the average age of the stock which reflects the relatively high level of capital expenditures in the post-war decade. As a consequence, the increase in the gross stock of structures and equipment in 1936/39 prices is considerably lower (35 per cent) than the growth in the net stock (55 per cent).

There are also, as Table XI shows, a few differences, mostly of the expected direction and size, in the distribution of the gross and net stock of reproducible tangible wealth among the different types of assets. Thus, the share of inventories and livestock is considerably lower in the gross stock as their absolute value is the same on both bases. For the other types of assets the differences are generally small.

3. The structure of national wealth

The picture is reasonably clear, if we regard the estimates of 1903, 1915, and 1929 as comparable among themselves, as we are probably entitled to do; if, a much stronger if, we feel that we have an idea of the direction of the adjustments which have to be made between the estimates of 1929 and 1947; and if we are satisfied with current prices as basis of the calculations,[2] Table XIV, which provides the basic data for private wealth, may then be briefly summarized as follows:

(a) The outstanding change in the structure of private tangible wealth is the decline in the share of land from almost two-fifths in 1903 to one-fifth in 1956.

(b) The movements of the share of 'improvements', a regrettably broad category, including dwellings, stores, office buildings, and very varied types of structures, are difficult to interpret. They increased considerably between 1903 and 1915 and probably also from 1947 to 1956 if allowance is made for various public improvements. These are probably genuine changes, reflecting in part two

---

[1] The net stock figures used for comparison are those in Table I, i.e. those based on straight-line depreciation.

[2] At present no deflation is possible for components of private wealth before 1947.

A A

periods of heavy home-building activity. The sharp percentage decline between 1929 and 1947, on the other hand, is probably to a large extent, though not entirely, due to the change in methods of estimation, viz. a relatively higher valuation in 1929 already encountered in the discussion of trends in aggregate national wealth.

TABLE XIV

*Structure of Private National Wealth of Australia
at Depreciated Replacement Cost*

	Current Prices: £A million					Percentage Distribution				
	1903 (1)	1915 (2)	1929 (3)	1947 (4)	1956 (5)	1903 (6)	1915 (7)	1929 (8)	1947 (9)	1956 (10)
1. Land . .	374	475	900	1,540	3,600	38·6	29·6	27·1	27·7	22·0
2. Buildings .	310	631	1,351	2,034	5,587	32·0	39·4	40·7	36·5	34·0
3. Producer durables .	71	106[1]	180[1]	570	1,962	7·3	6·6[1]	5·4[1]	10·2	12·0
4. Agricultural machinery .		23	57	128	514		1·4	1·7	2·3	3·1
5. Livestock .	97	100	194	288	915	10·0	6·2	5·8	5·2	5·6
6. Motor vehicles .			147	87[2]	744[2]			4·5	1·6[2]	4·5[2]
7. Consumer durables .	31	77	127	272	1,208	3·2	4·8	3·8	4·9	7·4
8. Inventories .	60	148	316	595	1,773	6·2	9·3	9·6	10·7	10·1
9. Coin Bullion .	26	44	48	50[4]	108[4]	2·7	2·7	1·4	0·9[4]	0·7[4]
10. Total private wealth .	970	1,605	3,320	5,564	16,411	100·0	100·0	100·0	100·0	100·0
11. Public wealth .	327	517	1,005	1,484[3]	5,425[3]	33·7	32·2	30·3	26·7[3]	33·0[3]

[1] Plant and equipment in manufacturing, mining, shipping, private railways and tramways.
[2] Passenger cars only.
[3] Only public works (structures and equipment).
[4] Includes monetary gold as well as silver and copper coin bullion.

Source:

Lines 1–10

　Col. (1) Coghlan's estimates (*Official Yearbook*, 1933, p. 491, 'Personal effects' (£A12 million) omitted.
　　,,　(2) Knibbs' estimates (*ibid.*, p. 492) except separation of land and buildings which is a very rough estimate; 'Clothing, and personal adornments' (£A15 million) omitted.
　　,,　(3) Wickens' estimates (Official Year, *loc. cit.*) except separation of land and buildings which is a very rough estimate; 'Clothing and personal adornments' (£A31 million) omitted.
　　,,　(4) (5) From Table IX (except line 9).

Line 11

　Col. (1), (2) Benham, *loc. cit.*
　　,,　(3) Rough estimate based on Benham's ratio of public to private wealth for 1921 and 1923.
　　,,　(4), (5) From Table IX.

(c) Producer durables show the expected sharp upward trend, though this movement seems to start only after World War I and is probably somewhat exaggerated in the figures for the period between 1929 and 1947 as a result of the change from census-type to perpetual-inventory method.

(d) The share of livestock – primarily sheep – remains fairly stable at about 6 per cent from 1915.

(e) The share of inventories shows a slight, but steady upward trend from 1915, after a sharp increase – possibly the result of poor figures in the earlier period – between 1903 and 1915.

(f) Coin and bullion lose rapidly in importance beginning with World War I.

(g) The share of consumer durables, including all motor vehicles, increases as expected steadily (with only a break in motor vehicles due to World War II) and substantially, from only 3 per cent in 1903 to 12 per cent in 1956.

(h) Public wealth – for which only very rough global estimates exist before 1947 – seems to have maintained approximately the same relationship to private wealth of close to one-third throughout the period. The more pertinent comparison of public structures, accounting for most of public wealth, with private improvements discloses an even closer parallelism, now, however, at the level of about one to one.

A closer look at the changes in the structure of reproducible national wealth in the last decade is justified both because this

TABLE XV

Distribution of Reproducible Tangible Wealth, 1947 and 1956 at Depreciated-Replacement Cost – Current and Base (1936/39) Prices

(Per cent)

	Current Prices		1936/39 Prices	
	1947 (1)	1956 (2)	1947 (3)	1956 (4)
1. Dwellings	24·0	20·6	19·6	16·5
2. Other private structures . .	13·3	10·2	10·8	8·2
3. Government structures [1] .	27·2	30·0	29·1	29·3
4. Non-agricultural equipment [2] .	10·7	11·6	9·7	12·3
5. Agricultural equipment . .	2·4	2·8	2·1	2·8
6. Livestock	5·3	5·1	7·7	6·4
7. Inventories	10·8	9·7	13·0	10·9
8. Passenger cars [3] . . .	1·3	3·3	1·1	4·2
9. Other consumer durables .	5·0	6·7	6·9	9·4
10. Total	100·0	100·0	100·0	100·0

[1] Including equipment.
[2] Including one-fifth of cars and all other vehicles.
[3] Estimated at four-fifths of cars.

Sources: Cols. (1) and (2) from Table II.
Cols. (3) and (4) from Table I.

is a period of unusually rapid growth in total wealth and because for that period we have figures both in current and base (1936/39) prices. The relevant estimates, shown in Table XV, indicate the following main changes, some of them fairly marked if it is remembered that we are dealing with only one decade.

(a) a sharp increase in the share of consumer durables, both passenger cars and other items;

(b) some rise in the share of producer durables;

(c) a slight decline in the share of inventories and livestock;

(d) a decline in the shares of private structures, both dwellings and other;

(e) a slight increase in the share of government structures.

4. *Wealth–income ratios*

The use of the plural in the title is deliberate – it is intended to draw attention to the obvious fact that there is more than one ratio of this type, though economists are as yet far from having thoroughly explored the particular problems connected with the different forms of the ratio and far from agreed about the form to use for different analytical purposes. We shall limit discussion to the two most common variants, the ratio of total national wealth and of reproducible tangible assets (including and excluding consumer durables) to gross national product. For closer analysis less aggregative ratios would be preferable, but they require figures for the value of tangible assets and of the contribution (however defined) to current income of economic sectors, figures that are not yet available except possibly for agriculture during the last decade.

The relevant figures now available have been brought together in Table XVI. They seem to permit, with all due caveats, the following conclusions:

(a) The overall wealth – income ratio has shown a sharp fall from the turn of the century to the end of World War II, most of the decline occurring in the decade before World War I and again – one may surmise – during World War II. No trend in the ratio is observable during the last decade.

(b) The more significant ratio of reproducible wealth to gross national product has behaved a little differently. It also declined from 1903 to 1915, but considerably less than the overall ratio. It was at much the same level in 1929 as before World War I. It declined sharply, as did the overall ratio, between 1929 and 1949. In the last decade, however, it showed a slow upward trend. As a result the present ratio of approximately $3\frac{1}{3}$ is only one-fourth below that of 1903, while the overall ratio has declined by about two-fifths. (The difference, of course, is mainly the result of the reduction of the share of land in national wealth.)

TABLE XVI
Wealth–Output Ratios

Year	Wealth (£A million) at Depreciated Replacement Cost			Gross National Product (£A million)	Wealth–Output Ratios		
	Total National Wealth	Reproducible Tangible Assets			(1)/(4)	(2)/(4)	(3)/(4)
		Total	Excluding Consumer Durables				
	(1)	(2)	(3)	(4)	(5)	(6)	(7)
1903	1,309	900	870	204	6·40	4·41	4·26
1915	2,137	1,550	1,473	380	5·62	4·07	3·88
1929	4,350	3,300	3,026	844	5·15	3·91	3·59
1947	7,018	5,458	5,099	1,819	3·86	3·00	2·80
1956	21,763	18,128	16,176	5,460	4·00	3·32	3·00

Source: Cols. 1 and 2. From Table X.
  Col. 3.   Col. 2 less consumer durables and motor vehicles from Table XIV.
  Col. 4.   1903 to 1929 Clark's Estimates (*Conditions of Economic Progress*, 3rd ed.) raised by 11 per cent, the average ratio between Clark's and White Paper estimates in 1946–53. For 1947 and 1956 White Paper estimates. All figures are average of estimates for the two fiscal years ending 30 June of year indicated and of the following year except that for 1903 Clark's 1901–3 average is used. (Fiscal year 1956/57 rough preliminary estimate.)

(c) The elimination of consumer durables from the numerator does not alter the movements of the ratio substantially, though it does somewhat accentuate the decline before 1947 and reduces the recovery during the last decade. Both effects follow from the increasing share of consumer durables in national wealth and reproducible assets.

But we do not wish to put too much weight on these estimates. The conclusions we are offering are intended to be tentative, and (we hope) the basis of future discussion and investigation. If we seem to have been somewhat arbitrary and adventurous in our methods, we must plead that we have been painting in the modern manner, with broad strokes, and stark colours, and that the objective we set ourselves was sometimes more impressionistic than photographic.

APPENDIX

Notes on the Estimation of the Expenditure Series and the Price Indexes

Expenditure estimates

Consumer durables. The nearest approach to a series for expenditure on consumer durables in the primary sources was the sub-group 'Hardware, electrical goods, furniture etc.', of the personal consumption estimates in the official estimates of national income and expenditure. For the post-war period, 80 per cent of expenditure on this sub-group was taken; for the war period, figures for the sub-group were not available and an arbitrary division between expenditure on durables and non-durables was made of the total for personal consumption.

Building. For the period 1928/39–1938/39, the series for total expenditure on building was taken from Dr. (now Sir) Roland Wilson's ANZAAS paper for 1939. For the earlier years back to the turn of the century, total expenditure on building was estimated in two ways; on the basis of:

(i) the relation between total building and the value of buildings completed in the area served by the Sydney Water Board, and

(ii) the relation between dwelling and total construction,

the relations applied being in accordance with the trends shown in them over the years for which they were calculable on an independent basis.

Expenditure on dwelling construction was then estimated separately and the series for expenditure on non-dwelling construction taken as a residual. The dwellings series for the period prior to 1938/39 back to 1928/29 was mainly based on figures of the value of dwellings completed each year, supplemented by the information available from building-permit figures. These latter were also the main basis for the dwellings series for the earlier years back to the turn of the century; for this period, the series was derived by applying an average price to the numbers of new dwellings for whose construction permits were issued by Local Government bodies. The number of dwellings thus derived was adjusted to take account of information shown in census data; average values were obtained by applying the construction cost index to average values for 1936/37–1938/39, these in turn being derived by applying the number of permits issued to expenditure in those years.

Agricultural equipment. The estimates of expenditure on agricultural equipment were made on the same basis as set out in the paper by Wilson already mentioned, on 'Public and Private Investment in Australia'. Expenditure, excluding tractors, was taken as the sum of the value of domestic production and imports (plus duty and primage) less exports of selected commodities. Allowance was made for duplication in other investment series; and 30 per cent was added to cover indenting and other distribution costs. The items and the proportion of the value of their output assumed to be used on farms were:

  (i) agricultural implements – 87·4 per cent;
  (ii) saddlery, harness, and whips – 73·1 per cent;
  (iii) small tools – 50 per cent;
  (iv) wire, including nails – 35·3 per cent.

The unit values of tractor imports (by types) applied to the increase in the numbers (by types) of tractors on rural holdings (as shown in the Commonwealth Statistician's annual bulletins) formed the basis of the estimates of expenditure on tractors; an allowance for import duties was included.

To some extent, this series is deficient in its coverage. It takes no account, for instance, of costs of installation where those should be included; a case in point is fencing, where account is taken of material costs, but not of erection. The series also leaves out of account such items as well-sinking and dam building, which involve only labour.

Livestock. Livestock numbers were readily available, but it was difficult to obtain an adequate pricing basis. The prices used were for average values of livestock slaughtered as published by the Commonwealth Statistician up to 1953/54, brought up to date fror 1954/55 and 1955/56 with information obtained from the Australian Meat Board. This probably constitutes an under-valuation.

Farm inventories. For wool, the prices and quantities used were those quoted by the National Council of Wool-Selling Brokers. All wheat stocks were assumed to be held by the Australian Wheat Board, whose stocks were valued at the export price in the last month of the financial year, except for recent years, when they were valued at a price estimated to approximate that finally realized.

Barley stocks were estimated from crop figures, less exports and estimated consumption; the estimate was checked against export figures for the first months of the financial year up to the time of harvesting a new crop. They were valued at the prices realized for exports in the first months of the succeeding financial year.

No allowance was made for other farm inventories because of the absence of relevant statistics, and this constitutes a deficiency in the coverage for this item.

Non-farm inventories. Figures for non-farm inventories were derived by adding to an estimate for 1948/49 the annual change in book values shown in the official estimates of national income and expenditure. The estimate for 1948/49 was derived by adding an allowance for the uncovered field to an estimate made by the Commonwealth Statistician. The Statistician's estimate related to stocks held by private business subject to pay-roll tax, derived from a sample survey and published in the Statistician's *Quarterly Business Surveys.* The allowance added was 25 per cent of the Statistician's estimate, which was believed to cover 80 per cent of private non-farm business. No allowance was made for stocks held by Governments, this constituting another inadequacy of coverage in the estimates.

Public works. For the period from 1919/20 back to the early years of the century, rough estimates were made from the information shown in the Commonwealth Statistician's *Finance Bulletins.* For the Commonwealth and Local Governments, the available figures related to gross works expenditure; for the States, they related to net loan expenditure. In the first case, the figures would be over-estimated and in the second, probably under-estimated.

Price Indexes

The price indexes used were:

For consumer durables. The Commonwealth Statistician's 'C' series index of retail prices.

For dwellings and other structures. A 'construction cost' index linking three series – for the period from 1925 to 1956, an index constructed by the Rural Bank of New South Wales; for the period 1901–24, one constructed by the State Statistician in New South Wales; and for the years prior to the turn of the century, an index of the costs shown in Bullen's monograph mentioned previously. The indexes for the period 1901–56 relate to costs in the Sydney Metropolitan area.

For motor vehicles. Average unit values derived from applying registration figures to expenditure.

For equipment (both agricultural and non-agricultural). A section of the import-price index constructed by the Commonwealth Bank of Australia. The index relates to the f.o.b. price of goods leaving the country of origin in the periods for which it is shown; the section used covers the commodity groups 'metal manufactures', 'electrical machinery and equipment', and 'other machines and machinery'.

For non-farm inventories. The mean of the official indexes of wholesale prices and average weekly earnings, the latter linked to the index of nominal average male wage-rates for the war and earlier years.

For public works. The mean of the building-materials component of the official wholesale price index and the index of average weekly earnings, the latter again linked to the nominal average male wage-rate index for the war period and earlier years.

Price indexes were not required either for livestock or farm inventories.

13

AN ESTIMATE OF THE TANGIBLE WEALTH OF INDIA [1]

By M. Mukherjee and N. S. R. Sastry

I. THE ESTIMATES

AN estimate of the value of tangible wealth of India is presented in Table I below. The various items of reproducible assets have been shown separately from the value of land. The figures, in concept, always relate to current market value and refer to the end of the financial year 1949–50.

II. METHOD OF ESTIMATION

The various estimates included in the table have been obtained by following different methods, depending mostly on the nature of available data. It will be convenient to describe the procedure followed by certain broad categories of method of estimation. The following five categories have to be distinguished for this purpose:

(1) adjustment of data on assets thrown up by recent nation-wide surveys;

(2) price adjustment of available data on book value of fixed assets by using a historical series of paid-up capital and a relevant price-index number;

(3) to use a time series of actual capital expenditures rather than of paid-up capital and arrive at the estimate by price adjustment with the help of an index number;

(4) to use figures of net assets or accumulated total expenditures and adjust them in an overall way whenever possible; and

(5) to use miscellaneous methods, such as direct evaluation on the basis of number or quantity and price, capitalization of income, aggregation of hypothetical series with current investment figure as the base, etc.

[1] The paper draws heavily upon a draft prepared for the preliminary Indian Conference on Research in National Income (New Delhi, 28–30 January 1957) by our colleagues, Miss Uma Datta and Vinod Prakash. We have also benefited considerably from the discussion on the preliminary draft in the Indian Conference, in particular, from Professor Kuznets' observations. The estimates given in this paper, however, are materially different from those presented in the preliminary paper.

The views expressed by the authors are not necessarily those of the institutions which they serve.

TABLE I

Tangible Wealth in India in March 1950

(Rs. crores) [1]

1. Agriculture, animal husbandry, and allied activities:

(1) Agricultural implements, including tractors . .	363
(2) Livestock used in farms	2,428
(3) Sheds, barns, etc.	880
(4) Improvement of land and irrigation works: private .	1,304
(5) Improvement of land and irrigation works: public .	229
(6) Plantations other than tea plantations . . .	20
(7) Forestry and fishery.	12

(8) Sub-total   5,236

2. Mining and manufacturing (large scale):

(1) Mining	110
(2) Electricity generation and transmission . . .	240
(3) Tea plantations	133
(4) Other factory establishments: private . . .	1,206
(5) Other factory establishments: public . . .	1,206
(5) Other factory establishments: public . . .	127

(6) Sub-total   1,816

3. Small enterprises   763

4. Transport and communications:

(1) Railways	1,574
(2) Communications	93
(3) Roads and bridges	522
(4) Vehicles	281
(5) Transport animals	356
(6) Shipping and navigation companies . . .	18
(7) Public and semi-public capital in ports, docks, light-houses, etc..	71
(8) Airways companies	17
(9) Public capital in aerodromes and aerodrome equipments	8
(10) Other transport companies	48

(11) Sub-total   2,988

5. Trade and commerce:

(1) Wholesale and retail trade	1,704
(2) Banks, co-operatives, and insurance companies . .	68

(3) Sub-total   1,772

6. House property:

(1) Urban: private	2,644
(2) Rural: private	1,761
(3) Public	106

(4) Sub-total   4,511

7. Reproducible tangible wealth (RTW) in India . . .	17,086
8. Value of land in India	17,854
9. Value of tangible wealth in India	34,940

[1] 1 crore = ten millions.

It should be noted that these categories are relevant only for describing the procedure of estimation, and it is not necessary to ensure that they are distinct in a logical sense.

III. ESTIMATES BASED ON SURVEYS

The survey estimates cover a fairly large percentage of the total value (about 33 per cent of RTW and 67 per cent of total wealth), and this naturally adds to the reliability of the overall estimate presented. It is indeed reassuring to get estimates in a number of sectors which are more or less independent of arbitrary decisions. Such estimates include the values of agricultural implements, livestock, rural house property, including sheds and barns and land.[1] The estimates used in this paper are drawn from the Rural Credit Survey (RCS) [2] conducted recently by the Reserve Bank of India (RBI). But in several cases it has been possible to check the estimates used by us against estimates based on data thrown up by alternative surveys, such as the National Sample Survey (NSS) or estimates prepared on some other basis.

While using survey data, it is necessary to ascertain how the value reported has been reckoned. If the value is reckoned at current prices and we are certain that the price used takes cognizance of the age of the asset, then the survey value can be accepted as such. This is generally true for RCS data, which we have used extensively. When the value of an asset is reckoned at current market prices but the age distribution of the asset is not taken account of, it becomes necessary to deduct an estimate of accumulated depreciation from the value thus worked out. When, however, the survey data, in addition, refer to original cost, it becomes necessary to adjust both for depreciation and for the change in price level. These considerations will become relevant when we come to discuss the sector estimates.

---

[1] Reliability here has to be interpreted in a relative sense. We regard these estimates as more reliable than possible alternative estimates under these categories based on other available statistics. Secondly, these estimates are not regarded as less reliable than the estimates in many other sectors.

[2] The following abbreviations have been used in the subsequent text:

RCS: Rural Credit Survey
RBI: Reserve Bank of India
NSS: National Sample Survey
LC: Livestock Census
NIC: National Income Committee
NIU: National Income Unit
SSMI: Sample Survey of Manufacturing Industries

Agricultural implements. It is possible to estimate the current value of agricultural implements in India on the basis of three different bodies of data and also the counts available in the Livestock Census (LC). Firstly, there are many studies on cost of cultivation which enable one to work out an estimate of the value of implements per acre of cultivated land. These studies relate to different regions and different years, and price adjustments are necessary to bring the figures up to date. Estimates of the value of all implements (including bullock carts) per acre given in the *Final Report of the National Income Committee* (NIC) adjusted for 1949–50 prices range between 20 to 25 rupees.[1] Such a figure inflated for the net cultivated area of the Indian Union yields an aggregate of the order of Rs. 500 crores. The second body of data is available in the Poona report of the NSS which puts the value of implements per agricultural household at Rs. 69.25. Adjusted for prices and inflated for the total agricultural population, we get a figure of Rs. 415 crores from this source. An alternative estimate making use of the number of implements reported in the LC, 1951 and the purchase price of implements given in the Poona report of the NSS is also possible, though this is likely to lead to under-estimation because the coverage of the LC in so far as different varieties of implements are concerned is somewhat limited.[2] The all-India estimate on this basis works out at Rs. 400 crores.

The third body of material relates to the RCS conducted by the RBI. The report of the survey clearly states, 'while recording the value of implements and machinery . . . care should be taken not to record their purchase prices. Their approximate value in their present state, that is after some allowance is made for wear and tear, should be taken. The values will, of course, be as given by the cultivator but it should be made sure that he does not give the prices at which the articles were originally purchased' (pp.

---

[1] For example:

J. P. Bhattacharjee, West Bengal	(1945–56):	Rs.22
G. P. Aggarwal, Uttar Pradesh	(1948–49):	Rs.25.4
D. S. Chauhan, Uttar Pradesh	(1948–49):	Rs.22
D. R. Gadgil, Bombay	(1936–38):	Rs.23.6

Quoted from the *Final Report of the National Income Committee*, p. 41. The figures in the *Report* were adjusted for 1948–49 on the basis of wages of rural artisans.

[2] The implements included are wooden and iron ploughs, carts, sugar-cane crushers, oil engines, electric pumps, and ghanies (i.e. oil crushers). Also, NSS Poona Report records purchase prices which need adjustment for working out current market value.

14–15, RCS, Vol. III). Obviously the estimate obtained from the survey needs no adjustment for depreciation. But the survey figure, which is an average value for the period November 1951 to March 1952, has been adjusted for prices so as to relate to the end of the financial year 1949–50. Secondly, the adjusted survey figure of Rs. 130 per rural cultivating household has been used to work out an estimate for urban cultivating households, the number of such households being known. The aggregate value of agricultural implements works out at Rs. 475 crores.

The estimated value of implements includes the value of bullock carts. For arranging the figures of capital stock by industrial categories according to which national income is given, it is necessary to have a separate estimate of the value of carts. This has been done on the basis of number of carts given in the LC and purchase prices given in the Poona Report of the NSS. As the Poona Report reckons value at purchase prices, the figure has been adjusted for prices and also for depreciation yielding a figure of Rs. 112 crores as the depreciated market value of bullock carts.[1] The residue of Rs. 363 crores has been taken as the value of agricultural implements. The value of carts is included in item 2.4 of Table I, vehicles.

Livestock. Animal husbandry constitutes the largest single item of reproducible capital stock of Indian farmers. It is possible to estimate this value on two independent bases. First, it is possible to estimate the number of animals as on March 1950 on the basis of LC data relating to 1945 and 1951. These figures then can be evaluated by making use of the all-India sample estimates of purchase prices available in the Poona Report of the NSS. As the prices rose, the purchase prices are likely to be lower than the current prices, and hence there is some amount of under-estimation implicit in the procedure. The estimate works out at Rs. 2186 crores on this basis, including a separate estimate for urban animals evaluated at a higher price. We have not, however, used this figure in Table I.

The alternative estimate used by us is based on the RCS, which gives value of animals per rural cultivating household (Rs. 564) and is preferable to the former because this involves only minor adjustments. The RCS report states, 'in the case of large animals, the value should be ascertained from the

---

[1] The net effect of price adjustment and allowance for depreciation has been a reduction by about one-third.

cultivator. Usually the value will be estimated from the price the cultivator will have to pay if he has to buy a similar animal' (pp. 14–15, RCS, Vol. III). Thus it is not necessary to adjust for appreciation here. The only price adjustment needed is to translate the figure to our reference date from the survey date of the October 1951 to June 1952 average. The value of animals owned by rural cultivating households worked out in this fashion is Rs. 2,093 crores. For rural non-cultivating households the average value of livestock owned per household is taken in proportion to the ratio of land holdings of cultivating and non-cultivating households. The aggregate for rural areas thus works out at Rs. 2,529 crores. The value of livestock in urban areas is taken to be 10·08 per cent of the value of rural animals from the records of the National Income Unit (NIU) relating to calculation of the increment in stock of animals. The total value of livestock in India works out at Rs. 2,784 crores. We have accepted this figure because it is much more satisfactory than our first estimate based on LC and Poona Report of the NSS. It may be of some interest to note that the RCS neglects the value of smaller animals unless they are owned in large numbers. Any correction on this count would not, however, alter the estimate very much.

For reasons of classification, it is necessary to get an estimate of the value of animals used for traction. This has been worked out on the basis of a percentage (12·8) given in the Final Report of the NIC (p. 54). The residual Rs. 2,428 crores is taken as the value of livestock required for purposes other than transport. The value of draught animals works out at Rs. 356 crores, and is shown as item 4 (5) of Table I.

Rural house property. The Final Report of the NIC gives a figure of Rs. 2,656 crores as the depreciated current value of rural house property (p. 101). This figure has been arrived at by multiplying the number of rural houses given in the census by an average cost of construction of a new house obtained from some preliminary tabulation of the NSS and then depreciating the figure on the basis of NSS data on age composition of rural houses. The total amount of depreciation works out at 42·65 per cent of the undepreciated value. Instead of accepting this figure, we have worked out a separate estimate from RCS which gives a figure of Rs. 1,082 as the average value of rural house property per cultivating household. This figure has been adjusted for our reference date, and an aggregate has been worked out for the rural cultivating families. The ratio of average land holdings (as in the case of livestock) has been used to work out the average for rural non-cultivating families. The aggregate thus works out at Rs. 4,848 crores. A deduction has been made from this for accumulated depreciation using the overall percentage (42·65) noted above. Lastly, a notional deduction of 5 per cent has been made to allow for the value of land included in the estimate yielding a figure of Rs. 2,641 crores.

Residential house property is taken as two-thirds of the above aggregate, i.e. Rs. 1,761 crores, and the residual, Rs. 880 crores is supposed to cover the value of sheds, barns, and parts of houses used for productive purposes. The relevant percentage has been obtained in the following rough-and-ready manner. The RCS gives average value of house property per household by deciles. It has been assumed that the average value for the lower five deciles is the minimum residential requirement for all households, and what remains over and above this is available for production purposes. This assumption gives a somewhat higher figure for non-residential property, which has been rounded off to 33 per cent, because in any case not much confidence can be placed on the assumption. However, it is well known that the residential houses of the rural population are used extensively for productive purposes, as barns, cowsheds, etc., and 33 per cent used need not necessarily be an overestimation.

Land. The value of land in rural areas has been obtained directly from the RCS. RCS gives Rs. 3,515 and Rs. 1,391 as value of land holdings respectively for rural cultivating and rural non-cultivating households. These figures are first adjusted to our reference period by making use of a suitable index number, the price index of food grains. Then use has been made of the estimated number of rural cultivating and non-cultivating households to obtain the value of rural land. This figure amounts to Rs. 15,753 crores. To obtain the value of land owned by urban cultivators, the average for rural cultivators has been used, while for the rest of the country the rates relevant for rural non-cultivating households have been used. It is not known how far this procedure is correct. But it may be said in favour of the procedure that while the average size of holdings in urban areas is smaller, the average value per acre is considerably larger. The aggregate value of land in the country works out at Rs. 17,854 crores.

It should be mentioned that the basis of valuation is the prevalent village rate, and the following quotation from the RCS report is useful while interpreting the results: 'Valuation can only be approximate and it may be necessary to assist the respondent even to arrive at the approximate value of his land. For this purpose, the average land value prevalent in the village should be ascertained from the respondent and unless he is insistent that his lands are either considerably inferior or superior to the average land, the average land value rate should be applied. Dry and wet areas are to be separately valued' (pp. 14–15, RCS, Vol. III).

IV. ESTIMATES BASED ON INVESTMENT COST INDEX AND SERIES OF PAID-UP CAPITAL

The estimates to be considered next are those for which the available current data on book value of either assets or paid-up capital are adjusted by making use of an index number of investment cost. This class of estimates can be divided into two sub-classes: (i) manufacturing industries covered by the Sample Survey of Manufacturing Industries (SSMI) and some other enterprises for which the current book value of assets is available but the historical series relate to paid-up capital only; and (ii) railways, and postal and telegraph service, for which it is possible to get a historical series of investment expenditures, and hence no dependence on the paid-up capital series is necessary for price adjustment. In this section we shall consider estimates of category (i), category (ii) being taken up in the subsequent section. But it is necessary to describe the general procedure before passing on to sector estimates.

The general method of price adjustment followed by us is as follows: Where a paid-up capital series is available over a number of years, the figure in the earliest year considered is multiplied by a relevant price inflator, and after this each increment in paid-up capital is adjusted by an appropriate price inflator until we come to the last year, 1949–50, for which the multiplier is unity. At the end of this, the adjusted values are added to give an estimate of the paid-up capital reckoned at prices of the reference period and the ratio of this to the current book value of paid-up capital is the appropriate multiplying factor to adjust the current book value of net fixed assets. This, of course, holds only on the assumption that the firms themselves did not adjust their book values upwards due to price rises – an assumption likely to be generally true in India. Undoubtedly a more satisfactory procedure is possible when a book-value series is available for either net assets or gross capital expenditures year after year. In the former case the procedure would give the value at current prices in a straightforward way, while in the latter case a further adjustment for depreciation would be necessary.

But as long time-series data on either net assets or gross assets are not available for many major industrial groups it becomes necessary to press into service the time-series data on paid-up capital in spite of all their limitations. The paid-up capital need not necessarily bear a fixed relation to the net assets of a concern. Some companies may have a preference for borrowed capital rather than equity capital, and in such cases the ratio of net assets to paid-up capital will be low. Secondly, a part of the assets may be purchased out of own savings of the enterprises, and this tends to increase the ratio. Quite apart from this, data on paid-up capital relate only to joint-stock companies, and hence miss those concerns which are not thus organized. But in spite of all this, growth in paid-up capital is likely to reflect some growth in investments in the country in the joint-stock sector, and hence the adjustment described in the last paragraph is likely to have some amount of validity. Also, as joint-stock enterprises cover a sizable part of all enterprises, the use of these adjustment factors to inflate book-value figures of enterprises which do not come under the category of joint-stock companies cannot lead to any considerable error.

We have made some preliminary studies on the stability of the net assets/paid-up capital ratio. Firstly, it is possible to get considerable material on net assets and book value in individual enterprises from the *Investors' Encyclopaedia* and similar publications. We have computed the ratios and observed their variability. It is interesting to note that the averages are not widely different from unity, while the coefficients of variation are generally less than 50 per cent. Thus, even at the level of individual enterprises, some correspondence is to be noticed between the magnitudes of paid-up capital and net fixed assets.

This affords an additional justification of our use of the paid-up capital data. The relevant figures are given in the table [1] below:

Class Range of the Ratio	Number of Establishments					
	Cotton	Jute	Coal	Planta-tions	Sugar	Tea
(1)	(2)	(3)	(4)	(5)	(6)	(7)
0·10–0·49	13	5	3	3	7	..
0·50–0·69	14	10	10	6	6	9
0·70–0·89	26	15	9	17	12	16
0·90–1·09	8	12	9	23	8	32
1·10–1·19	7	7	9	24	9	14
1·30–1·49	7	3	4	14	4	14
1·50–3·09	26	8	16	20	6	19
Average	1·1225	1·0000	1·1325	1·2226	0·9654	1·1753
Coefficient of variation: per cent	53·3	38·7	42·7	23·8	34·9	28·9

The second analysis is based on detailed material on paid-up capital and net assets for the years 1947 and 1950–54 available in the study of balance sheets of joint-stock companies conducted by the RBI. This material has been used to study the variation of the ratios as well as to obtain estimates of net investment on the basis of data on paid-up capital whenever necessary. The work has been done separately for thirty-five industry groups, and the results do not warrant a rejection of our procedure.

For price-adjustment purposes we have taken series starting from 1938/39. The reason for not going beyond this date is that while the period for which adjustments were made, i.e. 1938/39–1948/49 witnessed almost a quadrupling of the general price level (wholesale), the period 1930–39 showed very little change in prices in spite of the depression years. Also in the two decades before 1930, the general price level rose for the first half and fell in the second half, the initial and final values of the index being

[1] The ratio of paid-up capital to net fixed assets worked out for individual units are summarized in the table in the form of frequency distributions by the size classes of the ratio. The averages $(\bar{x})$ and the coefficients of variation $(100\sigma/\bar{x})$ where σ's are the standard deviations, have also been shown. The main idea in presenting the table is to disclose the nature of relation between paid-up capital and net assets. This is necessary for assessing the level of reliability of the class of estimates prepared by this procedure. If the relation between these magnitudes were quite chaotic, then there would not have been any ground for our adopting this particular procedure of estimation.

of the same order. It was expected therefore that the book value of assets in 1938–39 would not be very different from their current market value. This surmise proved more or less correct. First, the current market value of total paid-up capital of all joint-stock companies in 1938–39 has been worked out by using a series running up to 1900 and a wholesale price-index number. Data on paid-up capital starting from 1900 have been culled from the publication, *Progress of Joint Stock Companies in India*. The adjusted value thus worked out is slightly lower than the book value for 1938/39. Then the procedure has been repeated for sixteen groups of industries for the period 1920/21– 1938/39, and the results are generally not unsatisfactory. It may therefore be concluded that the procedure of using a short series may lead to some under-estimation or over-estimation, but probably the magnitude of error is not large.

Before going into the individual estimates, it may be worth-while to describe the investment cost-index number, which forms a corner-stone of our estimation procedure. In concept, an investment made *t* years ago has been multiplied by a factor giving the ratio of the investment price level now and the investment price level *t* years ago. Thus the overall level of capital stock we show now is very much dependent on the index number used.

As no such index is readily available, it was necessary to construct the index. For this purpose, the import component of investment has been considered separately. A study of the current estimate of capital formation by the NIU indicates that roughly one-fourth of gross investment in recent years is composed of imports. The remaining three-fourths is very largely construction, but some domestic output of investment goods is also included. We have attempted to construct an index of import prices on the basis of quantities and prices of such capital goods for which this information is available. The index thus constructed severely lacks in coverage, the most important types of goods being left out of its purview because of absence of data. Also, quality difference in the assets imported affects this index number, sometimes in an obvious way. We have considered it desirable therefore to use the index of unit values of all imports prepared by the Directorate General of Commercial Intelligence and Statistics, which is available over the period we need, in preference to the index number constructed by us. To the extent the average price of all imports differs from the average price of imported capital goods, this procedure is likely to lead us to error. On the other hand, the import-price index constructed by us is subject to known limitations and in any case by no means comprehensive about capital-goods imports.[1]

We have then worked out a construction-cost index by making use of price quotations relating to steel, cement, bricks, and timber, as well as wages of construction workers. The weights assigned to these series have been worked out on the basis of fairly extensive material on the analysis of cost of construction available from several sources.[2] We have used this index number to represent not only the construction counterpart of investment but also the domestic output of investment goods. This is justified on the grounds that such domestic output is small and that some of the components of the index (such as steel and timber) may in fact represent the movement of the price of domestic output of capital goods.

The index as worked out by us is presented below along with the available wholesale price-index numbers:

Year (1)	Investment-cost Index			Wholesale Price Index	
	Overall (2)	Building Cost (3)	Import Price (4)	Calcutta (5)	All India (6)
1938–39	100	100	100	100	100
1939–40	104	103	106	113	113
1940–41	119	117	127	127	125
1941–42	140	136	153	153	143
1942–43	169	161	193	219	180
1943–44	247	264	196	310	232
1944–45	254	275	189	301	250
1945–46	251	267	205	303	258
1946–47	254	252	262	345	284
1947–48	291	287	302	395	325
1948–49	314	301	356	423	383
1949–50	325	318	346	464	399

The fact that the index is well below the wholesale price-index numbers shows that the use of this index is unlikely to lead to over-estimation. On the other hand, the possibility of some

[1] Recently, the RBI has started publishing an index number of import prices of investment goods. But this index dates only from 1953 and cannot be of any help for our purpose.

[2] For example, *Report of the Committee of Experts for Building Works*, *Report of Environmental Hygiene Committee*, and various unpublished data in the Central and State public-works departments.

under-estimation cannot be dismissed. This is particularly true because two components of the construction-cost index, steel and cement, show rather a small rise because of controlled prices. It is probably true that people had to pay more for these items during and after the war than the official prices. However, the import price index of capital goods which we originally constructed depicted a considerably lower rise in the prices than the import-price index used by us. Thus, there may be some amount of compensation, i.e. over-estimation of the value of imported components may be balanced by under-estimation of domestic output. We may now consider briefly the various sector estimates obtained in the manner indicated above. It may be noted that the same index number of investment cost has been used in all cases.

Mining. For mining, the estimation has been made separately for coal-mining, gold-mining, and all other mining. Instead of working out the price-adjustment factor on the basis of paid-up capital series, the investment-cost index has been used to work out a price-adjusted figure of the paid-up capital in 1949–50. This figure is then multiplied by a ratio of net assets to paid-up capital obtained from the analysis of balance sheets of mining companies conducted by the RBI. The resulting figure is of fixed assets inclusive of land, and a deduction of 15 per cent has been made for land. The RBI balance sheet analysis gives the composition of fixed capital showing the share of land separately. But this ratio cannot be used in a straightforward way because the change in value of land is likely to be different from the change in value of other assets during the period considered. The percentage adopted therefore is notional, but it takes account of the RBI data on composition of fixed assets. Finally, the working capital has been estimated by making use of ratios obtained from the RBI balance sheet analysis. Thus for coal-mining a figure of 35 per cent has been used, while for other companies 40 per cent is taken as the ratio of working to fixed capital inclusive of land. The aggregate capital stock in the mining sector works out at Rs. 110 crores.

Factory establishments. For factory enterprises, price-adjustment factors have been worked out for twenty-four industry groups covering 82 per cent of the book value of fixed capital given in the SSMI. For the industries not thus covered, the average adjustment factor for the groups covered has been used.

The value of net fixed assets given in the SSMI are then multiplied by these factors to arrive at the adjusted market value of the fixed assets. The figure at this stage includes the value of land. To this, the value of inventories given in the SSMI has been added to arrive at the aggregate capital stock in factories covered by the SSMI. Only electricity generation and transmission, for which coverage of the SSMI is not adequate, has not been considered here.

Capital stock in the public enterprises included in the SSMI works out at about Rs. 89 crores. This figure has been obtained on the basis of capital employed per person and employment in public enterprises for which separate data are available. Not all government enterprises could, however, be covered in this way, and a figure of about Rs. 42 crores has to be added to get the capital stock in government industries. The method of arriving at this figure of Rs. 42 crores will be described in a subsequent paragraph because this involves a different method of estimation. It should be mentioned here that we have not included ordnance factories and mints under government industries for conceptual reasons. It may be noted, however, that ordnance factories provided more than half of government industrial employment in 1949–50.

While the method of estimation for getting the capital stock in the tea industry is the same as that for any other factory industry, this has been shown separately for analytical reasons.

Lastly, an adjustment was made in all cases for taking out land from fixed capital. For all factory industries, a fixed ratio of 5 per cent has been used on the basis of RBI data on composition of fixed capital. This method, however, is not appropriate for the tea industry, for which the land area under plantations has been evaluated at the average rural land price worked out from the RCS.

We have tried an alternative procedure in the factory-establishment sector which may be briefly described here. There is a good deal of data available in various government and other projects which enable one to work out ratios between capital requirement and value of peak production. These ratios when applied to the actual production figures of 1950–51 give estimates of capital requirement corresponding to the level of output. The figure thus obtained would give an estimate of the upper limit of the capital stock in the individual sectors, while the current unadjusted book values would give a lower limit. It has been ascertained generally that the estimates accepted by us lie between the two extremes. But corresponding to our estimate of about Rs. 1,500 crores in the factory-establishment sector, this procedure gives a figure of as much as Rs. 3,000 crores, the current book value being of the order of Rs. 1,000 crores.

Miscellaneous sectors. The other sectors in which paid-up capital data have been used in conjunction with the investment-cost index are the following: plantations other than tea plantations, navigation companies, airways companies, other transport companies, such as tramways, trading companies (for ascertainment of fixed capital), and miscellaneous other joint-stock companies. In every case the procedure has been to work out a price-adjusted figure of paid-up capital on the basis of a time series of paid-up capital and the investment-cost index and then to multiply the figure by a ratio of net fixed assets to paid-up capital obtained from the RBI analysis of balance sheets. Whenever necessary a notional adjustment was made to deduct the value of land from that of fixed capital. Also, in all cases except in the trading sector, the estimate of working capital has been worked out by applying a ratio of fixed to working capital obtained from the RBI balance-sheet analysis. For final presentation, the capital in plantations (other than tea) has been shown along with agriculture and allied activities, shipping and navigation companies lumped together and a small item (Rs. 1.24 crores), miscellaneous other joint-stock companies, included in trade.

Trading inventories. The inventory in the trading sector has been calculated on the basis of data furnished by the RBI balance-sheet analysis but in a different way. For this a figure of net output in the trading sector has been worked out and a relation has been established between this and the value of inventories. This relation, together with the estimate of trading income in 1950–51 prepared by the NIU, gives the estimate of inventories in the trading sector. An arbitrary adjustment has, however, been made to split up a fairly large balance-sheet item on 'other expenses' and to postulate that a part of this really constitutes factor income. This procedure gives a figure of Rs, 1,619 crores as the value of stock of all wholesale and retail traders. A figure of Rs. 75 crores for government stocks, mostly of grains, can be estimated on the basis of data on physical stocks and prices. But this figure is conceived to be included in Rs. 1,619 crores given above.

In the preliminary paper on capital stock referred to earlier, the corresponding figure was Rs. 1,520 crores. This was worked out arbitrarily in the following way: From the figure of trading incomes taxed obtained from taxation sources, the total outlay of such traders was worked out on the assumption of a 10 per cent return, and then the figure of stocks was calculated on the assumption of complete replacement of stocks every three months. The rest of the trading income accruing to small traders was obtained as a residual, and the corresponding estimate of stocks was worked out on the assumption of a return of 12 per cent and complete replacement of stocks eight times every year. The object of citing this example is to show that if our present procedure is valid, the earlier phantasy was also not altogether absurd.

V. ESTIMATES BASED ON SERIES OF CAPITAL EXPENDITURES AND INVESTMENT COST INDEX

We may now consider a group of estimates which depends on the investment-cost index but not on any series of paid-up capital. This group comprises railways, and postal and telegraph services. In these activities it is possible to obtain figures of net or gross assets year after year, and hence straightforward adjustment with the investment-cost index is possible.

Railways. For railways, figures of net assets are available year after year, and hence the price adjustment can be applied in a straightforward way and no deduction for depreciation is necessary. The only adjustment we have made is a notional deduction of 10 per cent for land.

Communications. The procedure followed for communication services such as postal, telegraph, etc., is exactly the same as that used for railways. The sector includes capital stock used in broadcasting and in overseas communication services considered in the next section.

VI. ESTIMATES BASED ON ADJUSTMENT OF ACCUMULATED EXPENDITURES

We now pass on to a group of sectors in which no time-series data are available, and adjustments whenever made are to be made in some overall way. The bulk of these estimates relate to government investments and are culled from government accounts. As most of the government figures are given gross, the adjustments would generally entail a scaling down of the figures on this count and a scaling up of the figures for price changes. When the items are small we have frequently accepted the figures given in the government accounts without any adjustment, hoping that the two corrections will offset one another. Further, in some cases we have used unadjusted book values on the supposition that the use of our inflating method would lead to over-estimation. The sectors coming under this category are the following:

(i) government capital stock in irrigation works and agricultural improvement projects; industries not included in SSMI; public buildings; ports and docks including port trusts; aerodrome and aerodrome equipment; overseas communications and broadcasting; water-supply works and forestry;

(ii) mostly private capital stock in banks; co-operatives; insurance companies and shipping companies.

Public irrigation works. In so far as public irrigation works are concerned, the increase in value of investment over the period 1938/39–1949/50 has not been large. Hence, the accumulated aggregate for 1949/50 available in the government accounts has been scaled up by the investment-cost index. From this a deduction has been made for accumulated depreciation using the rate adopted for private irrigation and land-improvement projects. Lastly, a notional adjustment has been made for land included in the asset. The estimate includes capital stock in embankments, drainage works, etc.

Government industries outside SSMI. Accumulated gross expenditures on government industries not included in the SSMI are taken from the Combined Finance and Revenue Accounts of the Central and Provincial Governments in India, 1946/47, and Demands for Grants for the Expenditure of the Central Government (excluding Railways) for the years 1949/50, 1950/51, and 1951/52. The figures thus obtained are accepted without any adjustment, though a deduction has been made for land on notional grounds. The industries thus covered include the penicillin factory, Indian rare-earths factory, government housing factory, Sindri fertilizer factory, etc.

Public buildings. The accumulated expenditure on public buildings has been obtained from the Combined Finance and Revenue Accounts up to 1946/47. To this has been added the gross investment on government buildings in the years 1947/48, 1948/49, and 1949/50 worked out by the NIU. The resulting figure has been accepted as such on the supposition that degrossing and price adjustment would be offsetting one another. A deduction has, however, been made for land. A small item on central water-supply works has been included in this head.

Other government capital stock. The procedure followed for arriving at the capital stock of port trusts and accumulated capital expenditures on ports, docks, and light-houses is exactly the same as in the above case. For presentation all the heads have been combined into one item in Table I. Out of a total of Rs. 71 crores port trusts account for as much as Rs. 66 crores. The estimate for aerodromes and aerodrome equipments, overseas communications and broadcasting, and forestry are also obtained in this fashion. While the first of these has been shown under a separate heading in the main table, the second has been included in communications, and the third, a very small item, has been lumped with fishery.

Banks, co-operatives, insurance companies, and shipping companies. The estimate of assets of banks has been worked out on the basis of figures available in the RBI balance-sheet analysis and another RBI publication, *Banking and Monetary Statistics of India.* The figure of assets which relates to all commercial banks, the Imperial Bank, and the Reserve Bank of India has been taken as such without any adjustment and has been inflated to cover the co-operative societies by ratio of net output of banks to net output of co-operative societies obtained from NIU records. Similarly, the figure of assets of Indian life-insurance companies obtained from the *Life Insurance Year Book,* 1950, has been adjusted upwards to cover all insurance companies by the ratio of premium income of all companies to the premium income of Indian life-insurance companies only. The resulting figure is Rs. 14 crores. No price adjustment has been made in the above cases, but the figures have not been adjusted for depreciation either. The only adjustment relates to a deduction for land. In so far as 'assets' of banks include an intangible item, 'branch adjustments', the figure is perhaps over-estimated. On the other hand, the procedure followed by us probably leads to some under-estimation in the co-operative sector, as is indicated by calculations based on some alternative sources. Lastly, regarding shipping companies, the procedure has been to scale up the figure of fixed assets and inventories for the eleven companies available in the RBI balance-sheet analysis to cover all the nineteen existing companies on the basis of some data available in the *Investors' Encyclopaedia*, 1951–52. Here also no further adjustment has been attempted. For presentation purposes, the assets of banks, insurance companies, and co-operative societies have been aggregated, while the assets of shipping companies have been shown together with those of navigation companies.

VII. ESTIMATES BASED ON MISCELLANEOUS METHODS

The remaining estimates have been derived by miscellaneous methods. This group includes values of vehicles, roads, and bridges, and capital stocks in electricity generation and transmission and in fishery obtained by applying price or cost data to the number or amount of assets; urban house property and small enterprises for which the stock has been obtained by capitalizing income;[1] and the value of private land improvement and irrigation works arrived at on some hypothetical considerations.

Vehicles. Data regarding the number of motor vehicles taxed in India in the year 1949–50 are obtained from the *Statistical Abstract*, 1951–52. Average prices of the relevant types of vehicles have been obtained from the Ministry of Transport. The total market value of all vehicles has been calculated on the basis of these prices and the number of vehicles of each type. As the prices relate to vehicles of average age, no deduction has been made for depreciation. No statistics are available either on the total number or on the value of horse-driven and similar other types of vehicles, and a notional figure of Rs. 33 crores has been taken to cover all such items missed.

Roads and bridges. Statistics relating to the length of roads classified under various heads are available in the *Basic Road Statistics of India*, 1954, and the approximate cost of construction of different types of roads are given in *Transport in Modern India*. The value of roads thus obtained has been adjusted for depreciation on the basis of data on age structure and useful life

---

[1] The procedure followed for trading inventories was the same, but they are included in fixed capital in the sector.

period of Indian roads from the above publications. The total value of bridges has been calculated on the basis of a ratio of recent capital expenditures on roads to bridges obtained from available data.

Electricity generation and transmission. The estimate has been worked out on the basis of available data on aggregate installed capacity in the country and the cost of installation. Data on cost of installation are available for nineteen States, and we have used a simple average of Rs. 2,200 per kW of capacity in preference to a somewhat lower weighted average. The value thus obtained is gross and relates to fixed assets. An estimate of accumulated depreciation (29·3 per cent) worked out from the RBI balance-sheet analysis has been taken out of this to arrive at the net figure. To get the figure presented in Table I, an estimate of working capital based on the Public Electricity Supply, *All India Statistics*, has been added and a notional deduction (5 per cent of net fixed assets) for land has been made. The estimate of net assets works out at about Rs. 240 crores. The main reason for adopting this method is the availability of a large body of data on current cost of installation, a category of material not extensively available for other industrial sectors.

Fishery. Capital assets used in the fishery sector are in the form of boats, canoes, catamarans, power vessels, and nets, besides inventories. Data relating to vessels of various types used for sea fishing in the whole of the Indian coast (except Bengal and Orissa) are available in the *Report of the Marketing of Fish in the Indian Union*, 1951. The number of vessels used on the Bengal and Orissa coasts is estimated in relation to the share of the total catch in these areas. Likewise, vessels required for inland fishing have been estimated, due weight being given to the fact that the number of boats used for the same catch is likely to be more in sea-fishing than in fresh-water fishing.[1] The number of nets used either in sea-fishing or in fresh-water fishing has been roughly estimated on the basis of the capacity of the different types of vessels to carry men. The average prices of vessels of different types are not available, and notional estimates have frequently been used. Inventory value has been taken at 10 per cent of the fixed assets, the aggregate capital stock amounting to Rs. 11 crores.

Urban house property. For urban house property, the method used was capitalization of rentals as given by the Final Report of

---

[1] Boats are needed only for a part of the fresh-water fishing.

the NIC on the assumption of a net rate of return of 7·5 per cent.[1] The sector is one of our weakest, considering particularly the large share of total value covered by it. The percentage adopted is probably not unrealistic, but its empirical basis is not strong.

Small enterprises. An estimate of fixed capital stock in small enterprises at purchase prices is available in the NSS fourth-round preliminary tabulation results. This figure is roughly adjusted to stand for present book value of net fixed assets by making use of a ratio derived from some studies made by the Bureau of Industrial Statistics, Calcutta. This figure is then scaled up by the overall price-adjustment factor for the factory establishments considered earlier. A ratio of total capital to fixed capital was then applied to this figure, giving an estimate of total capital stock corresponding to the sample coverage of net output. When this is adjusted for the entire net output of the sector used by the NIU we get the value of capital stock in the small-enterprises sector, the figure being Rs. 763 crores. As the sample estimate of capital stock covers a large part of the sector, this method is hardly one of income capitalization, though blowing up for the entire sector is of this nature. Alternatively, use may be made of the sectoral capital–output ratios obtained from sources such as the NSS; *Report on a Survey of Cottage Industries in Aligarh Town and Surrounding Rural Area for the Year 1949* (Ministry of Commerce and Industry, 1949–50); *Rural Economic Enquiries in Hyderabad State*, 1949–50, by S. K. Iyenger; *Economic Enquiry of Saurastra*, by C. N. Vakil; *Development of Industries in U.P.*, 1949, prepared by Uttar Pradesh Directorate of Cottage Industries; *Report of the Fact-finding Committee (Hand-looms and Mills); Rural Problems in Madras* – Monograph by S. Y. Krishnaswamy; etc. These ratios

[1] Some further material on the rate of return is presented below. A study of transactions in evacuee property in the Uttar Pradesh indicates orders of gross rentals ranging between 5 and 8 per cent. The Planning Commission used a net figure of about 5 per cent for industrial housing. The Delhi Tenants Association considered a net figure of 6 per cent reasonable. S. C. Aggarwal, in his *Industrial Housing in India*, gave a figure of gross return of 6 per cent. In Bombay City gross rent is allowed by courts at the rate of 8·3 per cent of the cost of the building structure plus 6 per cent of the cost of land. Taking this into consideration and also the fact that one-sixth to one-fourth of the total cost is ascribable to land, a figure of about 7·5 per cent could be worked out for urban house property. A recent case study in Calcutta indicated that net returns are above 9 per cent for new houses but 6 per cent or lower for reassessed old houses. None of these studies have a proper sampling base, and hence can only furnish a notional figure. Finally, it is well known that new houses or even new tenants in old houses fetch a larger return. But old tenants, as a rule, pay less, mainly due to rent-control measures.

used in conjunction with output in various sectors worked out by the NIU give an estimate of Rs. 718 crores. The earlier estimate has been used in our main table.

Private land-improvement and irrigation works. The estimate of value of private land improvement and irrigation works has been worked out on the basis of a hypothetical time series of investments. The procedure followed closely corresponds to the method used in the current estimation of capital formation by the NIU. The method involves carrying backward the benchmark figure of per household investment under these heads by index numbers of rural population and value of agricultural production. The long time series thus constructed at constant prices when aggregated yields a figure of as much as Rs. 1,304 crores after adjustments for depreciation (life having been reckoned at forty years) and land.

VIII. CAPITAL–OUTPUT RATIOS

An examination of the relation between the capital stock estimated by us and the net national output is naturally of considerable interest. The following table presents the estimates of capital stock and net domestic output in 1950–51 by some broad sectors and the resulting capital output ratios:

TABLE II
Estimates of Reproducible Capital Stock by Industrial Origin and Capital–Output Ratios

	Reproducible Capital Stock, End of 1949/50 (Rs. crores)	Net Domestic Output, 1950/51 (Rs. crores)	Capital–Output Ratio
1. Agriculture, animal husbandry, and allied activities	5,236	4,890	1·07
2. Mining . . .	110	70	1·57
3. Factory establishment . .	1,706	550	3·10
4. Small enterprises . .	763	910	0·84
5. Communications . .	93	40	2·32
6. Railways . . .	1,574	180	8·74
7. Other transport . . .	1,321	146	9·05
8. Trade and commerce . .	1,772	1,324	1·34
9. House property . .	4,511	410	11·00
10. Government services, professional services, and other sectors	—	1,030	—
Total . . .	17,086	9,550	1·79

Note: Items in first column correspond to entries in Table I, p. 366.

We get an overall capital–output ratio of 1·79, or a ratio of 3·66 if the value of land is also included. Regarding individual sectors, house property tops the list with a ratio as high as 11, while railways and transport other than railways also have very high ratios, each having an order of 9. Large-scale factory establishments have a ratio of 3·1, followed by 2·3 in communication services and 1·6 in mining. The unorganized sectors have very low ratios, the lowest being 0·8 in small enterprises, followed by 1·1 in agriculture [1] and allied pursuits and 1·3 in trade and commerce.

An attempt has also been made to compute capital–output ratios by making use of estimates of fixed capital only in the numerator. The aggregate estimate of fixed capital is Rs. 11,789 crores, and this gives a capital output ratio of 1·23 when land is excluded and 3·10 when land is included. Sector estimates of fixed-capital–output ratios are less reliable than the total-capital–output ratios presented earlier. The following table gives the two types of ratios for a few sectors in which the comparison is considered to be valid in spite of the limitations in data:

	Fixed Capital–Output Ratio	Total Capital–Output Ratio
1. Agriculture, animal husbandry, and allied activities	0·57	1·07
2. Mining	1·09	1·57
3. Factory establishments . . .	2·16	3·10
4. Small enterprises	0·48	0·84
5. Transport and communications .	7·15	8·16
Overall . . .	1·23	1·79

It is not our purpose here to draw any conclusion from these figures. Knowing the reliability of our estimates, we do not think it will be desirable to read too much from them. However, the figures are worth presenting for their obvious importance. This attempt at a numerical hypothesis, it is hoped, will lead to critical appraisal at a quantitative plane, and only in such atmosphere of criticism can more reliable estimates emerge.

[1] It may be of some interest to work out a ratio for agriculture, in which the capital stock includes land. This can be approximated by adding the value of land owned by the cultivating households to the reproducible capital stock in the sector. The figure works out at 3·88.

FIFTH CONFERENCE OF THE INTERNATIONAL ASSOCIATION FOR RESEARCH IN INCOME AND WEALTH

Held at De Pietersberg near Arnhem in The Netherlands
from 19 to 25 August 1957

LIST OF PAPERS UNDER EACH TOPIC

I. PROBLEMS OF MEASURING THE NATIONAL CAPITAL

Sessions organized by Raymond Goldsmith:

O. Aukrust and J. Bjerke: 'Real Capital of Norway, 1900–56'

M. Balboa and A. Fracchia: 'Fixed Reproducible Capital in Argentina 1935–55'

T. Barna: 'Alternative Methods of Measuring National Capital'

K. Bjerke: 'Composition of Properties in Copenhagen, 1949'

P. J. Bjerve and M. Selsjord: 'Financial Accounting within a System of National Accounts'

J. M. Garland and R. W. Goldsmith: 'The National Wealth of Australia'

F. Grünig: 'An Estimate of the National Capital Account of the Federal German Republic'

National Accounts Division, Netherlands Central Bureau of Statistics: 'Preparation of a National Balance Sheet, Experience in the Netherlands'

M. Mukherjee and N. S. R. Sastry: 'An Estimate of the Tangible Wealth of India'

A. Sauvy: 'Sur la Notion de Capital Accumulé' (Summary available in English)

Anthony Scott: 'The National Wealth of Canada'

Ivo Vinski: 'The National Wealth of Yugoslavia at the End of 1953'

J J. D. Willers and D. G. Franzsen: 'Capital Accumulation and Economic Growth in South Africa, 1870–1955'

S. Yoshiue: 'The National Wealth Estimates of Japan'

II. SIZE DISTRIBUTION OF INCOME

Sessions organized by Milton Gilbert:

W. Beckerman: 'Size Distribution of Income in the United Kingdom'

R. Bičanič: 'Personal Income Distribution of Peasant Families in Yugoslavia'

O. Lindahl: 'Size Distribution of Income in Sweden'

J. L. Nicholson: 'Social Redistribution of Income in the United Kingdom'

N. S. R. Sastry: 'The Distribution of National Product in India'

III. CONTRIBUTED PAPERS

Sessions organized by Kjeld Bjerke:

R. C. Geary and Rupert Burge: 'Balancing of a System of National Accounts in Real Terms'

J. Idenburg: 'Quarterly National-income estimates'

C. T. Saunders: 'Problems in the Compilation of Quarterly National-income Accounts'

G. Stuvel: 'The Recording of Interest in the National Accounts'